# FREEDOM ON THE HORIZON

THE UNITED LIBRARY
2121 Sheridan Road
Evanston, Illinois 60201

THE HISTORICAL SERIES OF THE REFORMED CHURCH IN AMERICA
NO. 65

E
184
.D9
K7213

# FREEDOM ON THE HORIZON
Dutch Immigration
to America, 1840-1940

**Hans Krabbendam**

WILLIAM B. EERDMANS PUBLISHING COMPANY
Grand Rapids, Michigan / Cambridge, U.K.

© 2009 Reformed Church Press
All rights reserved

Wm. B. Eerdmans Publishing Co.
2140 Oak Industrial Drive S.E., Grand Rapids, Michigan 49503 /
P.O. Box 163, Cambridge CB3 9PU U.K.
www.eerdmans.com

Printed in the United States of America

Print Management by
HeuleGordon, Inc.
Grand Rapids, MI

Krabbendam, Hans, 1964-
　[Vrijheid in het verschiet. English]
　Freedom on the horizon : Dutch immigration to America, 1840-1940 /
Hans Krabbendam.
　　p. cm. -- (The historical series of the Reformed Church in America ; no. 65)
　Includes bibliographical references and indexes.
　ISBN 978-0-8028-6545-8 (cloth : alk. paper) 1. Dutch
Americans--History--19th century. 2. Dutch Americans--History--20th
century. 3. Dutch Americans--Middle West--Social conditions. 4.
Immigrants--Middle West--History. 5. Dutch Americans--Middle
West--Religion. 6. Christian Reformed Church--History. 7. United
States--Emigration and immigration--History. 8. Middle West--Emigration
and immigration--History. 9. Netherlands--Emigration and
immigration--History. I. Title.
　E184.D9K7313 2009
　977'.0043931--dc22
　　　　　　　　　　　　　　　2009040146

## The Historical Series of the Reformed Church in America

The series was inaugurated in 1968 by the General Synod of the Reformed Church in America acting through the Commission on History to communicate the church's heritage and collective memory and to reflect on our identity and mission, encouraging historical scholarship which informs both church and academy.

General Editor
>   Rev. Donald J. Bruggink, Ph.D., D.D.
>   Western Theological Seminary
>   Van Raalte Institute, Hope College

Associate Editor
>   George Brown, Jr., Ph.D.
>   Western Theological Seminary

Copy Editor
>   Laurie Z. Baron

Production Editor
>   Russell L. Gasero

Commission on History
>   Douglas Carlson, Ph.D., Northwestern College, Orange City, Iowa
>   Mary L. Kansfield, M.A., East Stroudsburg, Pennsylvania
>   Hartmut Kramer-Mills, M.Div., Ph.D., New Brunswick, New Jersey
>   Jeffery Tyler, Ph.D., Hope College, Holland, Michigan
>   Audrey Vermilyea, Bloomington, Minnesota
>   Lori Witt, Ph.D., Central College, Pella, Iowa

# Contents

# Maps and Tables

# Photographs

# Preface

If one goes searching today for recognizable Dutch manifestations in the Midwest of the United States, one will certainly find them in places with names such as Holland, Zeeland, Vriesland, Pella, and Orange City. Place names, historical buildings, societies, and festivals point to Dutch roots. At first glance most of these sites appear to be purely local—a historical monument, a windmill, a canal, or a tulip festival. However, these examples are related to each other, as a result of the waves of Dutch immigrants who came to America in the nineteenth and early twentieth centuries, and who formed a subculture. The Dutch in different locations keep in touch with each other in various ways. Thus there are a number of Holland Societies in many localities, bound together by cultural and historical relationships to the Netherlands, often harking back to the seventeenth and eighteenth centuries; festivals of recent date that have a commercial and nostalgic flavor; and churches that want to continue a theological tradition.

Careful observation of these manifestations demonstrates that the current relationship with the Netherlands is actually rather thin, and that their main purpose is to strengthen the mutual connections among Dutch Americans. The bond with the Netherlands, of whatever kind, offers these groups an identity. Their transatlantic contacts are usually informal, brief, and incidental. A few groups, however, are cohesive and intense, and they have always taken the bond with the Netherlands very seriously. They stand in a broad tradition of Protestant emigrants from Europe who moved to America since the middle of the nineteenth century. In the general American immigration pattern these groups were not exceptional—other ethnic groups have also reinforced their identity with religious bonds. This similarity to other groups could lead to the conclusion that there is no story to tell about the Dutch in America. Obviously there is.[1] The Dutch had their distinctive characteristics. This book seeks to understand the settlement process of an unproblematic and relatively small immigrant group during the century when the door to America was wide open and Dutch emigration reached its apex. It takes a closer look at the transatlantic ties to explain the formation of a new Dutch-American identity.

My fascination with this topic began in the mid-1970s when as a young teenager I met an American family of Dutch descent that temporarily lived in my hometown. It was Robert P. Swierenga, who, together with his family, spent his first semester in the Netherlands to lay the foundation for his comprehensive statistical analysis of Dutch emigration. In the meantime he planted a seed of historical curiosity in my young mind. This seed germinated during my studies at Leiden University and Kent State University and continued to grow new branches. I harvested these fruits in a Dutch book, *Vrijheid in het verschiet. Nederlandse emigratie naar Amerika, 1840-1940*, of which this is the English translation, adapted for an American audience.

The main theme of this book originated during a term of study at the Van Raalte Institute in Holland, Michigan. The generosity, hospitality, and expertise of the staff in the heart of this Dutch colony gave this book a significant impetus, especially because by their interest they made clear that I should describe and elucidate the permanence of their subculture, which was self-evident to them. I never knocked in vain on the doors of Elton Bruins, Jack Nyenhuis, Bill and Nella Kennedy, Karen Schakel, and Robert P. Swierenga for facts, photographs, and files. The assistance of the archivists of the Joint Archives in Holland, Larry Wagenaar and his successor Geoffrey Reynolds, was indispensable as well. I found the staff of Heritage Hall of Calvin College in Grand

---

[1]    Hans Krabbendam, Cornelis A. van Minnen, and Giles Scott-Smith, eds., *Four Centuries of Dutch-American Relations, 1609-2009* (Amsterdam/Albany: Boom/ State Univ. of New York Press, 2009).

Rapids equally helpful, and I was always welcomed as an old friend. Dick Harms, Wendy Blankenspoor, Hendrina Van Spronsen, and Boukje Leegwater offered assistance and coffee. It is thanks to this connection that Harry Boonstra and Gerrit Sheeres offered their services to translate the book into English. I am grateful for their excellent job. Thanks to the unparalleled editorial skills of Margriet Bruijn Lacy the manuscript was cleared of errors and glitches.

The connection between the Netherlands and the Midwestern Dutch immigrants fits naturally into the mission of the Roosevelt Study Center, a research institute for American history and European-American relations in Middelburg, the Netherlands. Housed in a twelfth-century abbey and surrounded by medieval monuments, the center offers a near-perfect residence for research. I am indebted for these stimulating circumstances to Kees van Minnen, Leontien Joosse, Giles Scott-Smith, and the doctoral students who came and went. The doctoral research project of Enne Koops on post-World War II Dutch immigration and the multifaceted connection between religion and immigration once again confirmed the importance of the immigration tradition that emerged in the nineteenth century. That is the theme of this book.

**Overisel Reformed Church, Michigan.**
Archives, Calvin College, Grand Rapids, Michigan

# Introduction

Graafschap, Overisel, and Vriesland are small villages on the edge of a cohesive Dutch immigrant community in the western part of the state of Michigan, with Graafschap to the west, Overisel to the southeast, and Vriesland to the northeast of the city of Holland. Each of these three villages at one time had a monumental, white-washed Protestant church. The congregation of Vriesland sold the old building, built in 1869, to a Spanish-speaking Pentecostal congregation and built a new multipurpose building a few hundred yards up the road. The Overisel congregation moved into a still more attractive church, right behind the old one, complete with kitchen, library, and sports hall. The original building of 1866 became superfluous, and, after some discussion, it was torn down. In spite of the fact that the Graafschap Christian Reformed Church was the cradle of the denomination and the site of its first ministerial training school, this historic building was also replaced by a new one. Only the steeple was retained. The requirements of contemporary American church life make ownership of historic churches a liability rather than an asset. An appeal to historical consciousness is insufficient to save the original buildings.

This leaves the Pillar Church, the church of the founder of the Dutch colony, Albertus Van Raalte, built in 1856, the main monument of the sturdy ecclesiastical past of the Reformed immigrant colony.[1]

However, at the same time that monuments have disappeared, new construction in western Michigan has expanded. In the past several decades thousands of new residents, among whom are many Latin Americans, have come because of labor opportunities. It is expected that within twenty years the rural area with independent villages will be changed into a conglomerate of mutually exchangeable suburbs. The memorial year of 1997, packed with festivals, parades, lectures, publications, exhibits, memorials, concerts, and church services, was perhaps the final marking point of a homogeneous past. Although that thought can lead to some melancholy, it is truly astounding that a small group of Dutch pioneers was able to maintain its own subculture for a century and a half. This book describes how it was possible.

In the Netherlands, emigration to America continues to fascinate a wide public. The success of hotel "New York" in Rotterdam is a striking example of this. Historians are interested in the phenomenon of emigration, because it means much more than simply a demographic movement of people who build a new life in another country. The phenomenon demonstrates moments of crisis in the country of origin, possibilities in the country of settlement, but most especially the human capacity for imagination. Would a move bring about improvement? Everyone who thought about emigration formed an image of the new country, of the journey, of the future, of the loss of home. People projected ideals and expectations on the screen called "America," which promised freedom and prosperity. Once they had arrived and settled, the immigrants reshaped their new environment and compared their American lives to their earlier lives in the Netherlands. Had it been a good decision to emigrate? How are family and friends doing? In turn, the relatives left behind tried to form a picture of life in America. Established Americans also pondered the effects of the massive immigration. Some saw the immigrants as an asset for the country, a welcome strengthening of the nation, as an indispensable labor force or as potential customers. More often Americans feared that the arrival of hordes of paupers who maintained their non-American lifestyle and imported ideas that undermined democracy threatened the unity and prosperity of their country.

---

[1]    *Grand Rapids Lakeshore Press*, April 2, 1998. Janet Sjaarda Sheeres, *Son of Secession: Douwe J. VanderWerp* (Grand Rapids: Eerdmans, 2006), 126-30.

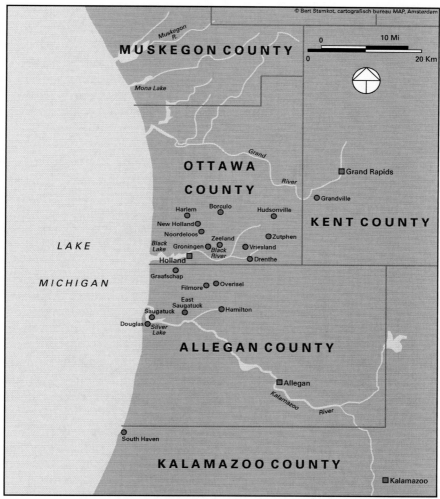

Map 1: The Dutch settlements in West Michigan.

To this day the debate about immigration continues to affect the core of the American nation, just as it does in the Netherlands and the rest of Europe.[2] This often grim discussion is usually conducted in terms of "us" against "them." The history of Dutch immigration to the United States reminds us that "we" once were "they." A long-term

[2]    Samuel P. Huntington, *Who Are We? The Challenges to America's National Identity* (New York: Simon and Schuster, 2004). Ian Buruma, *Murder in Amsterdam: The Death of Theo Van Gogh and the Limits of Tolerance* (London: Atlantic Books, 2006).

perspective teaches that immigrants come in waves of different composition. Immigration policy therefore returns regularly to the political agenda. In the eighteenth century immigrants mostly from the British Isles crossed the Atlantic, followed by Europeans from the north and west in the first half of the nineteenth century, and by Europeans from the south and east at the end of the century. Between 1921 and 1965 the influx of immigrants was limited to a maximum of several hundred thousand, but in 1965 the American Congress passed new legislation that increased immigration greatly in the remainder of the twentieth century. After the Second World War the center of gravity moved from European to Asian refugees, and Latin-American immigration became the most numerous. Even though the number of immigrants in the 1980s and 1990s reached new absolute heights with five to six million newcomers per decade—considered in relative terms there never were as many newcomers as in the 1890s, when nearly 15 percent of U.S. citizens were born abroad.[3]

The apex of Dutch emigration to the United States was in this very period. Between 1846 and 1914 at least two hundred thousand Dutch citizens crossed the Atlantic, while approximately one hundred thousand Dutch followed them between 1948 and 1960. The early immigrants settled in western Michigan, Wisconsin, and southeast Iowa. The next waves moved further north to northern Michigan and westward to Minnesota and the Dakotas. Immigrant communities also developed in cities such as Chicago, Detroit, Paterson (New Jersey), and Rochester and Buffalo in New York State.[4]

Even after migration from the Netherlands had dwindled in 1930s, the phenomenon continued to appeal to the imagination. This was true for those involved, as well as for scholars and writers who were curious about people's motives, their circumstances, and the human capacity for adaptation. Those studying immigration each highlighted a different aspect—for example, by emphasizing the "special character" of the Dutch immigrant, defending the role of church and faith, correcting the neglect of forgotten groups, or tracing either the communal mentality or its alternatives. In the historiography of nineteenth-century Dutch emigration to the United States this

---

[3]    U.S. Bureau of the Census, "Nativity of the Population and Place of Birth of the Native Population: 1850-1990," http://www.census.gov/population/www/documentation/twps0029/tab01.html., visited March 3, 2009. In 1990 this was nearly 8 percent.

[4]    Robert P. Swierenga, *Faith and Family: Dutch Immigration and Settlement in the United States, 1820-1920* (New York: Holmes & Meier, 2000).

Map 2: The Dutch settlements in the Midwest.

variation in viewpoints is especially noticeable. The interest in the religious aspect has always occupied a prominent place, not only in historical writing of American descendants of these immigrants, but also among Dutch writers.

The memory of nineteenth-century migration played a remarkable role in the twentieth century among self-conscious Calvinists in the Netherlands (first called Seceders, later *Gereformeerden*), who commemorated their centennial in the midst of the depression of the 1930s. In 1834 the first Protestants had seceded from the privileged Reformed Church (*Hervormde Kerk*). On October 12-14, 1934, hundreds of kindred spirits came together in Utrecht in an atmosphere of great thankfulness, mixed with some pride. After all, who could have imagined in 1834 that one hundred years later a descendant of the Seceders would be prime minister of the Netherlands (Hendrikus Colijn), and that a few years earlier a grandson of a Separatist emigrant (Gerrit Jan Diekema) would be appointed as the American ambassador to the Netherlands?

On the first day of the event Professor A. Goslinga, historian at the *Gereformeerde* Free University in Amsterdam, opened an impressive exhibit about this history. One of the visitors was bank employee and writer Piet Risseeuw from The Hague, who was deeply impressed by the material on display and especially by the forty brochures and four illustrations about migration to America. Risseeuw became so captivated by the brochures of the ministers Anthony Brummelkamp and Albertus C. Van Raalte, who had defended the early emigration, that he decided to write a novel about the relationship between the Secession and the migration of 1846 to the United States. During the Second World War he found time to turn his collection of historical sources into a historical fiction series; the first two volumes appeared in 1946—*Vrijheid en brood* (*Freedom and Bread*) and *De huilende wildernis* (*The Howling Wilderness*). The third and last volume, *Ik worstel en ontkom* (*I Struggle and Escape*) appeared in 1951. Together they were published in 1959 as the trilogy *Landverhuizers* (*The Emigrants*).

This topic scored a bull's eye. Immediately after publication in 1947, the Dutch Christian radio station NCRV produced the book as a radio drama, and new editions were printed until 1982. *The Emigrants* formed the image of emigration for the postwar generation.[5] The Netherlands slowly recovered from the deprivations of economic crisis and World War II. Parallels with the setbacks and difficulties of the pioneers in the land of freedom were readily at hand. Moreover, after two generations, emigration had once again gained momentum, with one-third of Dutch families considering departure in 1948. Risseeuw based his sturdy main characters on actual people and quoted regularly from their correspondence. As a novelist he was especially interested in family relations and in various survival strategies. As a committed Calvinist, he wanted to give a new impetus to Christian literature. In his trilogy he allowed the Christian faith to play a central role, even though he also gave notable secondary roles to those who were not Christians.

Risseeuw stood in a historical tradition that paid much attention to the religious aspect of migration. However, this emphasis ran the risk of pushing aside other aspects. In response, later publications underrated the religious dimension. If one looks at the statistical data that one-third of Protestant Dutchmen had joined a Dutch-American denomination, one could conclude that the influence of church and faith was limited. This is, however, a premature conclusion that does

---

[5]    An English translation was finally published in 2008: *Landverhuizers* (*The Immigrants: Historical Trilogy Novel of Dutch Emigration of the Mid-Nineteenth Century*) [trans. and condensed by C.L. Jalving] (Sheboygan Falls, Minn.: Sheboygan County Historical Research Center, 2008). See my article, "De optelsom moet kloppen. P.J. Risseeuw's trilogie *Landverhuizer*," *Transparant* 10.2 (April 1999): 9-15.

not take into consideration the many Roman Catholic immigrants who did not found their own denomination, but were absorbed in the American Catholic Church, and the many immigrants who joined other American churches. Religion played a role in the immigrant experience in various ways, but it needs to be matched with the other aspects that shaped a Dutch-American subculture.[6]

This book has sprung from my wonder about the fact that a relatively small group of Dutch immigrants was able to maintain its own identity for such a long time. In the explanation of this phenomenon religion plays a significant but not exclusive role. Earlier studies about Netherlanders in America have described a number of aspects of the Dutch emigration movement: Jacob van Hinte and Henry Lucas published massive works that described local settlements in detail. The American historian (and third-generation Dutch-American) Robert P. Swierenga provided a solid statistical basis for research on the composition of the waves of emigrants till 1880, and he described the Dutch community in Chicago in minute detail. He inspired a generation of immigration historians who dealt with subjects such as regional concentrations, Roman Catholic emigrants, Frisians, women, and the development of Dutch communities in the Midwest. In the Netherlands, Pieter Stokvis marked the beginning of this emigration movement in 1846 with his dissertation about *De Nederlandse trek naar Amerika*.[7] These recent research results, augmented with original sources, make it possible to reconstruct the Dutch-American emigrant culture in the nineteenth century. This book does not offer an exhaustive overview of all Dutch communities—for that purpose one can consult the works of Van Hinte and Lucas and the many articles in the periodical *Origins*—but will expose the patterns that have guaranteed

---

[6]    These forms are described in a number of collections: George Harinck and Hans Krabbendam, eds., *Sharing the Reformed Tradition: The Dutch-North American Exchange, 1846-1996* (Amsterdam: VU Univ. Press, 1996); George Harinck and Hans Krabbendam, eds., *Breaches and Bridges: Reformed Subcultures in the Netherlands, Germany, and the United States* (Amsterdam: VU Univ. Press, 2000); Hans Krabbendam and Larry Wagenaar, eds., *The Dutch-American Experience: Essays in Honor of Robert P. Swierenga* (Amsterdam: VU Univ. Press, 2000); George Harinck and Hans Krabbendam, eds., *Amsterdam-New York: Transatlantic Relations and Urban Identities Since 1653* (Amsterdam: VU Univ. Press, 2005); George Harinck and Hans Krabbendam, eds., *Morsels in the Melting Pot: The Persistence of Dutch Immigrant Communities in North America, 1800-2000* (Amsterdam; VU Univ. Press, 2006).

[7]    See Appendix 2.

the continuity of these communities. More than the American studies, this investigation is focused on the bonds with the Old World.[8]

Dutch immigrants received the same welcome in America as did many English immigrants. As a group they were not discriminated against, as were many others who came to America from more exotic areas. In 1847 the Presbyterian minister George Duffield already called the Dutch immigrants "a very interesting and valuable foreign population."[9] The congressional commission which, under the leadership of Senator William P. Dillingham, examined the situation of immigrants between 1907 and 1910, made an extremely positive judgment about the Dutch: "In social customs the Dutch show greater affinity to the English than to the Germans. They have been called the Englishmen of the mainland. Like the English, the Dutch have been great colonizers."[10] Even after the Second World War an American Republican senator from Wisconsin said that he gladly saw Dutch immigrants come, because they would improve the quality of the American people: "They are a good breed; we can use them."[11] Whatever the political motives for these statements, they illustrate the fact that the Dutch Americans did not have to overcome political obstacles or fight for their acceptance. Nevertheless, as individuals they faced alienation similar to many British immigrants and yet they did not disappear in the melting pot without a trace.[12]

That the Dutch communities with a Reformed character did not seek integration head over heels was a result of the communal ideals that they wanted to realize. The Seceders were a despised minority in the Netherlands and became a leading group in America. This transition stimulated a strong self-consciousness that differentiated itself from both a Dutch and an American awareness. The Dutch immigrants

---

[8]  David A. Gerber, "Forming a Transnational Narrative: New Perspectives on European Migrations to the United States," *The History Teacher* 35.1 (2001): 61-78.

[9]  See P.R.D. Stokvis, *De Nederlandse trek naar Amerika, 1846-1847* (Leiden: Universitaire Pers Leiden, 1977), 135.

[10]  *Reports of the Immigration Commission*, Vol. I. *Summary* (Washington, D.C.: Government Printing Office, 1911), 232.

[11]  Senator Alexander Wiley (Republican from Wisconsin) in *Hearings Before a Subcommittee of the Committee on Foreign Relations United States Senate, Eighty-Second Congress, First Session on United States Economic and Military Assistance to Free Europe* (Washington, D.C.: Government Printing Office, l951), 249.

[12]  William E. Van Vugt, *Britain to America: Mid-Nineteenth Century Immigrants to the United States* (Urbana: Univ. of Ilinois Press, 1999).

were not unique in this respect; other ethnic subcultures formed new identities as well. The ethnic groups did not form natural, permanent units from the beginning, but brought them about themselves.[13] It is not accidental that this history mainly took place in the Midwest. This region, including the states of Michigan, Illinois, Iowa, Wisconsin, Minnesota, and North and South Dakota, promised space for group settlements and farming and offered freedom to remain true to oneself. This freedom also had a reverse side. Immigrants could easily decide to leave or to split the community. An ethnic enclave that was able to keep the old authority structures in place because of American freedom saw with dismay the unraveling result of that same freedom. These circumstances hindered the immigrants from copying their society from the Old World. Even the virtue of freedom could produce internal tensions in communities that wanted to continue their own lifestyles as much as possible.[14]

If a group was successful in satisfying the needs of its members within the boundaries of its own community with the help of economic and social institutions, then it strengthened its continuity considerably. Through the establishment and maintenance of the boundaries between its own group and outsiders, through formal membership and informal rules regarding language, clothing, behavior, and custom (whether or not formulated by authorities), the group remained distinct from other groups. This permanence was further strengthened by successive generations identifying with this tradition in various cultural expressions, such as literature, festivals, and commemorations.[15]

The establishment of a Dutch-American subculture in the nineteenth century in the American Midwest is sketched out in this book according to ten building blocks that overall follow a chronological sequence. The first three chapters describe the prelude of the emigration movement, which led to the actual departure in the period 1846-1850. This segment of the history is known best because of its adventuresome nature, but it becomes more structurally significant by viewing it as a

---

[13] Werner Sollors coined the term the "discovery of ethnicity," in *The Invention of Ethnicity* (New York: Oxford Univ. Press, 1989), ix-xx.

[14] See my article, "The Return of Regionalism: The Importance of Immigration to the Plains for the History of the Ducth in America," in Paul Fessler, Hubert R. Krygsman, and Robert P. Swierenga, eds., *Dutch Immigrants on the Plains* (Holland, Mich.: Joint Archives of Holland, 2006), 1-21.

[15] Rudolph J. Vecoli, "An Inter-Ethnic Perspective on American Immigration History," *Mid-America* 75 (1993), 223-35.

condition for community formation in America. The organization of the departure and the building of immigrant communities in America demonstrate how the immigrants had developed ideals and plans at home, and thus laid a basis for a firm network.

The next three chapters (4-6) describe the three building blocks for internal cohesion—church, family, and work. This series is followed by the means of communication that are described in chapters 7-9. The cement between the building blocks constituted the internal communication by maintaining and adapting the language and the media, and the external communication with the Netherlands, which was preserved through extensive correspondence and visits, and with American society, especially through politics. These factors eventually led to a Dutch-American identity, which is described in chapter 10. In the conclusion, these ten interwoven developments are placed in a wider perspective that begins with New Amsterdam and continues through the postwar emigration. It then becomes clear that the Dutch-American group culture was a temporary phenomenon that reached its climax in the first half of the twentieth century. Around 1920 all the elements were fully developed. After that time, the pattern would not change essentially until the last emigration wave of 1948-1960 had ebbed away and all kinds of modernizing developments replaced the local autonomy with regional and national bonds.[16]

Dutch Protestant immigrants are more prominently represented in this book than other religious groups because they best satisfied the requirements for continued existence as a group: a strong identity, shared experiences, geographic concentration, internal and external communication channels, a discussion among themselves about their own identity, and the urge to pass on the identity to succeeding generations. The Netherlanders who chose to build their lives outside the Protestant or Catholic enclaves were, of course, no less "Dutch American"—except that they did not contribute (or very little) to the new phenomenon of the Dutch American.

---

[16]    James D. Bratt, *Dutch Calvinism in Modern America: A History of a Conservative Subculture* (Grand Rapids: Eerdmans, 1984), 220: "The slowness of accommodation also deserves note. Having all the marks of the WASP profile, the Dutch did not melt into American society on schedule; in fact, they vociferously resisted the same. Socio-economic dysfunction cannot explain the anomaly, for in these areas the Dutch have adjusted well enough. The reason must lie in considerable part in the realm of 'outlook,' religion and 'mind.'"

Map 3: The Netherlands in the nineteenth century.

# CHAPTER 1

# Origin of an Emigration Tradition

Writing from Boston in December 1846, the Dutch immigrant couple Derk and Louise Arnaud urged their minister, Anthony Brummelkamp of Arnhem—and indirectly their compatriots—to emigrate. They paraphrased an Old Testament text: "Make haste to leave Sodom, with Lot, and go to America, which I consider as a Zoar for the protection of my people." This sentence appeared in a series of letters that Brummelkamp published in 1847 and that were read by many people.[1] This urgent appeal is a typical example of the emotional tone of news coming from America through which emigration came to national attention in the period 1846-1850. It laid the basis for a strong emigrant tradition.

The positive expectations expressed about emigration to America among the middle class and laborers, and the departure of the first large groups of emigrants to America, provoked public discussion

---

[1] A. Brummelkamp, *Stemmen uit Noord-Amerika* (Amsterdam: Hoogkamer, 1847), 95. English translation: *Voices from North-America: With Introductory Words from A. Brummelkamp*. Trans. John J. Dahm (Grand Rapids: Calvin Copy Center, 1980).

about the advantages and disadvantages of a departure and about the consequences for the old country. The fear of a large exit of citizens prompted the government to chart the migration carefully, by which it expanded further into a social phenomenon. Thus, emigration became a tradition that reached further than the tens of thousands who actually left. Although hundreds of thousands of residents in the Netherlands found themselves in the same harsh socioeconomic situation, only a portion of them decided to emigrate. What motivated one to leave and the other to stay? What information about America was available, and how much weight did this information have if one considered the advantages and disadvantages of the Old and the New World? How did emigration become part of the Dutch national heritage?[2]

**Freedom in the Distance**

The first Dutchmen who had the opportunity to travel across the independent nation of America and send their reports home were young sons of aristocratic families who had been attached to the first diplomatic missions that the Netherlands Republic sent to its sister nation on the other side of the Atlantic Ocean. Gijsbert Karel van Hogendorp and Carel Baron de Vos van Steenwijk were in the privileged position that they could visit the new nation in 1784. They were received hospitably everywhere in the homes of the affluent, and they noticed that the network of the American elite was linked seamlessly to that of Europe.

These travelers soon discovered that American class distinctions were founded only on wealth. The newcomers thus had access to the affluent and dominant class and could avoid unnecessary contacts with the common people.[3] To their relief, the Dutch travelers thought they saw that the new federal structure had curbed the influence of the common people, while democracy still came through. Their idea of freedom was especially a protection from the influence of too many lower-class elements on the government.

The affluent folks who could make these journeys returned to the Dutch Republic with mixed feelings. Ordinary citizens had neither

---

[2]  See for instance the inclusion of emigration in the recent listings of key events in the histories of the provinces Zeeland, Friesland, and Groningen.

[3]  J.W. Schulte Nordholt, *The Dutch Republic and American Independence* (Chapel Hill: Univ. of North Carolina Press, 1982; orig. Dutch ed. 1979), 252-63; Carel de Vos van Steenwijk, *Een grand tour naar de nieuwe republiek: Journaal van een reis door Amerika, 1783-1784*. Ed. Wayne te Brake (Hilversum: Verloren, 1999).

time nor money to become acquainted with America, and the poor could not even afford to go there on their own. For them freedom was far away. When half a century later (thanks to cheap travel) they were able to see the United States with their own eyes, they were much more positive about the position of the ordinary American than the aristocratic travelers had been. The Dutch immigrant Alexander Hartgerink expressed his satisfaction with America in 1845: "There is no aristocracy here, but in a certain sense there is equality and freedom." In the meantime, the democratic rights had been increased considerably under President Andrew Jackson. Hartgerink, like many of his fellow immigrants, was especially struck by the absence of social status in America.[4] That characteristic contained a promise of fair relationships, the promise of a better life and of upward mobility that would become known as "the American dream."

America attracted the attention of Europe, which looked expectantly to the west as the direction from which new perspectives would blow east. The independent American nation benefited the most from this centuries-long myth.[5] Day-dreaming sages and hunted refugees fixed their hope on the American continent, as the Old World once again disappointed them. The expectation that life in the New World would be better was fed by several factors—the inspiration that radiated from the myth of the West, the generous gestures of the American government to promote the expansion of its domain, and the heroic struggle for independence that had created a very promising political system. Even though the European elite after some time developed reservations about the "system of freedom and equality that gives free rein to the mischief and passions of the huge masses," the masses themselves especially saw the benefits. Nineteenth-century Europe offered ample reasons to long for this freedom: wars, calamities, compulsory military service, inequality before the law, heavy taxes, economic restrictions, religious persecution, and poverty were more often the rule than the exception. News about America, supplemented by guidebooks, travel accounts, and translated novels, provided for the increasing need for concrete information about the land of promise. And emigrants left their shores.[6]

[4]   G.H. Ligterink, *De landverhuizers. Emigratie naar Noord-Amerika uit het Gelders-Westfaalse grensgebied tussen de jaren 1830-1850* (Zutphen: De Walburg Pers, 1981), 96.

[5]   J.W. Schulte Nordholt, *The Myth of the West: America as the Last Empire* (Grand Rapids: Eerdmans, 1995; orig. Dutch ed. 1992).

[6]   R.G. van Polanen to Bagman & Zoon, May 16, 1830, in J.J. Westendorp Boerma, "Briefwisseling van mr. R.G. van Polanen, (1828-1832)," *Bijdragen*

## The Phenomenon of Migration

Transatlantic migration was of course not brand new, but the term "migrants" (*landverhuizers*) first appeared in official Dutch documents in 1817 to designate a foreign phenomenon: "like an army the foreigners [especially Germans] are coming here, and desiring to leave for America from a Dutch harbor."[7] This definition was based on travel through the Netherlands by more than one hundred thousand German emigrants from the Rhineland between 1720 and 1770, who traveled via the main rivers and Rotterdam harbor to Philadelphia. Only when the Dutch also left their country in organized groups did the term acquire national significance, but it always retained a negative flavor. The extent of Dutch emigration never reached the level of the other West European countries, which experienced the departure to America of many more inhabitants. The number of Dutch emigrants fluctuated around an average of 3,000 per year. Between 1846 and 1850 about 12,000 Dutch persons left for the New World, compared to 450,000 Germans and as many as 950,000 Irish. In total, 220,000 Dutch people emigrated to America in the period 1820-1920, or 72 per 100,000 residents. Crises in Dutch agriculture (industrialization got underway around 1890) resulted in several peaks in 1846-1847 and around 1890. Financial crises in America in 1857, 1873, and 1893, and the Civil War of 1861-1865 put a strong brake on the flow, until economic recovery a few years later caused the emigration to catch up again. These waves helped the tradition of emigration survive the low tides.[8]

---

en *Mededelingen van het Historisch Genootschap* 68 (1953): 102. P.R.D. Stokvis, *Nederlandse trek naar Amerika, 1846-1847* (Leiden: Universitaire Pers, 1977), 76-81.

[7] *Woordenboek der Nederlandsche taal* 8.1 ('s-Gravenhage /Leiden: Martinus Nijhoff/A. W. Sijthoff, 1916), 1031.

[8] Jan Lucassen, "The Netherlands, the Dutch, and Long-Distance Migration in the Late Sixteenth to Early Nineteenth Centuries," in Nicholas Canny, ed., *Europeans on the Move: Studies on European Migration, 1500-1800* (Oxford: Clarendon, 1994), 186; P.R.D. Stokvis, "Dutch International Migration 1815-1910," in Robert P. Swierenga, ed., *The Dutch in America: Immigrant, Settlement, and Cultural Change* (New Brunswick: Rutgers Univ. Press, 1985), 48; and "Nederland in de internationale migratie, 1815-1960," in F.L. van Holthoon, ed., *De Nederlandse samenleving sinds 1815. Wording en samenhang* (Assen: Van Gorcum, 1985), 71-92. Demographically this process was linked to the seventeenth and eighteenth centuries. See Ad van der Woude, "De betekenis van de migratie voor de demographische situatie in de Republiek der Zeven Verenigde Provincieën," in Ad van der Woude," *Leven met geschiedenis. Theorie, praktijk en toepassing van historische kennis* (Amsterdam: Balans, 2000), 225-45.

This transatlantic tradition existed alongside moves to other European countries, which three out of five Dutch emigrants chose. The neighboring countries of Belgium and Germany were especially popular. In 1899 there were 88,000 Dutch in Germany and 54,500 in Belgium compared to 95,000 in the United States. In 1909 there were even more Dutch in Germany (144,000) than in America (120,000). This appears at odds with the massive emigration to America from Germany, but it is not. Many of the Dutch found (temporary) work in specific areas, usually in border regions, where industry offered work opportunities.[9]

The transatlantic journey was a break with past trends. For centuries the Republic of the Seven United Provinces had been a land of immigration. From the sixteenth century to the beginning of the nineteenth the Netherlands attracted hundreds of thousands of immigrants because of the economic opportunities, favorable geographic connections, political stability, and international (especially colonial) contacts. This position as a net immigration country in Europe changed in the first half of the nineteenth century, so that by 1850 more people left the country than entered it. The population growth of the second half of the century was due to lower death rates and consistently high birth rates. The pressure to find means of existence increased because the population growth doubled from 17 percent between 1850 and 1870, to 26 percent between 1869 and 1889, to at least 35 percent between 1909 and 1930. The country counted 3 million people in 1850, 5.1 million in 1900, and 7.8 million in 1930.[10] The sporadic migration to the United States changed in 1846 into a structural movement. The quick succession in the departure of large groups triggered a public debate. Since these departures had the character of a social protest as well, after 1847 the government began to keep an eye on the movement by requesting separate reports on overseas emigration from municipalities and provinces. This directive remained in force until the end of the century. Here one could see the birth of a new phenomenon that was defined by bureaucratic means and thus received an official status.

Of the overseas destinations of the Dutch, the United States was the most important; nine out of ten emigrants went there. The country

---

[9]   Jan Lucassen, *Migrant Labour in Europe 1600-1900: The Drift to the North Sea* (London, etc.: Croom Helm, 1987; orig. Dutch ed. 1984).

[10]  Clé Lesger, "Noord-Hollanders in beweging. Economische ontwikkeling en binnenlandse migratie, ca 1800-1930," CGM Working paper 4 (Amsterdam: Centrum voor de Geschiedenis van Migranten, 2003), notes 21-23.

had a reputation that spoke to everyone's imagination. Departure to European destinations captured less attention, because it usually meant a less definitive break with familiar surroundings than settling in America. The journey in Europe was less spectacular than the Atlantic crossing. The motives behind migration within Europe were economic—usually concerning seasonal labor or other temporary work. The greatest difference between European and American destinations was that with an overseas move ideological motives came into play, so that Dutch enclaves with their own identity developed, which offered a broad range of services. Dutch communities in European cities, however, were mostly connected with commercial posts, and apart from an occasional congregation, they hardly had any of their own institutions.

There was still a final reason for the attention the migration phenomenon received, in spite of its relatively minor extent, and that was the role of a homogeneous group—the Seceders. In 1834 this group had separated itself from the Hervormde Kerk because of the lack of freedom it experienced to propound an orthodox response against the liberal and centric tendencies in the established church. The Seceder leaders Hendrik P. Scholte (1805-1866) and Albertus C. Van Raalte (1811-1876) provided a clear motivation for their departure and determined the image of the emigration movement for a long time.[11]

## Causes

The earmark of Dutch emigration was the rational deliberation about chances for improvement. Without the depressing circumstances in the Netherlands of the 1840s, which formed a sharp contrast with the prospects in America, the exodus would not have happened. Economic stagnation, poor harvests, and high national debts because of the aftermath of the war of 1830 that led to Belgium's independence were to blame for this situation. In five years' time the number of the needy rose from 10 to 15 percent of the population, a sizeable group of a half a million in a population of three million. And there was no change in sight. High taxes in the form of excise duties caused the burden on the

[11]  Because of this clear interpretation of the past, an inflated impression has arisen in popular historical writing that the Seceders dominated the emigration. See G. B. van Dijk, "Geloofsvervolging of broodnood: Hollanders naar Michigan," *Spiegel Historiael* 5.1 (1970): 31-36. For a recent interpretation see Karel Blei, *The Netherlands Reformed Church, 1571-2005*, Historical Series of the Reformed Church in America, no. 51 (Grand Rapids: Eerdmans, 2006).

ordinary citizen to rise sharply. Some cities even financed three-quarters of their budget with indirect taxes. Many laborers were exhausted due the failure of 80 percent of the potato harvest in 1845, followed by the harvest failure of rye the following year, and several severe winters. As a result they became extra susceptible to cholera and other contagious diseases. The national government took no extra initiatives to mitigate the hardships, except for the importation of a thousand guilders worth of corn, for which the climate proved to be unsuitable. To compensate for rising farm rentals, farmers economized on the wages of their laborers. In the provinces of Zeeland, Groningen, and Overijssel, with many large farms and many day laborers, the growing population could not be provided for. Only in areas with many small farms was the situation somewhat bearable.

For most people there was no prospect of climbing up the economic ladder, while the threat of sliding down into poverty became ever greater. The elite society still remained proudly erect, but many economic certainties had disappeared. In the province of Zeeland only one-third of the rural population had year-round steady work. The rising prices hurt the small craftsman and laborer directly, but the middle class was also affected because of the diminishing purchase power. The population became so restless that town councils charged the night watchmen to watch especially for thievery. In the countryside of Zeeland soldiers patrolled to intervene if farms were in danger of being robbed of their food supplies. In the city of Zierikzee attempts to collect unpaid taxes in February 1845 led to several days of demonstrations with the banging of pots and pans. Elsewhere in the country riots broke out against the high price of bread.[12]

Besides the economic stagnation, the country also suffered from political paralysis, because the voice of the opposition that demanded more democracy was throttled, liberal ideas were rejected as dangerous to the state, and the status quo was harshly enforced. An anonymous commentator expressed the spectrum of motives for emigration strikingly in an imaginary conversation among a rich farmer, a doctor, a blacksmith, a teacher, and a government official, while sailing down the most important river connecting Rotterdam and the port of departure. Pressing circumstances made life in their country difficult: the threat of loss of professional jobs, the lack of fertile soil, the arbitrariness of compulsory military service, the corruption of the higher classes,

---

[12]  Paul Kroes, "Sociale onrust in Zeeland, 1845-1846" (MA thesis Nijmegen Univ., 1986), 90-91.

the contempt of the government for its subjects, the arrogance of the educated, the suspicion against every form of influence of the people, the bureaucracy, and the lack of freedom. They bemoaned the fate of the little guy who was monitored by officials even in his own house to determine whether he had paid the tax on slaughtering his own pig.[13]

The sympathy of this critical author was clearly with the laborers who were the ones who were really productive, but were hardly given any recognition. This stifling atmosphere was in sharp contrast with the aroma of freedom that wafted over from the United States: "The luxury, the refined morals, the good taste, the genial relations among rich Americans are not inferior to those of England. However, the wide gap that here separates the elite from ordinary people is not known in America; one does not treat the laboring man with such indifference, and keep him at a distance as is done by us. Manual labor is honored and rewarded according to merit. This respect for labor shines through everywhere, because it is regarded as the real source of general prosperity."[14] The liberal author optimistically displayed to his readers the "new Society" that had been born in America without bloodshed—although he did ignore the injustice toward Indians and the cruelties of slavery.

The participants in this imaginary discussion did not form the largest group of immigrants. Prosperous farmers and citizens constituted on the average only 13 percent of the adventuresome travelers in the period of 1835-1880. Neither did the very poorest leave, since they could not pay for the trip or finance the initial period without help from others. Their contingent was 22 percent. Those who had no or few means were therefore dependent on the readiness of others to advance the costs of the passage. Nearly two-thirds of the emigrants had some resources. They formed the core of the emigration flow.[15]

---

[13] Remieg Arts a.o., eds., *Land van de kleine gebaren. Een politieke geschiedenis van Nederland, 1780-1990* (Nijmegen: Sun, 2001), 83-95. *De landverhuizers in het kanaal door Voorn, in mei 1847* (Amsterdam: Hoogkamer, 1847).

[14] Ibid., 16. The national tax on slaughtering was terminated in 1852 and on the grinding of grain in 1855; local taxes disappeared in the following ten years.

[15] Robert P. Swierenga, *Faith and Family: Dutch Immigration and Settlement in the United States, 1820-1920* (New York: Holmes & Meier, 2000), 63, table 2.14. These figures give a global picture, but do not offer a general conclusion about poverty. J.M.M. de Meere estimates that in 1849 a maximum of 8.3 percent of the Dutch trade population was structurally unemployed and dependent on poor relief, but in addition there was an unknown group that were temporarily dependent. See his *Economische ontwikkeling en*

Table 1: *Religious Background and Economic Class of Heads of Family and the Unmarried, 1835-1857 (percentages)*[16]

| Religion (number) | Well-to-do | Middling | Poor |
|---|---|---|---|
| Reformed Church (3956) | 9 | 64 | 28 |
| Seceders (1041) | 18 | 63 | 19 |
| Roman Catholic (1620) | 12 | 69 | 19 |
| Jewish (178) | 9 | 62 | 29 |
| Total (6795) | 11 | 65 | 24 |

Neither were the emigrants between 1835 and 1920 evenly divided among the various social classes and regions. The exodus was the greatest in the three "clay provinces" of Zeeland, Groningen, and Friesland; these accounted for 39 percent of the emigrants. The provinces of Drente, Gelderland, Limburg, Noord Brabant, and Overijssel provided 37.5 percent, and the most urban and highest-populated provinces of Noord- and Zuid-Holland and Utrecht only 23.5 percent. These proportions were stable until the end of the century and then changed in favor of the urban areas.[17]

The church affiliation of the first emigration wave until 1857 also showed a remarkable composition. The *Hervormden* (members of the established or state church) and Seceders (members who separated from the state church in 1834), who represented 55 and 1.3 percent of the population, were overrepresented with 65 and 13 percent respectively of the total emigration. Roman Catholics were underrepresented with 20 over against 39 percent, while the Jewish share of 2 percent corresponded to their portion of the population. Two-thirds of the emigrants—that is, the greatest majority—belonged to the Hervormde Kerk.

Roman Catholic emigration was even more regional than that of the Protestants. The Catholics came from the provinces of Gelderland (especially in the mid-1840s), Noord-Brabant, and Limburg. Educated

---

*levensstandaard in Nederland gedurende de eerste helft van de negentiende eeuw. Aspecten en trends* ('s-Gravenhage: Martinus Nijhoff, 1982), 55. He points out that in the first half of the nineteenth century there was economic growth (with the exception of the crises years 1845-1846), but for the first time there were many publications and discussions about poverty as a serious social problem.

16  Ibid., 178, table 6.4. Robert P. Swierenga, "Local-cosmopolitan Theory and Immigrant Religion: The Social Basis of the Antebellum Dutch Reformed Schism," *Journal of Social History* 14 (1980/81): 119.

17  Swierenga, *Faith and Family*, 46-48, table 2.4.

laborers among them were better represented, and there also were more farmers than laborers. Limburg delivered especially farmers and farmhands, who often came from mixed farming; the other regions had more skilled trades people.

It is plausible to assume that the overrepresentation of the Seceders can be explained by the more burdensome circumstances they experienced in the 1840s. We shall discuss this later. However, it becomes clear from Table 1 that the Seceder emigrants were not poorer than the average emigrant. On the contrary, among the Seceders there were more prosperous people than among other emigrants. During the first wave of 1835-1857, 18 percent of the emigrating Seceders were well to do, the same percentage were needy, while 63 percent were in between. For the Roman Catholics those numbers for the same period were somewhat less favorable, while for the *Hervormden* and the Jews the percentage of needy people (around 29 percent) was similar (see Table 1).

In the following periods (1858-1865 and 1866-1873) the portion of well-to-do Seceder emigrants declined to below average—to 16 and 9 percent respectively—but the portion of needy also remained low. Thus, the middle group became larger. With the other groups the portion of the well to do increased.[18] There was no direct relationship between Secession, poverty, and emigration, although the Seceders' mutual solidarity made it possible for the poor to go along.[19] Next to economic factors, social and ideological factors contributed to the emergence of an emigrant culture.

## Social and Religious Factors

The Seceders were not the only ones to emigrate collectively, nor were they a majority, but their ability to link local groups to a national network made their contribution to an emigration tradition substantial. Though the statistics may show that the Seceder emigrants' prosperity did not deviate much from that of other emigrants, financial burdens did weigh more heavily on them. The Secession was a movement of the common man. Developing their own church life demanded great sacrifices. They were on their own for building and furnishing their

[18]   Robert Swierenga and Yda Schreuder, "Catholic and Protestant Emigration from the Netherlands in the 19th Century: A Comparative Social Structure Analysis," *Tijdschrift voor Economische en Sociale Geografie* 74 (1983): 35.
[19]   Robert P. Swierenga and Harry S. Stout, "Dutch Immigration in the Nineteenth Century, 1820-1877: A Quantitative Overview," *Indiana Social Studies Quarterly* 28 (Fall 1975): 7-34, esp. 21.

churches, paying fines for illegal church services, and supporting ministers. Many church council meetings were devoted to devising plans for support of the poor. In order to prevent a spiral of poverty, people were counseled not to take items to the pawn shop to secure a loan. The poor received in-kind help as much as possible, rather than money, so that they would not be tempted to squander the money. The deacons often paid school tuition for children, and several ministers even financed small projects in home industries, so that the poor could become productive. But the means were too limited to be able to help everyone, especially because structural improvement of the situation was not forthcoming. Many people were depressed about the future of the Netherlands because of the buildup of economic stagnation, social regress, church disagreement, increased criminality, and the inability to solve the problems of population growth.[20]

Two widely accepted misperceptions have been making the rounds about the Seceders who emigrated: that they fled because of persecution and that they were extremely conservative. However, the direct cause could not be persecution, because since 1841 many Seceder congregations had requested, and received, official recognition from the government, which meant that being forced out of illegal church buildings, imprisonment, and the billeting of soldiers were issues of the past. King William I had finally come to terms with the separation of the Netherlands and Belgium, and therefore the grim attempt to keep the national church together (which had created the opposite effect) was relaxed. The result of years of oppression was a great loss of trust between the government and the orthodox Christians. The government had turned out to be a strong opponent of new initiatives. Even after 1841 it issued fines to Seceders for conducting meetings. Society treated the Seceders with disdain, and from the Protestant church hierarchy one could not expect much understanding for a more democratic organization.[21]

---

[20] Hans Krabbendam, "Emigration as Protest? Opinions about the Relation between Church and State as a Factor in the Dutch Emigration Movement," in Hans Krabbendam and Larry Wagenaar, eds., *The Dutch-American Experience: Essays in Honor of Robert P. Swierenga* (Amsterdam: VU Univ. Press, 2000), 61-70.

[21] Jasper Vree, "The Dominating Theology in the Nederlandse Hervormde Kerk after 1815 in its Relation to the Secession of 1834," in George Harinck and Hans Krabbendam, eds., *Breaches and Bridges: Reformed Subcultures in the Netherlands, Germany, and the United States* (Amsterdam: VU Univ. Press, 2000), 33-47. After 1867 Reformed [*Hervormde*] male members were allowed to vote for church councils and calling ministers.

It took at least half a century before Seceders were fully accepted by Dutch society.[22] This social isolation strengthened solidarity among the Seceders, even though internal quarrels disrupted their unity. The basis for a separate denomination was created by the official government recognition after 1841; however, internal quarrels—for example, about the church order and the acceptance of official recognition by the government—broke the unity and led to smaller factions of several thousand members. The group that fostered the most reservations about a strict organization of the new denomination, which was to be governed by the rules dictated by the authoritative Church Order of 1619, was less dismissive of the kindred souls who remained loyal to the Hervormde Kerk. However, they lost out to those who assumed a more exclusive posture toward those who thought differently and established strict codes of conduct for the denomination. This group was especially strong in the northern part of the country. Emigration took place in the early stage of the Secession, when this strict movement was still gaining strength. An exclusivist view of their own history had not yet taken root.[23] This flexible mentality of the immigration leaders also translated into a readiness to adjust to life in America. The most conservative party remained behind.

The Seceder emigrants did express their displeasure about the divisions within their own circles but did not offer their isolation as an argument to justify their departure.[24] The Reverend Simon van Velzen, the leader of the strict group opposing the preachers Hendrik P. Scholte and Albertus Van Raalte, accused them of emigrating for personal reasons, either caused by lack of respect (Scholte) or disappointment about the failure to obtain more freedom in the churches (Van Raalte):

> [Scholte] had little influence in the Church at this time. Most of the believers no longer respected him. He seems to have been moved to emigration by ambition to become an influential person

[22]    Jasper Vree, "Van seperatie naar integratie. De Afgescheidenen en hun kerk in de Nederlandse samenleving (1834-1892)" in Reender Kranenborg and Wessel Stoker, eds., *Religies en (on)gelijkheid in een plurale samenleving* (Leuven/Apeldoorn: Garant, 1995), 161-76.

[23]    Ibid.

[24]    M. te Velde explains that the early Seceders were indeed divided into factions, but that the anti-synod people had no reason to feel isolated. See M. te Velde, *Anthony Brummelkamp (1811-1881)* (Barneveld: De Vuurbaak, 1988), 179; also, M. te Velde, "The Dutch Background of the American Secession in the RCA," in Harinck and Krabbendam, *Breaches and Bridges*, 85-100.

in North America, and the need to diminish his affluent life style here. He left here unreconciled, censured after having revealed many heretical ideas. Most of the members who went to North America harbored Scholte's ideas. They were not fully devoted to the doctrine of our forms of unity, but were licentious. A few who were true to pure doctrine also went along.[25]

About Van Raalte's departure Van Velzen wrote, "He was disappointed here and his attempts were not successful."[26] These judgments say more about Van Velzen than about his colleagues. The organization of the church was very important to him and he must have regarded the departure of the obstructionists with a certain relief.

Personal experiences and nuanced ideas about the arrangement of society prepared the way to leave the country. The experience of a life-threatening illness made Van Raalte feel removed from his environment. The independent Scholte thought that the Seceders strove too much for the restoration of the old Reformed Church and too little for renewal. The formulation about the relationship between church and state was still in progress, but already two opposing factions could be delineated. On the one side stood Simon van Velzen, who pleaded for protection of true Reformed doctrine by the government. On the other side stood Scholte, who pleaded for complete separation between church and state, and, in a more moderate form, Brummelkamp and Van Raalte, who desired that the state should not favor any denomination, not even by the granting of subsidies. This second group felt the attraction of the American relationship between church and state.[27]

Scholte was the Seceder with the widest international scope. His periodical *De Reformatie* (The Reformation) reported on religious conditions from all over the world, broadened the horizon of his readers, and made the step to another country not only easier but also more attractive. Scholte's followers, the minister Cornelis van der Meulen and the farmer Jannes van de Luijster, had the same interest

---

[25] A note of van Velzen in the Minutes book of de Christelijk Afgescheiden Gemeente te Amsterdam, cited in C. Smits, "De Afscheiding bewaard (De strijd van ds. S. van Velzen te Amsterdam)," in D. Deddens and J. Kamphuis, eds., *Afscheiding-wederkeer. Opstellen over de Afscheiding van 1834* (Barneveld: De Vuurbaak, 1984), 215.

[26] H. Reenders, "Albertus C. van Raalte als leider van Overijsselse Afgescheidenen 1836-1846," in Freerk Peereboom, a.o., eds., *Van scheurmakers, onruststokers en geheime opruijers: De Afscheiding in Overijssel* (Kampen: N.P., 1984), note 369.

[27] Te Velde, *Brummelkamp*, 345-48.

**Statue of Albertus C. Van Raalte in Holland, Michigan.**

Hope College Collection of the Joint Archives of Holland, Michigan

in international news. In America, Scholte maintained his rejection of a Christian government. "The world is still the world, even if it is called Christian and will not subject to Christ until the Anti-Christ has come and been brought into subjection."[28] The emigrants approvingly cited a hymn composed by the Jewish convert Isaac Da Costa about America, which he held up as a star of hope for the "old and worn-out and crowded Europe." He had encouraged emigration in his poetry collection,

> Go there! From where the fresh sound of "be free," came first,
> and thundered through Europe. Go there! Whoever needs air and
> light,

---

[28]    Letter of H.P. Scholte to J.J.L. van den Brugghen, October 22, 1857, cited in Johan Stellingwerff, Robert P. Swierenga, ed., and Walter Lagerwey, trans., *Iowa Letters: Dutch Immigrants on the American Frontier*, Historical Series of the Reformed Church in America, no. 47 (Grand Rapids: Eerdmans, 2004), 432.

**Henry P. Scholte, leader of the Dutch immigrants in Iowa.**

Western Seminary Collection of the Joint Archives of Holland, Michigan.

who wants to float above stuff and society...
Whether for abundance and treasure. Pull out the stakes
of Europe's tent—whoever loves God and freedom!
Freedom of the church, freedom of the state,
of pen, of press, of will—to everyone's desire or benefit.[29]

The Seceders experienced this contrast between the Old and the New World more intensely than most other Protestants. Moreover, their spiritual kin who remained in the Hervormde Kerk, such as scholar

---

[29]   A. van Malsen, *Achttal brieven mijner kinderen uit de kolonie Holland in Amerika* (Zwijndrecht: J. Boden, 1848), 6. For an English translation see John Yzenbaard, "'America' Letters from Holland," *Michigan History* 32 (March 1948): 43. He cited from Isaac Da Costa, *Wachter! Wat is er van de nacht? Bij de uitgangen van 1847*. The poems of Da Costa were loved by orthodox people and offered comfort to the emigrants, as noted by Ds. Van der Meulen. *Ter nagedachtenis aan Rev. Cornelius van der Meulen* (Grand Rapids: De Standaard Drukkerij, 1876), 58-59. On the advice of Anthony Brummelkamp the emigrants took along Da Costa's poetry collections. However, Da Costa also mentioned the other side of American freedom—lynching laws, the tension about slavery, and individualism.

and politician Guillaume Groen van Prinsterer (1801-1876) and social reformer Ottho G. Heldring (1804-1876), initially rejected emigration completely. Groen saw the migration movement among the Seceders as an emergency exit from a failed ideal. The separation of church and state as it was avowed in America stood in direct opposition to his own antirevolutionary vision of government. Heldring thought in more practical terms, but he also wanted to bring government and people together. He saw no future in emigration and found it a waste of energy. Times were difficult, but emigration was a bridge too far. He preferred to find the solution in the development of new polders or in settling on the island of Java—as long as the project remained under the Dutch flag.[30]

## Social Responsibility

The social involvement of the Secession ministers also argues against the supposed conservatism of this group. Alexander Hartgerink, mentioned above, was an important link in the emigration chain; he told the Secession minister Anthony Brummelkamp of Arnhem that he was also leaving, because he had received favorable reports about America. His decision set Brummelkamp thinking. This minister was one of the pillars of the seceded denomination. The theological training institute that he led with his brother-in-law, Albertus van Raalte, brought him into contact with a broad circle of fellow believers. Moreover, Van Raalte was pastor of a congregation and attempted to relieve immediate needs with his own funds as much as possible. The Secession ministers were closer to their parishioners than most of the *Hervormde* ministers who were gentlemen of social standing and who, in some cities, even established separate churches for the poor.[31]

---

[30]  *Groen van Prinsterer Schriftelijke nalatenschap. Zesde Deel. Briefwisseling vijfde deel 1827-1869*. Ed. J.L. van Essen. Rijks Geschiedkundige Publicatiën. Grote Serie 175 ('s-Gravenhage: Martinus Nijhoff, 1980), 159 (August 25, 1847). *Groen van Prinsterer Schriftelijke nalatenschap. Derde deel. Briefwisseling tweede deel 1833-1848*. Ed. C. Gerretson and A. Goslinga. Rijks Geschiedkundige Publicatiën. Grote Serie 114 ('s-Gravenhage: Martinus Nijhoff, 1964), 810-81. Letter of Heldring to Groen, September 30, 1846, ibid., 746-47. Groen accepted the American Revolution as a movement against injustice. See Arie van Dijk, "Groen en de Amerikaanse Revolutie," in J. de Bruijn and G. Harinck, eds., *Groen van Prinsterer in Europese context* (Hilversum: Verloren, 2004). H. Reenders, *Alternatieve zending. Otto Gerhard Heldring (1804-1876) en de verbreiding van het christendom in Nederlands-Indië* (Kampen: Kok, 1991), 87-89, 103-06.

[31]  Gerben Heitink, *Biografie van de dominee* (Baarn: Ten Have, 2001), 92-111.

Van Raalte's involvement with the poor gave him qualms of conscience. He believed that healthy people should not depend on public support; if they could work they should do so. If that was not possible in the Netherlands, they should try elsewhere. Out of the various possibilities, the United States appeared to be the most promising: comparable living conditions, accessibility, space, freedom of religion, and regular travel decided the question. However, the readiness to leave did not just happen; first, objections of principle as well as practicality had to be overcome. Various factors persuaded Van Raalte to start looking abroad—an illness that brought him to the brink of death, the message that his congregation could no longer support two pastors, and that he would not be held back if he found a position elsewhere. The hardly flourishing personal circumstances, his sense of responsibility, and also his adventuresome spirit made him decide in summer 1846 to join the emigrants.[32]

Van Raalte clearly explained his rationale: "We have been forced to this decision because of emptiness and slavish work, suffocating cares and oppression because of crowding together of people, with all those anxieties and the development of the evil that lives in people's hearts, and the destructive competition—all these are a fertile womb for many sins."[33] Here the economic need clearly had a spiritual dimension. Van Raalte decided to go with the emigrants to keep them together, so that they would not be scattered and thereby lose their Dutch spirit and especially lose their faith. At the same time, Van Raalte saw that America offered possibilities for Christian education, which was, for the time being, not in sight in the Netherlands. His disappointment with his native country and his fellow Christians opened the door for departure. The interpretation of circumstances, the somber expectations for the future, and the contrast with the hopeful perspectives in America helped him cross the threshold. His colleague Hendrik Pieter Scholte experienced a similar process.

Even more so than Van Raalte, Scholte was positive about America; he especially had great admiration for the political arrangements and the separation of church and state. He came to the conclusion that emigration to America could well be the best solution for his present and future problems. When he met someone from America who confirmed the feasibility of his plans, he began to plan for departure

---

[32] Jeanne Jacobson, Elton J. Bruins, and Larry J. Wagenaar, *Albertus C. Van Raalte: Dutch Leader and American Patriot* (Holland: Hope College, 1996).

[33] H. Reenders, "Van Raalte," 191-94, citation on 194.

in May 1846. He interpreted a case of Seceders being fined in 1846 as a confirmation of his fear for the future of the Netherlands. On May 15, 1846, he wrote to Groen van Prinsterer:

> There is lively discussion about colonization in the United States of North America in various areas of our country and among Christians who are not yet poor. The stubborn opposition of the government against freedom of religion and education encourages the desire for emigration. In these areas also, prosperous people are talking about it. After an honest overview of the condition of our country, I can no longer speak against that desire. Here people are crowded together. Especially for Christians who do not have many resources, the longer they are here, the more difficult it becomes to get through life honestly. In North America the land is empty, there is complete freedom of religion and education; even when the size of the group is sufficient, and stays together, with the purchase of several large tracts of land, local government remains in the hands of the colonists.

Initially Scholte had hoped that the churches would help the emigrants as a sign that they were not forgotten, but he leaned more and more to joining those who were leaving the country.[34]

In the middle of July 1846, before his departure, Scholte had a meeting with Thomas De Witt, one of the leaders of the Reformed Protestant Dutch Church, who happened to be in the Netherlands to gather documents about the history of his church. De Witt would play a crucial role in the reception and support of the emigrants, together with his colleague Isaac N. Wyckhoff of the church in Albany. The channels for future settlement were put into place.[35] On May 25, 1846, Van Raalte and Scholte informed these Americans of Dutch origin about their coming.[36]

---

[34]    *Groen van Prinsterer Schriftelijke nalatenschap. Derde Deel. Briefwisseling tweede deel 1833-1848.* RGP 114:740 (October 9, 1846) and 748.

[35]    Report of Thomas De Witt in June 1847. *Acts and Proceedings of the General Synod of the Reformed Protestant Dutch Church in North America,* Vol. 7 (New York: J. A. Gray, 1849), 133-34. De Witt mentioned that he had spoken with Scholte. "The tide of emigration has commenced, and soon two important colonies from this class [i.e., the well-to-do class] will be founded in the West."

[36]    "Appeal to the Faithful in the United States in North America," Henry S. Lucas, ed., *Dutch Immigrant Memoirs and Related Works* (Assen: Van Gorcum, 1955; repr. Grand Rapids: Eerdmans 1997), 1: 14-20. Isaac N. Wyckhoff

## The Spread of Emigration Fever

News about the United States as a suitable destination reached the Dutch via several channels. In the spring of 1845 the coastal town of Cadzand in the province of Zeeland was excited by the "delicious" letters of three carpenter laborers, and as a result 170 people sold their belongings so that they could leave.[37] In the Achterhoek area of the province of Gelderland, the emigrants from Westphalia, Germany, on their way to the Rotterdam harbor, inspired the local people to do the same. The initiatives of Van Raalte and Scholte put the wheels in motion in the whole country.

The situation in the province of Zeeland shows clearly how the emigration virus spread and how social and ideological factors led to joint emigration of the well to do and the poor. The gentleman-farmer Jannes Van de Luijster was the leader of the Seceders in the province, and his spacious yard and large barn were the ideal meeting place, because his house was close to the small harbor of Borssele, from where there were regular connections to Goes, Walcheren, and Zeeuws-Vlaanderen. Without fail he paid the fines for prohibited meetings and supported the poor generously. He shared Scholte's ideas about the threat that hung over Europe, because the masses had rejected the gospel, and he interpreted the economic deterioration as a sign of God's judgment. Because of his prominent place in the community and the region, his decision to leave and to finance the trip for seventy-seven people, was an enormous stimulus for other interested families. He also prevailed over the practical objections of the Reverend Cornelius Van der Meulen (1800-1876), who had served a group of ten Secession congregations in Zeeland since 1841. Although we cannot trace exactly how Van der Meulen's change occurred, it is likely that he was concerned at first about the worldly motives and the exaggerated expectations of wealth, but later realized emigration was a solution for collective challenges. The minister functioned as the social conscience of the enterprise and emphasized that no one should remain behind for lack of money, because life would become even more difficult for those who stayed. Therefore the minister pressed for publication of the emigration plans.[38]

published an English translation of this letter in the weekly magazine of the Reformed Church, the *Christian Intelligencer*, October 15, 1846.

[37] Kroes, "Sociale onrust in Zeeland," 91. *Vlissingsche Courant*, April 4, 1845.

[38] Minutes of the Particular Synod of Zeeland January 6, 1847, Municipal Archives Goes, Archieven Particuliere Synode Gereformeerde Kerken in Nederland, inv. 3.

**Cornelius Van der Meulen, Seceded minister in Zeeland.**

Collection Roosevelt Study Center, Middelburg, the Netherlands.

The actual departure of the early groups of emigrants from the Netherlands opened Van der Meulen's eyes to the possibilities offered in America to his poor congregation. After reading about religious revivals elsewhere in the world he realized that in America he could work just as well on his mandate to work for the kingdom of God. He still considered the encouragement from Genesis "to be fruitful and multiply," and from Mark, "to go into all the world and preach the Gospel to every creature" relevant and applied it to the actual situation. In spite of his criticism of the Dutch government, he did love his native country. However, the strong bond with the Netherlands became weaker when he realized that Christianity was universal. Faith offered him and the other emigrants compensation for the loss of the bond with their birthplace. They left "from a sinking country, whose sources of prosperity the Lord had visibly ended."

In their justification of emigration, they expressed fear of God's judgment on the Netherlands, and they emphasized that they did not want to help support "false religious ministers." They longed for deliverance from "the constricting bonds of the Church," and neither could they justify that their children could not be taught in Christian schools. To preclude the criticism that they were looking for an imaginary lazy life of plenty, they acknowledged that they "were not looking for paradise on earth, but for a country where their conscience would not be bound." Finally, they remembered that the Christian's true country was not on this earth, but on the new earth, so that they could leave the Netherlands with a peaceful heart.[39] Thus, their criticism about affairs in the Netherlands opened the door to another place, where freedom beckoned.[40]

## Roman Catholics

The establishment of an emigration tradition among Roman Catholics shows a very different pattern. Among Protestants, ministers went along with their congregations when they decided to emigrate, and mission work was taken up much later. With the Romans Catholics, however, the priests went ahead with a mission, to be followed later by groups of lay people who settled near the mission. After the French occupation (1795-1813), the Roman Catholics reclaimed their civil rights and monastic orders returned to the Netherlands. The Dutch archdiocese strengthened its ties with Rome, and the church became increasingly involved in social and intellectual life. The seminaries generated a surplus of students. At the same time interest in other countries blossomed. While the American Roman Catholic Church had a great shortage of personnel, the Netherlands brought over sixty-five Jesuits and several Dominicans, Crosiers, and Capuchins who concentrated in the cities and in the west. In letters and articles they informed their Dutch fellow believers about their work.[41] At the same time Commissioner-General Henricus van den Wijmelenberg blew new life into the Order of the Holy Cross by directing them to mission work

---

[39] *Reglement der Zeeuwse Vereeniging ter verhuizing naar de Vereenigde Staaten van Noord-Amerika* (Goes: Wed. P. Crombouw, 1847).

[40] In the middle of the nineteenth century the word *vaderland* pointed first to the place of birth and thus had especially a regional/local significance. Next, it also indicated the historical home, of which you were the heir, and finally, a communal goal. This last element, the willingness to take part in the common good, did not bind this group strongly to the Netherlands because of lack of opportunities. Cf. Remieg Aerts and Henk te Velde, "De taal van het nationaal besef, 1848-1940," in N.C.F. van Sas, ed., *Vaderland. Een geschiedenis van de vijftiende eeuw tot 1940* (Amsterdam: Amsterdam University Press, 1999), 391-454, esp. 399-400.

[41] A.J.J.M. van den Eerenbeemt, *De Missie-Actie in Nederland (1600-1940)* (Nijmegen: Berkhout, 1945), 58-70.

and by founding a monastery community in America. Many Crosiers had family members among the emigrants.[42]

The closest tie between Dutch priests and emigrants developed in northeast Brabant. Until 1842 this region fell outside the Dutch diocese Den Bosch, and the priests there had studied in other countries. A number of them joined the group of nearly one hundred priests from the province of Noord-Brabant who went to America to carry out mission work. The Dutch church hierarchy would have preferred them to stay in the Netherlands but went along with the situation. The emigrating priests stimulated the local population to go to America. The Crosiers especially, who had their base around Uden, went to America with the purpose of supporting the emigrants.[43]

In 1857 American bishops with a European background founded the American College in Leuven, Belgium, with the purpose of providing priests for the United States. These priests and the accounts of their adventures heightened the interest in the United States. The well-known Flemish Jesuit and missionary Pieter de Smet published regular reports in *De Godsdienstvriend* about life and his mission work in America. Although the priests who left did not do much to prepare the emigration of fellow citizens, they did take care of essential contacts and information, whereby they could reassure their fellow believers with the news that although America was Protestant, it still was a "safe" country.[44]

Around 1850 the interest moved from mission work among the Indians to serving the Catholic immigrants, and, where possible, the conversion of Protestants. In the period 1820-1880 eighty-eight priests and eight monks from Noord-Brabant were active in America, with the Dominican priest Theodorus van den Broek (1784-1851) as the best-known representative. He formed the first link of group migration of Roman Catholics from Brabant. His parish in Wisconsin, which he had established in 1836, emptied out because in 1843 the Menominee tribe was forced by the American government to settle in a different area. He

---

[42]   Guy Deboutte, "Pater Franciscus Eduardus Daems, O.S.C (1826-1879) en de eerste kruisheren in de Verenigde Staten. Verwezenlijkingen en problemen" (MA thesis, Catholic University Leuven, 1982), 79-83.

[43]   H.A.V.M. van Stekelenburg, *Landverhuizing als regionaal verschijnsel. Van Noord Brabant naar Noord-Amerika, 1820-1880*) (Tilburg: Stichting Zuidelijk Historisch Contact, 1991), 79.

[44]   Ibid., 45-79. For a biography of another prominent Dutch priest, see Annemarie Kasteel, *Francis Janssens, 1843-1897: A Dutch-American Prelate* (Lafayette: Center for Louisiana Studies, 1992).

Theodorus van den Broek, leader of Dutch Roman Catholic immigrants in Wisconsin.

Van Stekelenburg Collection, Roosevelt Study Center, Middelburg, the Netherlands

could no longer pay the debts that he had incurred in setting up the mission post. In addition, he had to think of a solution when he learned that an inheritance on which he had counted and for which he had returned to the Netherlands did not amount to anything. He thought that he could breathe new life into his settlement with a shipment of immigrants, and he hoped that with their support he could start a monastery.

With that purpose in mind he wrote a brochure to explain his plan and to describe his area. In the late summer of 1847 he got the ball rolling and in March 1848 three groups left for Wisconsin, with a total of more than 400 people from Oost-Brabant. An earlier group of 120 people, mostly from Nijmegen, had left for Iowa under the leadership of attorney and ex-seminary student Christiaan Verwaijen, but left no traces.[45] Other groups followed, among which, in 1850, a company of

---

[45]    Harry van Stekelenburg, "Dutch Roman Catholics in the United States," in Robert P. Swierenga, ed., *The Dutch in America: Immigrant, Settlement, and Cultural Change* (New Brunswick: Rutgers Univ. Press, 1985), 66-67.

80 people, under the leadership of the priest from Boekel, Gerhardus van den Heuvel. Because of their small number they did not succeed in establishing their own colony and they were scattered in Wisconsin.

It appears from these cases of organized emigration of Roman Catholics that the religious motif played a role only with the clergy who left for the United States individually. Personal initiatives inspired groups to make the journey to America.[46] Actually, the bond with "the Netherlands" hardly existed; most Catholics felt closer ties with their regional counterparts in Belgium or Germany.[47] Only recently, in 1848, they had had to resign themselves to the fact that they belonged to the Netherlands. Historian J.A. Bornewasser wrote significantly, "For most of the members of the people of Limburg at this time, the designation 'my native country' must have been as real as the concept of 'parents' for a foundling."[48]

Between 1851 and 1877, about 1,700 Catholics from Noord-Limburg and the area around Sittard left for America. These were mostly farm laborers and farmers who were attracted by the offer of the Homestead Act (1862), which offered pioneers the prospect of land ownership at low cost, if they would clear and cultivate the rough land. They settled in areas where Dutch and Flemish Catholics had settled earlier—Green Bay, De Pere, and Little Chute in Wisconsin. The city of Venlo even named one of its new districts "Depere," indicating the popular destination in Wisconsin.[49]

The time of massive emigration among Catholics arrived only after the Civil War (1861-1865) and was concentrated in Noordoost-Brabant (Boekel and Zeeland), Noordwest-Brabant (Zevenbergen), and de Kempen (Oirschot). The most popular settlement areas were

---

[46]  J.A.. Bornewasser, "De Nederlandse katholieken en hun negentiede-eeuwse vaderland," in J. A. Bornewasser, *Kerkelijk verleden in een wereldlijke context. Historische opstellen, gebundeld en aangeboden aan de schrijver bij zijn aftreden als hoogleraar aan de Theologische Faculteit Tilburg* (Amsterdam: Van Soeren en De Bataafsche Leeuw, 1989), 262-83. Perhaps the need to prove that Catholics (like Protestants) were also good Dutchmen hampered their emigration.

[47]  Rico op den Camp, "Towards one nation: The Province of Limburg and the Dutch nation during the eighteen-seventies," in Annemieke Galema, Barbara Henkes, and Henk te Velde, eds., *Images of the Nation: Different Meanings of Dutchness, 1870-1940* (Amsterdam: Rodopi, 1993), 81-86. Political disappointment, financial issues, and neglect of the infrastructure discouraged identification with the Netherlands.

[48]  Bornewasser, "De Nederlandse katholieken," 278.

[49]  G.C.P. Linssen, "Limburgers naar Noord-Amerika," *Economisch- en sociaal-historisch jaarboek* 35 (1972): 209-25.

in Wisconsin (Fox Rover) and cities in the Midwest, such as Detroit. The overpopulation in the south of the Netherlands was not so critical that emigration offered the only escape. Land-clearing projects and emerging industrialization in the Netherlands provided economic alternatives. The most valid explanation for emigration in general is the succession of structural changes that clearly led to tensions in daily life. Emigration offered a way out of such tensions. However, there was no sign of such structural tension in the Land van Cuijk region. The major reason for emigration from Brabant did not lie in religion, nor politics, nor extreme poverty, nor overpopulation, nor disasters. Brabant did suffer from the potato blight, just as in Zeeland, but more than a harvest disaster was needed to decide on emigration. The most heavily hit areas, such as the areas of Heusden and Altena, hardly produced any emigrants.

It was especially the need for improvement or the desire to forestall economic deterioration that prompted the people of Brabant to leave. The decline in home industry and the lack of economic alternatives stimulated migration. Many went to the cities where several industries had been established, such as Tilburg, Eindhoven, and Helmond, while others chose to go to America, if they saw the possibility to remain within a Roman Catholic environment. The attraction of America was more important than the pressure in the Netherlands, and during the 1860s neither force was very strong. Emigration slowed down because of the American Civil War, and at the same time the import of American cotton from the South stopped, the demand for wool increased, enabling that industry to grow in Tilburg. Migrants who under different circumstances would have sought their welfare across the ocean, could now come to this city.[50]

Reflection about the relationship between church and state, thus, did not play any role. Here again there is a significant difference between Catholics and Seceders. The latter harbored the idea that they belonged to the center of the nation and cherished the ideal to of returning the country to the old ways. The Catholics did not know such ideals and expectations. Among them the mission culture was much stronger than the culture of collective emigration.

---

[50]   Van Stekelenburg, *Landverhuizing*, 164-65 and 189-209; J.P.M. Peters, "De migratie naar Tilburg (1860-1870 en de Amerikaanse Secessie-oorlog," in *Noordbrabants Historisch Jaarboek* 1 ('s Hertogenbosch/Zutphen, 1984), 143-77.

## Liberal (Anti) Emigration Culture

Reliable information played a crucial role in the rational process of Dutch emigration. The potential emigrant had to weigh the frequently conflicting accounts of the circumstances of those who had gone before. Examples of successful migrants were contradicted by just as many stories about fellow countrymen who left with some money and later returned penniless.[51]

Proponents and opponents clashed vehemently in newspapers and brochures. Emigration fever stirred up the expectation of a better life, so that prospective emigrants lost sight of the risks and drawbacks. The poet O.J. Eekma from Zaltbommel ridiculed the exaggerated expectations of the migrants:

> Go! Go! Brothers, take action!
> What good is it here if you're slaving and toiling?
> Here they will take or tax everything.
> Here they will hardly give you a piece of dry bread,
> There riches await you, there you can treat yourself.
> When a new mother country embraces you.

He made an emotional appeal to their love for their country:

> Can nothing bind you to your own country?
> And have you no love for your Netherlands soil?
> Don't you have everything here—plus friends and relations?
> Didn't the Sun first shine on your face here?
> Can nothing prop up your crumpling courage?
> Oh! Why do you betray your mother?[52]

A poet who published under the pseudonym Jeremias sketched a humorous contrast between the structure in the Old World and the chaos in the New. He reminded his public that America had no safety net, so that there was a real risk that one would die poor and alone. Moreover, the much-lauded freedom appeared to be tied to the color of one's skin:

---

[51]   Henry S. Lucas, *Netherlanders in America: Dutch Emigration to the United States and Canada, 1789-1950* (Ann Arbor: Univ. of Michigan Press, 1955; rep., Grand Rapids: Eerdmans, 1989), 63-67.

[52]   O.J. Eekma, *Amerika-Loevestein. Twee Zangen des tijds* (Maastricht: W. J. van Haren Nomen, 1846), 6.

We travel on—who will come along
To the land of welfare and peace?
We will merrily escape all the trouble
Like Eneas of Troy,
And take our own along.

Here we dream about a good society,
By creating *order.*
Here we put great value
On religion, discipline and education,
And other *silly* matters.

There they flit from belief to belief,
Like moral beetles.
They munch, without shame or scruple
A leaf from the Quaker tree,
Or dance with the Shakers.

Here we twaddle about humanity
 And loving hearts,
Here we talk nonsense about Christian duty...
There they train dogs
To chase the blacks.[53]

The press warned against profiteers and pointed to the criticism of America already uttered by Charles Dickens and other opinion makers.[54] The liberal newspapers especially judged the emigration projects of the Seceders critically. "We say...that the leaders in this project put great responsibility on themselves. We also believe that, even if in the beginning the *Reformed Hernhut on the Mississippi* was portrayed as a patriarchal paradise, that the farmer from Winterswijk would not soon be recreated as an American-Dutch angel."[55]

An elite feared that emigration was an expression of the get-rich-quick desire. When gold was discovered in California in 1848, which

[53] Jeremias, *Naar Amerika. Toeroep aan allen die 't geluk zoeken* (Rotterdam: Mensing & Van Westereenen, 1840), 7. A footnote explained who the Shakers were: "A well-known religious sect in North America. So-called because of their (apparently insane) movements and shaking during their worship."

[54] A. Lammers, *De jachtvelden van het geluk. Reizen door historisch Amerika* (Amsterdam: Balans,1998), 74-77.

[55] *Goessche Courant,* January 25, 1847.

attracted fortune hunters from everywhere, the famous Dutch author Jacob van Lennep wrote a play specifically to warn against hubris: "It is true that in our calm and sedate country there are fewer heads than elsewhere that are turned crazy by the dreams of fortune and luxury which gives them ideas of treasures scattered over there; nevertheless, we have no shortage of people here who imagine that they only have to go there, and then return rich and prosperous." He decided to warn the public by putting this comedy on stage.[56]

In more affluent circles, emigration functioned as a warning. Emigration was a criticism of society, but not in itself to be recommended, especially not for their own group. Liberal spokespersons used the commotion about emigration to increase the pressure for reforms. Orthodox Protestants also saw the emigrants as allies, because by their departure they judged current laws. Liberal folks from Amsterdam even toyed with the idea of publishing a weekly periodical with the title *De Landverhuizing* (Emigration), which would serve as a lever for changes, such as freedom of religion and education.[57]

The influential Rotterdam newpaper *Nieuwe Rotterdamse Courant* (May 4, 1847) also warned the government that if it remained inflexible and aloof, many countrymen would leave. "How could the manner in which the so-called Seceders worship God harm the government? Why take these people to court and apply a Napoleonic provision of criminal law to them? Why not give them complete freedom to establish congregations according to their pleasure, without subjecting them to provisions that do not exist for other denominations? In this way complaints are piled on top of complaints."

More conservative newspapers realized that the emigration phenomenon was used to express criticism about society, but they rejected the accusation that the departure of many countrymen as such demonstrated that life in the Netherlands had deteriorated, because international migration had always taken place. They pointed to the results of overpopulation. The press also denied that religious persecution was taking place, by pointing to the possibility for new denominations to receive recognition. Actually, it might be a good thing that the Seceders were leaving the country: now, they were a threat to freedom of conscience because they wanted to prohibit

[56] J. van Lennep, "De droom van California (1849)," *Poetische werken.* Vol. 10.3 (Rotterdam: M. Wijt en Zonen, 1862), 231-75.

[57] Letter J.A. Wormser to Groen van Prinsterer, Dec. 19, 1846, G. Groen van Prinsterer, ed., *Brieven van J. A. Wormser* 2 Vol. (Amsterdam: Hoveker, 1874-1875), 1:91.

inoculation, as well as lightning rods, and, one writer speculated, in the future they probably would allow rabid animals to roam freely. Besides, they wanted to destroy the public schools and place the state under the church. Only in the years after the American Civil War did the elite of Amsterdam and Rotterdam come under the sway of America, as the result of the propaganda to purchase land in Minnesota, a process that would be repeated in 1889, with California as the attraction.[58]

Apart from these views, which really were political commentaries, printed material brought more practical advice. In 1846, a small-town publisher offered a substantial brochure that listed people's chances of success in America on the basis of their skills and professions. People who had mastered a trade, such as bakers, brewers, masons, carpenters, and farmers could look forward to a good future. However, people who worked with their heads would not find anything suitable. "Learned professionals should never decide to become emigrants..., because in that country people have no time for much scholarly learning." An exception to this advice was made for (progressive) preachers: "Ministers have always found a good position in North America, and really, the situation of the clergy is plentiful and happy...."[59] At least, if they show a healthy combination of common sense and of faith, because that's how Americans are. But this category of ministers appeared the least inclined to emigrate.

Other writers urged people to be more careful and advised them to make an assessment of essential investments. The liberal newspaper *Goessche Courant* of February 15, 1847 wrote: "Every eager emigrant must first read Robinson (Crusoe) and ask himself if he can do what Robinson could." The emigrant must also realize that besides money to purchase land, he also would need oxen, wood, building materials, and labor in order to survive the pioneer days. Financial reserves were indispensable. The editors advised the organizers of emigration to go to the Dutch East Indies (the "Great East"). In addition, the editors raised a matter of principle—could one go to a country that condoned slavery and where immigrants themselves were able to own slaves? The Seceder leaders consciously settled in states without slavery, in order to

---

[58]  Jacob Van Hinte, *Netherlanders in America: A Study of Emigration and Settlement in the 19th and 20th Centuries in the United States of America*, Robert P. Swierenga, gen. ed., Adriaan de Wit, chief trans. (Grand Rapids: Baker, 1985), 621-27, 641-61.

[59]  *Aan welke personen is de landverhuizing aan te bevelen? Een woord aan allen, die het voornemen hebben, om hunnen geboortegrond te verlaten en naar Noord-Amerika te verhuizen* (Zwijndrecht: J. Boden, 1846), 32-33, 35.

avoid that problem.[60] The many forms of lack of freedom in their own country functioned as arguments in the discussion about emigration, which showed a sharp contrast with America.

## The Stream Begins to Flow

The promise of freedom in America had an enduring attraction for Europe, which was also felt in the Netherlands. At first the appeal had been tempered by the governing elite; however, when emigration from neighboring countries got underway, the pull was also felt by the middle class and farmers. The extent and the demographic distribution of emigration from the Netherlands demonstrate that besides socioeconomic factors and information about the United States, one's outlook on life also played an important role in the creation of an emigration culture. The departure of the emigrants was more than a solution for the problem of lack of physical space. The Netherlands was not nearly full—in the south and east of the country there were large areas of uncultivated heath land, sand dunes, and marsh land. However, these areas did not only have an unfavorable reputation, they also failed to provide room for change for those colonists who, besides economic possibilities, were looking for social reform. The new *polders*, such as the Haarlemmermeer, did not offer such possibilities either (no more than the Dutch colonies) and were too expensive for families with limited means.

Bureaucratic regulations by the government put the phenomenon of migration on the map. The strongest justification for emigration came from the Secession Protestants. This conscious deliberation loosened the bond to their birthplace, and laid the basis for an ideal that made emigration attractive. In Roman Catholic circles the motivation based on one's outlook on life was not as strong, and the initiative to emigrate came more often from outside, without elaborate plans for a new society. For that reason few Dutch Catholic settlements came into being. The stimulating role that arose from plans for settlements is the subject of the next chapter.

---

[60]    *Goessche Courant*, January 25, 1847; see also the *Drentsche Volks-Almanak* of 1847. *Goessche Courant*, March 11, 1847.

CHAPTER 2

# Organization and Emigration Climate

The sudden public interest in emigration in 1846 and the following years was in itself not a guarantee that that this phenomenon would continue. The future of the movement depended on the structures that would encourage the emigration process. How did the emigrants organize their departures? What possibilities for continuity did their organization offer? What expectations did the pioneers in the designated country have, and how well did they succeed in realizing their intentions? In addition, the emigration flow depended on government policies, especially those of the American authorities. Which obstructions hindered the flow and how did government agencies stimulate (or discourage) emigration? The success of the whole operation finally depended on cooperation in America. What influence did the American contact persons have on the outcome of this process?

## Organization and Selection

A communal approach to emigration offered the emigrants the best guarantee of continuity. They could thereby make use of the

31

relatively new organizational form of an association. The Netherlands in the 1840s witnessed the birth of many voluntary associations for businessmen, domestic servants, insurance agents, educators, Christian schools and libraries in particular, and for philanthropic projects, mostly for the benefit of the ill and poor.[1] The Seceded ministers Van Raalte and Brummelkamp took the lead in establishing a formal organization April 15, 1846, when they founded the "Society of Christians for Dutch Emigration to the United States of North America" in Arnhem. In August of that same year Scholte completed his design for the "Society for Moving to the United States," even though this organization was not ratified officially until Christmas Day of that year. A group from Zeeland used both examples to found the "Zeeland Society for Moving to the United States of North America" February 1, 1847.

The formalities necessary for establishing a society forced the emigration groups to consider their purpose and means carefully. The express purpose of the societies was to regulate collectively those matters that individual emigrants could hardly manage, such as booking a passage, choosing a settlement, purchasing land, and arranging public facilities such as a church, a school, roads, and medical care. The three societies borrowed components from each other but also showed regional differences in the selection criteria and the rights of the participants.

Membership in the societies was open to adult men above age twenty who could contribute one guilder (or forty dollar cents, an average day's wage). Scholte rejected only those who clearly showed immoral or antisocial behavior, as well as all Roman Catholics. Van Raalte's society formulated the requirements more positively and in the selection of emigrants used the criterion of "...seeking a salting element for the colony, which is necessary to have a Christian preponderance present there." Those interested must give evidence that they "are willing to subject themselves to the Word of the Lord, so that in that way a Christian government can be present." The Zeeland regulations excluded only those who were "guilty of immorality and offensive behavior, or those who harbor errors about the doctrine of salvation."[2]

---

[1]    The government newspaper and the registers of societies announced the founding of many trade and ideological societies between 1845 and 1847.

[2]    *Reglement der Zeeuwsche Vereeniging ter verhuizing naar de Vereenigde Staaten van Noord-America* (Goes: Wed. P. Crombouw, 1847); Henry S. Lucas, "De artikelen van Scholte's Vereeniging ter verhuizing naar de Vereenigde Staten," *Nederlands Archief voor Kerkgeschiedenis* 38 (1952): 179-87; "Grondslagen der Vereeniging van Christenen voor de Hollandsche Volksverhuizing naar de

It is noteworthy that none of these societies had an exclusively Secessionist membership, although Seceders took the initiative and guarded the necessary homogeneity. The Zeeland society was organized loosely as an ecclesiastical congregation and called a Seceded minister, Cornelis Van der Meulen. This example was followed by a group of Frisians who would leave later in 1847 with the Reverend Marten Ypma, even though they did not choose the society format. The participants in both of these groups knew each other well. The other societies postponed regulating church issues until they had arrived at their destination. Scholte emphasized the principle of separation of church and state authority, while Van Raalte accepted a practical separation between these two.

The Zeeland society was the most democratic and took explicit measures to protect widows and orphans and guarantee the right of the poor to vote, while Scholte rejected that idea. The groups of Van Raalte and Van de Luijster on the one hand, and Scholte on the other, show differences in economic and social positions. Scholte calculated fifty dollars per adult for the steamship passage, including meals. For the passage via sailing ship, without meals, Van de Luijster figured seventeen dollars per person and fourteen dollars per child, with families receiving a discount. So the groups imagined the life of the new settlement, adapted the rules to their regional needs, but it was still to be seen whether those plans would survive the test of real life.

**Contacts**

The plans of Brummelkamp and Van Raalte were the talk of the day among all kinds of people and ideologies. In spite of the careful preparations, Van Raalte remained concerned about the threatening secularization and dispersion of the immigrants. He therefore could not avoid going along himself. In June 1846 he sent ahead a group of explorers, carrying a letter with a request for support from the Christians in the United States, thus preparing the way for newcomers to America. In September 1846 he put into practice what he preached, and with his family boarded a ship to America. About one hundred people from the provinces of Gelderland and Overijssel left with him.

---

Vereenigde Staten in N. Amerika," in A. Brummelkamp, Jr., *Levensbeschrijvig van wijlen Prof. A. Brummelkamp* (Kampen: Kok, 1910), 205-09. The manuscript is located in Box 1, Folder 8, of the Van Raalte Papers, Calvin College Archives, Grand Rapids, Michigan.

Upon arrival in New York they received generous support from ministers of the Reformed Protestant Dutch Church [subsequently, the Reformed Church in America], that is, from Thomas De Witt, and later, when traveling through Albany, from Isaac N. Wyckhoff, who had excellent contacts for finding people jobs. Wyckhoff was one of the most orthodox ministers in his denomination. He still preached regularly from the Heidelberg Catechism and was therefore a real kindred spirit of his Dutch colleagues. He was always ready to help others and especially welcomed the Seceders because their presence meant a strengthening of his denomination. Wyckoff directed Van Raalte to friendly connections in Michigan, who in turn invited him to explore the western part of that state.[3] In the future this minister would also remain a counselor for newcomers and usher them into the Dutch settlements. Showing an increasing American sense of self-importance, the *Christian Intelligencer*, the weekly magazine of the Reformed Protestant Dutch Church, declared that the established church in Europe and especially in the Netherlands was on the wrong track: papists and heretics had free play, but a revival movement such as the Secession was suppressed. What better place to come to than America, where real freedom waited?

### The Settlement Climate in America

The contact persons in New York had a decisive influence on the location of the settlement of the organized immigrants. The northern part of America was a natural choice. The harbor of New York became ever more important and had excellent connections by water and rail with the West, where in lightly populated and undeveloped areas many connected sections of land became available. In the South, most of the land was in the hands of great landowners, slavery ruled there, and the climate was very different from the Netherlands. Even though the

---

3    S. Osinga, *Tiental brieven betrekkelijk de reis, aankomst en vestiging naar en in Noord-Amerika, van eenige landverhuizers vertrokken uit De grietenijen Het Bildt en Barradeel in Vriesland* (Franeker: T. Telenga, 1848), 12-13; H. Reenders, "Albertus C. van Raalte als leider van Overijsselse Afgescheidenen 1836-1846," in Freerk Peereboom, a. o., eds., *Van scheurmakers, onruststokers en geheime opruijers: De Afscheiding in Overijssel* (Kampen: N.P., 1984), 195. Allan J. Janssen, *Gathered at Albany: A History of a Classis*, Historical Series of the Reformed Church in America, no. 25 (Grand Rapids: Eerdmans, 1995), 76. *Christian Intelligencer*, November 26, 1846, June 3 and 10, 1847. They probably based their negative judgment about the Netherlands on news reports in Scottish newspapers.

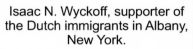

**Isaac N. Wyckoff, supporter of the Dutch immigrants in Albany, New York.**
Western Seminary Collection of the Joint Archives of Holland, Michigan.

farmers in the North took more business risks than most immigrants, they shared the attitude of the Dutch, who were used to producing for a market and investing in innovation on behalf of their businesses. Just at the time that the Dutch groups arrived in America, the circumstances for founding agricultural communities were favorable. The expansion of agricultural areas had just entered a new stage. After the new American republic had decided in 1785 and 1787 that the state could sell land in large connected sections, with the certainty of ownership and the prohibition of slavery, many pioneers traveled to the west. They largely followed horizontal lines—northerners traveled to northeastern Ohio and then to the territories of Michigan, Wisconsin, and Minnesota; southerners from Kentucky and Tennessee traveled to the south of Ohio and Indiana and to Illinois, while inhabitants of Pennsylvania nestled between the two groups.[4]

This movement placed the various Indian tribes under pressure. After 1795 the tribes in Michigan were forced by treaties to turn over their territories to the federal government in Washington, which sold the land to individuals. The first white inhabitants of these areas were

[4]     Robert P. Swierenga, "The Settlement of the Old Northwest: Ethnic Pluralism in a Featureless Plain," *Journal of the Early Republic* 9 (1989): 73-105.

descendants of the colonists of the East Coast. Farmers followed fur traders and trappers, even though the area was known for a long time as marshland and therefore unhealthy and dangerous. Thus, the western section of Michigan, where the Dutch would settle later, came into federal hands in 1821. Just before Michigan was admitted to the Union as the twenty-sixth state in 1837, the territory of the Ottawa tribe was opened for settlement, in exchange for money, goods, and a mountain of promises. The Indian tribes had left the southern parts of Michigan, all but an estimated eight thousand who remained behind, in 1837. By 1847, the Ottawas who lived at the mouth of the Black River and were divided between Catholic and Protestant missions had decided to move north in order to maintain what was left of their nomadic way of life.[5]

Iowa, the other state where many Dutch immigrants would settle, had been part of the United States since 1803. That same year, President Thomas Jefferson purchased from France the state of Louisiana, everything west of the Mississippi, for fifteen million dollars. Through this transaction the territory of the still young republic of the United States was more than doubled. A series of forts had to keep the West safe for the white people. On December 29, 1846, Iowa entered into the Union as the twenty-ninth state. Even more quickly than elsewhere in the West, colonists and speculators bought the fertile prairie land from the state for $1.25 per acre. In 1873, forty years after the first white people had settled there, the average population density was two or more people per square mile. That meant that the frontier phase, the imaginary line between wilderness and civilization, had been formally closed.[6] This is how fast settlement took place.

Two years after Iowa, Wisconsin became part of the Union. This heavily wooded state adopted a very progressive constitution that stipulated that everyone, after swearing an oath, was guaranteed voting rights. It filled all public offices through elections, granted small farms respite when liquidating debts, and granted women the right to own property.[7]

[5]   Willis F. Dunbar and George S. May, *Michigan: A History of the Wolverine State*, 3rd rev. ed. (Grand Rapids: Eerdmans, 1995), 146. Larrie B. Massie, *Haven, Harbor and Heritage: The Holland, Michigan, Story* (Allegan Forest, Mich.: Priscilla Press, 1996), 23. Robert P. Swierenga and William Van Appledorn, eds., *Old Wing Mission: Cultural Interchange as Chronicled by George and Arvilla Smith in their Work with Chief Wakazoo's Ottawa Band on the West Michigan Frontier* (Grand Rapids: Eerdmans, 2008), 11-54.

[6]   Dorothy Schwieder, *Iowa: The Middle Land* (Ames: Iowa State Univ. Press, 1996).

[7]   Ray Allen Billington, *Westward Expansion: A History of the American Frontier*

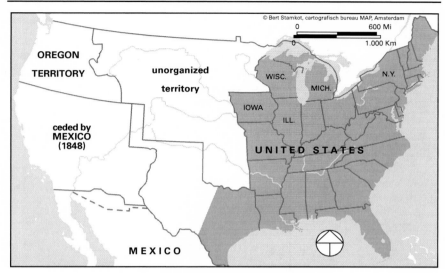

Map 4: The United States in 1848.

The governments of these young states were interested in a steady stream of newcomers, in order to collect more taxes, to be able to finance more services, and to increase their influence in the Union. In addition, private business people, such as land speculators, veterans, and railway agents, hoped to earn money, and farmers who had arrived earlier expected a rise in the value of their property as the demand for land increased. The first settlers came from states in the East. Around 1850 only one-eighth of the population in the area of the Great Lakes came from outside America. This number would increase quickly and shift the political center of gravity to the west when after 1840 the states outside the original thirteen would form a majority in the Senate, and after 1860 also in the House of Representatives.[8]

**The Choice of a Settlement Location**

Before the decision had been made to go to America, the immigration leaders had considered and rejected several destinations elsewhere because of lack of religious freedom (Dutch East Indies), undesirability of the climate (Suriname), poor accessibility of the

---

(New York: MacMillan, 1960), 309. La Vern J. Rippley, *The Immigrant Experience in Wisconsin* (Boston: Twayne Publishers, 1985), 1-8.

[8]    Margo J. Anderson, *The American Census: A Social History* (New Haven: Yale Univ. Press, 1988), 7-31.

interior and lack of personal opportunities for development (South Africa). Initially, Van Raalte and Scholte had attempted to establish one large Dutch colony in the Mississippi basin. Van Raalte had indicated in his plan that he considered Milwaukee, Wisconsin, as the area of concentration; the others did not determine their destination in advance. Forerunners of the immigrants traveled to scout the terrain: Scholte sent people to the area above St. Louis, and Van Raalte to Milwaukee and Illinois.[9] Scholte had read in German travel accounts that fertile agricultural land was available in Iowa.

Van Raalte and his party arrived in New York in November 1846 and were cordially welcomed by a specially established support committee. Scholte's group of scouts left the Netherlands on October 2 and traveled via the southern harbor of New Orleans in the direction of St. Louis. The groups from the north and the south were supposed to meet in St. Louis, but things went differently than anticipated. Scholte's wife became ill, and he postponed his departure to spring 1847, when four ships left with a total of more than eight hundred emigrants. Van Raalte, in the meantime, hurried to the Great Lakes to travel in the direction of Milwaukee. However, a severe winter arrived early, so that he was grounded in Detroit. Van Raalte did not necessarily want to go through with the intended meeting with Scholte and in the meantime looked at alternative destinations. From Detroit he took an orientation trip to the West, to go to St. Louis via Illinois and Wisconsin. He could go no further than the city of Kalamazoo, the end of the railway connection, and he allowed himself to be persuaded by a local Presbyterian minister, Ova P. Hoyt, to visit western Michigan.

While Scholte formally organized his society in Utrecht on Christmas Day 1846, Van Raalte was traveling with Judge John Kellogg. Kellogg took the trouble to show him the area around Allegan, where there were six townships, each nearly eighteen thousand acres, for sale at $1.25 per acre; Kellogg himself had substantial property here. Van Raalte wrote to his wife Christina in Detroit, "...I am thinking more and more that the State of Michigan may become the state of our home."[10] Accompanied by Judge Kellogg, Van Raalte plowed for weeks through the knee-high snow in the virgin forests, at times near exhaustion. Before the end of the year it became known among those caught by the

---

9   Antonie Brummelkamp and Albertus C. Van Raalte, "To the Faithful in the United States, May 25, 1846," in Henry S. Lucas, ed., *Dutch Immigrant Memoirs and Related Writings*, repr. (Grand Rapids: Eerdmans, 1997), 1:14-20.

10   Leonard Sweetman, ed., *From Heart to Heart: Letters from the Rev. Albertus Christiaan Van Raalte to His Wife Christina Johanna Van Raalte-De Moen, 1836-1847* (Grand Rapids: Calvin Heritage Hall, 1997), 67.

winter in Detroit and Albany that their destination would be Michigan, and they realized that this meant the end of the joint colony.[11] Less than three weeks later, Van Raalte yielded to the persuasive power and hospitality of the Americans and cut the knot—Michigan would be the destination. He trusted his own observation and the judgment of the Americans who had already lived there for several years. The woods of Michigan were affordable for poor immigrants. Land was cheaper than in the prairie states and the trees could be used for lumber. The climate was reasonable and the connections with the East (railways by land and Lake Michigan by water) were better than in Iowa or Missouri. Moreover, charitable Americans in Detroit and Kalamazoo had founded support committees that had already purchased land for the Dutch. Also, in Illinois there was a Dutch Reformed Church member who was contemplating founding a society and helping the Dutch acquire land. He called out: "Come on, friends. Though we have no money to bestow, we can direct you to suitable locations, give employment to your mechanics, furnish land for your farmers to cultivate till they will get lands of their own, and aid you in various ways."[12]

The interest shown by these Americans appeared to provide advantages for the colonists. Van Raalte had no time to undertake more distant trips, because the waiting immigrants in the cities wanted certainty quickly. Michigan was relatively close, the land was virgin forest, and the region offered all kinds of possibilities with a harbor and industry. Van Raalte hoped to develop industry based on agricultural products and with the financial help from his contacts.[13] These considerations provided the deciding factor for settling in Michigan.

Once Van Raalte had decided in favor of Michigan, the roles were reversed—now he tried to persuade Scholte to settle in the same area. However, Scholte was not about to change his mind. He believed the (untrue) reports that all the forests in Michigan made it unsuitable for agriculture, and that speculators owned too much of the land. He let it be known that his group had not left home in order to chop wood. He therefore stuck to his original plan. He accused Van Raalte of being a booster, who "in his design to get people there, had already completely become an American."[14] Scholte paid more attention to the proven quality of the land, while Van Raalte looked for future possibilities. Scholte was convinced that Iowa offered a healthier climate than

---

[11]  Stellingwerff, *Iowa Letters*, 51.

[12]  *Christian Intelligencer*, November 26, 1846.

[13]  A. Brummelkamp, *Stemmen uit Noord-Amerika* (Amsterdam: Hoogkamer, 1847), 73 and 90.

[14]  Stellingwerff, *Iowa Letters*, 63.

Michigan. This argument weighed heavily with people in the nineteenth century, who believed that surroundings especially determined health. High and dry was better than low and wet, uniformity better than variety or change, since change in surroundings also required a different physical disposition.[15] The group from Utrecht had more capital to invest in the more expensive prairie land that had already largely been reclaimed for agriculture by Americans. This condition increased the chance of getting through the early years. No matter how understandable the differences were, hopes of having one colony were gone, and from now on everyone who would leave the Netherlands had to make a choice between Iowa and Michigan. This internal competition between the immigrant colonies turned out to be a blessing in disguise, because it soon encouraged the spread of specific information about the various options for the following waves of immigrants. From the beginning, free market capitalism enveloped the Dutch immigrants, as the large group from Zeeland would experience.

### Spreading Out and Concentration

The experiences of the immigrants from Zeeland demonstrate how precarious and uncertain the journey was, even for a well-prepared group. Farmer Jannes Van de Luijster had carefully prepared the departure of the 457 people who had joined his society. He had at his disposal a budget of over nine thousand dollars, from which he had paid the passage, purchased food, and bought a hundred English Bibles. But before the party could board, the most recent American regulations obstructed their leaving as one group. On February 22, 1847, the American Congress had passed a law that stipulated that each passenger had to have a minimum of fourteen square feet of space on board. This law was passed to increase the safety of passengers, after it had become known that in the previous three months immigrant ships had carried two hundred dead passengers when docking in New York harbor.[16] Because of this stipulation, the society's board could not find a ship large enough to transport the whole party.[17] People decided to split into three groups under the direction of leaders who knew each other well. On April 8, 1847, two ships left from Antwerp under the

---

[15]   Conevry Bolton Vancius, *The Health of the Country: How American Settlers Understood Themselves and Their Land* (New York: Basic Books, 2002), 86-93.

[16]   E.P. Hutchinson, *Legislative History of American Immigration Policy 1798-1965* (Philadelphia: Univ. of Pennsylvania Press, 1981), 35-36.

[17]   *Nieuwe Rotterdamse Courant*, May 4, 1847.

leadership of Van de Luijster and elder Jan Steketee, and six weeks later a group left Rotterdam under the leadership of the Reverend Cornelius Van der Meulen. Along the way this last group met Scholte, who tried without avail to persuade them to settle in Iowa.

Van der Meulen's leadership proved indispensable. Even before his party left the Netherlands, disaster struck. There was an outbreak of measles in the harbor of Hellevoetsluis, and twenty children died; on the ship there was a "foul smell of death." A person from Middelburg who passed the disaster ship wrote on May 12 that he had wanted to stop by and chat, "but we were forbidden to go on board because of the illness on the ship. And while I'm writing this there is news that 2 more have died. That makes 17 in the 3 weeks that the ship has been here. And now half of the people have to leave the ship to board another."[18] However, Van der Meulen was able to prevent his 114 followers from falling apart, a constant threat that continued when his party arrived as the last of the three in New York. He heard that Scholte had nearly been able to talk Van de Luijster into going to Iowa. Van de Luyster had even bought train tickets, but he had second thoughts when his fellow travelers were not persuaded of Iowa's superiority and had higher expectations about Michigan. The desperate experiences during the passage, especially for Van der Meulen's party, had strengthened the group's solidarity. Still, one-third of the party left the group along the way. Some remained in the cities of Rochester or Buffalo, working there temporarily in order to build up funds for future land purchases; others traveled farther to Wisconsin or Iowa. However, in July 1847 most of the people from Zeeland joined Van Raalte's colony in Michigan, which had been established in February.[19] The names of the settlements fit the sense of continuity that so many immigrants pursued. Van Raalte called the settlement "Holland"—he could not imagine a more appropriate name. Several kilometers to the east Van de Luijster founded the village of "Zeeland."

---

[18]  Osinga, *Tiental Brieven*, 7. M. Frederiks aan J.S. Frederiks, May 12, 1847. Calvin College, Heritage Hall, Immigrant Letter Collection. In the burial records of Hellevoetsluis, C. Smits found twelve dead children from ages six weeks to five years and one woman of twenty-six, but eye witnesses reported higher numbers. C. Smits, "Secession, Quarrels and Personalities," in Herman Ganzevoort and Mark Boekelman, eds., *Dutch Immigration to North America* (Toronto: The Multicultural History Society of Ontario), 109.

[19]  See my "Forgotten Founding Father: Cornelius Vander Meulen as Immigrant Leader," *Documentatieblad voor de Geschiedenis van de Nederlandse zending en overzeese kerken* 5.2 (Fall 1998): 1-23.

For the Dutch Americans of colonial descent continuity proved important as well. For them, the Dutch immigrants were a gift from heaven. A certain "E" wrote in the *Christian Intelligencer* that the growth of the Dutch Reformed Church had, till then, been greatly hindered by the designation of "Dutch" in its name—which did not have any appeal to the varied people in the West. Only a few families from New York and New Jersey had been able to form core congregations in a few western states The Dutch came at precisely the right moment to the right places, and he added, "Here is the wonder of the movement: they are pious men." Moreover, these immigrants could offer an inexpensive solution to the spread of the Dutch Reformed Church. "The immigrants of whom we speak are the cheapest missionaries, they support themselves." This view spurred on the Old Dutch to offer the newcomers a helping hand. Their pity was stirred by the reports about their experiences in the Netherlands and their pathetic situation.[20]

This help was sorely needed, because the circumstances in the first years were deplorable. Severe winters, accidents, fevers, lack of food, and contagious diseases took their toll and made many people doubt a favorable outcome. The colonists learned the hard way how they had to use their strengths; for example, cutting down trees in such a way that one falling tree would drag along the next one—lessons they learned from returning Ottawa Indians.

In the meantime, new groups of Seceders left the province of Friesland, under the leadership of the Reverend Martin A. Ypma, and from Overijssel, led by the Reverend Seine Bolks from Hellendoorn, with Michigan as their destination. Immigrants from Groningen founded a village east of the Holland settlement, while a group from the German border region of Bentheim baptized their village "Graafschap," on the western side of Holland. Because the acquisition of land was not centrally regulated, and the different provincial groups each wanted to establish a geographic center, the people from Friesland and Zeeland made a mutual agreement to coordinate their land purchase. There were, however, other competitors in the market. Two days after this agreement, three families bought parcels of land in the neighborhood of the intended territory of the Frisians. It appeared later that these were families from the province of Zuid-Holland. The Frisians then considered the contract broken and chose land from the territory intended for the Zeeland people. In pioneer days, distrust could develop

---

[20]    *Christian Intelligencer*, May 13, 1847. For an emotional call for support from Grand Rapids, see the issue of May 6, 1847.

easily. The Frisians discovered later that the three families involved did not belong to the Van de Luijster Zeeland group and adopted them into their community.[21]

The separation between Iowa and Michigan did not mean that the original destination, the state of Wisconsin, was lost sight of. Wisconsin became the place of settlement for Rudolph Sleijster, who had been sent out as a forerunner by Van Raalte. Families from the Achterhoek area in the province of Gelderland had found their way to Milwaukee. A number of them stayed in this rapidly growing city, where the Germans were dominant. Others used the city as a point of departure for settling further north. Groups from Zeeland and Gelderland purchased land in Sheboygan County and in Holland County, which were organized in 1846 and 1848. The villages of Cedar Grove and Oostburg, and later Sheboygan Falls, drew newcomers, some straight from the Netherlands, others from the Zeeland settlements in western New York, from the villages of Pultneyville and Sodus, on Lake Erie.[22] The soil was good and cheap, and the immigrants could receive spiritual care from the Secession minister Pieter Zonne, who lauded the advantages of Wisconsin. He was joined in this praise by the first Dutch language newspaper, *De Sheboygan Nieuwsbode,* an enterprise of Jacob Quintus of Zeeland. Even without careful, early plans such as Scholte and Van Raalte had made, it was possible to found a viable settlement. However, these settlements did not expand as much as Holland, Zeeland, and Pella because they lacked leadership.

**Experiences of Roman Catholic and Jewish Emigrants**

Circumstances did not discriminate against immigrants of different faiths. Catholics and Jews experienced the same pioneer perils as Protestants. The Roman Catholic emigrants from the province of Noord-Brabant, who left for Wisconsin in 1848, were influenced by the initiatives of the Seceders and followed more or less the same boat route to Lake Michigan but landed on the other side in Green Bay, north of Sheboygan. They also experienced problems with money for the passage, ships that were overbooked, and unexpected delays. They were severely disappointed in their great expectations when they

[21]  Undated letter from Jan Elsma in the Gerhard de Jonge collection of the Joint Archives of Holland, Michigan.

[22]  Hans Krabbendam, "Independent Immigrants? The Position of the Wisconsin Dutch in the Dutch-American Network," paper presented at the conference, "The Dutch-American Experience in Wisconsin 1840-present," Sheboygan, Wisconsin, September 25, 2008.

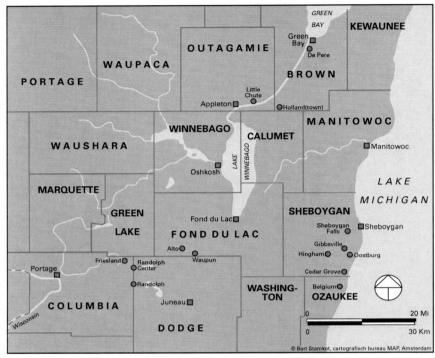

Map 5: Dutch Roman Catholic settlements in the north
and Protestant settlements in the south of Wisconsin.

reached their destination—Little Chute was remote, the soil poor and
still full of trees, and there was not a house in sight. A number of the
party went farther and founded "Franciskus Bosch" (later rebaptized as
"Hollandtown"). They kept up their courage with religious processions
and church feasts. The priests provided leadership that was different
from the Protestant ministers' style. On the one hand, they were more
mobile than the ministers, because they did not have to take care of
a family or property; on the other hand, they were sent to a more
extended field of labor by their superiors. Even though the Protestant
clergy were often on the road, they had deeper roots in the community
because of their economic interests, their leadership involvement, and
their involvement in family networks.[23]

Jewish emigrants found themselves in still a very different
situation. Around 1840 more than 80 percent of the fifty thousand Jews

[23]    H. van Stekelenburg, *Landverhuizing als regioneel verschijnsel. Van Noord-Brabant
naar Noord-Amerika 1820-1880* (Tilburg: Stichting Zuidelijk Historisch
Contact, 1991), 37-79, 116.

in the Netherlands lived in cities, with Amsterdam as the uncontested center, while fewer than 37 percent of the total population lived in cities. The Jews, more than other ethnic groups, had suffered under the economic and financial pressure of the French period because many of them were (small) merchants and store keepers. Lack of leadership, impoverishment, loss of the Yiddish language, and resistance to orthodoxy ruptured their mutual solidarity. To consider emigration for religious reasons was out of the question; their departure was economically motivated. The emigration of 6,500 Jews who left the Netherlands for America between 1800 and 1880 differed in time (they went earlier than their compatriots), destination (to cities), and route (usually with a stopover in London).[24]

The Dutch Jews had an extensive international network. Their urban network directed them to American cities, where they were quickly absorbed in American-Jewish communities, especially in New York, Boston, Philadelphia, and New Orleans. The first wave of Jewish emigrants from the Netherlands in the period 1790-1825 consisted of wealthy business people, who assumed leading positions in the early Jewish communities in the young republic. The second wave, between 1825 and 1870, represented the economic middle groups. They spoke Yiddish and were orthodox. The Dutch Jews formed their own synagogue in only three cities—New York, Philadelphia, and Boston. The orthodox B'nai Israel congregation in New York City kept going for fifty-five years. In the third period, 1870-1915, the proletariat emigrated. They did honor a number of customs but were much less interested in religion. The nearly unavoidable stopover in London hastened their assimilation because they learned English there. Concentration of their trades in clothing and tobacco, and especially in the diamond industry, promoted the ethnic cohesion as a Jewish community.[25]

**The Role of Government**

The Netherlands was an exception among European countries for not having legal obstructions for emigrants. Travel documents could be obtained simply by showing an abstract from the birth registry. With that information the officials could annually provide the

[24]   Robert P. Swierenga, *The Forerunners: Dutch Jewry in the North American Disaspora* (Detroit: Wayne State Univ. Press, 1994), 18-64. Karin Hofmeester, *Jewish Workers and the Labour Movement: A Comparative Study of Amsterdam, London and Paris (1870-1914)* (Aldershot: Ashgate, 2004).
[25]   Swierenga, *Forerunners*, 87-97.

province and the national ministry with an overview of the number of emigrants. Thus, the Dutch government remained informed about the interest in emigration. This regulation was instituted in 1846, so that the government could intervene if, in its opinion, the exit of emigrants was excessive.

The American government intervened after disasters struck immigrant ships. In 1847 the Zeeland Emigration Society had already encountered the effects of the requirement to have sufficient space on board. In 1855 the American government continued in this direction by stipulating that immigration ships had to provide sleeping accommodations, and that ship owners had to make available medical care, laundry and cooking facilities, and food (ten pounds of salted boneless beef per person). Before this time every person on board had to provide for his own victuals. The food was kept in numbered bags and boxes. Every few days the immigrants, under the watchful eye of a sailor, could fetch food from the ship's hold to cook it on a large stove that had room for ten pans at one time.[26] For every passenger eight years or older who died on board because of illness, the captain had to pay a ten dollar fine. These requirements were intended in the first place to improve the horrendous conditions especially on ships transporting the Irish, but they also served the American need for healthy immigrants. The first attempts of politicians to place limits on the entry of paupers and criminals via federal law were foiled because Congress delegated these procedures to the states, but the call for national coordination was not silenced. [27]

In the same period in which the central government took measures to protect the immigrants against exploitation, the western states appointed immigration officers. In 1852 Wisconsin appointed the Dutchman Gijsbert Van Steenwijk to inform immigrants in New York City about the favorable circumstances in the state. From his office in the midst of the bars in Greenwich Street where the newcomers were received, he distributed twenty thousand brochures in German, five thousand in Norwegian, and four thousand in Dutch on the ships in the harbor, in hotels, and on the street. He also placed advertisements and articles in European newspapers and visited consulates and shipping offices. Much of his energy was devoted to warn against agents

---

[26] Johannes Izaak Bril from Town Holland in Wisconsin to his brother Pieter Johannes Bril to Zuidzande, Zeeuws-Vlaanderen, November 13, 1854, *In de vreemde* 5 (March 1994): 83.

[27] Hutchinson, *Legislative History*.

of railroads and bar owners who tried to sell expensive travel tickets to Wisconsin; at the same time he was busy persuading the immigrants that he himself was honest and did not receive a direct profit from their settlements in this particular state.[28]

Indirectly, the American government stimulated immigration to the country by passing the Homestead Act on May 20, 1862. This act granted the possession of 160 acres to heads of families and individuals over twenty-one after they had lived there for five years and had cultivated the land. If people did not want to wait this long, they could get the land for $1.25 per acre. This law extended earlier laws that had offered federal land cheaply. To landless farmers this prospect seemed hard to resist, but they were not the ones who emigrated the most. The railroads received large tracts of public land from the state, as a subsidy for laying the tracks. Universities also received land to cover their expenses. These companies and schools were allowed to choose the best parcels. Speculators had abundant opportunities to acquire land. The homestead lands for individuals were often located farther from the railroads or in less desirable areas. Because these drawbacks only came to light later, the strong attraction remained for a long time.

Railroad companies advertised their land and services through their agents in Europe.[29] H. Ubbens, a farmer from Groningen, was such an agent, and in 1881 he pulled out all the stops to overcome the doubts of his compatriots and to persuade them to move to the west.[30] He drew from his own experience and cited a report from a Grand Rapids newspaper to persuade his readers that temporary work in a factory could be defended, but that a permanent job in a factory was unnecessary self-torture that undermined spirit and body. Inexpensive land was waiting for the pioneer, while he could always sell that land for good money. If he worked on the field himself, he would reap the benefits of his own labor without increasing the fortune of a

---

[28]  G. van Steenwijk, "Milwaukee," *De Recensent. Algemeen Letterkundig Maandschrift* (1851); also printed as a separate brochure. G. van Steenwijk, *Report of the State Commission of Emigration* (1852). Also see my "Consuls and Citizens: Dutch Diplomatic Representation in American Cities, 1800-1940," in Robert P. Swierenga, Don Sinnema, and Hans Krabbendam, eds., *The Dutch in Urban America* (Holland: Hope College, 2004), 59-75.

[29]  Paul Wallace Gates, "The Homestead Law in an Incongruous Land System," in Vernon Carstensen, ed., *The Public Lands: Studies in the History of the Public Domain* (Madison: Univ. of Wisconsin Press, 1962), 315-48.

[30]  H. Ubbens, *Amerika! Kan de landverhuizing niet op betere voet worden geregeld en op voordeeliger wijze worden ondernomen? Eene vraag met het oog op het landgebruik toegelicht en beantwoord* (Veendam: E.J. Bakker, 1881).

boss. Ubbens called on interested parties to found a society, and after sending an investigation team, to proceed to establish a colony together. The commercial character of his information became clear in the advertisement of the firm of Prins & Zwanenburg in Groningen, which in its brochure promoted passage with the Royal Dutch Steamship Company (Koninklijke Nederlandsche Stoomvaart Maatschappij).

After the conclusion of the American Civil War had consolidated the power of the national government, "Washington" strengthened its grip on the immigration process, especially since the higher courts rejected the laws of separate states. Besides a further refinement of the measures to protect passengers, the call for selection of immigrants became ever louder, out of fear that needy newcomers would have to be supported by public aid. In 1875 Congress passed a law that stipulated that American consuls could grant approval for departure to America only after they had made sure that there were no prostitutes or criminals among the applicants, or people with a job contract with an American employer. This last provision created much confusion among the immigrants who thought that a job contract would help them enter America; however, such a contract actually worked against them, since the American labor organizations were against such contracts because they upset the free labor market.

Immigrants did not have to be protected only against profiteering shipping companies; as soon as they stepped on American soil, they risked falling into the hands of other profiteers. The immigrant ships were besieged by agents who wanted to take the newcomers to their offices in order to sell them (very expensive) boat and train tickets to the West. For example, in 1847 the Frisian S.T. Krap thought that he had bought a cheap ticket from New York to Lafayette, Indiana, when he paid twenty-five guilders to the captain of a ship who got him from the sailboat. However, he soon discovered that he had been booked on a canal boat instead of a train, and therefore the journey took much longer and the trip on the boat was as noisy as "a regular European village carnival."[31] In order to avoid such hardships, in 1847 the Old Dutch in New York established a "Netherlands Society for the Protection of Emigrants from Holland." But even this society was not always trustworthy, because some of the protectors had business interests in the transportation and sale of land to immigrants.

---

[31]  Osinga, *Tiental brieven*, 23; P.R.D. Stokvis, *De Nederlandse trek naar Amerika, 1846-1847* (Leiden: Universitaire Pers Leiden, 1977), 137-43.

## Passage and Arrival

Immigration travel became an exciting and profitable business during the nineteenth century. The transporting of large numbers of people from Europe to America made commercial traffic between the two continents more balanced. Immigrants "filled" the gap of European return loads for the ships from America that had brought bulk goods, such as grain, tobacco, and cotton, and often had to return in ballast. The first generation of immigrant ships were no more than cargo ships, with some temporary provisions.

For most of the passengers the journey was an extraordinary experience because they had never been on a ship that long. The real tension, however, was caused by the unknown nature of the destination. As long as the passage was made by sailing ship, the journey lasted a long time, on average thirty days, with exceptionally long ones taking sixty days. Some captains and crew were not very "customer friendly," but others were caring. Whoever was not sick, caught a good ship, stayed in a cabin, and knew that he was on his way to a safe place with family, could even enjoy him- or herself during the voyage. This happened to Geertje Frederiks, who traveled for forty-three days from Hellevoetsluis to New York in 1848. As a single twenty-five-year-old woman she was under the protection of the captain. She reported the following to her grandpa in Middelburg:

> Oh, Grandfather, I can't tell you what an enjoyable trip I had. I was not bored for a single day, and the Captain was a good man. He was like a father to us. He gave us all the enjoyment he could. I lived like a princess in that cabin, and as cousin Galderke said, I certainly could not have lived in steerage. Oh, Grandfather, one has to see that miserable life in order to imagine it even a little....We received wine from the captain every day...; that good captain gave us everything. If you would sometime speak to immigrants coming here, certainly recommend captain Mijers from Baltimore, because good people on board are important to make sea life pleasant, as I have experienced. We often had the wind against us while at sea (but no heavy storm), hard wind and much rain, so that everything on board went helter skelter. We often had those funny events when we were eating soup at noon, and during the passing of the plates it rained soup on our heads. This caused so much laughter that even the minister (who was very serious) could not help laughing. Then, on another night, the wind blew so hard that the fat Lady was pitched out of her

bunk on to the floor, much to the delight of the onlookers. And an old Lady, who was in a different cabin (and always thought she was going to die, whether or not there was danger) sat in a corner on the floor, and was about to throw up into a basin next to her; just at that time we felt a bump and the basin flew to the other end of the cabin, and broke into a thousand pieces. The old lady was frightened and hollered nothing but "My last hour has come," and along came the wonderful puke on the carpet of the cabin. Oh! We had hundreds more of these funny episodes; if I were to tell you all of those, I would fill six pages. I will only say that a sea voyage such as this one is more pleasure than disagreeable.[32]

Twenty-five years later, in 1873, W.H. de Lange made his trip from Deventer to Grand Rapids, Michigan. As a steerage passenger he came at the end of the sailing ships period and had very different experiences:

The food was poor. For twelve days we ate moldy bread, and during July we got only [bad] potatoes with sauerkraut or pea soup and these with spoiled American fat. On top of that, my luggage was stolen in Rotterdam. All our provisions and other articles were in there, and we missed the box just as we sailed away, so that we had no chance to still buy something. And so we lived in complete poverty, and could truly say that we had to bite through the sour apple before we got a sweet one. We spent 27 days at sea, so that it was a happy moment when we spotted the mountain of Jersey—it was a wonderful sight. When we arrived in New York (or Nieuw Urk, as some over-educated Dutchmen call it), we were busy again, because our goods had to be unloaded and inspected. We spent 24 hours there, but could not see much of it, because of the trouble with our goods, but [New York] is large, dirty, and restless.[33]

Because of the change from sailing to steam ships, immigrant transportation became more and more an industry with substantial competition between the European harbor cities, companies, and

---

[32]  Geertruida Frederiks to her grandfather Johan Frederiks in Middelburg, October 20, 1848, Immigrant Letter Collection, Heritage Hall, Calvin College, Grand Rapids, Michigan (hereafter abbreviated as ILC HH).

[33]  W.H. de Lange from Grand Rapids to H. Houck in Deventer, October 4, 1873, ILC HH. See also Herbert J. Brinks, ed., *Dutch American Voices: Letters from the United States, 1850-1930* (Ithaca: Cornell Univ. Press, 1995), 412. Urk was a traditional Dutch fishing island in the former Zuiderzee.

governments. In 1873 the Nederlands-Amerikaansche Stoomvaart Maatschappij (NASM, better known as the Holland-Amerika Lijn) began a regular departure by steamship from Rotterdam, causing a revolution in the duration of the journey, safety, and comfort. This commercialization led to a more anonymous relationship. Individual captains and ships were no longer praised or cursed in newspaper articles; rather, the shipping companies were judged. Because of the more rapid connections, the journey was more safe and predictable. This resulted in the reduction of deaths during the passage. In 1840, on average 1 percent of the passengers (especially children under fourteen) died; thirty years later the number was one-third of 1 percent.[34] The fare for the steamships was somewhat higher than for the sailing ships, because coal increased the cost, but the comfort and speed offered enough compensation for the higher price. The average time of the passage was reduced from five weeks to twelve days, and even to nine days in 1914. The companies preferred to invest in enlarging the capacity, rather than further reducing the duration of the trip or lowering the prices, because more passengers produced more income. Wealthy passengers strengthened the reputation of the service.

The new generation of immigrant ships became impressive sea castles. Thus, the famous *Rotterdam* of the Holland America Line could accommodate two thousand steerage, five hundred second-class, and five hundred first-class passengers. Shipping companies saw that they could increase their profit more with the improvement of first- and second-class accommodations. After 1900, more and more passengers chose comfort.[35] The passage price was $25 per person in the lowest class (steerage), $40 for second class, and $125 for first class. More and more Dutch immigrants traveled second class, because third class really was outfitted just for the very poor. Periodic price reductions could save the travelers one-half of the price, but the opposite could also happen. Between 1892 and 1914 the shipping companies made mutual price arrangements that pushed the passage prices up 30 percent. After the First World War the companies quadrupled prices for third class from $36 to $132 guilders, since the war had caused a backlog.[36] Thus,

---

[34]   Robert P. Swierenga, *Faith and Family: Dutch Immigration and Settlement in the United States, 1820-1920* (New York: Holmes & Meier, 2000), 140.

[35]   Drew Keeling, "The Transportation Revolution and Transatlantic Migration, 1815-1914," *Research in Economic History* 19 (1999): 39-74.

[36]   C. Zevenbergen, *Toen zij uit Rotterdam vertrokken. Emigratie via Rotterdam door de eeuwen heen* (Zwolle: Waanders, 1990), 79-80, 89, 98. Torsten Feys, "Business Approach to Transatlantic Migration: The Introduction of

immigration was more and more streamlined, and the immigrant became more and more a product.

## Dutch Lack of Response

The Dutch government was more interested in stimulating the transportation business and avoiding the care for stranded travelers than in the comfort of travelers. The laws always trailed behind the facts. The first emigrant law of 1861 controlled the passing through of emigrants from outside the Netherlands, who could enter the Netherlands without a passport if they left the country within two months. In addition, the facilities of the departure harbors of Rotterdam and Amsterdam needed improvement through municipal oversight of lodging and boarding by means of registration of the passengers.[37] Because the foreign migrants crossing the Netherlands greatly exceeded the Dutch emigrants in numbers and visibility by the end of the nineteenth century, they also largely determined the negative image of the emigrants, who walked around the harbor areas, loaded down with baggage, afraid and unintelligible. The poor image of emigrants was demonstrated when the mandate to gather statistical data stipulated that only steerage passengers were counted as emigrants. The acronym N.A.S.M. (Nederlandsch-Amerikaansche Stoomvaart Maatschappij) was interpreted as *Neemt Alle Schurken Mee*.[38] The government was interested in emigration as a means of combating unemployment, but this positive expectation was neutralized by fear that the best workers would be lured to other countries. This consideration also confirmed the image of emigration as a problematic issue. No one came up with the idea that the emigrant in the country of settlement could make a contribution to the Dutch economy.

The limited imagination of the government in using emigration as a policy tool combating unemployment, while English examples became known, prompted representatives from the agricultural sector to found their own organization in 1913—the Dutch Society

---

Steam-Shipping on the North Atlantic and Its Impact on the European Exodus 1840-1914" (Ph.D. diss., European University Institute, Florence, 2008).

[37]    J.A.A. Hartland, *Geschiedenis van de Nederlandse emigratie tot de Tweede Wereldoorlog* (The Hague: Nederlandse Emigratiedienst, 1959), 236-57.

[38]    Walter Lagerwey, ed., *Letters Written in Good Faith: The Early Years of the Dutch Norbertines in Wisconsin* (Green Bay: Alt, 1996), 155 (1894). [The rude change in the meaning of the acronym meant, "Take All the Crooks Along."]

for Emigration (Nederlandsche Vereniging "Landverhuizing" [NVL]). They were joined by several cabinet members with relevant portfolios, such as foreign affairs, agriculture, commerce, and industry. This broad organization, however, lacked decisiveness because of internal disagreement about whether emigration should be stimulated or discouraged, in addition to a shortage of funds and the outbreak of the First World War. Only in the 1920s a network of correspondents throughout the Netherlands enabled the commission to provide potential emigrants with information about possibilities of settlement and to help them further.[39]

A second organization, the Emigratie Centrale Holland (ECH) assumed responsibility for the economic aspect of emigration. This central organization was led by business leaders who wanted to bring down unemployment rates. They hoped to finance their operation from the fees emigrants paid them for assistance to find work abroad, but this did not happen. However, the businesslike approach helped in the long run as a means of reducing exaggerated expectations. The government also added its two cents. In 1923, it hesitantly provided loans to poor emigrants, even though the number remained on average limited to one hundred people per year. In 1931 the two emigration societies (NVL and ECH) merged into one foundation, Stichting Landverhuizing Nederland.

Mutual distrust between the official government commission and the private societies (especially the NVL) impeded a rapid implementation of the emigration law of 1861, which was not accepted till 1936. The officials who were especially involved in the shipping business did not want to intervene in emigration itself. They did want to oppose the misleading propaganda and the labor contracts in which emigrants had to give part of their wages to their bosses, to pay for the passage. The private societies wanted above all to guard the interests of the emigrants by protecting them against all kinds of profiteers, regulating the many details regarding emigration, and conducting an active information plan. The law came too late, because in the 1930s emigration ran in the opposite direction and Dutch emigrants returned from America. Even the founding of ideological societies that wanted to coordinate the emigration of members from their party came too late for American destinations. The Rooms-katholieke Emigratie Vereeniging (1925) and the Gereformeerde Emigratie Vereeniging in 1927 (enlarged to a Protestant Christelijke Emigratie Centrale in 1938)

---

[39]  Hartland, *Geschiedenis*, 45-110.

did come in time to formalize the emigration tradition and to secure the transfer of experiences in the periods when emigration came to a virtual standstill, that is, in the 1930s and early 1940s.[40]

### From Protection to Limitation in America

During the nineteenth century, the authorities in America became much more involved with the immigrants. The nature of this involvement moved from concern for the immigrant to fear of the unwanted results of massive immigration. Since between 80 and 90 percent of the immigrants entered America via New York harbor, the city of New York designated the old fort Castle Garden on the south point of Manhattan as an immigrant reception place in 1855. Here, the immigrants came on shore and were assisted in gathering reliable information for finding work and living space, exchanging money, and purchasing train tickets. During the 1880s Castle Garden could no longer accommodate the flood of immigrants, and the federal government decided to build a new center in front of the Manhattan shore, for the arrival of immigrants on Ellis Island. When Castle Garden closed its doors in 1890, 7.5 million people had entered America at this point. Castle Garden suffered from a poor reputation, and Izaak Janse, a laborer from Zeeland, feared its conditions in 1881 but discovered that this was unnecessary because actual conditions were not so bad. Instead, he reported back home about the modern appearance of the center; he was especially impressed with the faucets "that provide water all the time."[41]

The completion of Ellis Island January 1, 1892, marked the conversion from regional to national control of the immigrant stream. Through the years, the facilities of this reception station were constantly enlarged. The immigrants waited in the enormous hall until they could appear before the official who asked them a number of questions about their identities and backgrounds, and who checked if they had a minimum of $25 available. Whoever could not give a satisfactory answer, demonstrated physical or mental disabilities, or acted suspiciously was taken to the specialists. He or she might possibly stay on the island several days or even weeks until the problem

---

[40]    Mari Smits, *Met kompas emigreren. Katholieken en het vraagstuk van de emigratie in Nederland (1946-1972)* (Nijmegen: KDC, 1989), and Pedro de Wit, *Wegen wijzen overzee. 65 jaar christelijk emigratiewerk* (Kampen: Kok, 1993).

[41]    Letter from Izaak Janse from Grand Rapids to the Polderdijk family in Nieuw en St. Joosland, May 30, 1880, ILC HH.

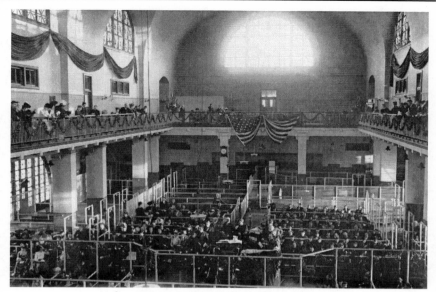

Central reception hall at Ellis Island.
National Park Service, Statue of Liberty National Monument, New York

was solved or until a deportation decision was made, with the costs to be born by the shipping company. This way, profiteers were warded off, and assistance organizations could offer their services.[42]

In spite of these protective measures, ominous rumors about America continued to circulate for a long time. In 1907, for example, the young Dutch immigrant Gerard van Pernis took along a revolver at the insistence of his brother who had been in military service, in order to protect himself in wild America against train robbers, freely roaming Indians, and wild animals. He soon found out that he had wasted four and a half guilders on an unnecessary and awkward bump on his hip.[43]

Most of the Dutch immigrants had little to fear because they were in good physical condition, could read and write, and often knew their destination. The greatest threat to unobstructed passage came from America. American society began to see unbridled immigration more and more as a problem when the main stream of immigrants went to the cities instead of the countryside, and all kinds of social problems, such as poverty, crime, corruption, and labor unrest, were blamed on the immigrant.

[42]  For a description of an immigrant physician, see Victor Safford, *Immigration Problems: Personal Experience of an Official* (New York: Dodd, Mead, 1925).

[43]  Gerard M. van Pernis, *According to Thy Heart: A True Story of an Immigrant's Life* (privately published, 1967), 29.

At the other side of the country, in California, the Chinese were the first group that began to feel the change from caring for to worrying about the immigrant. In 1882 the American government halted immigration from China for a period of ten years. With this decision the government accommodated the anti-Chinese mindset in California, where many Chinese worked in the mines, on railroads, and in industry. Their "strange" behavior and their isolation led to the suspicion that they were not able to integrate, endangered a free labor market, and formed a threat to good morals. The swelling stream of immigrants also amplified the call for selectivity on the East Coast. New York threatened to close Castle Garden if the city did not receive funds out of the Public Treasury to improve the situation for immigrants. Unrestrained immigration that burdened the cities especially worried many Americans. Neighborhoods bursting at the seams were a danger for public health, and poverty and crime became ever more evident. Attacks by alleged German anarchists increased the feeling that foreigners were a danger to democracy. Laborers who had been lured to America by employers to work on a contract basis depressed the wages of other workers. Proposals to select the best candidates for immigration on the basis of reading and writing tests passed, only to meet presidential vetoes. Since anarchists and radicals were not illiterate, the presidents saw no value in this stipulation, which hurt bona fide immigrants.

As the pressure continued to mount, Congress found a solution in the creation of a commission that was to inspect the circumstances of the immigrants carefully. In 1906 the U.S. Immigration Service sent officials to Europe to investigate whether shipping companies observed the rules and were really monitored by the American consuls. It became clear from the inspection that there was little to fear from the Dutch ports. The inspection commission gave a passing grade to the consul general, Soren Listoe, in Rotterdam. Listoe, accompanied by an American naval physician and a policeman, personally inspected five hundred immigrants who boarded a ship from the HAL in the summer of 1906. The consul checked the passengers who had to walk through a narrow, brightly lit corridor to discover possible signs of illness. Babies in particular were observed carefully, after it had become known that on a previous journey a woman had exchanged her deformed child for a healthy child during the inspection, to take it back just before departure. The child was discovered in New York and sent back. Every year hundreds of passengers, especially from Russia and Hungary, were not allowed on board because they showed signs of the infectious eye disease trachoma.[44]

Between 1907 and 1910 a broadly representative U.S. Immigration Commission, under the leadership of the Republican senator from Vermont, William P. Dillingham, carried out a large-scale investigation into the origin, passage, settlement, and further developments of the immigrants. The commission concluded that the problem was not the supposed inferior quality of recent newcomers (no proof of such inferiority was found), but lack of space in America to accommodate such great numbers. This conclusion was sufficient reason to limit the number of immigrants.

The outbreak of the First World War fanned American nationalism and branded as unpatriotic those who wanted to maintain their foreign citizenship. In 1918, because of the war, the American authorities asked everyone who wanted to visit the country to show a passport. In Congress the proponents of limiting immigration finally got the upper hand. They used a broad range of means to persuade public opinion of the need for this measure, by organizing programs for the assimilation of newcomers and by inflaming the fear of Bolsheviks and other foreign radicals. The progressive politicians also hoped to improve American society with these measures. In 1921 Congress tied immigration to an annual quota of 3 percent of the population from any country that already lived in America. Three years later, that percentage was lowered to 2 percent. Between 1920 and 1929 immigration shrunk from 805,000 to 280,000 people.[45]

How selective the authorities had become was shown in a report of the Dutch socialist N.A. de Vries, who made a trip through America in 1923 to investigate whether the prohibition of alcohol was effective. With a sense for irony he described the easy treatment he received, in contrast to the third-class passengers, who had to wait a long time and were thoroughly searched.

> The medical examination is a farce—they look into your eyes for a moment! Apparently that tells them everything. They were as

---

[44] "Powderly Report, European Investigation, 1906-1907," July 1906. Microfilm, U.S. Immigration Service, Bureau of Immigration Records, reel 1, pp. 20-22. *Reports of the Immigration Commission.* Vol. 4. *Emigration Conditions in Europe* (Washington, D.C.: Government Printing Office, 1911), 111. Between January 1, 1904, and September 4, 1908, 2,523 emigrants were refused, although in decreasing numbers, from 800 to 200 per year.

[45] Robert F. Zeidel, *Immigrants, Progressives, and Exclusion Politics: The Dillingham Commission, 1900-1917* (De Kalb: Northern Illinois Univ. Press, 2004).

meek as lambs. All the paper work we had to submit, did not mean a thing! My physical and mental handicaps were not discovered, and the American nation is therefore not sufficiently protected against me, the immigrant. I did not even declare that I would not attack the government of the United States, nor the lives of its officials. I did not even declare myself against polygamy; apparently I may *continue* to believe in it.[46]

From now on the Dutch quota of newcomers could not be more than 3,106 persons per year. Since this number was close to the average number of applicants, this was not considered a serious problem. Moreover, most compatriots could pass a reading and writing test. The Dutch considered themselves superior to the emigrants from southern and eastern Europe and requested, along with Belgium, Germany, Sweden, and Denmark, to participate in a short-lived experiment that was conducted in August 1925 with English-speaking immigrants. They were examined in the harbor of their homeland and were allowed to pass through Ellis Island without further examination. Solidarity with other immigrants was far from their minds.[47]

However, the quota law, which remained in force until 1964, did have repercussions for the Dutch-American community. It ended free settlement in the United States. Around 1930, the number of Dutch Americans of the first and second generation reached its highest point with 414,000 people. This peak coincided with the highest number of Americans born in other countries.[48] The stagnation of the influx of new immigrants, continued through the economic crisis of the 1930s, hastened the Americanization process because communities did not have to reckon as much with people who knew only Dutch. At the same time, the spread of Dutch colonies to the west came to a natural end when California was reached in the 1920s; the pattern of the colonies did not change very much after that. The consolidation phase had begun. The nature of this consolidation process is the subject of the following chapters.

---

[46]    N.A. de Vries, *De Nieuwe Wereld. Amerika 1923. Reisbrieven* (Groningen: Wolters, 1924), 18.

[47]    Bertha M. Boody, *A Psychological Study of Immigrant Children at Ellis Island* (New York: Arno Press, 1970 [c.1926]), 2 (on November 5, 1925).

[48]    E.P. Hutchinson, *Immigrants and their Children, 1850-1950* (New York: Wiley, 1956), 5. The calculation for the Netherlands: 280,333 people with at least one parent who was born in the Netherlands, and 133,133 people who were born there themselves.

# CHAPTER 3

# Formation of an Immigrant Network

The first Dutch immigrants who came as a group had left with a plan for an orderly colony but had not thought about a grand countrywide network. That network could come into existence only when the strategically chosen places of the first settlement became the central point of a circle of new colonies or the starting point of a line along which new communities were established. In several places in America connecting lines appeared among the areas of concentration, so that within sixty years a broad framework of Dutch immigrants was established. This pattern first became visible in rural communities, but later it appeared also in urban areas. Even unsuccessful colonies were part of this network. This pattern would not have developed without the early footholds.

## Holland and Zeeland as Footholds

When the first Dutch immigrants landed on the coast of Lake Michigan, they set foot in pristine forest, soon to be connected to the "civilized" sections. Their first task was to prepare housing for the

59

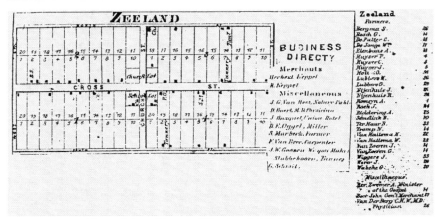

Map of the village of Zeeland, Michigan, in 1850.

hundreds of compatriots who were on their way. They built two log cabins, five by ten meters, with roofs of leaves, and they moved into the huts that the Indians had built. Next, they carved signs in trees so that connecting routes were established between the landing place at Lake Michigan and the sites of villages. The first groups arrived in March 1847 from their winter lodging elsewhere in Michigan, from Detroit and the village of Allegan. A planned settlement offered the best guarantee for the continuity of the community of immigrants. Both Van Raalte and Van de Luijster planned their layouts of Holland and Zeeland on American models, even though there were points in common with new designs in the Netherlands, such as the village of Borssele in Zeeland. They did not replicate the Old World but immediately adjusted to the New. The immigrant parties grouped themselves in settlements around these two central places, which they named after their provinces (Vriesland, Groningen, and Drenthe) or their previous towns (Borculo, Noordeloos, Harderwijk). These places did not have town plans, such as Holland and Zeeland, and without vision they remained small.

In the summer of 1847 the Zeeland people erected their first public building in the middle of the village—the log cabin church, ten by twenty meters, that was also used as a school and meeting hall. In the fall the colonists of Holland came together in a community meeting, their own version of local democracy. Until 1849 these assemblies met weekly to reach, if possible, unanimous decisions about church and civic issues of the "town" of Holland. The other villages did not need these formal meetings, since the colonists used the time between the morning and afternoon worship services on Sunday for practical matters.

Van Raalte, who had accumulated large debts in order to purchase thousands of acres, had ambitious plans that could become reality only if they were tackled collectively. The location of the meetings rotated among the largest homes with alternating chairmanship. Everyone could present agenda items.[1] The decisions had to be carried out by those present. Thus, a certain R. Schilleman was sent to Saugatuck, a small coastal village just south of Holland, to learn the art of fishing from the Americans. R. van der Veere got the task of meeting newcomers at the mouth of the Black River and accompanying them to the colony. The meeting also made a decision to carve more signs in the trees, so that the people could find their way to each others' homes. Bernardus Grotenhuis, a friend of Van Raalte's, and the more experienced Dutch American Elias De Young, were sent to Albany and New York to purchase materials that were later sold in the colony store. The money earned that way was used to buy meat and flour. Another community venture was the purchase of a ship, the *Knickerbocker*, which was to move not only goods but also immigrants from Chicago. Both plans were sunk because of the irregular contributions of the colonists and the absence of means to enforce payments. The immigrants fetched from Chicago thought that they did not have to pay because the ship belonged to the community; the store had insufficient capital and could not deliver the goods on time.

The colonists put their village of Holland collectively in order. In the fall of 1847 the town was surveyed and the parcels were sold under community supervision. Essential projects such as a road, a bridge, a church, a school building, a harbor pier, and an orphanage received priority. The colonists divided the costs among themselves and paid in dollars, *gouden willempjes* (gold ten-dollar coins with the image of King Willam II), in work, or in lumber to keep the money within the community. Everyone was aware that they could remain independent only if they themselves took care of matters and paid for them. The residents gathered quarters and dimes for a total of $25 for the purchase of a church bell. Because so many items had to be paid for, the village money chest was soon empty. By charging fines to latecomers and shirkers to the village meeting, they strongly encouraged a common effort, but there continued to be a critical shortage of cash. The result was that a church was built and a road to Grand Rapids constructed (in 1854), but for the time being no bridge or harbor. A number of the

---

[1]    G. van Schelven, "Historische Schetsen uit het Koloniale Leven," *De Grondwet*, September 17, 1912.

plans were not realized or were modified, but at least they gained a decision-making process, which at the same time produced training for participation in a democracy.

Working on communal goals impeded the progress of one's own business. Some people tried to dodge their responsibility by reporting sick and then working for themselves; others were in need of work. On November 8, 1848, Van Raalte gave an address at the community meeting with the central idea of "American work, American payment, and a strong encouragement for self-employment, so that you are your own boss."[2] He encouraged private initiatives in small and large businesses. For example, Lambertus Scholten obtained cats from "English" villages and sold them to families to battle the mice plague.[3] Others built mills to grind grain or to cut lumber.

Albertus Van Raalte clearly continued as the leader of the community. He purchased land from American war veterans who had accepted their wages in land and from other investors; retained contacts with politicians; played on the feelings of the church officers in the East; and functioned as the answer man, trusted person, and, of course, as pastor. He had the support of the shopkeeper Binnekant, hotel owner Doesburg, and his ministerial colleagues. In case of dissatisfaction he was the "fall guy." The other side of participation was, of course, that each person had to work voluntarily for the common good, and that did not suit everyone. Those with capital were asked most frequently for money and ran the risk of losing their investments. If a plan did not work out, such as the unsuccessful construction of a harbor, Van Raalte was heaped with criticism.[4]

The situation improved when local government was professionalized. The community meetings were discontinued in 1849 and replaced with a municipal organization. The eight Americans who lived in the area assumed the first public offices—such as postal official—gave advice and goods, and were very helpful: the Reverend George N. Smith provided housing, farmer Isaac Fairbanks gave agricultural instruction, Judge John R. Kellogg advised on land purchase, and Edward Harrington taught how to fell trees and also translated. These Americans were well disposed toward the Dutch. The "English" in the

[2]    Van Schelven, "Historische Schetsen," *De Grondwet*, September 24, 1912; English version in issue of January 26, 1915.
[3]    Lambertus B. Scholten in Lucas, *Dutch Immigrant Memoirs*, 1: 94.
[4]    Robert P. Swierenga, "Albertus C. Van Raalte as a Businessman," in Jacob E. Nyenhuis, ed., *A Goodly Heritage: Essays in Honor of the Reverend Dr. Elton J. Bruins at Eighty* (Grand Rapids: Eerdmans, 2007), 281-317.

Log cabin in Holland, Michigan, ca 1900.
Archives, Calvin College, Grand Rapids, Michigan

area eagerly sold the Dutch cattle and food, because they paid with real gold coins at a time when cash was scarce. The first group of men received official citizens' voting rights in the spring of 1851, after they had lived in America for at least two and a half years.[5]

Thus, a government, structured on the American model, was introduced as soon as possible. This provided local township government with a school inspector, road supervisors, and other public positions, later as a separate city. Township Holland, along with thirty-five surrounding townships, formed a county, with the small town of Allegan as the government center. The courthouse was located here. The counties were under the jurisdiction of the state of Michigan, which not only had its own laws but also its own constitution. Together the states formed the United States. When they became citizens, the immigrants received voting rights on all four governmental levels. With this right they were ahead of their compatriots by more than half a century. While their orthodox fellow church members in the Netherlands for a long time harbored reservations about general (male) voting rights, the immigrants accepted that right without objections and participated enthusiastically in various elections.[6] The promise of freedom was fulfilled.

5    G. van Schelven, "Historical Sketch of Holland City and Colony Delivered July 4, AD 1876," Van Schelven Collection, Joint Archives of Holland, Holland, Michigan. Dingman Versteeg, *De Pelgrim-Vaders van het westen* (Grand Rapids: C.M. Loomis & Co., 1886), 177-79.
6    *De Hollander*, October 13, 1852. The ministers did not hesitate to give advice about voting. In October 1852, The Rev. C. van der Meulen defended the candidacy of the Democrat Samuel Clark for the House of Representatives. See also chapter 9.

### Connections

The aim to make the settlements as independent as possible did not mean that the Dutch wanted to isolate themselves. They could not afford to do so anyway. Young people found work in Grand Rapids, where they could earn needed cash. The immigrant Jacob Harms Dunnink from Rouveen informed his family how the colony was being built up:

> Many people from the province of Zeeland arrived here this year. Most are from the laboring class and others paid for their transportation. But there is not enough work for them in the colony so they have to earn their living among the Americans. It is good there, but because of the language they have difficulties in understanding each other and in worshiping. Potatoes are planted on newly cleared land in this way. Two or three are placed together and then the soil is heaped up over them with a small hoe between the stumps of the trees, just like your mole hills. The trees are cut off here about three feet above the ground....The people we meet most here are the Zeelanders, because we sell our butter in their town. We also gather for worship on Sundays and after the service the children recite their catechism. They are a reverent and God-fearing people.[7]

In the first year many people died from malaria, a situation against which Scholte had warned. Severe winters and the failed harvest of 1851 forced still more people to go to the surrounding towns to get food or find work. The winter of 1849 was so cold that the water froze inside the homes, and the potatoes in the cellar. After that year the tide turned. By surviving the critical initial five years the village had proved its right of existence to the colonists who could not survive on their own. This had happened because of the communal solidarity of the congregation, the extra support from outside, and the development possibilities in this location.[8] In 1852 the village exported $28,000 worth of wood products (roofing materials, boards, and short poles) and this was only the beginning of a blossoming industry that generated thousands of dollars of income. Enterprising villagers

---

[7]　Letter from Jacob Harms Dunnink to family, January 24, 1850, ILC HH. See also Brinks, *Dutch American Voices*, 31.

[8]　Martin Ridge, "Robert Hine and Communitarianism," *Pacific Historical Review* 70 (2001): 478. Swierenga and Van Appledorn, *Old Wing Mission*, 349.

Mansion of Albertus C. van Raalte in Holland, Michigan.
Archives, Calvin College, Grand Rapids, Michigan.

bought machines for the leather tanneries in Grand Rapids, obtained the needed expertise and set up small leather factories.[9] The contacts among the Dutch in the colony and the surrounding places were intensive and continued as the years went on. When life in the colony had proved to be possible, immigrants who had pitched their tents in the eastern part of the country traveled west. Dunnink reported on the attraction of the colony in 1855:

> Many people have arrived at our settlement this summer. Some came from Europe, but many also from New York, Albanie and Buffalo. These are people who first could not travel farther because of their poverty....Many houses are being built on the road between us and Zeeland. During the summer six of them were already completed and many other people are beginning to clear the trees and are planning to come here to live. There is a large congregation here in Zeeland, which I believe has about 400 members. The building is already becoming too small. On Sundays thirty to forty people cannot find a seat.

The government also contributed to the growth in 1857 by making land available at a reduced price, with the stipulation that the buyers indeed would settle there. "The land is at a low price, the State has assessed the land that has not yet sold at 50 ct per acre, and many

9    Robert P. Swierenga, "'Better Prospects for Work': Van Raalte's Holland Colony and Its Connection to Grand Rapids," *Grand Valley History* 15 (1998): 14-22.

who still had money went to the State to buy land. But those who did not want to live there, could not get it.[10] These land sales tied Dutch immigrants to the area. They stayed in Holland twice as often as non-Dutch people."[11]

## Pella: Springboard in Iowa

In August 1847 the second group of Dutch immigrants, under the leadership of the Reverend Hendrik Scholte, established the village of Pella in the state of Iowa, where several farms had already been developed by Americans. Pella was situated in a fertile part of Iowa that, besides prairie land, also contained deposits of coal, clay, lime, and sandstone, and, just as Holland and Zeeland in Michigan, was laid out in square plots. The Dutch group that settled here was well to do, but that did not mean that there always was much money at hand. Cash funds were scarce in the first two years, since the money they had taken along was used for buying land. Until a new group with cash for purchasing arrived in 1849, the colonists had to buy goods by bartering.[12] A temporary source of income came from the trading with gold seekers who in these years were passing through on their way to California.

The people of Pella were just as eager to take the oath on the constitution as were the people of Holland. Just as in Holland, the first priority was to establish good connections with the surrounding area. A first effort to finance a plank road was not successful, because the people of Pella rejected the intended charging of tolls. They had more faith in a connection by water via the Des Moines River. In the fall of 1847, Scholte planned a new town of Amsterdam in a bend in this river, three miles southeast of Pella. This was meant to become the harbor for Pella, and at first it seemed to be an attractive location for which the colonists plunked down one hundred dollars per building plot. When a flood swept away this "town" four years later, Pella's leaders staked their future on a railroad connection. This connection took more time than they had envisioned. By 1858 the railroad had reached Pella at a distance of thirty-five miles, when the economic crises that preceded

[10]   Jacob Harms Dunnink, Zeeland, November 26, 1855, and December 27, 1857, ILC HH. Brinks, *Dutch American Voices*, 36.

[11]   Gordon W. Kirk, Jr., *The Promise of American Life: Social Mobility in a Nineteenth-Century Immigrant Community, Holland, Michigan 1847-1894* (Philadelphia: American Philosophical Society, 1978), 53-54, calculated for the 1870s.

[12]   Richard L. Doyle, "The Socio-Economic Mobility of the Dutch Immigrants to Pella, Iowa 1847-1925" (Ph.D. diss., Kent State Univ., 1982), 53-55.

the Civil War erupted. It was not until 1865 that Pella got its railroad connection with Des Moines, with the residents themselves investing in the project.

Pella did not have the magnetic attraction that went out from the satellite villages around Holland, which attracted a varied public. Thirty percent of the Pella population came from the province of Gelderland, and 31 percent from Zuid-Holland. Most of the city folks from Utrecht and Amsterdam lived in the center of the village, along with subdivisions occupied by Friesians and from rural communities in the provinces of Utrecht and Gelderland. The colony in Michigan had a much broader recruitment area in the Netherlands.

The greater initial capital at the disposal of the Iowa immigrants, allowing them to purchase existing farms, and the benefit of the fertile prairie soil around Pella that produced quick profits gave the Dutch in Iowa a head start on those in Michigan. The circumstances in the colony around Holland were less favorable, both in climate and in fertility (the land in Pella on average produced twice as much as in Holland). This situation stimulated the population of Michigan to consider alternatives to farming. Although Holland had only three factories in 1850, versus thirteen in Pella, the combined production in Holland was higher than in Pella. In 1880 the industrial output of Holland was five times as much as Pella, which continued to be much more dependent on agriculture. When economic growth in Pella stagnated after 1880, the population decreased because of the exodus to more western settlements. In the meantime Holland continued to grow.[13]

Scholte's ideal was not to establish a purely Dutch colony. He encouraged Americans to settle in Pella and he sold them land in the town. During his lifetime the Dutch constituency of Pella went down from 91 percent in 1850 to 70 percent in 1870, and then it rose again slowly to 86 percent by 1925.[14] Scholte did not strive for continuity but for renewal. His unorthodox involvement in politics, law, business, banking, and his refined lifestyle alienated him from his compatriots, who preferred to retain their old ways. He did not hesitate to sell a parcel of land that had been promised for a church building to two businessmen, and to propose another site for the church. Next, he

---

[13]   Richard L. Doyle, "A Comparison of Economic Development and Wealth Mobility in the Dutch colonies of Pella, Iowa and Holland, Michigan 1850-1880," in Elton J. Bruins, comp., *The Dutch in America*. Papers presented at the Fourth Biennial Conference of the Association for the Advancement of Dutch-American Studies (Holland: Hope College, 1984), 14-27.

[14]   Ibid., 111.

organized a religious revival and invited a Baptist college to town. Because he did not receive a salary from the church, he deemed himself independent and was often absent. His congregation felt neglected and missed his leadership. Because he did not join an existing denomination, his congregation lacked support. Tensions in the church and in the community, because of murky land transactions, supported each other. Moreover Scholte's wife, who continued her aristocratic lifestyle in a mansion with twenty-seven rooms and a concert piano, had little sympathy for the people.

In 1854 Scholte and his church parted ways. The Dutch rejected him and his rapid Americanization. Scholte was an example of an immigrant leader who, through his rapid adjustment to the American milieu, lost the trust of his group. This was expressed in the disintegration of the church into a motley mixture of small groups, which, after they had deposed Scholte, remained independent until they joined one of the two Dutch immigrant denominations.[15] This rift created space for other Protestant denominations, such as Baptists, Methodists, and Presbyterians, who competed successfully with the Dutch churches. In 1850 nine out of ten residents belonged to a Reformed church. Thirty years later this number had been reduced to 75 percent, and in 1925 to even less than 50.[16]

Between 1865 and 1897 Pella was the last station of the Des Moines Valley Railroad, which brought other groups to town. The contrast was great between the Dutch who observed Sunday rest carefully and the more relaxed Irish. The older generations kept their distance, but the younger developed friendships, although it did not lead to true ethnic blending.[17] Fewer than 10 percent of the Dutch married outside the ethnic enclave. The Dutch were mostly farmers or laborers, while the Americans occupied higher positions. Pella remained dependent on farming, although brick yards and stone quarries offered a limited number of industrial jobs. Nearly all industry was related to farming or produced for local use. Corn (for cattle feed), wheat, and oats were the main crops. Around 1870 there was no more federal land available and there were only forty-four employment positions outside farming. Without economic alternatives, the next generation had to seek farm land in the West, where they founded sister colonies in

---

[15]  Lubbertus Oostendorp, *H.P. Scholte: Leader of the Secession of 1834 and Founder of Pella* (Franeker: Wever, 1964), 169-73.

[16]  Doyle, "Socio-Economic," 119.

[17]  Cyrenus Cole, *I Remember, I Remember: A Book of Recollections* (Iowa City: State Historical Society of Iowa, 1936), 36-37.

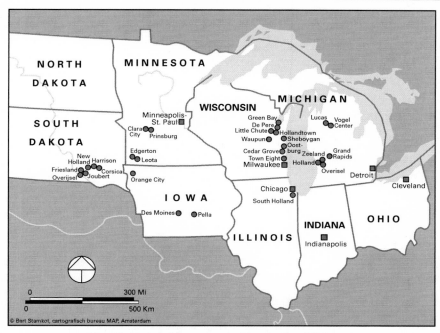

Map 6: Dutch towns and cities in the Midwest.

northwest Iowa. This move leveled the growth rate of the city after 1870, and after 1880 it even dropped below five thousand. Production could rise only through more intensive cultivation.[18] The farmers reached good results, and during the growth period until 1880 laborers could climb to farmer or renter, but when all the available land was gone, newcomers and younger people had fewer and fewer opportunities to advance economically. New companies settled in Pella only after 1900 and created somewhat more variety in the economy.[19]

In the meantime the lack of internal mobility exerted a conservative influence on the population. The effect of this conservatism could be seen in the retention of Dutch as a spoken language that was maintained longer in Pella than in other Dutch settlements. This characteristic can be traced to the continuity of (especially agricultural) family businesses, and it was reinforced by a more explicit resistance against the ever-present Americans and by the quality of Dutch education. Among the numerous immigrant groups in Iowa, the Dutch were conspicuous because of their exceptionally close relationships.[20]

[18]   Doyle, "Socio-Economic," 63.
[19]   Ibid., 156.
[20]   Schwieder, *Iowa*, 104.

## Wisconsin

The state of Wisconsin did not appear to be a bad choice for the settling of the original colony. The climate was mild, the soil fertile, and natural disasters usually did not occur. For these reasons stable communities were started that were dependent on agriculture. Originally it appeared that the central Dutch colony would develop in Milwaukee, the largest city in the state. The lay preacher Pieter Zonne, an enterprising man, had arrived there in May 1847, but he had become involved in several business conflicts and had forfeited much goodwill. Just as Michigan had been portrayed negatively by Scholte because of its bad climate, Wisconsin got the reputation that there were too many Germans and Roman Catholics.[21]

For Dutch Catholics this was, of course, a recommendation. In exactly the same period, therefore, they settled in Green Bay and De Pere, and in the villages of Little Chute and Holland(town). These villages were comparable to the rural Dutch Protestant colonies. In 1895 there were, respectively, 529 and 240 Dutch people in De Pere and Green Bay, while Outagamie County, the location of Little Chute, housed another 772 compatriots.[22] A number of immigrants had by then traveled farther on their own. In 1875 six families from De Pere, under the leadership of John Verboort and John A. van der Velden, settled in the Willamette River valley in Oregon, but these places remained small.[23]

The Protestant communities were fed both by immigrants straight from the Netherlands and by people from elsewhere in America.[24] Pieter Daane, the founder of Oostburg, came from Pultneyville in New York and became the most important shopkeeper of the village. He saw to it that Oostburg became connected with the railroad by moving the village three miles to the west to get a station on the Sauk Trail Road between Milwaukee and Sheboygan. Jacob Quintus, from the province of Zeeland, chose Sheboygan as his home to develop his political

---

[21]   Lucas, *Netherlanders*, 196-225.

[22]   "State Census of 1895," *Tabular Statements of the Census Enumeration...of the State of Wisconsin....* (Madison: Democrat Printing Company, State Printer, 1895), 60-111; the size of the Dutch community was much larger, since the census counted only the people born in the Netherlands, minus their children. See also chapter 4.

[23]   Nieuwenhuis, "Orange City," 30 and Lucas, *Netherlanders*, 444-59.

[24]   Robert J. De Smith, "Jacobus De Rooy, Rural Wisconsin Diarist and Preacher," *Origins* 2.2 (1984): 27-31, 36. Steve J. Van Der Weele," Growing Up in Sheboygan County," *Origins* 11.1 (1993): 13-23.

**Mainstreet Cedar Grove, Wisconsin, ca 1910.**
Hope College Collection of the Joint Archives of Holland, Michigan.

and journalistic activities. Thus, each community had an ambitious entrepreneur.

Further inland was Roelof Sleijster, the "scout" sent by Van Raalte, at the base of Waupun, which, along with Alto, Randolph, and Friesland formed a second concentration of the Protestant Dutch in Wisconsin. But these settlements remained small, just like Town Eight (also called Bethlehem) north of Milwaukee, and the coastal place of Amsterdam, where Henry Walvoord founded a trading post. Neither of these developed into a geographic magnet like Holland, Michigan. The first was flooded with other nationalities, and Walvoord drowned before he could set up a business. An observer described the difference between dream and reality: "Amsterdam, the great city, with seven houses and a water hole."[25] The remaining people moved the village to Cedar Grove, between Milwaukee and Sheboygan. This was the central area dominated by the immigrants from the provinces of Zeeland and Gelderland, followed in 1861 by the Frisians, with their own ministers.[26]

Real entrepreneurs found the possibilities in Wisconsin too limited. Pieter Lankester, a baker from Middelburg, discovered this,

[25]    Henry Harmelink in Lucas, *Dutch Immigrant Memoirs*, 2:113-14. William C. Walvoord, *Windmill Memories: A Remembrance of Life in a Holland-American Community Before the Turn of the Century* (Cedar Grove, Wis.: Villager Publications, 1979), 12. [This description is an ironic reference to the well-known Dutch description, "Amsterdam, that great city, is built on (wooden) piles." Trans.]

[26]    Willem Wilterdink, *Winterswijkse pioniers in Amerika* (Winterswijk: Het Museum, 1990).

and in 1850 he led a group of twenty-five families to Franklin, a village southwest of Milwaukee. He invested significantly in land and farms, but he was more of an entrepreneur than a farmer, and after about ten years he moved to Milwaukee. The Dutch community there counted eight hundred inhabitants and lived in an area called "the Dutch Mountain." He also had contacts with Rochester and Buffalo. In the next decade he, like Jacob Quintus, moved to Grand Rapids, where his friend Frans Van Driele was the hub of the Second Reformed Church, a congregation of many business people.[27]

The state of Wisconsin recruited immigrants actively in the 1850s and also included the Dutch in that effort by hiring a Dutch banker and consul, Van Steenwijk, as its immigration agent. However, Van Steenwijk did not succeed in initiating a large-scale settlement, although he did help make the state better known. The total number of Protestant villages remained limited. In 1860 there were 1,323 Dutch people in Holland Township, about 60 percent of its population. In 1895 the county had 580 people born in the Netherlands (besides numerous children of Dutch parents), which indicates fewer immigrants. This was not due to lack of prosperity. In Sheboygan County, Holland Township had the highest number of acres (22,322) of developed land, which represented a value of 1.3 million dollars, but with relatively few farming machines and few people as wage earners.[28]

The Dutch colony in Wisconsin was more relaxed than the one in Michigan and operated somewhat independently from Michigan; this was reflected in the number of Dutch Presbyterian churches in addition to the Reformed Church and the Christian Reformed Church. Maybe this relaxed attitude was the reason why the colonies in Wisconsin were viable but not as successful as those on the other side of Lake Michigan. The local communities, especially Oostburg, Cedar Grove, and Sheboygan Falls, could develop well because of the early land purchases, and they enjoyed a close social structure because of churches and schools. However, they lacked the superregional function of a strong city such as Grand Rapids. Only when Oostburg and Cedar Grove received stations on the railroad to Milwaukee in 1872 did their village centers develop further. Before this time the area was known as Township Holland, without having a genuine center.[29]

---

[27]    Brinks, *Dutch-American Voices*, 338-62.
[28]    *State Census of 1895. Agricultural Statistics*, 648-49.
[29]    Gustave William Buchen, *Historic Sheboygan County* (no place, no pub., 1944), 298-301.

Reformed Church minister John H. Karsten, who served in Oostburg as well as Alto, remarked that Wisconsin lacked an obvious leader. The immigrants avoided the cities and went their own way. Even the approximately three thousand Americans with Dutch roots who lived in Milwaukee in 1895 did not form an especially close or supportive community. The stagnation of additional immigration reduced the viability of churches.[30] The pioneers were content with the pietistic climate of the Reformed Church and the space they found in the Presbyterian Church. They felt less pressure to distinguish themselves from others or to isolate themselves. Even without sympathy for the prevalent pietist religion, the immigrants could take care of themselves if they had sufficient family and other Dutch in the area. Pieter van Ouwerkerk, who had emigrated in 1851from Zuidzande in the province of Zeeland to Town Holland in Wisconsin, had not joined a church seven years after his arrival. He wrote on May 18, 1858, "In America we have until now not joined a church, because here they are all Seceders. Uncle Kees is also quite pious and from that church. There are also many converts, but they are mostly from the Seceders and they'll be glad to tell you. I consider those conversions hypocritical."[31]

**The Trek to the West**

Besides concentration and stability, the Dutch communities also needed dynamism to create a place for new groups of immigrants. If insufficient farm land was available in the area, the colonies created daughter colonies. From the Holland colony the next generation spread out over western Michigan. When land became too expensive there, families moved to the north of the state and founded villages such as Vogel Center and Lucas, where the lumber industry especially offered additional income.[32] From Grand Rapids, farmers spread out into a wide area.

The areas with the best soil were bought first.[33] The Dutch bought the areas around Graafschap, Zeeland, Vriesland, and Drenthe directly from the state. The soil there consisted of brown clay and sand. Within four years all the land in Ottawa County was purchased and developed.

---

[30]   Karsten in Lucas, *Dutch Immigrant Memoirs,* 2:129-39.
[31]   Letter published in *In de vreemde* 5 (1994): 123.
[32]   Lucas, *Netherlanders,* 301-04; Van Hinte, *Netherlanders in America,* 535-41.
[33]   Henry Aay, "The Making of an Ethnic Island: Initial Settlement Patterns of Netherlanders in West Michigan," *The Great Lakes Geographer* 2.2 (1995): 61-76.

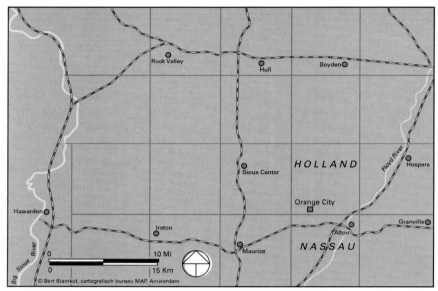

Map 7 Townships of Sioux County, Iowa.

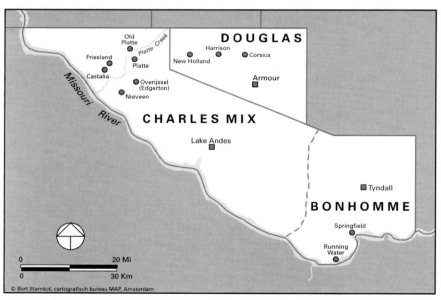

Map 8 Counties in South Dakota where Dutch immigrants settled in the late nineteenth century.

The area around Holland and along Lake Michigan had already been purchased by others (Americans and speculators), who were happy to sell their property to the Dutch. The colonists had obligated themselves to sell land only after approval of the board of the emigrant society, and certainly not to people who would undermine the Christian basis of the community. In reality, this agreement did not need to be maintained, since the board no longer functioned after a city council was elected. Moreover, the immigrants bought more land than they sold. The last expansion consisted of poor soil along the Macatawa, the Black River, where the town of Holland was located. By the beginning of the Civil War there was no more agricultural land available.

The "provincial" naming of the towns makes one assume that everyone looked for his or her province. That was especially true of the people from Drente and Friesland and for emigrants from Graafschap Bentheim, who had strong regional or linguistic ties. Immigrants from Groningen, Zeeland, and Overijssel spread out more across the area, although the center of the villages continued to be populated by people from the same province. Until 1850, at least one-third of marriage partners married someone from the same province.

Around 1870 the sons and daughters from the Pella colony settled in the northwest of the state, in villages such as Orange City and Sioux Center. Orange City was laid out by surveyors at the behest of a society founded in 1868 by citizens of Pella. The risk of carrying out these plans before a railroad had been laid soon became apparent when the track of the Sioux City and St. Paul Railroad bypassed Orange City at a distance of five miles. Mayor Henry Hospers saw to it that a side track approached the village at three miles; this station became the center of another town, Alton. The town of Maurice (a reference to the Dutch Prince Maurits) was a place on still another railroad and became an independent town in 1882. Most of these pioneers came from other settlements in the West, while a small number came directly from the Netherlands. The first residents of Sioux City came from Iowa, Minnesota, or Wisconsin, as well as from the Dutch provinces of Gelderland, Friesland, and Overijssel.[34]

---

[34] G. Nelson Nieuwenhuis, *Siouxland: A History of Sioux County, Iowa* (Orange City: Sioux County Historical Society, 1983), 109-62. Nella Kennedy, "The Sioux County Dutch," in Elton J. Bruins, "The Dutch in America: Papers Presented at the Fourth Biennial Conference of the Association for the Advancement of Dutch American Studies" (Holland: Hope College, 1984), 29-40.

These places, supplemented by Hospers and Rock Valley, developed in cooperation with the railroads, which were extended westward from Milwaukee. The churches followed the first pioneers and created the needed cohesion. Some farmers took to the road as early as Saturday afternoon to cover the twenty miles to the closest church in Hull.

Even though most of the residents in Orange City had roots in Pella, their orientation resembled that of their compatriots in Holland, Michigan. The local college, Northwestern, resembled Hope College in Holland rather than Central College in Pella. Northwestern was clearly Reformed and recruited its faculty from Hope. Politically Republican Orange City also looked more like Holland than Pella, which continued to vote Democratic. In fact, the daughter deviated from the mother, and looked more like her aunt in Michigan.[35] In the other counties, such as Sioux Center and the villages in the Dakotas, the population was more of a mix of new immigrants from the Netherlands and people passing through from other parts of America.

But the high expectations of the results in the West were cruelly disrupted. Between 1873 and 1878 grasshoppers devoured the harvests in Sioux County, while hail storms ruined the rest. These disappointments discouraged many farmers and they therefore returned to the East. The decade between 1877 and 1887, during which there were exceptionally heavy rains in this dry area, drew many new inhabitants. The pendulum then swung again to the other side with ten extremely dry years till 1897, followed again by a wet period between 1897 and 1910. In that year a serious drought started, which was, again, followed by favorable years in terms of climate and sale prices. This wave continued until the end of the First World War.[36]

Ten years after the development of Sioux County, land in the western part of Iowa also began to get scarce, and colonists traveled from there across the border to South Dakota, where they settled in the villages of New Holland, Corsica, and Harrison. With each step westward the organization became more professional—research teams investigated the area with speculators, ministers made recommendations, the newspapers printed grandiose advertisements, and the railroads offered reductions for the journey. But the circumstances in the daughter colonies were often much harsher than in the mother colonies. Farmers were even more at the mercy of the

35    Kennedy, "The Sioux County Dutch," 36-39.
36    Henry Van der Pol, Sr., *On the Reservation Border: Hollanders in Douglas and Charles Mix Counties* (Stickney, S.D.: Argus, 1969).

**Sod house in Dakota.**
Archives, Calvin College, Grand Rapids, Michigan.

elements than in Iowa. While the fertile soil in Iowa was a meter deep, in Dakota the fertile layer was superficial, the rainfall less, and groundwater shallow. In Dakota, farmers needed four times as much land as in Iowa, and people therefore lived further apart, and life was much lonelier.[37] A segment of the population consisted of unmarried young men, who worked their claimed land for a few months during a five-year period, to obtain complete ownership.[38] The high mobility in this part of America regulated the rhythm of people's lives. Every year on March 1 the rent contracts in Iowa expired, and a large number of people moved to another farm; many marriages were therefore conducted in February. The middle-class shopkeepers did a good business then in furnishing the new households. Those who traveled farther could take only cattle and machinery, and there was little room for luxury items. [39]

[37]  Dorothy Schwieder and Deborah Fink, "U.S. Prairie and Plains Women in the 1920s: A Comparison of Women, Family, and Environment," *Agricultural History* 73 (Spring 1999): 197.

[38]  Izaak Janse (Grand Rapids) to F.P. Polderdijk, Nieuw-en St. Joosland, February 22, 1887, ICL HH.

[39]  Mike Vanden Bosch, *A Pocket of Civility: A History of Sioux Center* (Sioux Falls, S.D.: Modern Press, 1976), 28.

Platte, South Dakota.
Archives, Calvin College, Grand Rapids, Michigan.

Around 1880 potential emigrants in the Netherlands could obtain enough comprehensive information about America to discover where land was for sale at affordable prices, but the exact way of life on the plains in the Midwest was not yet known. The life story of Hendrikus van der Pol, from the town of Ermelo in the province of Gelderland, confirms this situation. He and his friends studied the map of America to choose a destination and weighed all the information in the recruitment folders.[40] In 1882 he left for Dakota with his wife, three children, and a father-in-law—without funds but full of faith in the future. The journey west revealed the immigrants' way of life. Trains full of immigrants arrived at the stations. Families joined in renting a wagon for their belongings, which they unloaded at the station near their land claims. The conditions in Dakota were much more primitive than in Michigan and the east of Iowa. The first houses were built from sod, with a rough wooden roof, covered with tar paper. The Dutch imitated a few Russian families. They ripped the prairie ground open and sowed corn, wheat, and flax, and planted potatoes for their own use and for selling.[41] The two Dutch denominations stimulated the voyage by their mutual competition. Ministers from both denominations exerted themselves to visit the new settlement, to organize a congregation, and to erect a church building. After the first Dutch had settled in South Dakota in 1882, the Reformed Church established a congregation in New Holland May 3, 1883, and in Harrison June 28. A year later, the Christian Reformed Church also had a congregation in Harrison. In 1890 the state of South Dakota had thirty-five "Dutch" churches with

[40]  Van der Pol, Sr., *On the Reservation Border,* 10-11.
[41]  Ibid., 24-25.

nearly two thousand members who supported each other, especially in difficult years.[42]

The settlements in Michigan and Iowa supplied the colonists going to North and South Dakota, Minnesota (Mille Lac County), and Montana. In the spring of 1885 a company of at least twenty people left Michigan to investigate Dakota; they trusted the Dutch-American land agent, and all bought land. They encouraged other interested parties to buy land quickly, because it was going fast. Land agent P. Ellerbroek had gained their trust and they recommended him blindly. In the 1890s people from Iowa moved to the state of Washington. Frank Le Cocq from Orange City traveled ever farther west. He had first planted a Dutch community in South Dakota and there he had gained leadership experience. He had a large house built in Harrison and played an important role in the young state as representative to the first constitutional meeting of South Dakota in 1890. In 1917 he and his eight sons left for the state of Washington. Residents of Iowa also explored other areas for new colonies. W. van Amerongen and A.J. Kemper, both from Iowa, founded the Texas Colonization Company, which brought six hundred Dutch to "Nederland," a place in the Houston area, in 1900.[43]

In the West the colonists met wandering Indians who, partly because of the Dutch immigrants, had been driven from their land. Despite sensational stories in the press, there were no real confrontations. In 1895 a new Frisian immigrant wrote about his meeting with the native population: "I have also met some Indians; they are a strange people, the men have long hair with braids and they are dark brown. They live close to the road and they pass us and sometimes stop by for a thing or two. I am not at all afraid of them. They will not hurt anyone as long as you treat them well." Actually the two groups benefited from each other's presence by mutual trading. The Indians exchanged ponies, horses, and blankets for bread, milk, and copper items.[44]

[42]  Ibid., 31-32.

[43]  *De Grondwet*, March 17, 1885; Nelson Nieuwenhuis, "Orange City and the Western Movement," (Proceedings of the Conference of the Association for the Advancement of Dutch-American Studies, 1985), 16-33.

[44]  Ulbe B. Bakker, ed., *Zuster, kom toch over. Belevenissen van een emigrantenfamilie uit Friesland. Brieven uit Amerika in de periode 1894-1933/ Sister, please come over: Experiences of an immigrant-family from Friesland/The Netherlands. Letters from America in the period 1894-1933* (Kollum: Trion G.A.C., 1999), 101. Pieter Hovens, "Moccasins and Wooden Shoes: Indians and Dutchmen on the Plains Frontier, 1830-1940," in Paul Fessler, Hubert R. Krygsman, and Robert P. Swierenga, eds., *Dutch Immigrants on the Plains* (Holland, Mich.: Joint Archives of Holland, 2006), 37-55.

## City Communities

It was not the intent of the first wave of emigrants to settle in cities. The purpose of their temporary residence there was to build up their funds in order to be able to buy land. Nevertheless, city communities with a Dutch character did develop. These city communities also were part of the pattern of circles and connecting lines. The line is visible from New York City, although the city itself did not retain many Dutch Protestants. One of the first city communities began in Rochester, New York, where two hundred Dutch had already settled before Van Raalte and Scholte reached their destinations. Considering the uncertain situation in Wisconsin, many immigrants had changed their plans and remained in the cities that were on the route to the West.

There they made contact with the descendants of the seventeenth-century Dutch immigrants who had founded small English-speaking churches and who gladly assisted the newcomers. The Dutch found immigrants from their own provinces in these cities. The newcomers then spread farther out into the country, often to settlements with Dutch names. A fine example of this kind of circulation is the itinerary of Adriaan Zwemer (1823-1909), who became a minister in the Reformed Church. In 1849 Zwemer emigrated from Oostkapelle in Zeeland, with the colony in Michigan as his destination. He changed his mind when he discovered, just married to his fiancée from Zeeland, that he would have better opportunities in Rochester. He started a family there, learned English, and stayed to work for five years, until he received a scholarship for the just opened Holland Academy in Holland, Michigan, to prepare for the ministry.[45] He became a minister in the Reformed Church and served consecutively in Vriesland (near Zeeland, Michigan), South Holland (Illinois), Milwaukee (Wisconsin), Albany (New York), Graafschap (Michigan), Middelburg (Iowa), and Spring Lake (Michigan). His fifteen children, among whom were well-known professors and missionaries, spread out over the whole world.[46]

The great majority of Dutch immigrants who had arrived in New York harbor traveled on. The Erie Canal explains much about this pattern. This canal was connected to the Great Lakes areas and,

---

[45]    Adrian and Samuel M. Zwemer, *Genealogy and history of the Zwemer-Boon family* (Harrisburg: privately printed, 1932), 42-45.

[46]    Zwemer personally wrote his biography for each son and daughter. Because two children preceded him in death, a copy of the document was sent to Walcheren in the province of Zeeland. In 1932 the expanded biography was translated into English and published.

in combination with the expanding railroads, attracted new industries and opened up larger markets.[47] On the line Albany, Utica, and Buffalo industry centers developed for the production of textile, steel, locomotives, and machines. The supply of minerals, specifically iron ore, and fossil energy, such as coal and wood, was stimulated yet again by the extra demands of the Civil War. Thus, these industries offered many opportunities for work in the cities.

Old and new Dutch met each other on the piers. In Albany Isaac Wyckoff picked out the Dutch from the mass of people disembarking and found work for them. As soon as the emigrants arrived in the city, other people visited them.[48] That Albany was a transitional place was shown in the fact that their ministers often remained for only a year and then traveled farther.[49] The contacts with the other cities along the Erie Canal were good, but no new viable Dutch communities developed in any of these cities, except in Rochester. This line of cities with small Dutch centers continued in Cleveland, Ohio, and Detroit, Michigan. Rochester itself was the center of a circle. Before the arrival of Van Raalte and Scholte and their groups, immigrants from the province of Zeeland had landed there in 1840, but their desire was to farm in the area. They had founded stable settlements in the villages of Clymer, Marion, East Williamson, Pultneyville, and Palmyra on Lake Ontario, which resembled the atmosphere of the Wisconsin villages.

Both in Rochester and in Cleveland small groups of Dutch Catholics joined their fellow believers. In Rochester, the Catholics from Zeeland joined the "French Church of St. Mary's." The Dutch Catholic immigrants in Cleveland came from the province of Gelderland and settled on the west side of the city, where they were absorbed in the German parish of St. Stephen. The Protestants from Zeeland settled on the east side, and only after the Civil War did they have sufficient members to form their own congregation.[50] Of all the cities with a Dutch element, Grand Rapids certainly became the uncontested leader.

---

[47]  Walter Licht, *Industrializing America: The Nineteenth Century* (Baltimore: Johns Hopkins Univ. Press, 1995), 103-17.

[48]  See the article of Johannes Remeeus in Lucas, *Dutch Immigrant Memoirs* 2: 103-05.

[49]  Only when A.M. Donner joined the Reformed Church in 1857 was an independent congregation established, where the ministers then remained an average of two years. A.M. Donner, "De Hollanders in Albany, New York," in Lucas, *Dutch Immigrant Memoirs*, 2:294-300.

[50]  Swierenga, *Faith and Family*, 226-36.

**Grand Rapids**

Grand Rapids was founded in 1833 and by1850 had about 2,500 residents, 400 of whom were Dutch. These came primarily from the province of Zeeland and, under the leadership of Frans Van Driele, met for worship. They grew into a congregation that profited from contacts and assistance from the small English-speaking Reformed Church, which had been active in the city since 1840.[51] When the year 1851 turned out to be a disaster for the farmers, with crop failures and epidemics, many young people came from Holland and Zeeland to Grand Rapids to find work to supplement their family income. Initially spread out over the young city, they soon moved toward each other in the business center east of the Grand River. Gradually this area was filled with hundreds of families. In 1880 46 percent of the people of this area were of Dutch descent. Especially people from the provinces of Zeeland, Groningen, and Gelderland found homes here.[52]

This city community offered solidarity similar to that in the villages. W.H. de Lange had been in Grand Rapids for only half a year when, in the winter of 1874, he was hit by a sled that crushed his legs— an accident that proved fatal. Family and sympathetic people collected $400, and the family also received 125 guilders from the Netherlands. Thus, the family could survive for a while.[53]

Grand Rapids functioned as a safe haven for Dutch Americans who, for whatever reason, could not succeed in "De Kolonie," as the area around Holland was called, who hoped to escape the economic setbacks, or who just sought better trade opportunities. George Steketee was one of the latter. He left the town of Zeeland to build a business empire in department stores in Grand Rapids. He was so highly respected that he was elected as the first Dutch mayor of the city in 1881 and 1882.

The new immigration wave after 1880 settled directly in the southern neighborhood near Grandville, which around 1890 was connected with streetcar lines to the industrial area in the center of the city. A separate community developed on the west side of the river, where Germans and Irish settled, and later many Poles. Among

---

[51]   David W. Vanderstel, "The Dutch of Grand Rapids, Michigan, 1848-1900. Immigrant Neighborhood and Community Development in a Nineteenth-Century City" (Ph.D. diss., Kent State Univ., 1986), 181.

[52]   Ibid., 185.

[53]   T. Jansen (Johnson) from Grand Rapids to H. Houck in Deventer, February 22, 1874, and letter of April 7, 1874. See also Brinks, *Dutch American Voices*, 417-18.

The center of the Dutch in the United States:
the city of Grand Rapids, Michigan, ca. 1875.

Archives, Calvin College, Grand Rapids, Michigan.

these groups was a small minority of people from Staphorst (in the province of Overijssel) and from the province of Zeeland, who represented 11 percent of the area in 1860, but later that proportion diminished. In the northwest of the city the Dutch formed a triangle, with a remarkable number of people from the provinces of Zeeland and Friesland, although these groups did not live in the same street as their former village acquaintances.[54] Similar patterns were visible in other neighborhoods. In 1880, nearly 35 percent of the population on the southeast side had a Dutch background. Although that proportion decreased to 27 percent in the next two decades, this neighborhood was known as the "Dutch Ward," because of the eight churches, the theological school, and two elementary schools.[55] It is noteworthy that in all areas with a Dutch concentration there were people from Zeeland, especially from the islands of Schouwen and Tholen. They constituted 40 percent of the Dutch population in those areas, until after 1880,

[54]  Vanderstel, "Dutch of Grand Rapids," 197-202.
[55]  Ibid., 223.

when a new wave of people from Groningen, Friesland, and Gelderland changed the provincial proportions.[56]

Around 1800 the Dutch lived in single dwellings (about one-half of them owned by the occupant) and had large families. By 1900 there were certainly twelve neighborhoods where the Dutch formed a distinct group. Grand Rapids offered them all kinds of advantages: steady growth, an ample labor market, and numerous contacts with the Holland colony. Those who were interested could manage small farms in the immediate area. Newcomers often landed on the edge of the city. From there they could move to neighborhoods with folks from their country or region.[57] The Dutch immigrants were satisfied with "their" city, where they could find work, their own shops, churches, and cultural societies, and, above all, could buy their own homes. This satisfaction was evident from the high proportion of 43 percent of all Dutch who after ten years still lived in their original neighborhoods. Even after twenty years this proportion was still 36 percent, and 20 percent after 30 years.[58] They did not flee the city to the suburbs in large numbers. Actually, a move to other places did not mean a weakening of the community. Just as the first generation had sought their welfare in Grand Rapids and helped build the community, so the ones who moved strengthened the Dutch network elsewhere in the United States.

Sometimes the boundaries with the non-Dutch world were guarded literally. In 1888 a company laid a tram line with a steam locomotive straight through the Dutch neighborhood around East Street Church, in the direction of a recreation area east of the city. The area residents were angry, because they feared for the safety of their children, the nuisance of the hustle and bustle, and a disturbance of the Sunday rest. As soon as the workers had fastened the rails, the neighborhood people loosened them. The next day the workers were pelted with stones, and the rails were again pulled up. The tram company finally gave up. The lines were firmly drawn.[59]

How natural it was for people from the same area to visit each other is shown in the letters of Krijn Goudzwaard to his family in

---

[56]   Ibid., 248.
[57]   Evidence of the search for people from their own region can be found in the correspondence of Brechtje Allewijn-Mieras from Kalamazoo with Johanna and Abraham Wisse-Westrate. A letter of March 11, 1913, deals with the people from the neighborhood of Yersekenaren living in Grand Rapids, ILC HH.
[58]   Vanderstel, "Dutch of Grand Rapids," 269.
[59]   Ibid., 469-70.

Oud-Vossemeer, Zeeland. Because there already were many people from the province of Zeeland in Grand Rapids, the city attracted many others from there. They helped each other and found suitable marriage partners. On September 30, 1873, he wrote:

> You probably know already that Janna of Uncle Piet also lives in America. When they arrived here, niece Janna had a fever. They moved in with me, and niece and nephew were very sick when at my house, but they recovered. They live only about three houses from us. And because they were so sick, Uncle Piet also stayed with us. He did not know me but I knew him at once. He was very happy to meet us. He took all the letters I had from you, because he asked for them.[60]

Two and a half years later he announced that his oldest son had married Johanna de Windt from Goes. He experienced the Dutch character of the city nearly as self-evident: "There is not an English store in the city or there is a Dutch clerk. There are also plenty of Dutch stores, as well as Dutch attorneys."[61] Krijn prospered in the city. In 1876 he sold his house for $3,000, and from the proceeds he bought thirty acres of pasture for $150 per acre on the edge of the city, where his three sons settled around him.[62]

The magnet continued to draw, as was evident from the emigration of the later peace advocate, Abraham Muste. As a boy he left Zierikzee, in the province of Zeeland, with his family for Grand Rapids, because his mother's four brothers had already preceded them and had opened stores. They advanced the cost of the passage for the family and welcomed them. Within two days his father had found a job in a factory, and even the six-year-old Abraham soon felt at home among his cousins. "They made me feel that I was the Traveler they had been waiting for."[63]

Dialects and accents easily betrayed where a person was from. The wife of Izaak Janse discovered this in 1886. She met the owner of a hat shop in Grand Rapids. When the milliner heard that Mrs. Janse hailed from Arnemuiden, she said that she herself came from

---

[60]   Letter from Krijn Goudzwaard to family in the Netherlands, September 30, 1873, RSC; also in ICL HH. He lived at 407 Ottawa Street.
[61]   Ibid., February 16, 1876, and 1883.
[62]   Letters from Krijn Goudzwaard to family in the Netherlands, February 16, 1876, and June 10, 1893, RSC.
[63]   Nat Hentoff, ed., *The Essays of A.J. Muste* (Indianapolis: Bobbs-Merrill Co., 1967), 22-23.

neighboring Nieuwland, but that she had never met anyone in America from her village.[64] The combination of regional concentration and constant additions strengthened the community in Grand Rapids. The movement from the city center to the suburbs took place only after the Second World War.

## Kalamazoo, Michigan

The city of Kalamazoo functioned similarly for the Dutch community. The Dutch subculture there continued also after the Dutch immigrants had moved out of their neighborhoods and spread throughout the city.[65] The Dutch element in this city in southwestern Michigan consisted of a mixture of dissatisfied immigrants from Van Raalte's colony, descendants of the colonial-era Dutch from New York, and new immigrants. Until 1846 Kalamazoo was situated at the end of the railroad from Detroit west—the reason why many immigrants settled there. In 1852 the railroad was extended to Chicago. Thanks to the capable Paulus den Bleyker, a substantial portion of the agricultural sections in the areas came into Dutch hands. Den Bleyker was a Dutch orphan who had earned his capital with the draining of *polders* on the island of Texel, and he financed many ventures. Around 1870 there were about a thousand Dutch immigrants throughout the city, which numbered at least 27,000 residents and offered work to the newcomers.

In the following decade the Dutch discovered the potential of the low-lying marshlands surrounding Kalamazoo for growing vegetables. Immigrants from Groningen bought cheap land in the north and those from Zeeland in the south; with their families they cultivated the land very intensively for the market in Chicago. They needed little capital to grow celery, and in the winters they could add to their income by working in the nearby lumber mills. The small ventures paid off because of the low cost of land and housing, cheap labor, and access to markets. From that time on, the Dutch stuck together near their vegetable gardens. Around 1900 they had built more than ten churches, schools, and their own businesses. The south and the north settlements

---

[64]   Izaak Janse (Grand Rapids) to P.F. Polderdijk, Nieuw-en St. Joosland, December 14, 1886, ICL HH. For a similar story about acquaintances from Drente, see Brinks, *Dutch American Voices*, 90-91.

[65]   John A. Jackle and James O. Wheeler, "The Changing Residential Structure of the Dutch Population in Kalamazoo, Michigan," *Annals of the Association of American Geographers* 59 (September 1969): 441-60.

Celery farm in Kalamazoo, Michigan.
Archives, Calvin College, Grand Rapids, Michigan.

operated apart from each other and used English when they talked about communal issues, such as mutual aid societies.

By around 1940 the population of Kalamazoo had doubled, and the Dutch population in the city had multiplied eight times but was spread out over the city. The availability of cars, the decrease of the immigrant flow in the 1920s, and the decline of the celery market took away the need for the Dutch to live close to their farms. Their increased prosperity and the growth of the suburbs tempted them to spread out across the city.[66] As a result, the regional clusters fell apart, even though the cultural and religious bonds remained. The ethnic enclave was therefore a temporary, yet defining, phase in the history of the Dutch in this city.

## Chicago, Illinois

A similar development occurred in Chicago, where the first Dutchman, Leonard Valk, arrived in 1839.[67] He was followed by a trickling of compatriots when, after the Civil War, Chicago became a major railroad junction. In 1870 the city already contained more than two thousand Dutch. The real flood came after 1880, and around the

---

[66]   The economic basis of growing celery disappeared after 1950 because of competition from California, mechanization, and the lack of usable land.

[67]   Robert P. Swierenga, *Dutch Chicago: A History of Hollanders in the Windy City*, Historical Series of the Reformed Church in America, no. 42 (Grand Rapids: Eerdmans, 2002).

turn of the century there were more than twenty-one thousand Dutch. The Americans of Dutch descent in this metropolis would grow to a quarter million by 1980. The wave of immigrants of the 1840s brought families together who formed the basis of the first church. To the south of the city immigrants from the province of Noord-Holland grouped together in Roseland as truck farmers, while those from Zuid-Holland and Friesland founded South Holland. These colonies could survive until the advancing city, rising land prices, and supermarkets that bought their wares elsewhere in the country literally took away their livelihood in the 1950s. The west side of Chicago had been urbanized much earlier, in the 1880s. Immigrants from Groningen had especially settled there. They were poor and made a living with horse and wagon in transport or in garbage collecting.

It was because of the church that a community arose out of this nonplanned immigration. The early immigrants came together at someone's home and read sermons, and in 1853 they formed their first congregation. They did not receive a regular pastor until six years later, in the person of Cornelis van der Meulen, the founder of Zeeland. He and his successors remained only a short time. The person who became the real leader of the Dutch community was Bernardus de Beij from Groningen; for twenty-three years he pulled the strings in Chicago's First Reformed Church. Just before he arrived the True Reformed (later CRC) had seceded in 1867. After a fitful start, this Seceded church drew a large share of the newcomers who preferred a slow-pace adaptation to the American lifestyle and language. The immigrants invested their meager resources in the community, which in exchange provided a sizable marriage market, a good selection of well-known business partners, opportunities for recreation, and mutual help in illness, old age, and death. After 1900, the members of both denominations began to work together and established their own schools, offered mutual assistance, and merged garbage companies.

### Paterson, New Jersey

Besides Grand Rapids, Kalamazoo, and Chicago, a fourth large urban community developed in Paterson, New Jersey. The first Dutch arrived there around 1850, attracted to the textile industry and later to the blast furnaces and silk factories, which after the Civil War provided work for thousands. In 1856 there were enough Dutch-speaking people in Paterson to start their own church.[68] The proximity of the New York

---

[68]    Lucas, *Netherlanders*, 235; Gerald De Jong, "Dutch Immigrants in New Jersey Before World War I," *New Jersey History* 94 (1976): 69-88.

harbor, where most of the immigrants first set foot in America, helped Paterson and the surrounding places in New Jersey (Clifton, Lodi, Passaic) to continue to grow. The distance to the harbor was short, and the local ministers sympathized with the difficulties of the immigrants. They met them at the docks and helped them along. Especially those who did not have a clear destination in mind found work and homes in these towns. New Jersey was especially attractive to immigrants from the Zuid-Holland island of Goeree-Overflakkee, where the cultivation of the madder plant had come to an end. Three-quarters of the immigrants from Flakkee settled in this state. The Prospect Park area had so many Dutch that it was called "Little Holland." This was not a land of plenty, because people had to work hard for a meager wage. Because all the members of the family were enlisted to bring in money, they could earn a reasonable family income.

Around the turn of the century, the ten Dutch immigrant churches, supported by two newspapers and a Christian elementary school, formed the backbone of their community. Until 1954 the Union Holland Reformed Church in Paterson retained a reference to the Netherlands in its name, and the Northside Christian Reformed Church continued Dutch services until 1949. The ministers from these congregations traveled to the Netherlands regularly, where they shared knowledge about their American communities. The proximity of the New York harbor was advantageous for attracting Dutch immigrants.[69] New York itself was only the place of arrival and a quick passing-through. Only Roman Catholic and Jewish immigrants settled in the "Big Apple."

## Land Agents

The expansion and modernization of the American economy after the Civil War created the conditions for founding new settlements. In 1869 a railroad connected the east and the west of the country and sprouted a national railroad network. New settlements could be planned in the opened areas, while the railroad companies gladly sold their land (granted by the state) for ready cash. After the Civil War, representatives of Dutch investors came to evaluate the situation in

[69]    Ibid., 80. This was confirmed by the experiences of J.M. Rutte, the minister of the Sixth Reformed Church in Paterson, who went on vacation for three months in 1868 and strengthened the bonds between his congregation and many immigrants from the Zuid-Holland islands and the people in that area of the Netherlands. J.M. Rutte, *Levensbeschrijving en verantwoording van en door Ds. J. M. Rutte* (Paterson, NJ: De Telegraaf, [1882]), 22.

theWest—sometimes to control the railroads that had been financed with Dutch capital, sometimes to evaluate the investment situation.[70] Land agents took over the task of starting colonies for the Dutch from the pioneer ministers.

The agents continued to maintain close relationships with church circles in order to gain the trust of their customers.[71] That trust was not deserved by everyone: Pieter Hodenpyl, a land agent who was too eager to sell land in New York to new Dutch immigrants, approached them in the name of a relief organization, until he was unmasked as an exploiter. But not every promoter put his own interest first. The mayor of Pella, Henry Hospers, who had lived there since 1847 and was active in local government, business, and politics, was appointed as immigration agent by the state of Iowa in 1870. Because of this commission, he was able to carry out his plan for a new colony in the northwest of the state (Orange City). He was especially qualified in this position to provide supervision, make investments, and lend support to newcomers. In appreciation for his efforts the residents named a village after him. During the last two months of 1870 he traveled through the Netherlands to recruit new colonists. For this purpose he wrote a brochure entitled "Shall I Go to North America?" in which he gave an affirmative answer.[72] The message of his promotion trip was simple: keep struggling in the Netherlands or climb the ladder in Iowa. Land cost $2 per acre, and $720 was sufficient to build a house and buy a team of horses, a plow, and equipment. Especially families with children, whose wages could help bridge the first year, would be able to expand their property gradually. The rich soil, the clear streams, the healthy climate, and the excellent schools offered an exceptionally favorable environment.

The most trustworthy advisors were those who themselves took the risk to pioneer. Albert Kuipers, land agent for the Holland

---

[70]    Muriel E. Hidy, ed. and A. Hermina Potgieter, trans., "A Dutch Investor in Minnesota, 1866. The Diary of Claude August Crommelin," *Minnesota History* 37 (1960), 152-60. Augustus J. Veenendaal, *Slow Train to Paradise: How the Dutch Helped Build American Railroads* (Stanford: Stanford Univ. Press, 1996), 37-98.

[71]    A good example of a land agent in Montana and Washington was Reinder E. Werkman; see Donald van Reken, "The Life and Actions of Reinder Edward Werkman," in Larry J. Wagenaar and Robert P. Swierenga, eds., *Dutch Enterprise: Alive and Well in North America* (no place, no pub., 1999), 23-42.

[72]    *Iowa: de Vraag: Zal ik naar Noord-Amerika gaan? Kort and practisch beantwoord door een geboren Nederlander* [Henry Hospers] (Gorinchem, 1875).

Amerika Lijn in Drenthe, was such an example. This son of a poor baker had himself discovered modern farming methods and saw them as a solution to the problem of poverty in his country. He passed this knowledge on to his son Hendrik and sent him to America to look for suitable land. Hendrik traveled to the Dutch settlements and came to the conclusion that Charles Mix County in South Dakota offered the best chances. He recruited a group of poor people from the north of the Netherlands. But even before their ship had landed in New York, they were surrounded by speculators who began to sow panic about snakes and Indians in Dakota. As soon as the ship arrived, these speculators persuaded them to go to Paterson or Orange City or Holland, and the group disbanded.[73] Kuipers returned to the Netherlands in 1883, 1887, and 1888, and found new families for the Dakota settlements Friesland, Nieveen, and Old Platte, where 310 Dutchmen lived in 1890.

Private plans in the Netherlands to offer poor families a chance to go to America did not succeed. While enough families were interested, the actual number of emigrants who came over under this arrangement was small. Investors who wanted to promote emigration to Minnesota established a national society for the support of poor people who wanted to emigrate. This example was imitated at the local level. In the small village of Ellewoutsdijk in Zeeland, interested people founded a local Emigration Society, in which the members paid twenty-five cents initially, followed by a ten-cent contribution every week. With these funds a person would be selected by lot every year to emigrate to Minnesota. However, because of the economic crisis in 1873, the initiative failed.[74] Even though few aspiring emigrants were helped by this method, the specialized emigrant newspapers, lotteries, and reports (all of which complemented private correspondence) collectively stimulated the desire to emigrate.[75]

In America, people also beat the drums loudly to sell land. In economically difficult times, such as the 1890s, farmers who had reached the end of their credit and laborers who wanted to leave the

---

[73]  Van der Pol, *Reservation*, 295-96.

[74]  *De Landverhuizer. Maandblad ter bevordering der emigratie naar de Noord-Amerikaansche staat Minnesota* (July 1873). In April 1874 the first (and probably last) emigrant, Jacob van den Berge, was sent to Minnesota.

[75]  Contacts between potential emigrants and Dutch businesses were maintained through magazines, such as *De Landverhuizer* and *De Wereldburger*. This weekly weighed the chance of success of emigrating to and investing in North and South America, South Africa, and the Dutch East Indies. See the autobiography of Van Pernis about the evaluation of these destinations.

cities constituted a grateful public for the sellers of new settlements in the west and north of the United States. In 1891 and subsequent years the interest was so high that many colonists could no longer meet their obligations to banks and government and left their farms. High expectations about other locations prompted the colonists to hurry. If the deals did not turn out right, they traveled just as fast to the next place. That pattern explains the rapid development of South Dakota. In 1880 one could not find a single Dutch person in this state; five years later there were 5,000, but by 1890 there were only 1,428 left.[76] Those who persevered bought the empty houses and converted them to one house. The quitters hurried to look for alternatives. There was heavy traffic all over the western states.

Each state had its promoters. In Montana the Dutchman Andreas Wormser was active. At age twenty-four he had emigrated to America with his sister Maria. He took ministerial training at Western Theological Seminary in Holland and served as a pastor in Iowa, Ohio, Wisconsin, and Michigan, after which he joined the Presbyterian Church and was active in church organizational work in Montana. In 1891 he took on an additional career and became land agent in the Gallatin Valley in Montana, which he hoped to develop through irrigation for a New York company. For this project he brought well-to-do Dutch immigrants from the northeastern part of the province of Groningen. When they complained about the lack of water, Wormser got them to work with a sermon on 2 Kings 3:16—"Thus says the Lord, 'Make this valley full of ditches.'" Eventually this colony turned out to be viable.[77]

The most driven land merchant was the Dutchman Theodore F. Koch, who could claim wide international business experience in Europe, and who did not just find financiers, but also immigrants whom he took to Minnesota. He asked ministers to win over their members. He especially found the Reverend Cornelius Bode ready to cooperate to find new colonists. Koch's interest was clear—he used ministers and

---

[76]   Van der Pol, *Reservation*, 43-45.

[77]   Delbert Delos Van Den Berg, "'Buildings Castles in the Air:' Andreas Wormser, Immigrant Locator and Land Developer," (M.A. thesis, Montana State Univ., 1996), 55. One of the immigrants who came to America because of Wormser was Ulbe Eringa; see Brian W. Beltman, *Dutch Farmer in the Missouri Valley: the Life and Letters of Ulbe Eringa, 1866-1950* (Urbana: Univ. of Illinois Press, 1996), 42 and 49. Rob Kroes describes the community in *The Persistence of Ethnicity: Dutch Calvinist Pioneers in Amsterdam, Montana* (Urbana: Univ. of Illinois Press, 1992).

church magazines to gain the trust of potential clients. Bode's interest was the expansion of the church. He was a church planter in the West for the Christian Reformed Church, and he himself had bought land in this undertaking. Both men were interested in a church in the colony. In the two decades between 1870 and 1890, these areas in Minnesota had been stripped of their white pine trees (some trees twenty-five meters tall). According to the assumption of that time, the presence of such tall trees indicated extremely fertile soil, suitable for cattle grazing and growing corn, wheat, rye, and potatoes.[78]

**The Chances in the West**

Even if the new colonies in the West survived the initial years, success was not guaranteed. Some people made it, others just plodded but never became prosperous. Stagnation in the arrival of new immigrants endangered the continuity of church and school, reduced the choice of marriage candidates, and forced the youth to earn money elsewhere. The task therefore was to retain the growth tempo. The settlements continued to be vulnerable because of the harsh climate and severe winters, which persuaded many families to travel farther to the much milder California. Failures were not always caused by the quality of the soil or the climate, but also by the reputation of the settlement. Only through enthusiastic tales could the prophecies of the developers become self-fulfilling. Negative reports undermined the trust. Prinsburg in Minnesota succeeded because it could quickly provide resources, and it attracted immigrants from all areas, but not so the small neighboring village of Friesland.[79] Andries Wormser also saw his dream of "Wormser City" in the north of Montana go up in smoke because of lack of financial support and a disappointing climate.

How great was the chance of success in the West forty years after the first colonies were established? On the one hand, the colonists profited from the experience of the pioneers; on the other hand, the circumstances were more difficult because the best lands were already taken, and financing became more risky. Usually a village got started because there were several farms that wanted a post office and a church,

---

[78]  Robert Schoone-Jongen, "A Time to Gather, a Time to Scatter: Dutch American Settlement in Minnesota, 1885-1920" (Ph.D. diss., Univ. of Delaware, 2007).

[79]  Robert Schoone-Jongen, "Friesland, Minnesota: A Little Town That Couldn't," *Origins* 15 (1997): 39-45. The folder *Beschrijvingen en inlichtingen over de nieuwe Hollandsche Kolonie Prinsburg in Renville, Kaniyohi, en Chippewas Counties, Minnesota,* 18-24, mentions 120 Dutch-American buyers.

Removal of the Christian Reformed Church building of Platte,
South Dakota, at that time called Overijsel, ca 1900.
Archives, Calvin College, Grand Rapids, Michigan.

and that needed a store and a blacksmith. Visionary men contacted a railroad company, which would be eager if the plan was feasible and if they could grab a piece of land as an investment. If the companies began with railway construction, they would see to it that they would build a station with a village every five to eight miles, because a farmer's loaded wagon could travel that distance back and forth in one day. A correspondent of a newspaper in the area provided news and glowing reports about the expected future growth. The organization of a celebration for the Fourth of July would put the town in the limelight. A school enhanced the attraction for young families.

The blessing of a railroad connection became a liability if the national market failed and the railroad companies charged a high price for transportation. In the Far West there usually were no settlements in place, and the companies created their own villages. If they did go through an existing settlement, they demanded free passage or an investment. The laying of a new railroad could disturb the future perspectives of a village. Harrison, South Dakota, lost much business when in 1905 a new railroad connected to the new town of Corsica. The same happened to the village of Old Platte, which put its stores and workshops on rollers and moved them a few miles to the new train station. In North Dakota virtually no new villages were established outside the railroad places.[80] If there was no competition from others, the railroad company made sure to limit the number of villages. The railroad directors did want to build grain silos, because these promoted activity and made the villages more attractive for business. Initially these villages could attract some work opportunities and stores, but the market soon became saturated. The recipe for a viable establishment went as follows: "Three to five lumber yards, one or two banks, two or three general stores and farm machinery dealers, plus as many more individual trades people as could be attracted—usually a single drugstore, hotel, newspaper, butcher, restaurant, and livery stable."[81]

Success stories about the West stimulated investment companies that smelled a chance for a quick profit; the welfare of the colonists was secondary to that aim. An infamous case occurred in Rilland, Colorado. In 1892 the Nederlandsch-Amerikaansche Land- en Emigratie-Maatschappij recruited a group of two hundred people to settle in Colorado.[82] Two clever businessmen, Cornelis van der Hoogt and Albertus Zoutman, had founded this company and were able to persuade the socially sensitive and politically active Maarten Noordtzij (professor at the Christian Reformed Seminary in Kampen) to assume the presidency of the company. When the immigrants arrived in Colorado toward the end of 1892, they did not find a colony, but only two barracks. The company hardly was able to make the payments needed to obtain the ownership of the land. Noordtzij traveled to America to investigate the business, but he could not offer a solution. The company was dissolved and the immigrants were dispersed all over. Within a year the whole enterprise gave up the ghost.

Not all failures were the result of fraud; some plans just expected too much from future developments. In the same state of Colorado, about 150 kilometers northeast of Denver, a small village, called Kuner, was planned as a supply area for raw materials for the cannery of Max Kuner of Denver. The intent was grandiose: churches received land, and the plans anticipated an irrigation lake, a train station, a factory for the canning of sauerkraut and pickles, and a sugar refinery. Dutch

---

[80] Van der Pol, *Reservation*, 314. John C. Hudson, *Plains Country Towns* (Minneapolis: Univ. of Minnesota Press, 1985), 47-62.

[81] Ibid., 100-101.

[82] Peter De Klerk, "The Ecclesiastical Struggles of the Rilland and Crook Christian Reformed Churches in Colorado in 1893" in Peter De Klerk and Richard De Ridder, eds., *Perpectives on the Christian Reformed Church: Studies in Its History, Theology, and Ecumenicity* (Grand Rapids: Baker, 1983),73-98.

immigrants came from all parts of America and found each other in the Christian Reformed Church. Here also, the future had been imagined through rose-tinted glasses, because it soon became apparent that the ownership of the land was not secure. To make matters worse, the water reservoirs dried up and the promised factories were never built. The Dutch did not know how to irrigate their dry land and started to leave after 1912. After less than ten years the majority had left the Kuner settlement to go to Denver, Colorado; Lynden, Washington; Luctor, Kansas; Amsterdam, Montana; Redlands, California, or even all the way back to the Netherlands. The congregation had only two families left, and in 1918 the church was discontinued and the building sold.

Around 1900, California offered a way out for Dutch who wanted to try their luck somewhere else. This state became an assembly point for colonists who had already made many in-between stops. In the early years of the 1890s several dozen prosperous city people had been tempted by unscrupulous compatriots to buy land in Merced County and Fresno County in the San Joaquin Valley. They had been promised that they could soon earn hundreds of dollars per acre by becoming fruit growers, which would require relatively little work. Imitating earlier successful colonizations, both of these projects started quickly—but they failed just as quickly for lack of proper preparation by the investors, the unexpected hard subsoil, and the easy-going attitude of the colonists.

A third colony, called Queen Wilhelmina, populated by people regretting their decisions about earlier failed colonies, did not prosper either, even though the preparations were more realistic. Other immigrants already had adventures in their past in Chili, South Africa, or the Dutch East Indies.[83] A significant number of the new immigrants from the Netherlands came from the Haarlemmermeerpolder, a reclaimed area southwest of Amsterdam. This had been a "colonization" area in the Netherlands since 1852, with the nickname "Little America," which suggests some similarity to circumstances in the United States. However, since only 14 percent of the farmers owned their land, and because of high farm rentals, difficult circumstances, illness, poverty, and housing shortages, many moved away from there.[84]

---

[83]   David E. Zwart, "Formed by Faith: The Dutch Immigrant Community in Kings County, California: 1890-1940" (M.A. thesis, California State Univ., 2004), 16-22.

[84]   H.N. ter Veen, *De Haarlemmermeer als kolonisatiegebied* (Groningen: Noordhoff, 1925), 30 and 46.

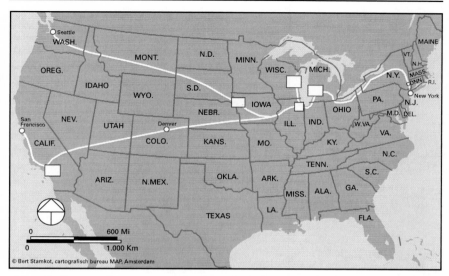

Map 9: Connections among the Dutch settlements in the United States.

## A Dutch Immigration Chain

The splitting up of the Protestant emigrants into settlements in Iowa and Michigan might have been a disappointment to those directly involved, but for future immigrants some good came out of it. Chances were real that the two powerful personalities of Scholte and Van Raalte would eventually have become opponents. As it was, distance avoided such a conflict, and two centers developed in Michigan and Iowa— centers with their own characters that attracted different categories of people and later offered two complementary patterns of spreading out. The difference in the role played by the two first settlements becomes clear by seeing Holland, Michigan, as the center of a circle and Pella, Iowa, as the starting point of a line. Holland was the middle of a circle formed by about ten satellite villages. Grand Rapids also was within the circle, and after 1880 it became a new center of the Dutch in West Michigan. Pella was the starting point of a line that traveled farther west, within the state of Iowa until 1870, and then farther, to North and South Dakota. That line was connected to smaller circles of Dutch immigrants farther to the west. The settlements in Wisconsin showed a mixed pattern, which was directed to the colonies in Michigan as well as to the settlements in and around Chicago and farther west. Even the failed settlements could form a temporary link in the chain that bound the Dutch closer to each other.

The dynamics of the founding and the spreading out of the Dutch settlements in America offered immigrants an ever increasing number of settlement opportunities. No doubt those who came early had the advantage that they could buy the best land and gain the most profits, but the price of hard work and heavy sacrifices, sometimes of their own lives, was correspondingly difficult. In addition to the planned villages, concentrations of the Dutch within cities also occurred rapidly. Thanks to this spreading out, new waves of immigrants could find a place within the boundaries of the network, or remain there temporarily, until they could go their own way. Most important were those communities that developed so much strength that they could offer support to their own members but also offer a contribution to the total network.

# CHAPTER 4

# Cement of the Churches

National religious organizations functioned on two levels in keeping immigrants together: first, they helped strengthen local communities and linked them to broader networks; and, second, these organizations were the focal points of reflection for immigrants needing to cope with a new environment. European religious trends that emphasized personal piety could more easily find a connection with similar individualistic traditions in America than religious groups that circled around the centrality of doctrines. The difference between these two directions was played out in a sequence of time that also applied to the Dutch immigrants—the early pietist Seceder immigrants were much more open to American influences than the later ones.[1]

The American system of separation of church and state created room for all immigrants to establish their own churches and religious associations. This freedom of choice had important consequences for the tempo of the process of integration of the newcomers. As

---

[1]  John Gjerde, *The Minds of the West: Ethnocultural Evolution in the Rural Midwest, 1830-1917* (Chapel Hill: Univ. of North Carolina Press, 1997).

an organization, the church offered the immigrant more than only spiritual support. It also offered social, material, and educational assistance. The immigrants could turn in three possible directions. Some used the church as a means to maintain their own group. Others saw the church as a mediating agency between family life and the outside world. A third category sought to find quick entry into the dominant culture via American denominations. All immigrants had to choose, because circumstances in America were different from those in their own countries—the laws were different, there were fewer religious holidays, greater pluralism, and more competition in the religious arena. Even those who wanted to maintain their old faith community as much as possible had to devise new structures, raise funds, and react to other traditions.[2]

## The Church in New Netherland

When the Dutch West India Company (WIC) founded a fortress and soon a town on the island of Manhattan in 1624, it was the beginning of an authentic piece of the Netherlands on the American continent. In a period of forty years the colonists built a community that in its main features corresponded to those in the Republic of the Seven United Netherlands.[3] Government, justice, social relations, and the church in New Netherland were continuations of the institutions and agreements in the motherland, even though a large number of people who came from elsewhere in Europe also lived in the colony. The Indian tribes, whose territories the WIC had bought, and the English colony that was more densely populated and more expansive, put pressure on New Amsterdam and prevented an exact copy of Old World society. New Netherland itself swallowed up the Danish and Swedish settlements, until its population in turn decided in 1664 not to offer resistance to the dominance of the English fleet that was sent out in the Second English War to wage war in the New World. Until that time, the continuation of existing customs had been self-evident—

---

[2]    Randall M. Miller and Thomas D. Marzik, *Immigration and Religion in Urban America* (Philadelphia: Temple Univ. Press, 1977); Timothy L. Smith, "Religion and Ethnicity in America," *American Historical Review* 84 (1978): 1155-85; John Bodnar, *The Transplanted: A History of Immigrants in Urban America* (Bloomington: Indiana Univ. Press, 1985), 144-68; Harry S. Stout, "Ethnicity: The Vital Center of Religion in America," *Ethnicity* 2 (1975): 204-44.

[3]    Jaap Jacobs, *New Netherland: A Dutch Colony in Seventeenth-Century America* (Leiden: Brill, 2005).

New Netherland was a product of the WIC. Its directors in the republic counted on short-term profits but were divided among themselves about whether conducting business or founding a settlement gave the best financial guarantee. For that reason, very little was invested in adjustment to the future. The transfer of power to the English left many civic institutions in place.

In the course of the eighteenth century, Dutch culture blended with English culture, even though the Reformed Protestant Dutch Church, established in 1628, remained under the authority of the Amsterdam Classis until 1772.[4] The Dutch language lost ground, architecture adapted itself, and the American War of Independence encouraged a new American consciousness. In 1770 the "Dutch Church" was one of thirteen denominations in New York City. Even though the city offered more religious freedom than many European cities, the tolerance was not unlimited. Anglicans received preferential treatment, Jews were tolerated, but Roman Catholics received little space, and groups that denied the central articles of the Christian faith were opposed. In the nineteenth century the margins became wider, but this broadening had to be contested.[5]

Within the "Dutch Church" this adjustment took place gradually, from generation to generation, first in New York, later in the countryside, but the church did not completely erase the traces of the New Netherland period. Until 1794 the minutes of the synod were written in Dutch, and in 1834 the minister in Tappan, New York, still preached in Dutch. In 1844 the majority of the Reformed Church members did not want to abolish the word "Dutch" in the denomination's name, but opposition to the term increased. The opponents saw the term as an obstacle for members who had no association with the Netherlands. After the Civil War had fueled American national consciousness, the label "Dutch" was dropped. Around this time, American liturgical customs such as choirs, funeral orations, and Christmas celebrations had entered into the life of the church, which from then on was called the Reformed Church in

---

[4]    A "classis" is an organization of a number of local Protestant congregations in a region that is autonomous. Dirk Mouw, "Recruiting Ministers: Amsterdam, New York, and the Dutch in British North America, 1700-1772," in George Harinck and Hans Krabbendam, eds., *Amsterdam-New York: Transatlantic Relations and Urban Identities Since 1653* (Amsterdam: VU Uitgeverij, 2005), 87-98.

[5]    Joyce Goodfriend, "The Limits of Religious Pluralism in Eighteenth-century New York City," in Harinck and Krabbendam, *Amsterdam-New York,* 67-86.

America (RCA).[6] The denomination that became independent in 1772 wanted to continue the framework of the church order of the Synod of Dordt but adjusted to American circumstances; this adjustment included an appreciation (although hesitant) for organized revivals and the acknowledgment of individual, free conscience, whereby heterogeneity within the denomination increased. This room for variety was attractive to the first wave of Seceder immigrants, who lacked this quality in the Netherlands. In the long run, this combination increased internal tensions already at work in the Reformed Church.[7]

**Tensions**

The nineteenth-century Dutch immigrants, who had left the motherland with the ideal of a new community, became involved in another culture, with its own legal, political, and educational institutions and its own religious relationships. They could, and had to, choose what they wanted to keep of their old baggage, and what they wanted to give up or adapt. Not everyone had the same priorities. This internal tension could become stronger by outside pressure, by reactions from other groups of immigrants, or by the local culture. The immigrants, with their respect for hierarchy and authority, suddenly found themselves in a republican environment where freedom, equality, and individualism were encouraged. In Protestant and Republican America the emphasis was on individual rights, democracy, and economic progress. These priorities influenced relationships

---

[6]    See, for example, Joyce Goodfriend, *Before the Melting Pot: Society and Culture in New York City, 1664-1730* (Princeton: Princeton Univ. Press, 1991); Donna Merwick, *Possessing Albany, 1630-1710: The Dutch and English Experience* (Cambridge: Harvard Univ. Press, 1990); and Firth H. Fabend, *A Dutch Family in the Middle Colonies, 1660-1800* (New Brunswick: Rutgers Univ. Press, 1991), and *Zion on the Hudson: Dutch New York and New Jersey in the Age of Revivals* (New Brunswick: Rutgers Univ. Press, 2000); Gerald F. De Jong, *The Dutch Reformed Church in the American Colonies* (Grand Rapids: Eerdmans, 1978).

[7]    Al Janssen, "A Perfect Agreement? The Theological Context of the Reformed Protestant Dutch Church in the First Half of the Nineteenth Century," in Harinck and Krabbendam, *Breaches and Bridges*, 49-60; Dennis N. Voskuil, "Strangers in their Own Land: Calvinists in an Arminian Culture," in Gerard Dekker, Donald A. Luidens, and Rodger R. Rice, eds., *Rethinking Secularization: Reformed Reactions to Modernity* (Lanham: Univ. Press of America, 1997), 93-110. Scholte, Brummelkamp, and Van Raalte did not belong to the group within the Secession that considered the church order of Dordt to be unchangeable.

within families, in society, and with the government.[8] Some European immigrants welcomed these changes, while others emphasized the solidarity of the family and isolated themselves.

Nearly all ethnic groups encountered internal struggles between fast and slow "assimilators," so that they had to assess their own uniqueness continually. Inevitably, the authority structures in their community shifted.[9] Conflicts arose when a specific development demanded a response, such as the struggle for women's voting rights and for labor unions, or new laws that affected one's personal life, such as Prohibition or Sunday rest. Parents noticed that education encouraged love for the new fatherland that could be at odds with loyalty to their faith tradition. Proponents of the American "public school" welcomed the influence of American culture. Opponents wanted to resist this influence but used the same American methods for that purpose, such as mobilizing volunteers through national conventions with uplifting lectures and their own bureaucratic organizations. The more strongly their own worldview was developed, the more clearly did the differences between Old and New World come to light, not only when immigrants rejected American phenomena, but also when they embraced a new situation.

Of the three strategies (quick integration, gradual adaptation, or keeping separate as much as possible) Scholte followed the first option, most other Dutch immigrant leaders of his generation the second, and the third strategy presented itself to the small group that split off from the Dutch Reformed Church in 1857. After a painful initial period during its first twenty years, this group created the basis for a second Protestant subculture, which was closely related to, but at the same time different from, the Reformed Church.[10]

In 1850 the local immigrant congregations in West Michigan had united into a classis according to the Calvinist tradition. This classis

---

[8]   Mark A. Noll, *America's God: From Jonathan Edwards to Abraham Lincoln* (New York: Oxford Univ. Press, 2002).

[9]   Gjerde, *Minds*, 107. For a description of the relationship between religious beliefs and agricultural practices, see Robert P. Swierenga, "The Little White Church: Religion in Rural America," *Agricultural History* 71 (1997): 415-41.

[10]   Al Janssen, "A Perfect Agreement?"; Robert P. Swierenga, "True Brothers: The Netherlandic Origins of the Christian Reformed Church in North America, 1857-1880"; Melis te Velde, "The Dutch Background of the American Secession from the RCA in 1857," all three chapters in Harinck and Krabbendam, *Breaches and Bridges*, resp. 49-60, 61-84, 85-100.

devised solutions for common problems but also shielded freedom of conscience against new man-made rules.[11] This form of organization offered important advantages. The structure took care of regularity, cooperation, and mutual control. At some point the immigrants had to decide whether they would join an existing denomination or form one of their own. The group was too small for the second option, and it therefore joined the Reformed Protestant Dutch Church (RCA) in 1850. Even though the procedure for this decision was not flawless, since not all the members were consulted, it was a reasonable step. This decision was based on agreement of doctrine, the expectation of democratic control, and especially appreciation of the warm welcome with which this denomination had received them. These feelings of sympathy were mutual. The contact persons in the Reformed Church did not see the Seceders as a nuisance, but as heroes. They observed developments in the Netherlands through American eyes and helped the Secession leaders gain a positive reputation. The *Christian Intelligencer* (the church weekly of the Dutch Reformed) knew from Scottish sources that the Reformed Church (*Hervormde Kerk*) in the Netherlands had slipped theologically and practiced a repressive rule. These reports confirmed the negative image the Americans had about unruly and undemocratic Europe. The immigrants received generous financial, organizational, and moral support for their plans. The first generation felt in minute detail the difference with the condescending treatment of the Reformed Church in the Netherlands. The Reformed Church in America actually had great respect for the orthodoxy of the immigrants.[12] Supported by the financially strong churches of the East Coast, Albertus Van Raalte founded an English-language school for secondary education, which he expanded into the Holland Academy, called Hope College since 1866. Without giving up the authority of the local church and the traditional Reformed Church structure, he did strive for a gradual adaptation to the American setting. This trajectory can be seen in his stimulating the use of English, his prompt application for American citizenship, and permitting revival meetings to be organized.[13]

[11]    *Classis Holland, Minutes 1848-1858* (Grand Rapids: Eerdmans, 1950), 21-23 and 54.

[12]    Ibid., 52-53.

[13]    For a clear overview of Van Raalte's expectations for the church, see J. Vree, "The Dominating Theology within the *Nederlandse Hervormde Kerk* after 1815 in its Relation to the Secession of 1834," in Harinck and Krabbendam, *Breaches and Bridges*, 32-47. For the felt need for stability among the immigrant churches as a reason for joining the RCA, see Christian Vander Veen, "The Immigrant Churches," in E.T. Corwin, *A Manual of the Reformed*

The consequence for the RCA was that the denomination acquired a western branch, where the Dutch character remained in force. In 1840 nearly all RCA members lived in the East, but by1880 the West accounted for at least 13 percent, and by 1920 this had grown to 28 percent. When Dutch immigrants settled in New Jersey, they also strengthened the Dutch character there.[14]

In addition to the tension that developed between the two regions, the communities also imported tensions from the Netherlands. The struggle that a group of the Seceder immigrants in the Netherlands had waged to keep their new denomination pure in doctrine was continued in America. The discussion concerned the boundaries of their community. Could only members of their own church participate in the Lord's Supper? Should they hold on to observing the day after Christmas, Easter, and Pentecost as religious holidays, as was the custom in the Netherlands? Could one honestly be a member of a denomination such as the RCA, which allowed members to be Freemasons? Did the singing of hymns not run the risk of being drawn along into unbiblical ideas? Just as in the Netherlands, pronounced viewpoints caused a rift in the community, in spite of the close village and family relationships.

The church split of 1857 was, as such, not a unique event. Dissatisfaction about ministers or about domineering people in local churches occasionally led to separate congregations, which sometimes continued independently or joined a Presbyterian denomination. What was unique in 1857 was that the local conflicts led to the formation of an alternative denomination. That year, four groups from Graafschap, Grand Rapids, Noordeloos, and Polkton withdrew from the Reformed Church and formed the True Dutch Reformed Church, later called the Christian Reformed Church (CRC). These congregations wanted to remain close to the traditions of the Dutch mother church, because they had no confidence in the (in their eyes) lax attitude of the central leadership of the Reformed Church, which allowed judgment about divergent behavior, such as membership in a Freemason lodge, to lie in the local church. Although most of the "True brethren" equated the American church split with the Dutch Secession of 1834, there also was an American component at work—the freedom to remain true

---

*Churches in America, 1628-1878* (New York: Board of Publication of the RCA, 1879), 74-82, esp. 81.

[14]   Donald A. Luidens and Roger J. Nemeth, "Dutch Immigration and Membership Growth in the Reformed Church in America: 1830-1920," in Krabbendam and Wagenaar, *Dutch-American Experience*, 169-88.

to oneself. They quoted a clause used in 1849 by the Reverend Isaac Wyckoff of Albany when the immigrant churches were contemplating whether to join the RCA, that is, they would be perfectly free to leave that church whenever they wished.[15] A CRC Seceder brother published a poem in the *Stoompost* justifying the church split:

> We no longer offer our hand
> To Dutch Misformed and Remonstrant
> Or Anabaptist or other lords
> Who do not teach pure truth.[16]

It is noteworthy that only one-third of the Dutch Seceders joined the split of 1857, while two-thirds remained in the RCA—a similar proportion of those who came from the *Hervormde Kerk*. Again, one-third of them joined "1857." Thus, in both denominations there were more members from the *Hervormde Kerk*.[17]

Initially the "True Brothers" sought to join other believers, such as orthodox Presbyterians, who admittedly offered room for the Dutch language and the church order of Dordt but did not take on that heritage themselves, and thus offered very little guarantee for the future. They also sought support from the Secession churches in the Netherlands. Thanks to the prestige of Van Raalte and Van der Meulen, most of the Seceders kept their trust in the RCA. However, when these two leaders died in 1876 and the "True Brothers" got their organization in order, thanks to their own ministerial training and the church magazine *De Wachter*, this trust and support caved in.[18] The articles in *De Wachter* certainly did not persuade everyone in the Netherlands that

---

[15] Elton J. Bruins and Robert P. Swierenga, *Family Quarrels in the Dutch Reformed Churches of the Nineteenth Century* (Grand Rapids, Eerdmans, 1999), 47-103.

[16] Cecelia Verhage, comp., "Grandfather Remembers These" (Manuscript Keppel Moerdyke Collection, 1989), 18. Zeeland Historical Society, Zeeland, Mich.

[17] Swierenga, "True Brothers," 72-79. Te Velde, "Dutch Background," 93. After the CRC had come into existence, it attracted more Seceders than *Hervormde* members. Until 1880 three-fourths of those who were Seceders in the Netherlands joined the CRC, but in 1880 60 percent of the total membership of the CRC were from *Hervormde* background. Considering that the growth of the Secession churches in the Netherlands consisted nearly completely of former *Hervormden*, it is not surprising that the same was true in America.

[18] Richard H. Harms, "Forging a Religious Identity: The Christian Reformed Church in the Nineteenth-Century Immigrant Community," in Krabbendam and Wagenaar, *Dutch-American Experience*, 189-206.

the church split had been right, but they did impair the reputation of the RCA. Dutch ministers were informed through personal contacts about the advantages of emigration to America for themselves and for their children and later dared to join the CRC, thereby giving support to the small denomination and increasing its prestige. Thus, the CRC became an alternative community for the new waves of immigrants who sought church continuity and felt at ease in a homogeneous Dutch community. The RCA leaders invested insufficient personal contact with the Seceded churches in the Netherlands and faced the impossible task of persuading the immigrants who wanted continuity with the Netherlands that their church was not American.[19]

## From Idealism to Realism

Thus, new immigrants had to choose between two denominations, both of which offered a Dutch-American identity. After 1880 the center of gravity of the flood of new immigrants shifted from the Reformed Church to the Christian Reformed Church. The new wave of Dutch immigrants who streamed into America between 1880 and 1893 had explicit expectations about church life. Many of them were not content with a church in which they could be Reformed without hindrance (such as the RCA); they wanted guarantees of purity of doctrine for the future. The generation of 1840 saw the eastern wing of the RCA as an ally, whereas the following group began to see the more liberal segment more and more as a potential threat. The new immigrants from the Dutch Secessionist churches had experienced a development toward

---

[19]    See e.g. the judgment of R.T. Kuiper, who immigrated to Graafschap, Michigan, in 1879, in Hans Krabbendam, "Een betrouwbare stem uit Amerika. Dominee R.T. Kuiper uit Wildervank," *Veenkoloniale Volksalmanak* 9 (1997): 33-35. For a description of the founding of local CRC congregations from an RCA perspective, see B. de Beij and A. Zwemer, *Stemmen uit de Hollandsch-Gereformeerde Kerk in de Vereenigde Staten van Amerika* (Groningen: G.J. Reits, 1871). The only two *Hervormde* ministers who immigrated found themselves on the extreme wings of the church: F.W.N. Hugenholz moved from Zierikzee to Grand Rapids to give leadership to the only liberal church for Dutch immigrants. J.M. Rutte had received part of his theological education at the RCA seminary in New Brunswick, New Jersey, and served the Sixth Reformed Church in Paterson for six years. He returned to the Netherlands in 1874 and served congregations in Arnemuiden, Maartensdijk, Bunschoten, Oene, Genemuiden, and Huizen. In 1887 he moved again to Passaic, New Jersey, but after a year returned once more to the Netherlands. Thanks to the database of Dutch ministers set up by Fred van Lieburg at the Vrije Universiteit Amsterdam.

a homogeneous denomination, according to the position of pioneer Hendrik de Cock, who gave much more importance to the church order of Dordt than did Scholte and Van Raalte. The emigrants of the first group of early Seceders had weakened the antisynodical element. Many later Seceders clung to a more exclusive church concept, which made it more difficult to integrate into America. In addition, the church climate in the Netherlands became increasingly polarized in the 1880s, leading up to the Doleantie, the second split from the *Hervormde Kerk*.[20] It was easy to associate the CRC with a dissenting church that reminded one of the church relations in the Netherlands, although relations in America were different.[21]

For most of the immigrants, however, theological questions did not determine their choice of a church, but rather practical issues did, such as the use of the Dutch language or contacts with acquaintances. The CRC wanted to be and remain a Dutch immigrant church. Its synodical meetings in 1884 and 1888 tried to form one denomination with the immigrant churches of the RCA in the West, but the latter did not want to give up their bond with the RCA in the East.[22] Discussions with English-language orthodox Presbyterians failed partly because of the language question, partly because of the absence of guarantees about the purity of that church.

Until 1890 the CRC was hardly involved in American events, focused as it was on the survival of the church. Between 1890 and 1918 the church developed from a Dutch, via a Dutch-American, to an American community. An ongoing debate about Reformed principles and their relationship to modern culture divided the community internally but also kept the church together through the communal questions and the theological orientation toward the Netherlands. After some time many people got tired of the discussion; they doubted the usefulness and the implementation of Reformed principles for

---

[20]   The Doleantie was a church split in 1886 that was led by Abraham Kuyper, who stood up against the rigid church organization of the *Hervormde Kerk*. In 1892 this group of "lamentators" fused with the Seceders to become the Gereformeerde Kerken in Nederland. In 2004 both denominations and the Lutheran Church merged into the Protestant Church in the Netherlands.

[21]   Herbert J. Brinks, "Henry Beets (1869-1947) Historian of the Christian Reformed Church," and George Harinck, "The Secession of 1834 as Frame of Reference: H. Bouwman and the Historiography of the Reformed Churches in the Nineteenth Century," resp. 125-40 and 141-53, in Harinck and Krabbendam, *Breaches and Bridges*.

[22]   John H. Bratt, "Ecumenicity in the American Setting. The Christian Reformed Church and the North American Presbyterian and Reformed Council," in De Klerk and De Ridder, *Perspectives*, 261.

social problems. Practical issues such as education and benevolence received priority and led to the establishment of their own institutions that fit into the American system.[23]

Whoever was a member of a faith community could count on generous help. Boudewijn Nieuwenhuisse of Franklin, in Wisconsin, experienced this when he did not feel well for a time. He told his family in the Netherlands, "My stomach hangs like a stone in my body," and it prevented him from working. His fellow believers did not leave him in the lurch. He assured his relatives: "Being convinced of our weak and pressing situation, our small congregation of Hollanders have together decided to carry out all essential work, such as mowing, harvesting the grain, etc., and to bear the cost of that as a community, so that I stand in awe of the Lord's goodness and forbearing, who still moves hearts to kindness."[24]

Without this extra bond of faith it was difficult to carry out a joint undertaking. This was experienced by Marien Frederiks, who, with several other Dutch fellow travelers, including his half-brother with a partner and child, went to the state of New York but was not able to get started as a baker. The plan to develop a section of land in the woods outside Utica (between Albany and Syracuse) and to build a log cabin with five other Dutch families failed because the neighbors charged each other a dollar per day for mutual help. Forced by need and disillusionment he left for Utica, where his daughter Geertje joined him a year later. From there they went to Louisville, where there were no other Dutch. They became members of a Wesleyan church, still ate some Dutch fare, because they did not like the strange American food, but spoke only English and maintained contact with the Old World only via letters.[25] A third brother, Hubertus, received support from an "an old Dutch family" in Utica, who donated clothes to his children and gave him an opportunity to develop a stable family life.[26]

[23] Henry Zwaanstra, *Reformed Thought and Experience in a New World: A Study of the Christian Reformed Church and Its American Environment, 1890-1918* (Kampen: Kok, 1973), 295-322. This Americanization process was temporarily strengthened by the pressure of patriotism during the First World War. After that time the church chose a moderate course.

[24] Bouwdewijn Nieuwenhuise to family in Kloetinge, August 26, 1853, ILC HH.

[25] Marinus Frederiks to Johan Samuel Frederiks in Middelburg, December 14, 1847; Reinier van Oosterhout to Johan Samuel Frederiks, December 21, 1858, and Geertje Oosterhout to same, August 14, 1852, and undated [1858], ILC HH.

[26] Huibertus Frederiks to Johan Samuel Frederiks in Middelburg, October 15, 1851, ILC HH.

Immigrants without an articulated world view thus entered the melting pot more readily than immigrants who were very conscious of their identity. During the nineteenth century, a segment of the Dutch Reformed population became more and more conscious of its position and refined its world view. This neo-Calvinistic group chose separation from the American culture in favor of a closely knit community that offered protection. The first emigration wave of the 1840s and 1850s was less reserved toward the Yankee culture than those of the 1880s and 1890s. These first groups were less dogmatic and had more room to maneuver in America. In the pioneer phase the government left many basic provisions up to the local citizens. For the first generation of pioneers this was something completely new, to which they responded positively. They could establish their own civic and church organizations, and in times of need they could mobilize their own support. No wonder that the first pioneers had a positive opinion about the United States, in contrast to many later immigrants who especially saw what was lacking in America. In the meantime their political rights in the Netherlands had improved. As the century came to a close, the growing influence of "Washington," the market revolution, and urban expansion increased the exchange between the Dutch settlements and their surroundings.[27]

A key example of the optimistic first generation was Hendrik Scholte, the eloquent singer of America's praise. In 1848 he asserted, full of expectation, from Pella, "Here we have no excuse about compulsion or hindrance from outside; we have unlimited freedom for exerting all attempts and means, given by God, for the development, revelation, and spreading of the kingdom of God.[28] However, someone like Jacobus Verbrugge from Chandler, Minnesota, who had participated fully in the orthodox church life in the Netherlands, kept missing depth of faith in America. In 1913 he noted:

> One cannot deny that there is a shadow side to life here....Even though America is religious, there is little depth in the fear of God; in that regard we have not yet found what we left in Holland. Yes, one meets good, dear Christians, but never try, for example, to awaken them from their nap about church life; [they think that] you're just a fighter, just arrived from Holland, or whatever, and I don't want to deny at all that in the long run this

27   Robert P. Swierenga, "The Dutch Urban Experience," in Swierenga, Sinnema, and Krabbendam, *The Dutch in Urban America*, 1-12.
28   H.P. Scholte, *Eene Stem uit Pella* (Amsterdam: Hoogkamer, 1848), 37.

has had a paralyzing influence on me, and I have learned pretty well to be quiet even if everything in me fights against it. Depth, devout depth in one's life—*ach*, one looks for it in vain. In short, the rushing current of American life is detrimental for me.[29]

## From Reaction to Initiative

The main reason for Seceder ministers to accompany their departing compatriots in 1846-47 was to prevent their dispersion, which could easily lead to the loss of their faith. Even though the first attempt was directed at the gathering of fellow Christians into a stable colony, still the immigrants soon fanned out according to the pattern sketched in the previous chapter. Traveling farther was the solution to lack of farm land. The possibility of moving west or to the cities meant an escape from economic setbacks or social conflicts. This mobility might have weakened specific localities, but the total network became stronger.[30] Because of this mobility, the American churches faced the same problem as when the first wave of emigrants left the Netherlands—retention. Their efforts offered a crucial contribution to the formation, development, and growth of their own subculture.

The interest of the RCA in mission work was awakened at the end of the eighteenth century, when it became apparent that many congregations no longer functioned well, while more churches were needed in newly established villages and cities. In 1822 a number of involved Reformed Church members founded the first Missionary Society, which functioned independently until the church took over this task in 1831 and installed its own board—the Board of Domestic Missions.[31]

The Reformed Church was especially concerned about the immigrants with a Reformed background who streamed into America. In 1845 the board noticed that a great number of Germans needed help and support to construct a church building and establish a congregation. The board decided to form closer ties with the German Reformed Church and to study the West, in order to locate places for

---

29    Letter from Jacobus Verbrugge to Jan Tijmer Vis, January 15, 1913, in Frank Verbrugge, ed., *Brieven uit het verleden/Letters from the Past* (Minneapolis: Dept. of Printing and Graphic Arts of the Univ. of Minnesota, 1981), 184.

30    Gjerde, *Minds*, 97.

31    *History of the Board of Domestic Missions of the Reformed Church in America, 1786-1921* (New York: Abbott [1922]), 1-11.

The "A.C. Van Raalte sod church" in Thule, South Dakota, in 1886.
Archives, Calvin College, Grand Rapids, Michigan.

new congregations.[32] Two years later the first group of Dutch came as "a new body of pilgrims" who also needed help. The decision to help them meant a decisive turn in the orientation of the churches. Up until that time most of the funds were spent on the churches in the New York area. From 1847 on, the resources were shifted to the West.[33]

The board soon concluded that "...the opportunities for doing good among them [the Dutch] are multiplying...." It sent missionaries to Chicago and Buffalo. The RCA expected, correctly, that these churches would soon be independent and that the assistance would be temporary. Under the leadership of the passionate secretary John Garretson, the Board of Domestic Missions founded 150 new congregations in ten years, and the funds for this purpose rose to $17,000 per year. Material aid also went directly to the Dutch churches, such as the church in Oostburg, Wisconsin, where the Reverend K. van der Schuur, at his request, was sent clothes for his members who were suffering from the cold weather.[34]

The existing RCA congregations were energized because they had to deal with two problems. The new congregations increasingly

[32]   *Acts and Proceedings of the General Synod of the Reformed Protestant Dutch Church in North America at New-Brunswick, June 1845* (New York: Post, 1845).
[33]   *Twenty-Second Annual Report of the Board of Domestic Missions of the Ref. Protestant Dutch Church* (New York: Gray, 1854), 16-17.
[34]   Ibid., 45.

appealed to their ministers and services, and at the same time there were more ministers who operated independently and who had not been educated properly or who led a dubious lifestyle.[35] America offered many more opportunities for such religious entrepreneurs than the Netherlands.

The ministers who had traveled along with their congregations from the Netherlands assumed the tasks of gathering the believers in newly developed regions and cities and providing a good education for their children. The responsibility they had felt in the Netherlands, they also felt in America. Van Raalte was on the road regularly to solve problems elsewhere. After they had set up their own villages, ministers often left their colonies to serve areas farther away. Thus, Van der Meulen left Zeeland, Michigan, in 1859 for Chicago to begin a church there; in 1872 Seine Bolks of Vriesland, Michigan, went to Orange City, Iowa. These same ministers strongly supported higher education. Van Raalte, with support from Van der Meulen, founded Hope College, and in 1882 Bolks laid the foundation of Northwestern College in Orange City.

In the last two decades of the nineteenth century the new wave of immigrants led to a more systematic approach to church work. Each western classis appointed a missionary to visit those congregations that were without a minister, where he led the worship services and directed people to the assistance available from the denomination. In the five western classes of the Reformed Church (Grand River, Holland, Wisconsin, Iowa, and Dakota), young ministers and an occasional old-timer worked as traveling preachers to support the church community. The permanent starting point was in New York, the arrival place for 90 percent of Dutch immigrants. Between 1891 and 1893, the Reverend Martin Ossewaarde worked there; he spoke to hundreds of immigrants every month, encouraged them, visited the sick in the hospital, protected them from profiteers, and put them on the train to the West. His was the first trusted face the immigrants encountered.[36]

In 1882 the women of the RCA organized a Woman's Executive Committee of Domestic Missions of the Reformed Church in America, with the wife of the prominent minister Paul D. Van Cleef as president. The most important purpose of this organization was "home-making—

---

[35]  *Classis Holland Minutes, 1848-1858* (Grand Rapids: Eerdmans, 1950) already lists six problem cases in 1851 and the following years: A.K. Kasse, Nysing, A.C. Tris, J. Koppejan, Roelof Smit, Jacob Duim.

[36]  *Sixty-first Annual Report of the Board of Domestic Missions of the Ref. Protestant Dutch Church 1893* (New York: Gray, 1893), 19, 20.

Women's Aid Society of Platte, South Dakota, ca. 1900.
Archives, Calvin College, Grand Rapids, Michigan.

providing parsonages for those missionaries who are connected with the Domestic Board."[37] In the first year the women collected $2,500, of which they sent $500 to Centreville, Dakota, for a parsonage and $1,250 to Sioux Falls in the same territory for a church building.

The ladies were touched by the reports about poverty in the western churches. One report described, "They have nothing *but souls*; they are out upon the prairies, shelterless; they need everything."[38] In their fourth annual report the women recognized the strategic importance of supporting churches in the West: "It is these faithful, God-loving, God-serving people on whom the future of our dear Church, West, depends. What is done for them now, especially for the young people, will be richly repaid." This last expectation was indeed realized; ten years later this women's organization had ten times as much to spend—$25,000. Even the just established small churches organized women's societies, which contributed in a modest way to the growth of the funds. For small churches these societies filled an important function because they strengthened the group spirit among the dispersed families.[39] The minimum level for an independent

[37] *First Annual Report of the Woman's Executive Committee of Domestic Missions of the Reformed Church in America 1884* (New York: Board of Publications of the RCA, 1884), 6.

[38] *Third annual report*, 1886, 9.

[39] *Fourteenth annual report*, 1897, 100. *Mission Field*, October 1891, 313.

congregation with its own minister was fifty members or one hundred souls.[40] In remote areas the church consisted of a few families, who were visited periodically by a traveling minister, or they could use the services of a theological student during the summer months. In the long term they needed to share a minister to guarantee their continuation, but in the meantime the Sunday gatherings offered a desperately needed contact.

Each classis had a vice president who mobilized the women in the churches. Their activities grew every year. They sent books for Sunday school libraries, organs for worship, and clothes as Christmas presents. A special program provided magazines for isolated families. The committees sent information to each other through the *Mission Field* magazine, which in 1900 could boast a distribution of 4,300 copies.[41]

This monthly magazine strengthened the bonds between the "civilized" regions and the pioneers. The traveling minister James F. Zwemer had the knack of transporting his readers to the prairies. In his descriptions of his experiences in Dakota in 1887, he intimated that his western adventures were much more exciting than the annual synod, and that his staying with the hospitable pioneers was a better motivation for him to do mission work than were days of meetings. He described how the families came together faithfully to read a sermon by Roelof Pieters or Cornelius Wabeke, or a translation of Spurgeon, while they received a visit from a minister only once a year.[42] Thus, the editors informed the readers that the western churches were reliable partners, while they gratefully accepted gifts as tokens of solidarity and unity.[43]

Zwemer's brother Samuel told his fellow church members that growth of the RCA could be expected only on the frontier. Two thousand Dutch entered America every year, and if these were not welcomed into the RCA, they would go to other churches. But then the churches in the West would have to be improved quickly—of the twenty-five RCA

---

[40]   *Jaarboekje voor de Hollandsche Christel. Geref. Kerk in Noord Amerika* (Grand Rapids: D.J. Doornink, 1881-1890). In those years Oostburg, Wisconsin, was the smallest congregation with its own minister. In 1900 B. Mollema served the Reformed Church in Charles Mix County, South Dakota, a congregation of fifteen families and thirty members.

[41]   *Sixty-eighth Annual Report of the Board of Domestic Missions to the General Synod of the Reformed Church in America* (New York, 1900), 22.

[42]   James F. Zwemer, "A Missionary Tour in Dakota," *Mission Field*, November 1888, 14-16. Pieters and Wabeke were both RCA ministers who died in 1880.

[43]   "Letter from an Elder of a Sod-Church in Dakota," *Mission Field*, November 1889, 17.

congregations in Dakota, eight did not have church buildings and five no parsonages.[44] The representative of the RCA awaited the Dutch at Castle Park, the New York entrance, to help them buy train tickets and ship baggage. They also received a folder with a spiritual message, a Bible, and a brief history of the Reformed Church, with names of the ministers or churches at their final destinations.[45] The efforts of the congregations on the East Coast for the churches in the West also was beneficial for themselves—a new zeal and better organization.[46]

The minister B.D. Dykstra, "God's greyhound," was motivated in his efforts as missionary minister by the ideal that every group of Dutch should have access to a Dutch church, even if the immigrants actually had no prospect of supporting a pastor by themselves. He was not ready to do the same cost-benefit analysis as the headquarters in New York, where bureaucrats figured out where the limited means could be best used. "B.D." was convinced that the pioneers should be able to identify themselves with a group that shared their historic roots.[47]

In order to give extra weight to their work, the ministers emphasized that by engaging in a cultural offensive they contributed to a national mandate. One minister declared proudly that within three months the newcomers had exchanged the clothes they brought (with exception of their underwear) for real American clothing. "They catch the spirit of this country right speedily." The leaders in the denomination saw an important patriotic role to be fulfilled with this kind of church-supported activity. The churches had to teach the newcomers reverence for divine and human authority and respect for the rights of others. The gospel would give hope to those who had escaped from a dull and hopeless existence in Europe. Thus, a safe environment would develop, where social unrest from inside and enemies from outside would not be able to get a hold.[48]

---

[44]    S.M. Zwemer, "A Plea for the Frontier," *Mission Field*, May 1888, 14-15.
[45]    J.W. Warnhuis, "Work at Castle Garden," *Mission Field*, August 1888, 18-19.
[46]    J.H. Karsten, "Our Western Work," *Mission Field*, February 1889, 15-16.
[47]    D. Ivan Dykstra, "B.D." *A Biography of My Father, the Late Reverend B.D. Dykstra* (Grand Rapids: Eerdmans, 1982), 78-85.
[48]    A. Vennema, "A specific work for the Reformed Church," *Mission Field*, March 1888, 18. Lecture of Dr. Thompson for the national synod, *Mission Field*, September 1889. RCA minister and former editor-in-chief of *De Hope*, J.H. Karsten translated Josiah Strong, *Our Country* into Dutch: *Ons land. Deszelfs mogelijke toekomst en tegenwoordige crisis*, inl. door Austen Phelps (Grand Rapids: Hollandsche Boekdrukkerij van H.A. Toren, 1889), because the book, better than any other work, explained America's responsibility for the course of world history and threats to that mission. These threats

The RCA attached much more importance to domestic mission work as a means for progress than the CRC. Thus, the RCA gave ministers much practical advice about the support of mission projects. Churches received the tip to distribute empty envelopes to church members on Fridays, which would be collected during the Sunday service.[49] Ministers had to preach about missions twenty times per year, always mentioning the theme at meetings, and gather much literature about the topic. The pressure increased and the church announced in the year of highest immigration (1907) that the immigrants first must become (Protestant) Christians before they could become good American citizens. As the immigrants more and more frequently moved to the cities, where they could not be reached as easily, church members felt a greater urgency.[50] The church increasingly sought more cooperation with the government and other churches, because around the turn of the century the presumption of a Christian America was disappearing and was replaced by the fear that America would change too much.[51] Church members had to be motivated with ever stronger means, and more and more money was spent on education. Fear of chaos replaced hopes of easy integration as a motive for domestic missions. Missions became a component of social policy. The methods fit exactly in the American tradition of addressing people about their individual responsibility. The experience of the earlier immigrants, who had also been poor but had climbed out of that poverty, persuaded them to counsel new immigrants to do the same.[52]

Not all new churches sought support from the denomination. Now and then, immigrants founded a Reformed church on their

---

consisted of new immigrants, Roman Catholics, Mormons, socialism, liquor abuse, materialism, urban concentration, and the disappearance of readily available land.

[49]   "The purpose of the Board [of Domestic Mission] is to make this periodical a representative of the progressive and aggressive spirit of the Reformed Church," *Mission Field*, December 1889, 3. *Mission Field*, January 1888, 16-17. See also the progressive title for a program of a mission circle in Orange City: "Effective Workers in Needy Fields," *Mission Field*, March 1907.

[50]   S.M. Hoogenboom, "Domestic Missions—Its Aims and Claims," *Mission Field*, December 1907, 300. W.T. Demarest, "A Survey of the Situation," *Mission Field*, July 1908, 110-14.

[51]   W.H. Vroom, "The Contest for the Christian Faith in America," *Mission Field*, February 1907.

[52]   Lynn Winkels Jappinga, "Responsible for Righteousness: Social Thought and Action in the Reformed Church in America, 1901-1941" (Ph.D. diss., Union Theological Seminary, New York, 1992), 308-22.

own. An example of such personal initiative occurred in 1867 in Silver Creek, Minnesota, thirty miles west of Minneapolis, where the engineer and investor J.H. Kloos from Rotterdam had enticed a well-educated, prosperous group of people from Amsterdam to purchase land. Especially Anton Braat, a thirty-eight-year-old architect, saw great potential and dragged his family and friends along. Kloos had pictured the situation much too brightly, because the house that was supposedly waiting for them did not deserve to be called a house. However, architect Braat was able to build a house himself that accommodated the whole group until they were all on their own. For years these immigrants took turns holding worship services together, which also attracted Americans. Some members of the family even were baptized at a revival, and only in 1894, twenty-seven years after their arrival, did they together found a Reformed church.[53]

In the beginning of the twentieth century, the enthusiasm for domestic missions began to wane, in spite of extra exertion to revive mission awareness among youths through special study books. Foreign missions drew twice as many donations as domestic missions. However, the presence and activities of the Christian Reformed Church continued as a stimulus not to give up the project completely.[54]

## Competition between the Reformed and Christian Reformed Churches

Although the two Dutch-American denominations differed little theologically, they did disagree on practical issues. Before 1889 the RCA in the West requested from *Hervormde* members that they be confirmed as members in a public worship service. After 1889 they were simply accepted following a satisfactory conversation about doctrine and conduct. The CRC raised the bar for new members by demanding a thorough knowledge of doctrine. If candidates could not satisfy this requirement, they could not become full-fledged members. Some newcomers therefore chose the RCA. Those who later wanted to move from the RCA to the CRC had to make a public profession of faith, while the reverse was not necessary.[55] Until 1920 the RCA and the CRC

---

53    Gertrude Braat Vandergon, *Our Pioneer Days in Minnesota* (Holland, Mich.: Holland Letter Service, 1949), 3, 23, 27, 36, 83, 123.

54    See *Mission Field*, October 1908, 225, and *Leader*, September 13, 1906, 40, for an overview of donations in the Midwest. Rural areas gave relatively more to domestic missions than urban areas.

55    See, for example, the council minutes of the Reformed Church in Berwyn, Illinois, February 20, 1889, (in Berwyn RCA), and those of the Graafschap

did not have a very accommodating official relationship. Up to that time each church justified its existence at the expense of the other. Because there were no fundamental theological differences between them (they differed only in their views on regulations, language, education, and culture), the wish to heal the breach never disappeared completely. Especially after 1892, when the Seceders in the Netherlands joined those who had followed Abraham Kuyper in the *Doleantie* (forming the *Gereformeerde Kerken* in Nederland), ministers in both denominations made attempts to unite.[56] Earlier, the RCA had made a gesture toward the CRC by agreeing that the denomination would not start new congregations if there already was a congregation of the other denomination in that place and would accept new members without reservations. Peter Moerdyke, a prominent member of the Reformed Church in the West, who had a great influence on younger immigrants who wanted to Americanize quickly, considered a fusion with the Christian Reformed Church unlikely, because the CRC wanted to be Dutch and provincial and would delay the progress of the RCA. Moreover, the RCA reminded the CRC that its members had been separatists, and that they should return to the old mother church. The CRC, in turn, reminded the RCA in the West that it had naively joined an impure church and therefore had better join the pure CRC.

Not nearly everyone who had been a church member in the Netherlands joined the RCA or the CRC. Nevertheless, these denominations also attracted people who previously had not been closely associated with a church. The Schoonbeek family, who had belonged to the liberal wing of the *Hervormde Kerk*, joined the Christian Reformed Church in 1873, thanks to helpful neighbors who belonged

---

Christian Reformed Church, March 5, 1884, Calvin College. Albert Tibbe requested his membership papers (*attestatie*) to join the RCA. His children had joined the RCA because they had not been able to "pass" the profession of faith in the CRC, because of insufficient knowledge. Tibbe wanted the whole family to belong to the same church.

[56] Herbert Brinks, "Henry Beets (1869-1947), Historian of the Christian Reformed Church," in Harinck and Krabbendam, *Breaches and Bridges*, 125-40. John Kromminga, "Abandoned at the Altar: Union Discussions Between the CRC and the Western Part of the RCA," in *The Dutch and Their Faith: Immigrant Religious Experience in the 19th and 20th Centuries* (Holland, Mich.: AADAS, 1991), 71-84. Pieter Moerdyke, "Chicago Letter," *Christian Intelligencer*, dated July 7, 1906. He evaluated the positive characteristics of the CRC: "It is often remarked that they are simply a generation behind us in Americanization. We hope this process will continue only along the line of careful, prayerful, orthodox acclimatization."

to the CRC, and because of the use of Dutch. Later, the daughters went over to the RCA because of their marriage to young men from that church. Thus, they became regular church members.[57]

How important the continuity of religious life was for the immigrants was evident in letters they sent to the Netherlands, in which they showed themselves nearly unanimously enthusiastic about the economic and social innovations in America. As a reaction to the wild image that America had in the Netherlands, they affirmed their orthodoxy. Joining an American denomination was justified with the argument that this church did not differ substantially from the *Hervormde Kerk* in the Netherlands, and that it was better for their children.[58]

The failure of the official efforts of the Reformed and Christian Reformed churches to merge did not prevent local churches from working closely together. When the Christian Reformed church in Chicago had to be renovated, many members temporarily visited RCA services. That church then invited the Christian Reformed minister to the pulpit, a gesture that was gratefully received.[59] As a matter of fact, in Chicago the two denominations always worked well together. At the opening of a new church building the ministers of both churches addressed each other cordially. While elsewhere in the country the RCA defended public schools as a matter of principle, just as the CRC defended Christian schools, in Chicago many RCA families supported local Christian education.[60] Reformed Church leaders respected the CRC, although they regretted the periodic outpouring of criticism in CRC headlines about modernistic trends in the RCA.

Members went from one to the other Dutch-American denomination when there were conflicts in their own church about a marriage, about language preference (English or Dutch), or about the accessibility of a church.[61] Although younger Christian Reformed

---

[57]  Brinks, *Dutch American Voices*, 252-82.
[58]  H.J. Brinks, "Immigrant Letters: the Religious Context of Dutch-American Ethnicity," in Herman Ganzevoort and Mark Boekelman, eds., *Dutch Immigration to North America* (Toronto: Multicultural Society of Ontario, 1983), 131-46.
[59]  Peter Moerdyke, "Chicago Letter," *Christian Intelligencer*, April 6, 1895.
[60]  Swierenga, *Dutch Chicago*, 448-49.
[61]  "Significant and noteworthy is the flourishing of the new Hollander Christian Reformed Church in this city...[offering] the prospect of a vigorous life for a purely Dutch church," P. Moerdyke in the *Christian Intelligencer*, "Chicago Letter," September 15, 1900. Ministers such as S. Fortuin also moved between the two churches. He served the RCA in

The Rev. Roelof T. Kuiper, minister of the Christian Reformed churches in Graafschap, Michigan, and South Holland, Illinois.

Calvin College, Grand Rapids, Michigan.

people usually went to the RCA because of the language and flexibility, the majority of new immigrants went to the CRC. This denomination was more attractive because of the greater degree of homogeneity, solid education for the youth, and closer involvement in congregational life. Thanks to its self-government (without direction from the East Coast, as in the RCA) the CRC retained its Dutch character. Much longer than the RCA, the CRC remained a church for foreigners who wanted autonomy.

In order to become an acceptable partner to the Seceders in the Netherlands, the CRC had to engage in some ecclesiastical diplomacy. Until 1870, the CRC did not count as far as the Dutch churches were concerned. The visits to the Netherlands by the ministers Van Raalte and Van der Meulen in 1869, as representatives of the RCA, were events that placed the CRC deep in the shadows. Of necessity several CRC leaders traveled to the Netherlands with the purpose of winning over

Middleburg, Iowa, for two years, and then returned to the CRC, upon acknowledgment of his wrong choice (*Christian Intelligencer*, April 4, 1903). In order to decrease the risk of losing younger members who wanted the English services in the RCA, CRC churches also began to hold services in English (*Christian Intelligencer*, November 7, 1903).

their fellow believers. In 1872, a three-man delegation from the First Christian Reformed Church in Grand Rapids went to the Netherlands to find a minister. Their mission succeeded beyond expectation, because after a hesitant reception by the *Christelijke Gereformeerde* (Secession) synod, they made contact with the Reverend E. Boer, who finally let himself be persuaded to come to America. Four years later he became the first "docent" at Calvin Seminary, and the favorable reputation of the CRC increased greatly.[62] Boer, just like other immigrants, noted that maintaining Dutch customs in America was awkward. Soon after his arrival he dropped the church services of the second Christian feast days, because members of his congregation could not get off from their jobs. Thus, the CRC eventually also turned toward assimilation.

The visit of the Christian Reformed ministers Roelof Kuiper and Leendert Riedijk in 1882 was of decisive significance for the acceptance of the CRC by the Seceders in the Netherlands. Two years earlier, the American denomination had changed its name to "Holland Christian Reformed Church" and thereby emphasized its relationship to the *Christelijke Gereformeerden*, as the Seceders were called since 1869. Their presence at the Dutch ecclesiastical meetings did not lead to a rejection of the RCA as a sister denomination (the prestige of Van Raalte was still too great), but it did lead to a condemnation of Freemasons and a warning to the RCA that it was treading on thin ice. The absence of a representative of the RCA at the *Christelijke Gereformeerde* synod, and an official letter from the RCA with a plea for tolerance of differences, decreased sympathy for Van Raalte's church. In the meantime, the CRC delegates gained more and more supporters by distributing publications about its history, and by speaking in Dutch churches. As a result, many Dutch congregations advised their members who were emigrating to join the CRC. The turnabout had been reached; this also became clear when thirty *Christelijke Gereformeerde* ministers went to CRC congregations in America.[63]

## From Opposition to Alternative

Until the First World War, the Christian Reformed Church remained focused on itself. This was demonstrated, for example, by the meager contribution of manpower and money to foreign missions,

---

[62]    *One Hundredth Anniversary 1857-1957, First Christian Reformed Church, Grand Rapids*, 23.

[63]    In addition to seven ministers from the related *Evangelische Alt-reformierte Kirche* in the German border area.

while the Reformed Church had missionaries stationed in Borneo, India, Japan, the Middle East, and China. The primary task of the CRC was to keep its own church pure. Mission work was incidental and good for motivated devotees. Emphasis on welcoming compatriots had priority. Although Dutch immigrants often felt at home in the RCA, before their departure they had already been influenced by the thought that joining the RCA would water down their faith and culture, so that in the long run these could even be lost. The orthodox Protestants were conditioned in advance to watch for signs of flabby sermons. In due course the members of the CRC began to feel superior to the RCA.[64]

In 1879 the synod of the CRC designated a minister specifically to encourage remote congregations, just as the RCA was doing. After an enthusiastic beginning by the eccentric pioneer Tamme van den Bosch, this initiative floundered for lack of regular successors. Ten years later there was a formal organization for home missions, following the same pattern as the RCA, with the establishment of new congregations, recruitment of new members, and provision of subsidies to new churches. In 1907 the CRC had created slots for nine itinerant ministers who shared an annual budget of $10,000.[65]

The life of John R. Brink (1872-1960), one of the most effective home missionaries in the CRC, showed how an immigrant could become a missionary and how the CRC could expand.[66] Brink's emigration began in the summer of 1882 when an American second cousin made a trip to the Netherlands as a tourist. This visit triggered a discussion in John's family about emigration to America. John and his three brothers were eager to leave, because that way they could escape their military conscription. Their mother had no desire to emigrate with her family, because she could not bear to leave her two oldest married daughters behind. When the oldest son was indeed called up for military service in the spring of 1884, he cut the knot and left. The rest of the family followed soon, thanks to the travel tickets that the American family had advanced. These relatives had rented a house for them and purchased a plot of land in Jamestown, a village between

---

[64] Jim Evenhuis, interview with Jacob Eppinga, December 3, 2002, 7, manuscript, Series 2, tape 1, Joint Archives of Holland.

[65] *Gedenkboek van het Vijftigjarig Jubileum der Christelijke Gereformeerde Kerk, A.D. 1857-1907* (1907), 135-40. Scott Hoezee and Christopher H. Meehan, *Flourishing in the Land: A Hundred-Year History of Christian Reformed Missions in North America* (Grand Rapids: Eerdmans, 1996), xii-xiii.

[66] John R. Brink, "Memoirs" (ed. Ralph J. Brink and Ruth Brink Hoekema, 1985), Box 3, Collection 24, J.R. Brink, Heritage Hall, Calvin College.

Holland and Grand Rapids. Initially, the family kept busy repaying the debt. John also contributed his share during the year, while he studied at Hope College to become a teacher during the summer months. After having taught school for two years, he returned to Hope College to build up his knowledge so that he would be able to study for the ministry at Calvin Seminary. This combination already shows that the relationship between the two churches had been normalized. With his own earnings and a scholarship he paid for his study at Calvin, where he studied with three other Brinks (the short one, the fat one, the big one, and the tall one, that is, John). During the summer months he did student ministerial work in remote areas, and after he finished his study, he served his first congregation. Here, he discovered that his first love was pioneering. Until his retirement in 1946 he alternated between being a congregational pastor and a home missionary—traveling to support new congregations, preaching, visiting people in their homes, urging them to attend worship, renting a building, or buying land for a church building. Everywhere he looked for Dutch people who did not belong to a church. In his active years he founded twenty-seven new congregations. He began in Michigan, in places where the Dutch had trickled in but had developed no initiative to start congregations.

The CRC kept all these activities under its umbrella and thus could also keep American influences out of the church in practical issues. The church did not have a separate magazine for home missions and reported about various activities in the congregations in the weekly magazines *De Wachter* and the *Banner*. A gesture of *rapprochement* between the two denominations took place in *De Heidenwereld*, which reported on CRC missions among the Indians and RCA missions overseas. Only in 1922 did the first CRC missionaries go abroad, to China.[67]

The concentration of money and manpower for home missions appeared to pay off. Probably without realizing it, the CRC adopted the American growth model. In the 1880s the CRC founded churches in Kansas, North and South Dakota, and Minnesota. The one hundredth church was welcomed in 1891. The growth continued on both coasts—in Massachusetts, Washington State, and California. The two hundredth church was founded in 1912, in 1940 there were three hundred, and four hundred in 1952.[68] The RCA had a head start, but

---

[67]  Peter Moerdyke in the *Christian Intelligencer*, January 3, 1906. In 1913 the Rev. Henry Beets (the impelling force for mission activities in the CRC) changed the title to *Missionary Monthly*. Dick Van Halsema, "Seventy-five Years of Home Missions," *Reformed Journal* (May 1954), 8-11.

[68]  *One Hundred Years in the World, CRC Centennial* (1957), 208-11.

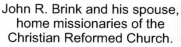

John R. Brink and his spouse,
home missionaries of the
Christian Reformed Church.

Archives, Calvin College,
Grand Rapids, Michigan.

around 1930 the CRC had caught up in the West. Only because of its strong position on the East Coast did the RCA remain the largest Dutch-American denomination; in 1980 it had 350,000 souls, with 300,000 in the CRC.[69]

## American Options

The lives of two emigrants from Zeeland show how their world views in the Netherlands determined their affiliation when the Dutch community did not attract them. A Seceder minister who emigrated in the first wave of Dutch migration in 1851 and a *Hervormde* farmer, who decided to leave thirty years later in the third emigration wave, illustrate the emigration tradition outside the RCA and CRC. Presbyterian churches offered many Dutch a church home.

Abraham C. Tris (1817-1907) was preparing himself for a career as an attorney when he was converted and decided to be trained for

---

[69]   James D. Bratt, *Dutch Calvinism in Modern America: A History of a Conservative Subculture* (Grand Rapids: Eerdmans, 1984), 222-23.

the ministry among the Seceders by Van Raalte in Arnhem.[70] He was put on the spot for his first sermon by his colleague Seine Bolks, who would emigrate from Hellendoorn in 1848. Tris's improvisation on Psalm 23 moved his listeners to tears and appeared to be proof of his exceptional gifts. In 1845 he was ordained as minister in Groede in Zeeuws-Vlaanderen. After disagreements about his preaching he moved to Heerjansdam and Zuid-Beijerland. Here he encountered the large-scale emigration of his fellow believers to the United States. He considered this a testing of his faith because those who remained behind had to bear the taxes and debts. The recruitment reports from America made the members of his church restless, and their departure weakened the vulnerable Dutch Seceder congregations. In 1850 Tris contracted smallpox and thought that he would die. This crisis broke down his opposition to emigration and made him feel positive about a call to America.

A specific theological viewpoint helped Tris to be attracted to America. In the Netherlands he had embraced a premillennialist view of the future, believing that Christ would return at the beginning of the Thousand Year Reign, and that the biblical prophecies therefore had to be taken literally. Apart from H.P. Scholte, few Seceders accepted this idea.

In the summer of 1851 Tris joined a congregation of Dutch immigrants in Albany, New York, but was soon disappointed. He had difficulty with the climate, he missed the experiential faith among the members of his congregation, and he despised their materialism. Moreover, he became disturbed by the presence of Freemasons, the singing of hymns, and the toleration of slaveholders in the RCA. Because of these aberrations from the traditional church order, he and his congregation joined the Associate Presbyterian Church. This was a small orthodox denomination with Scottish roots, which was closest theologically to the Dutch Seceders.

In the meantime his Dutch family, including his parents, had joined him. In 1854 he left as an itinerant preacher for Iowa to see if his two earlier Dutch congregations could live there. After all, at his departure he had promised his church members in the Netherlands to reserve a place for them. The economic crisis of 1857 slowed the

[70]   A.C. Tris, *Sixty Years Reminiscences and Spiritual Experiences in Holland and the United States of America* (Lebanon, Penn.: Report Publishing, 1908), 61, 86-91. J. Wesseling, *De Afscheiding van 1834 in Zeeland, 1834-69. Deel 1. De Bevelanden en Zeeuws-Vlaanderen* (Barneveld: De Vuurbaak, 1987), 343-56. Tris was known in America as an arrogant troublemaker in the Secession churches. *Classis Holland Minutes 1848-1858* (Grand Rapids: Eerdmans, 1950), 67.

execution of these plans, and the Dutch were out of sight and out of mind. He married a Scottish woman, served an evangelism post among Jews in New York for twelve years, and then settled in Lincoln, Nebraska, in 1876, as a member of the United Presbyterian Church. Even though he had sporadic contact with the Dutch, he became Americanized quickly and associated more and more with other people. For Tris, ethnicity was subordinate to doctrine. His strong eschatological expectation, which he found with Americans rather than his compatriots, made him join like-minded people in America. Tris's development shows that theological ideas about the role of feeling in one's faith, the expectations about end times, and his missionary drive brought him closer to American culture. His horizon reached beyond the Dutch and he became just as mobile as Americans. Tris could not find a place either in the RCA, which he found too lax, or in the CRC, which was still finding its way and where there was no room for his eschatological ideas. Joining the Presbyterians was therefore a logical step.[71]

Tris's choice could be explained by the frail Dutch immigrant culture in the middle of the century. The experiences of a farmer from Noord-Beveland in Zeeland, De Smit, thirty years later, demonstrates that the Presbyterians were an alternative at that time as well. Cornelis De Smit (1821-1887) was a councilman in Wissenkerke who sometimes preached in *Hervormde* churches, and he was a founder of a Christian school in that village. It was not poverty but curiosity that drove him to America in the spring of 1881. At the age of sixty, he left for America for a three-month orientation journey to research whether the risk of emigration would be better than waiting out the agricultural crisis that had plagued the Netherlands since 1880. He was not impressed with the city of Holland, but he found the farms and the friendliness of the people praiseworthy.[72] As a town councilman he was much more positive about the government than the Seceders, although he shared their pietistic inclination. He judged that America was far ahead of the Netherlands, and he thought it nonsense to try to teach Americans anything, as many Dutch tried to do by criticizing explicit abuses in America or by quietly hoping that the Americans would follow the good example of the Dutch.[73]

---

[71]  In 1920 the Rev. Harry Bultema was deposed from the CRC for preaching millennial ideas.

[72]  *Kalamazoo Gazette,* May 14, 1881, and *Kalamazoo Daily Telegraph* May 13, 1881.

[73]  C. de Smit, *Naar Amerika? Schetsen uit de Portefeuille, op reis naar en door de nieuwe wereld* (Winterswijk: H. Bulens, 1881), esp. 109.

After his return to the Netherlands, De Smit hit the lecture circuit with a practical presentation about emigration, which proved so popular that his lectures soon appeared in print. He wrote, "According to me it is a great mistake of most Dutchmen that they want to hold on tooth and nail to Dutch religious ideas in America. Strict Calvinism, whereby most Dutchmen are governed, is impossible to flourish in America." He foresaw that the only result would be that the children would go over to the more relaxed English churches. He praised the "recognition of God's rule by the public government in America (a country consisting of many nationalities), so that no one has to fear the government at all."[74] He also judged religious pluralism positively, because it suited human diversity.[75] De Smit criticized the exclusive attitude of the Reformed immigrants who shut out others without entering into conversation with them. He wrote: "The Dutchmen there [in South Holland, south of Chicago], just as everywhere I have been, are stiff and exclusive, much more than in the Netherlands. Actually, it could not be different; the old Hollanders who come to America, don't go along with the time, as we do at home. But the Hollander in America, if he wants to remain a Hollander, is suddenly stopped in his progress (which was already slow enough) and it is quite something that he remains as he was."[76] To his delight, De Smit also found exceptions and had a deep respect for the pioneers, for whom he wanted to erect a statue.

In his enthusiastic presentations he admitted that he would emigrate at once, if he were twenty years younger. Ultimately his age was not a hindrance, because on his successful American trip he had met many friends and acquaintances, and they gave him the courage to emigrate. He did not go alone. With four children and thirty-eight grandchildren he settled in Kalamazoo, where he became a lay preacher in the midst of people from Zeeland in the Holland Presbyterian Church, until his death in 1887.[77] His numerous descendants remained in the Kalamazoo area, while his published travel document resulted in attracting new emigrants.[78]

---

[74]   Ibid., 46-47.
[75]   Ibid., 69.
[76]   Ibid., 62.
[77]   *Kalamazoo Weekly Telegraph*, January 26, 1887, clippings in the copy of the English translation of *Naar Amerika*, in the library of Heritage Hall in Calvin College, Grand Rapids, Michigan, *De Grondwet*, February 1, 1887.
[78]   Christiaan Glerum from Schore wrote in 1888 that citizens left Noord- en Zuid-Beveland for Kalamazoo because they were in contact with the widow of C. de Smit. File 25, Box 21, ILC, HH.

De Smit is an example of someone who went to America with positive expectations, actually just like Tris. His journey was especially a result of the emigration culture, which he wanted to test for what it was worth. Just because he did this not for himself but as a reporter, and, moreover, returned to his own area, he could open the way for new emigrants. He offered an answer that was a perfect fit for the problems in Noord-Beveland. There, the latest polder draining had limited the potential for growth in agriculture and had weakened labor opportunities. America offered a solution.

Tris and De Smit had different goals that led both of them to Presbyterian churches. Through his missionary work among the Jews, Tris wanted to hasten the end times. De Smit intended to bring the people from his area into contact with American culture. The Presbyterians also were a serious alternative for others. Thanks to the close tie with Scottish fellow believers, the Presbyterians seemed similar to the orthodox Dutch churches in theology and liturgy. In addition, the Presbyterians did not find it difficult to open the office of minister or lay preacher to Dutch immigrants with ambition.[79] In places with other Dutch churches, the Presbyterian church was a variant that was not a threat to the Dutch-American network. In places without a Reformed church, it was the best alternative.

## Americanization

The transition from a pioneer situation to a more ordered society offered room for variety, as can be seen clearly in the churches in Holland, Michigan. After the first church (later called "Pillar Church")

---

[79] M. Borduin, "Het Hollandsche element in de Presbyteriaanse kerk," *De Gereformeerde Amerikaan* 8 (March 1904), 119-25. Around 1900 there were ten Dutch Presbyterian churches in the state of Wisconsin. Each church had a specific history of origin in a place where there was neither an RCA nor a CRC congregation. Some churches began because of dissatisfaction with the RCA. The tie with the denomination did not appear very close, and these Dutch churches had difficulty obtaining a minister. Ministers who did not want to join an RCA (or later a CRC) church, but still wanted to use Dutch, found a home in the Presbyterian Church. They usually joined the Associate Reformed Synod, or the Associate Synod of North America—the Presbyterian merger of 1858 that led to the formation of the United Presbyterian Church of North America. Hubert Keppel gives many examples of ministers or lay preachers who joined the Presbyterians after problems in their congregation. Cecilia Verhage, comp., *Grandfather Remembers These* (ms. Keppel Moerdyke Collection, 1989), Zeeland Historical Society.

was founded in 1847, a second one followed in 1862, which was the first English-language church and was intended especially for the staff and students of the Holland Academy (Hope College after 1866). In 1867 a third congregation was formed from the first, because the work had become too busy for Van Raalte.[80] Perhaps the coming to town of other denominations such as Methodists and Episcopalians was a stimulus to enlarge the reach of the Reformed Church. After two disasters (a devastating fire in 1871 and a tornado in 1873), the members rebuilt their church, and under the leadership of elder and businessman Isaac Cappon and the Reverend Uiterwick they launched a fast process of Americanization. Cappon was the owner of the largest tannery in Holland and served the town as the first mayor of Reformed background. "Third," the third congregation, was the first to adapt to American church practices, by initiating a church choir that sang hymns during the service, and by conducting a campaign against the use of alcohol, organizing revival services, and supporting public schools.

In 1870 Holland had a sufficient number of "Americans" to organize two Freemasonry lodges. The agitation against Freemasonry bubbled up in the town when people began to detect relationships between poor businesses and Freemasons. The president of Hope College was a minister from the East Coast and a Mason. The college's financial situation was lamentable, and people soon made a connection. A traveling lecturer revealed the secrets of two lodges. Two members of Van Raalte's church turned out to be members of the lodge and became the object of fierce discussions, which led to petitions to regional and national church authorities (classes and synods) to declare church membership incompatible with lodge membership. To the frustration of the western churches, the synods twice refused to make that declaration, with the argument that local church councils made decisions about church membership. In 1882 Pillar Church (Van Raalte's congregation) went over to the CRC. Third Reformed remained in the RCA because the majority agreed with the synod's position, but this congregation also lost about one hundred members.[81]

The encroaching Americanization came to expression most clearly in the use of English. The year 1872, when Holland was connected to the railroad network, was a turning point. That year the first English-language newspaper, *Holland City News*, also appeared and demanded a place next to the three Dutch-language weeklies. This newspaper was

---

80    Elton J. Bruins, *The Americanization of a Congregation*, 2nd ed. (Grand Rapids: Eerdmans, 1995), 9-10.

81    Harry Boonstra *The Dutch Equation in the RCA Freemasonry Controversy, 1865-1885* (Holland, Mich.: Van Raalte Press, 2008).

**Third Reformed Church in Holland, Michigan.**

Archives, Calvin College, Grand Rapids, Michigan.

proof that the first twenty-five-year period of relative isolation had come to an end. Initially, Third Reformed Church hesitated to begin English services, because the Freemasonry controversy had made it wary of new controversies. English evening services were temporarily suspended. The pressure for English increased, however, especially when enthusiastic young people started a youth society in 1889, and the church leaders feared to lose them. In 1891 the church made an arrangement with First Reformed Church to take turns having an English service, but in 1892 the afternoon service became English, and two years later the morning service as well, until Dutch was completely abolished in 1896. New immigrants joined the other churches in Holland, and Third Reformed became more and more the church of the elite. In 1905 Third Church called the first minister who owned a car, manufactured by the Church Manufacturing Company, although the Reverend Evert Blekkink did not use it on Sundays. During the First World War the church wrapped itself in unrestrained patriotic cloth. Further adaptation was demonstrated in the suspension of the evening service. In 1920 this process was completed with the calling of a minister without a Dutch background or knowledge of Dutch.[82]

The transition to English as the church language was usually a bumpy road. It was easier to establish a parallel English language congregation, as the CRC did in Holland in 1902 with Fourteenth Street Church.[83] With this change Holland lagged fifteen years behind

---

[82] This was James M. Martin.
[83] Jacob E. Nyenhuis, *Centennial History of the Fourteenth Street Christian Reformed Church, Holland, Michigan, 1902-2002* (Holland, Mich.: privately printed, 2002), 11-12.

**Edifice of the Christian Reformed Church in Hull, North Dakota.**
Archives, Calvin College, Grand Rapids, Michigan.

Grand Rapids, where the first CRC English-speaking church (La Grave) had already opened in 1887, and forty years behind the RCA. The more isolated a church was, the later the change to English took place.

American life also penetrated church life via other channels. In the architecture of church buildings, the Protestant Dutch followed the standard of Protestant American churches—a simple wooden construction with a pulpit or podium, without external display, and, if fortunate, a tower. The most common design (and the most copied because of its low cost) placed the pulpit in a corner, surrounded by pews in half circles. Thus one created a maximum number of seats without losing contact with the preacher. The most striking element in this design was the absence of space for a large Communion table, around which a large number of the congregation could be seated, as was customary in Dutch churches. After 1900, more and more CRC congregations passed the Communion chalice down the pew or provided small individual cups for Communion wine.[84] While the synod initially rejected the use of choirs during worship forcefully, because it would encourage the singing of hymns, apparently the

---

[84]  Donald Bruggink, "Ecclesiastical Architecture in the Christian Reformed Church," in De Klerk and De Ridder, *Perspectives*, 45-46. Richard H. Harms, "For the Humblest Worshipper," *Origins*, 20.2 (2000): 4-12.

new Communion rituals were not considered to affect the church's identity.

The buildings themselves had great worth, especially in the thinly populated West. Cooperation with others was therefore not exceptional. A Dutch newspaper reported in 1901 that in Platte, South Dakota, the renovation of a Christian Reformed church was so important that all kinds of nationalities, with other church loyalties, contributed financially: "English, Germans, French, Norwegians, Swedes, Danes, Russians...Roman Catholics, Baptists, etc. also contributed their gifts."[85] Apart from ringing bells on Sunday, the churches also accompanied the rhythm of the workday in the villages, where the bells were rung at 7:00, 12:00, and 6:00. The bell ringer received one dollar per week.[86]

In 1892 the Christian Reformed and Reformed churches in Grand Rapids joined hands in establishing an old people's home (Holland Home) with a Reformed orientation. They were inspired to do this by similar American charitable institutions.[87] Later, other institutions for the care of people with psychological problems followed, such as Pine Rest in 1916.

Social concern could also bring about separation from people's own immigrant group. The life journey of Abraham J. Muste demonstrates this.[88] Muste, born in Zierikzee, arrived in America in 1891 at the age of six. His uncles on his mother's side had financed the trip. Although the uncles were members of the CRC, Abraham's parents chose the RCA, but they allowed their children to benefit from Christian education for a number of years. Dissatisfied with the teachers and the high tuition, they sent Abraham and his sisters to the public school. After his undergraduate training at Hope College, he studied for the ministry at New Brunswick Theological Seminary on the East Coast. There he became acquainted with all kinds of modern ideas.[89] In his first congregation, the Fort Washington Collegiate

---

[85]  Bakker, *Zuster*, 227 (*Hepkema's Courant*).

[86]  Church Council Minutes, Graafschap CRC, March 1, 1881, Calvin College.

[87]  Suzanna Sinke, "Holland Home Beginnings: A Gendered Perspective," in *The Sesquicentennial of Dutch Immigration: 150 years of Ethnic Heritage* (Holland: Hope College, 1997), 79-87.

[88]  P.R.D. Stokvis, "Socialist Immigrants and the American Dream," in Krabbendam and Wagenaar, *Dutch-American Experience*, 91-101.

[89]  Jo Ann Ooiman Robinson, *Abraham Went Out: A Biography of A.J. Muste* (Philadelphia: Temple Univ. Press, 1981), 3-18. For his own memories see Nat Hentoff, ed., *The Essays of A.J. Muste* (Indianapolis: Bobbs-Merril, 1967), 14-47.

Church, he came into contact with the grinding poverty in the New York slums and shifted the accent of his reading of the Bible to socially relevant passages such as the Social Gospel movement emphasized, and he became sympathetic to socialism. He left the Reformed Church and joined the Congregationalists, who offered him more room to carry out his ideas.

## The Roman Catholic Church

Whereas the Protestant churches helped their members keep their own groups together, the Dutch Roman Catholic Church did less to concentrate its members in national parishes in America. At the high point of immigration just before the First World War, the Dutch Protestants had twenty times as many churches as the Catholics—five hundred versus twenty-five. Dutch Catholic immigrants in the period of 1831-1880 consisted of only 18 percent of the total number, while they made up 40 percent of the Dutch population; however, those data do not completely explain the difference in proportion.[90] Their social status as second-rate citizens did not constitute a strong motive to emigrate, even though they (just as the liberals) did use the first wave of emigration as an argument to press for equal rights.[91] Among Catholics also, poor financial circumstances were the most important incentive to leave. In social and economic terms there was no difference between the Catholic and Protestant provinces. It is true that in the south of the Netherlands, where most of the Catholics lived, there was more flexibility in dealing with population growth. The small farms on sandy soil became cost-effective with the use of fertilizer. In addition, the poor peasants added to their family income by doing textile work in their homes. When this home industry was replaced by factory production in the cities of the province of Noord-Brabant after 1860, many rural people moved to these cities. Besides, these areas were close to Germany and Belgium, where people could find employment. But areas with few alternatives for dealing with population growth, such as West-Brabant, did send many emigrants.[92]

[90]   Swierenga, *Faith and Family*, 156-60.
[91]   Van Stekelenburg, *Landverhuizing*, 116-17.
[92]   H.A.V.M. van Stekelenburg, *"Hier is alles vooruitgang,"* *Landverhuizing van Noord-Brabant naar Noord-Amerika, 1880-1940* (Tilburg: Stichting Zuidelijk Historisch Contact, 1996), 8. Between 1901 and 1920 only 14 percent of Noord-Brabant emigrants went to America, versus 82 percent to Belgium and Germany. See Yda Schreuder, *Dutch Catholic Immigrant Settlement in Wisconsin, 1850-1905* (New York: Garland, 1989), 33-34.

School, nunnery, and church of Holland(town), Wisconsin, ca. 1900.

*Katholieke Illustratie*, 1909.

Group settlements did not always follow preconceived plans. Some Dutch in Little Chute, where emigrants from areas around Uden, Boekel, and the village of Zeeland in Oost-Brabant had settled, were dissatisfied with the apportioning of the land. Eight families, under the leadership of Franciscan Adrianus Godthardt, therefore established a second colony, Hollandtown, which was surrounded by Irishmen.[93] Godthardt had gained experience in the Dutch East Indies before coming to America. He was not the easiest person to work with and regularly came into conflict with his superiors. But he did his best to take care of people's bodies as well as their souls. He himself thought that he received initially very little support from his compatriots, and even direct opposition from his closest colleagues.

> My life has never been more poor. I discovered what life is like for North-American missionaries. In the meantime I did receive totally undeserved general respect that flattered me, that is, from all people, French and English, whom I found in America. But not from the Hollanders, because those people are too rude to realize what is owed to a priest. I had farmers from Noord-Brabant around me, and those people are rude, stubborn, and selfish. They contributed nothing for my support, not even those who had money, and they also decided not to work for me.[94]

---

[93]   Van Stekelenburg, *Landverhuizing*, 64-67 and 87-110. Paul J. Spaeth, ed., "A Priest in the Woods: The Journal of Fr. Adrianus Dominicus Godthardt, O.F.M., 1848-1850," *Wisconsin Magazine of History* 75 (1991/1992): 117-40.

[94]   H. van Stekelenburg, transcription by A.D. Godthardt, "Reisbeschrijving," from his Missieboek, 127, map 21, Van Stekelenburg collection, RSC.

When the settlers realized that a church would strengthen their community, their unwillingness disappeared, and everyone contributed labor or materials to the building and furnishing of a church. Together with De Pere and Green Bay (the harbor city connected to Lake Michigan in northeast Wisconsin, where immigrants arrived and found temporary employment), these colonies would form the longest-lasting Dutch Catholic network.

Dutch Roman Catholics had, besides the church, stronger cultural ties than Protestants to support their community. Festivals brought people together in a pleasant manner. One of them remembered with pleasure the carnival dances in the large homes of the colony in Wisconsin. Every year the guild *De Schut* organized a traditional shooting contest, in which the winner could be king the following year, could choose a queen, and wear a great silver heart as a sign of honor. The men played cards, the women drank coffee and exchanged news items, and the kids played games. These traditions made for a close community. No one was ever arrested for disturbing the peace. At weddings and at the completion of a new house there was some drinking, but not in excess. The Flemish-Dutch community in Detroit also had a rich social life with musical performances, dancing parties, pigeon contests, and playing ball.[95]

## Antipapism

During all of the nineteenth century, Roman Catholics in the Netherlands were the object of ridicule, and in America antipapism also raised its ugly head periodically. This mistrust of Catholics was cultivated not only by aversion to their doctrine, but also by aversion to newcomers in general, such as the Irish, who often were Roman Catholic and also at the bottom of the social ladder, whereby they were more quickly involved in labor agitation. In the middle of the century such feelings were strongest on the East Coast, where most of the Catholic immigrants settled down. In 1844 Philadelphia was the stage of a violent outburst against Catholics. The twenty-four-year-old son of a ship owner from Rotterdam, Jan Rudolph Mees, happened to be on a trip through America to get acquainted with future trade partners, when he was caught in the middle of a riot between old-stock Americans (who called themselves Native Americans) and the Irish. He

---

[95]  Chrysostom Adrian Verwyst, "Reminiscences of a Pioneer Missionary," *Publications of the State Historical Society of Wisconsin, Proceedings, 1916* (Madison, 1917), 154-55.

recorded the anti-Catholic sentiment but observed that conflicting economic and political interests also intensified the pressure:

> Already at a considerable distance from Philad[elphia] on the Delaware one noticed that there must be an intense fire in Philad....Forty houses burned down in Kensington, an [Irish] suburb; this was the work of the *native American* party, which carried out revenge against the Irish. The brawl had begun the day before, when the *Native Americans* had a meeting that was disrupted by the Irish. The Irish made such a racket that the speaker could not be heard. They went to another place and carried the American flag, which was pulled down by the Irish and trampled down during the next quarrel. The *Native Americans* carried the flag through Philad, with a caption, "this is the flag that has been trampled down by the Popish Irish," and held another meeting in Kensington; this meeting was again disrupted by the Irish who twice shot at those who held up the flag, and at four more from that party. This day the others revenged themselves and the number of dead among the Irish was about 15. On the 9th they continued their rage and burned two churches, a nunnery and a parsonage.
>
> Actually, people were not very surprised that the riot happened, because gradually minor fights between the parties had taken place. The *Native Am* think that the foreigners are placed on the same level as they, and that the term of naturalization (which gives the right to vote) should be set at 20 years, while now they get it in 3 years, and by bribing they buy it often much earlier. Another cause for discord is in the laws about the schools; that is, the Roman Catholics want to prevent that the Bible is read in the *public schools*. To irritate the *Nat. Am.* they have already hindered them in many ways, among others, they have often broken up the railroad that runs through their quarters. Philad., although it is the City of brotherly love, is very troubled....[96]

Roman Catholic immigrants realized that these hostile sentiments would not disappear of themselves and they were on their guard. The thirty-two-year-old Father Adrianus van de Braak, who traveled from

[96] Jan Rudolph Mees, *Dagboek van eene reis door Amerika, 1834-1844*. Ingeleid en van aantekeningen voorzien door drs. B. Schoenmaker (Rotterdam: Stichting Historische Publicaties Roterodamum, 1988), 109-10. The Catholics opposed the prescribed King James translation of the Bible, which was not approved by the Vatican.

Le Havre to New York in 1852 to support his fellow believers, concealed his priestly office while on board because he had noticed that people harbored prejudices against Catholics. Only when the need of a dying emigrant pressured him did he disclose his office, so that he could administer absolution. His first experience in America was not so bad. When the custom officers came on board in New York harbor, they let Van de Braak pass, as soon as they realized that he was a priest.

The fear of anti-Catholicism loomed in the background for Van de Braak but was overcome by the practical needs that confronted him. His most important duties were to read mass in German; to hear confession in English and German; to give theology lectures; to visit dispersed Catholics with the host, candles, and wine; and to encourage them by preaching and serving the sacraments.[97]

Gradually Van de Braak arrived at a more positive judgment about America. He noticed that the church had fewer ranks and positions than in the Netherlands. To his surprise he heard that even the archbishop heard confessions. In Baltimore he visited a private hospital that was governed by "6 American unbelieving doctors, but staffed by Sisters of Love. That is how Americans are. They hate and curse Catholics, but if they can make money, they make use of whoever they can."[98] In a poorhouse, the priests who made weekly pastoral visits often had abuse flung at them. However, the gratitude of the Irish and German pioneers in the areas of the Cumberland Mountains when a priest came by compensated for these negative experiences. He found Protestants fickle: "They praise the Bible, but believe only what they like in it. What the one considers divine truth, another laughs at; and what they believe today, they mock tomorrow," and for a typical American denomination such as the Methodists, Adrianus could not generate any appreciation: "A cult from hell."[99]

Above all, the priest feared that many Catholic immigrants would lose their faith with the absence of clerical leadership in America. He therefore advised Hollanders not to go to the south. "In general the Hollanders here (there are exceptions of course) are unfortunate in soul and body, especially in soul...; the poor immigrants, who speak nothing but a little provincial Dutch or Flemish, find nothing here of all of this [stores, schools, churches, hotels]; they are left to themselves and are

---

[97]    Diary notes August 22 and 23, September 1 and 15, 1852. Manuscript of diary and letters of Father Adrianus van de Braak, August 1852-August 1853, Box 21, folder 136. H. van Stekelenburg Collection, RSC.

[98]    Ibid., diary September 21, 1852.

[99]    Ibid.

often rejected." Van de Braak had heard from a Dutch colleague, who walked through Brooklyn looking for Dutch people, that he had met nearly one hundred who had done nothing for their faith or not met a priest in years. The colleague read a mass for them regularly but advised others to go to Cincinnati, where the Dutch had founded their own church. Actually, the lack of Catholic churches was reason for the clergy to encourage the Dutch to remain in their own country.

In 1855 H.W. van der Bosch, a Catholic immigrant from Gelderland, experienced personally that a predominantly Protestant climate controlled America. He blamed this culture on the stream of non-Catholic immigrants from Catholic countries such as France, Italy, and parts of Germany, who resisted the church and especially the hierarchy. He wrote that as soon as someone noticed that you were Catholic, he would try to convince you of your error. Van der Bosch derived comfort from the beautiful churches, the monasteries, and the transfer of several prominent Protestants to the mother church, while he joined the German Catholic community in Auburn, New York.[100]

Three-quarters of a century later much had changed, especially in the cities, but Catholics in Iowa still wrote discouraging reports home: " I do not advise anyone who is RC to come here, especially not if the children are small. The education here is appalling, and that language, that is also dismal....You find Dutch ministers everywhere, but no priest, I think."[101]

## The Organization of the Catholic Church

These experiences show that the nature of church organization influenced the well-being of the immigrants and therefore also affected the information sent home. As Father Van de Braak wrote, Catholic immigrants were more dependent on the availability of a clergyman than Protestants. Protestants could conduct a complete worship service among themselves, without a minister, by singing, reading the Bible themselves, and reading a sermon. Catholics could not have church services without a priest, because they needed him for administering the sacraments. They could manage for a time without a priest by having a prominent parishioner conduct the Bible reading and prayers

---

[100] Brinks, *Dutch-American Voices*, 228-29.

[101] J. Geerlings, January 12, 1926, from Oskaloosa, Iowa, cited in Van Stekelenburg, *Hier is alles vooruitgang*, 36. See also folder 61, Van Stekelenburg Collection, RSC.

and using that gathering to make some business announcements.[102] The Catholics did invest much money and manpower into reaching the believers, but Protestants could afford their own training and prepare ministers much faster and more expediently, so that they could handle newly arising needs in a flexible manner. As soon as a Catholic church could function publicly with solemn masses on high holy days and with processions, involvement with the church increased. In 1880 J.T. van den Bergen acknowledged that trend when he wrote from Atchison, Kansas, that the climate was mild, the soil fertile..."and as to our RC religion, it is practiced freely. On feast days the processions go through town and are not hindered by anyone, everything is in order."[103]

The Netherlands Roman Catholic Church Council preferred to strengthen the bond with Rome and the international church community and to establish a clear internal structure. The policy to receive the crowds of new immigrants, who streamed into America especially after the Civil War, was carried out by the dioceses and not by the local parishes. The church hierarchy discouraged settling in distant places, and thus the American Catholic church increasingly acquired an urban character. In the cities, the English-language Catholics often pulled the strings, because they could communicate more easily than other nationalities, and they were more accustomed to bearing the financial responsibility for their church. At the same time a countermovement got underway, especially from German immigrants, who emphasized the interests of rural areas. This tension weakened the identification of the immigrants with the American church. In Wisconsin the two strategies collided—the Irish strategy of unity and integration and the German vision of independence.[104] The German-oriented bishop in that period encouraged maintaining their own language, popular devotions, and schools, which created the conditions for their own subculture, also for the Dutch.[105]

---

[102] Guy De Boutte, "Pater Franciscus Eduardes Daems, O.S.C. (1826-1879) en de eerste kruisheren in de Verenigde Staten. Verwezenlijkingen en problemen" (M.A. thesis, Katholieke Universiteit Leuven, 1982), 97. He cites the daily affairs and problems in 1850 in Hollandtown from P.C. Verwyst, O.F.M., *Life and Labors of the Rev. Frederic Baraga, First Bishop of Marquette, Michigan* (Milwaukee: 1900), 428-29.

[103] Letter to Pieter Johannes Francies van den Bergen, January 24, 1880, ILC HH.

[104] Schreuder, *Dutch Catholic*, 130.

[105] Virginia Yans-McLaughlin, *Family and Community: Italian Immigrants in Buffalo, 1880-1930* (Ithaca: Cornell Univ. Press, 1977), 119-20.

**St. Bonifacius Church
in De Pere, Wisconsin.**
*Katholieke Illustratie,* 1909.

## Catholics in the Cities

America's West offered the Dutch Catholics the same possibilities as the Protestants—land and employment opportunities in the cities, which especially attracted the young, the unmarried, and the less prosperous immigrants. These groups were more mobile than the older immigrants. Moreover, there was less anti-Catholicism in the West than on the East Coast. The second emigration wave after the American Civil War went to the cities. The newcomers had hardly any family connections there, so that in this period no Dutch Catholic communities developed. In the American cities the children of Dutch Catholic immigrants more frequently married non-Dutch, preferably Germans, than in the country. This happened especially among skilled laborers and among small business owners. The trek to the city in the late nineteenth century strengthened this intermingling. The Catholic churches in the cities received more support from outside the community, in terms of money, schools, teachers, and plans, than the Protestants, who were much more inclined to carry out their own initiatives. The few settlements of Dutch Catholics were isolated from each other and showed an image of small circles without many connecting lines. Numerically, immigrants in the cities offered the best chance for establishing ethnic churches, and that did happen in several places.

Thus, Green Bay had a community of Dutch Catholics and the city of Cincinnati, Ohio, included a Dutch parish with four hundred members. Cincinnati was dominated by German Catholics, with much lay involvement in governing the parish. In the Midwest the largest Dutch parish was St. Willebrord in Chicago. This parish was not founded until 1900 on the south side of the city, where many emigrants from the provinces of Noord- and Zuid-Holland settled. The priests came from De Pere, where they were educated in the Norbertine monastery and college. With their own school and eleven hundred souls in the 1920s, this was a lively community that fell apart in the 1960s when the trek to the suburbs began, so that the church had to be closed in the 1980s.

Dutch priests were already active in the middle of the nineteenth century in Chicago, but they served mixed English-language parishes. The most prominent priest was the dynamic Jesuit Arnold Damen (1815-1890). Damen came to the city in 1857, organized retreats for priests, founded many parishes and schools, and built a cathedral on the (then still open) prairies west of the city. He gathered priests from the Netherlands around him who heard confession from the immigrants in their own language, but he did not establish an ethnic parish. That could take place only in the early twentieth century, when the bishop gave in to pressure from German and Polish immigrants groups for their own church. By then, emigration was past its peak.[106]

In Grand Rapids the Dutch Catholics had the opportunity in 1882 to worship in their own parish, when the city became the center of a new diocese, led by the German immigrant Henry Joseph Richter. In 1887 Bishop Richter gave Father Henry Frencken the mandate to build a church. At the beginning of 1889 St. Joseph Church could be consecrated. The parishioners themselves provided the building, as well as furnishings and supplies for the classrooms, where nuns taught in English. Frencken's successor did not speak Dutch, while new parishioners had different national origins. The Dutch character was therefore of short duration.[107] Where possible, Dutch Catholics joined Flemish fellow believers in Moline, Illinois, and Detroit, Michigan.

---

[106] Swierenga, *Dutch Chicago*, 729-44.
[107] Cornelius Van Nuis, "Father Frencken's St. Joseph Parish, Grand Rapids, Michigan," in Richard H. Harms, ed., *The Dutch Adapting in North America* (Grand Rapids, Heritage Hall, 2001), 68-71.

In 1857 the Dutch Father Bernard Stoffers received the specific mandate from the bishop to look after Dutch-speaking and black Catholics in Detroit. For both groups he established chapels in the basement of the oldest parish church in the city, St. Anne. In 1884 around sixty Flemish and sixty Dutch families formed a community of Dutch-language Catholics who lived on the west and east side of Detroit. They bought a church building from the German Lutherans that was located an equal distance from both areas, and they were able to attract a Dutch-language priest who remained until 1907. His successor even stayed thirty-four years. The high point of this parish came in the years between the World Wars, when people experienced a rich social life, with their own church and their own newspaper, *De Gazette van Detroit*. Many members of the community worked in the construction business. The decline began after the Second World War, because of the move to the suburbs, when distances became too great to maintain mutual contact.[108]

In 1907 the network of Dutch-speaking priests was formalized by the founding of an "Association of Belgian and Holland Priests" in Chicago. The purpose of this association was to recruit Dutch and Flemish immigrants, to assist them, and to establish new settlements.[109] For ten years individual priests devoted themselves to establishing colonies. With the blessing of the episcopate in Minnesota, Dakota, and Montana, they worked together with speculators and developers to set up communities with churches and schools. Several priests were excused from other work to carry out this task. They placed advertisements and readers' letters in *De Volksstem* in De Pere, and organized trips to the Netherlands and Belgium to take emigrants along. However, the settlements in Chinook and Hollandville emptied out when the circumstances (drought, grasshoppers, isolation) proved too relentless to obtain good results.

## Wisconsin as a Center for Dutch Catholics

In most rural areas the Dutch Catholics were too small in number to achieve a homogenous community. They joined Flemish fellow believers, for example, in Ghent, Minnesota, and Rock Valley, Iowa. The only exception was Wisconsin. In 1848 Wisconsin was a young state standing at the beginning of its development. The government put a

---

[108] James Evenhuis, "Detroit's Motor City Dutch," in Swierenga, *The Dutch in Urban America*, 15-18.

[109] Van Stekelenburg, *Hier is alles*, 60-70.

St. Willebrord,
parish church of the
Dutch in Green Bay,
Wisconsin.

*Katholieke Illustratie*, 1909.

great deal of land on the market, and developers smelled opportunities
and began to construct roads and make the great rivers navigable. These
projects demanded many laborers. Europeans streamed in, beginning
at the coast of Lake Michigan.

Dutch Catholic immigration followed the pattern of the
Irish—new arrivals first worked on the railroad or the canal, and then
they bought land. Such was the situation when Father Van den Broek
arrived there. The safety of the community caused an immigration wave
every two to three years. An immigrant needed that period to establish
himself and, by writing positive letters, persuade relatives to emigrate.
Emigration thus followed a very orderly process; the structures of
family, relatives, and church of the Old World remained intact.

The Green Bay area went through various economic phases.
Until 1870 Wisconsin's population produced an abundance of wheat,
of which two-thirds was exported. The opening of states farther
west increased the competition. The Fox and Wisconsin rivers were
increasingly used as an energy source and less as a transportation route.
Water power provided energy for factories. The choice of work and
residence was determined by the development phase of the area. More
than one-half of the Dutch in Green Bay came straight from the old
country, while the other half came from the surrounding area. Around
1860, women found employment as domestic servants, while the men,
after a shorter or longer time as laborers in the timber industry in the
city, moved to the surrounding countryside or farther away.[110]

[110] Schreuder, *Dutch Catholic*, 117-19.

In 1864 the Dutch and Flemish together founded St. Willebrord as a separate Catholic parish in Green Bay, which in twenty-five years expanded to 220 families and governed its own school for 180 students. In adjacent De Pere, Father Verboort led a Dutch-language parish. Within a radius of twenty miles priests were active in the Dutch colonies in Green Bay, De Pere, Little Chute, Hollandtown, and Freedom. They rotated among these communities and strengthened them.[111] They received support from Father Eduard Daems, a Belgian who was educated by the Crosiers in Uden and who had undergone his first experience as a missionary alongside Father Van den Broek, during the last year of the latter's life. In 1868 he was appointed vice general of the Green Bay diocese. The Dutch benefited from the presence of many German immigrants in Wisconsin, who propagated national parishes.[112] In the nineteenth century, Wisconsin had nearly fifteen thousand Catholic immigrants of Dutch and especially Belgian (Walloon) origin, concentrated in the Green Bay area. A network of Norbertines and other Dutch priests visited each other on the high holy days.[113]

The churches served as centers of community activities, which continued to develop.[114] In the early twentieth century the church life in Hollandtown (now Holland), Wisconsin, included a mutual insurance company and a girls society that took Communion every other month as a group, encouraged each other in virtuous behavior, and collected books for the library. Young children belonged to a "Holy Childhood" group, the mothers met at the gatherings of the "Holy Heart." The men joined the "Holy Name Society" as a forum for church and social questions. The most important cultural import was the annual *Schut*, a shooting competition that was originally held October 4, the day of St. Franciscus, but was soon held earlier to have a better chance of good weather. Initially only Hollanders could participate, and later also Irish men who had married Dutch women, until in 1930 all ethnic restrictions were lifted.[115]

[111]  *The Catholic Church in Wisconsin* (Milwaukee: Catholic Historical Printing, 1895-1898), 587-90, 646-47.

[112]  Schreuder, *Dutch Catholic*, 131. Van Stekelenburg, *Landverhuizing*, 64-73. De Boutte, "Pater Franciscus Eduardus Daems."

[113]  Walter Lagerwey, ed., *Letters Written in Good Faith: The Early Years of the Dutch Norbertines in Wisconsin* (Green Bay: Alt Publishing, 1996), 132 (March 29, 1894).

[114]  Kathleen Conzen, *Immigrant Milwaukee, 1836-1860: Accommodation and Community in a Frontier City* (Cambridge: Harvard Univ. Press, 1974), 158-67.

[115]  Donna Geenen, "History of Hollandtown Brown County, Wisc." (Green Bay: Univ. of Wisconsin, n.d. [1971]), esp. 12-13. G. van den Elsen, *Twintig*

In 1923 Dutch Catholics estimated their number at forty thousand.[116] Of greater institutional significance was the founding of a priory in 1900, which in 1925 was elevated to an abbey, St. Norbert, in De Pere. The first Norbertines had arrived in 1893 to keep the immigrants connected to the church, and especially to keep them out of the hands of heretical preachers. The Norbertines were very successful in that venture. Together with the Crosiers, who had their center in Onamia, Minnesota, they provided 150 Dutch Roman Catholic clergy who worked in America. But the college did not play a significant role in the formation of a Dutch-American identity.[117]

## Churches as Intersections

Without exaggeration one can conclude that the churches were the most important shaping force of the Dutch-American subculture. They provided a center, homogeneity, continuity, social resources, and networks of communities. Immigrants who joined a church also chose a trajectory in the Americanization process. Pietistic Protestants had nestled comfortably in American culture. Insofar as this pietism remained moderate, it was an integrating factor that fit in with the traditions of American Protestantism. The first group of immigrants chose this track and joined the Reformed Church in America, which was deeply rooted in American society. Other immigrants, who experienced their faith especially in rational terms, intended to keep their distance from nonbelievers or those who believed differently. They tied strict stipulations to their contacts with the outside world, which caused the integration to slow down. This was the course of the Christian Reformed Church.[118]

Serious believers, Protestant and Catholic, were concerned about their spiritual future. This concern and the awareness of ecclesiastical responsibility motivated the first generation of immigrant leaders

*brieven uit Amerika* (Nederlandsche Christelijke Boerenbond, [1907]), 80-81. In 1956 Queen Juliana presented a silver parrot to the winner of the *Schut* competition.

[116] Jno. A. van Heerum, O.P., "Roman Catholics in the United States," *Regeeringsjubileum 1898-1923* (Chicago, 1923).

[117] It is interesting that the Roman Catholics feared the influence of the "*Scholtianen*," the Seceders who were led by "Brother van Raalte." De Boutte, "Franciscus Eduardus Daems," who cites the *Green Bay Advocate* of January 3, 1856.

[118] Gjerde, *Minds of the West*, 12-15 and 271-75. Gjerde used the term "particularism." In describing the Dutch Reformed the theological term "confessionalism" is more common.

to come along with the stream of immigrants and to create a safe environment. It turned out that this aim involved much more than they could have imagined initially. In addition to their tasks as ministers, they were expected to serve as travel guides, land agents, diplomats, education coordinators, social workers, public relations representatives, and judges. They built a framework that guaranteed continuity in this new environment and freely used the means that were available in America. The acceptance of modern means and the orientation toward the future advanced the process of adaptation. A number of the later immigrants, who expected a familiar piece of the Netherlands, were critical toward the course taken by the first generation. This internal tension was the price for the development of an immigrant tradition.

The division in the Dutch Protestant church community had advantages and disadvantages for the development of a Dutch-American identity. The chief advantage was the possibility of choice for immigrants who wanted a different course of assimilation—close to their Dutch source (in the CRC) or more space for American influences, either in the RCA, or in an American denomination, or in an independently operating Presbyterian church. The options offered a way out for those who, for whatever reason, turned away from their congregations, even though they did not want to end up outside the Dutch subculture. In addition, the competition stimulated reflection about their own identity, because they had to set priorities and formulate clearly how their church was different from other churches. Competition prompted the churches to recruit newcomers more actively and drew both churches inside an American framework in which growth was an important goal. At a distance of thirty to forty years, the CRC followed the changes that the RCA had imported in liturgy, societies, interchurch cooperation, missions, and social work. However, the division between the RCA and the CRC had the drawback of diminishing their strengths. Especially in the early period, two small churches in small settlements would drag out their existence until they had to close their doors, rather than unite in one ministry.[119]

The role of the churches in the formation of a Dutch-American community can hardly be exaggerated. Between 1840 and 1900, twenty-seven Dutch congregations were founded in Grand Rapids. Every Catholic or Protestant who took his or her faith seriously

---

[119] Tymen Hofman gives a description of that struggle in *The Strength of Their Years* (Knight Pub., 1983) about the Nobleford and Monarch churches in Alberta, Canada.

could find a church. Immigration and the high birthrate were nearly completely responsible for the growth, and therefore the ties with the Netherlands could not be ignored with impunity. Besides, the churches had a clear identity with a message in which the demarcation between church and state was confirmed, and the target audience could easily be found: every Dutch person! The Christian Reformed Church had a clearer profile for this group than the Reformed Church in America (the RCA was much more friendly toward the CRC than the other way around), and the CRC was on the offensive against the RCA. For immigrants who wanted to get away from their fellows, the RCA offered a "better" community. The Christian Reformed church leadership was in firm hands and was apprehensive about disorder and unbelief. That church community posed high demands in terms of knowledge and involvement. Membership meant a great investment in time and money, which led to strong identification.[120]

Roman Catholic immigrants had a more difficult time because their tradition in the United States was perceived with distrust. In only a small number of cities and rural areas could the Dutch Catholics build their own "national" subculture, but most of them mingled with fellow believers from Europe. For the Catholics there was room for ethnically mixed churches and, in a few instances, Dutch-language parishes. In Catholic circles, identity was also strengthened outside the church in cultural events, such as carnival celebrations and the *Schut*. The informal, and a few formal, mutual ties were too limited in extent and function to grow into a lasting organization of community networks.

It is estimated that only one-third of all adult Protestant Dutch immigrants were members of a Dutch-American church. However, this small number does not diminish the crucial role played by the churches in the forming of a Dutch subculture. The purpose had never been to bring all Dutch immigrants under one ecclesiastic roof. Of course, there also were meeting places for the Dutch outside the churches, for example, in cultural clubs such as the Holland Society. However, these organizations served only a limited group of prosperous men in the cities, who needed cultural and business networks. But it was the involvement of many families in the churches that provided the building blocks with which an impressive edifice could be designed and preserved.

[120]  Dean M. Kelly, *Why Conservative Churches Are Growing* (New York: Harper & Row, 1972). J.M. Mathison, "Tell Me Again: *Why* do Churches Grow? Looking for Answers in Demographics," *Books and Culture* 10.3 (May/June 2004): 18.

CHAPTER 5

# Immigrant Families

Whoever spends any time in the company of Dutch-Americans who belong to one of the two large immigrant denominations will sooner or later encounter the phenomenon of "Dutch bingo." That is the moment when two members of the group from different areas (till then strangers to each other) discover a common acquaintance or mutual family member. This phenomenon exists because of the ecclesiastical channels and the intertwined family ties. Together these created a strong mutual relationship that provided the subculture with sufficient size and supporting capacity.

More than other Europeans, the Dutch came to America as families, especially during the first waves of immigration.[1] In the period 1835-1880, four-fifths of all Dutch emigrants traveled in the company of family members, and of the many who traveled alone, a large number were on their way to family. It was customary that a

---

[1] Swierenga, *Faith and Family*, 52-57. Conzen, *Immigrant Milwaukee*, confirms the importance of families for the formation of a stable community. In this the Germans were much more successful than the Irish in Milwaukee, who tallied many more single people.

father or son (or sometimes a daughter) went ahead to earn money and to make arrangements for the passage for the rest of the family.[2] Even though these "home planners" were counted as single travelers in the statistics, they were single only temporarily—until the family reunion. The ship manifest of the *Princess Sophia*, making the passage from Rotterdam to New York in 1847, showed the pattern clearly. On this ship 14 passengers traveled alone and 105 traveled in families. In the 1840s the highest percentage during the nineteenth century left in family units, that is, 86 percent, while 13 percent belonged to a family that was related to other families.[3]

Most immigrant families were rich in children. Two-thirds of the couples who left had children already, and the latter constituted 40 percent of the total number of immigrants. The fundamental place of the family was also visible in the average age of the father (thirty-eight) and the mother (thirty-six) at the time of emigration. This average indicates families who were in the prime of their lives and possessed physical and financial reserves. Farmers especially had the benefit of this buffer. Before 1860 they constituted a greater part of the emigrants than after, and were older than the laborers. Nearly three-quarters of them were over thirty, while 80 percent of the farm laborers were under thirty. Moreover, one-half of the farmers were married, compared to 20 percent of the laborers, who still had this phase of life ahead of them.[4] In addition, in the period before 1880, 3 percent of Dutch emigrants traveled in family units of three generations. At least 14 percent of the families were accompanied by other relatives. Later, a mother or father might join them in order to spend old age in America.[5] After 1900 the number of single travelers increased, but this did not indicate a real

[2]    Yda Saueressig-Schreuder, "Dutch Catholic Settlement in Wisconsin," in Swierenga, *Dutch in America*, 119. She researched the influence of family relationships in the choice of settlement areas among Roman Catholics.

[3]    Swierenga, *Faith and Family*, 58.

[4]    Robert P. Swierenga, "Dutch International Labour Migration to North America in the Nineteenth Century," in Herman Ganzevoort and Mark Boekelman, eds., *Dutch Immigration to North America* (Toronto: Multicultural Society of Ontario, 1983), 21. Frank D. Lewis, "Farm Settlement with Imperfect Capital Markets: A Life-Cycle Application to Upper Canada, 1826-1851," *Canadian Journal of Economics* 24 (2001): 189.

[5]    Annemieke Galema and Suzanne Sinke, "Paradijs der Vrouwen? Overzeese migratie naar de Verenigde Staten van Friese vrouwen rond de eeuwwisseling," in Annelies Dassen, Christine van Eerd, and Karin Oppelland, eds., *Vrouwen in de vreemde. Lotgevallen van emigrantes en immigrantes* (Zutphen: Walburg Pers, 1993), 41.

*Johanna Dijkhoff, 40 – Holland – with 11 Chld. "Noordam" May 12 · '08. to Loretta, Minn.*

The Dijkhoff family in 1907 at Ellis Island;
the father of the family is just gone to buy train tickets.
National Park Service, Statue of Liberty National Monument, New York.

break in the trend, since in the meantime a network of communities of Dutch immigrants had been established, with a reservoir of marriage candidates. On Sunday evenings on Ashland Avenue, the center of the Dutch community in Chicago, the goal of every young person above seventeen was courtship. The Dutch young people came from far away to parade around and to find dates from their own circles.[6]

The efforts of the community to make emigration easier were directed especially to families. In 1852 a poetic resident from Oud-Vossemeer published a farewell poem for the departing emigrants urging them to support a poor family from the sale of their property. In the poem the good motif of improving one's life is contrasted with desire for change as a questionable motif in the decision to leave—assuming that it is self-evident that emigration for families offers a practical way to a better life:

> If only improving your lot in life
> Impels you to change,
> To gain bread honestly

---

6    Peter Huisman, *"A Little Minister"* (Columbus: Brentwood Christian Press, 1994), 14-15.

For your own family,
And your heart feels that
This is virtuous and dutiful,

If so—fulfill your desire,
Travel to the overseas coast.
Embark with your wife and children.
Nothing should hinder your trek.
After safe arrival,
May you find what you seek.[7]

After 1880 the number of unmarried emigrants increased, as the research in Frisian emigration demonstrates. Between 1880 and 1914, one-half of the emigrants from the north-Frisian clay areas left as bachelors. The percentage of unmarried men grew from 9 percent in the 1880s to nearly 23 percent in the five years before the First World War. For single women the percentage was at best half as much, and later even four times as low as for men.[8] This does not mean, however, that families were less important. Once they were in America, single men often found partners, when they had had enough of living without wives. Usually they found partners in one of the Dutch colonies and married quickly.[9] Ulbe Eringa, who emigrated from Friesland alone in 1892, at age twenty-six, met many distant relatives in the Sioux Center area, who invited him for dinner. Together with a friend from his youth he rented a farm. He married the friend's sister six months after she had come to America to take care of their household.[10]

Individual travelers were soon taken in by families in their own subculture. In 1880 Izaak Janse left Nieuw- en St. Joosland in Zeeland and came to Grand Rapids, where he found work in a lumber mill. In Grand Rapids he married a woman from Zeeland about whom he was full of praise: "...if a friend is as fortunate in his marriage as I am,

---

7   *Vaarwel aan eenige inwoners van Oud-Vossemeer bij hun vertrek naar Noord-Amerika* [1852]. Zeeuws Documentatiecentrum, Middelburg, clippings Oud-Vossemeer.
8   Annemieke Galema, *With the Baggage of the Fatherland: Frisians to America, 1880-1914* (Detroit/Groningen: Wayne State Univ. Press/Regio Projekt Groningen, 1996), 81-83.
9   E.J.G. Bloemendaal *Naar Amerika* (Arnhem: Arnhemsche Drukkerij en Uitgeverij, 1911), 131-32, 136.
10  Brian W. Beltman, *Dutch Farmer in the Missouri Valley: The Life and Letters of Ulbe Eringa, 1866-1950* (Urbana: Univ. of Illinois Press, 1996), 53, 58-59.

then he will not lack reasons for gratitude."[11] Izaak saw the growth in his in-law's family: "The sons and daughters of the Baas family (who traveled with me in 1880) had 14 children born to them in 6 years (of whom 2 died). The youngest is still unmarried. Thus my wife's mother now has 7 children and at the moment 18 grandchildren."[12] With his regular letters Izaak prepared the way to America for a laborer from the same farm, L. Fraat, who came to Sheboygan in Wisconsin twenty years later.[13]

These examples show that the increasing number of single travelers did not detract from the central place of the family. In 1900 only 1 percent of the Frisian households in America consisted of single people.[14] In this respect they differed greatly from other immigrant groups, especially from the Italians; in the first decade of the twentieth century 78 percent of them were men and only 22 percent women. Among these same Italians, marrying with compatriots was much more infrequent than with the Dutch.[15]

Only a few Dutch men came to America temporarily. Frans van Troost, from Zeeuws Vlaanderen, who had worked on a farm in Sluiskil, started seasonal work in Lodi, New Jersey, in 1911. From a cousin he heard that he could work year-round on a railroad, and he went to Stanley, New York, where he soon learned to speak English. He was delighted with the level of mechanization: "Sowing, weeding, cutting the grain, and threshing are all done with machines here." The negative items that he noticed were the poor care for the horses, the mediocre quality of the grain, and potatoes that did not taste as good as at home. In the meantime he kept his Dutch friendships alive.[16] Van Troost can serve as a prototype of the individual immigrant, who made up a much greater part of the whole in the twentieth century, but did not negate the firm basis of the family. A number of single men left to prepare for the passage of their families. This was noticed in the press, according

---

11   Izaak Janse (Grand Rapids) to F.P. Polderdijk, Nieuw- en St. Joosland, March 22, 1883, ILC HH.
12   Ibid., February 17, 1886, ILC HH.
13   L. Fraat (Sheboygan) to F.P. Polderdijk, Nieuw- en St. Joosland, December 2, 1900, ILC HH.
14   Galema, *Frisians to America*, 140.
15   Susanne Sinke, "Migration for Labor, Migration for Love: Marriage and Family Formation across Borders," *OAH Magazine of History* 14 (Fall 1999): 17-21.
16   Letter of Frans van Troost from Stanley, New York, to Alphons Begheijn in Sluiskil-Terneuzen, April 23, 1911, ILC HH.

to a report in the *Ter Neuzensche Courant* in 1913: "The emigration fever seems to have attacked our small town also. Within a short time about ten people left for Canada. On April 9 about 15 people will go on board in Antwerp, mostly fathers whose families will make the journey later."[17]

In 1907 the seventeen-year-old Gerard Van Pernis borrowed money from an uncle and traveled to Holland, Michigan. He sent his first wages home, accompanied by a jubilant letter in which the contrast between the grind in the Netherlands and the prosperity in America was portrayed so vividly that his parents and brother came across promptly. He had rented and furnished a house for them, looked for work, and made his wages available for the needs of the family.[18] When, in the twentieth century, Dutch organizations provided information and offered loans to emigrants, the explicit goal continued to be the unification of immigrants as complete families.[19]

## Changes in the Immigrant Family

Having arrived in America, families continued to grow. For example, in the period between 1850 and 1880, the average size of households in the village of Zeeland in Michigan increased by 35 percent, from 4 to 5.4 persons, including grandparents and workers. Families did not have to complain about the size of living space. Around the turn of the century, Grand Rapids families who earned their income in the furniture industry had on average six rooms per dwelling for 5.7 persons. Families in which the father was born in America even had 6.4 rooms available for an average of four persons.[20]

Such ample space was not limited to houses but was also evident in the community. The greater degree of equality between men and women in America, and the larger income of children in the family,

---

[17]  March 29, 1913, cited in G.J. Meijerink-Stegeman, "Emigratie uit Midden Zeeuws-Vlaanderen, 1900-1920. *Nehalennia* 137 (Fall 2000): 33. The number of individuals from Schouwen-Duiveland in the same period was 59 percent.

[18]  Gerard M. Van Pernis, *According to Thy Heart: A True Story of an Immigrant's Life* (privately published, 1967), 36-51.

[19]  J.A.A. Hartland, *Geschiedenis van de Nederlandse emigratie tot de Tweede Wereldoorlog* (The Hague: Nederlandse Emigratiedienst, 1959), 158.

[20]  J.L. Krabbendam, "Van Zeeland naar Zeeland. De ontwikkeling van het dorp Zeeland in Michigan, 1846-1860," *Nehallenia* 114 (September 1997): 41 table 1. *Reports of the Immigration Commission, Immigrants in Industry*, vol. 15 (Washington: Government Printing Office, 1911), 512.

offered family members greater freedom of movement. Some parents allowed this, but others protected their children out of fear that they would lose them to the American culture. In both instances the families had to make choices that did not (yet) present themselves in the Netherlands.

Thus, emigration captured Dutch families in the midst of the transition from the traditional to the modern family, which had been in full swing since 1830. Relationships between parents became more equal, parents and children related more freely to each other, becoming more emotionally involved with each other and showing an increase in affection, attention, protection, consumption, and individualization. Higher wages, better labor conditions, and healthier housing created the conditions for this process.[21]

The prototype of the modern American family showed more equality between the parents, who deliberately determined the number of children and who had a more intense emotional relationship with each other and their children. Members of the family received more space to lead their own lives and there was more distance from the outside world because of the decreasing influence of neighbors and relatives. The modern family was less directed toward joint production and became more of a consumer and caring unit. Dutch family advisers warned against American permissiveness toward children, but they praised the spacious, fresh bedrooms and the neat, warm clothing of Americans.[22]

The end result of this development was described with bewilderment by the twenty-four-year-old Dutch student Max Kohnstamm, when he spent a year (1938-39) in an academic and prosperous family on the East Coast in America.

> America's national enemy number one: Progressive Education. You cannot imagine how terrible the bedlam, the tyranny, the guerilla war is. As timid, fearful shadows the adults flounder through the homes, where the almighty child-dictators rule.

---

[21] Cf. Henk van Setten, *In de schoot van het gezin. Opvoeding in Nederlandse gezinnen in de twintigste eeuw* (Nijmegen: SUN, 1987), 9, 17. In the United States the transition to the modern family is dated as early as around 1830. See Carl N. Degler, *At Odds: Women in the Family in America from the Revolution to the Present* (New York: Oxford Univ. Press, 1980), 8. Melissa R. Klapper, *Small Strangers: The Experiences of Immigrant Children in America, 1880-1925* (Chicago: Ivan R. Dee, 2007).

[22] H. van Hoogen, "Het huislijk en familieleven der Hollanders in Amerika," *De Gereformeerde Amerikaan* 2 (August 1899): 303-04.

Three-year-old children have complete control over the radio; if they have time they are wise-cracking on the telephone with their friends, and when the oldest turns seven or eight, he or she has control of the car. Father can walk or buy a second car. Yelling and fighting, slamming doors or leaving them open, they chase through the house like a herd of elephants....The behavior of the children really defies all description....The noise, the messiness, and the rudeness, terrible manners ruin virtually every get-together....It is therefore terribly difficult for all parents to row against this American stream....Here you have an early maturity that stops your heart.[23]

For the time being this description of the behavior of children did not apply to the Dutch immigrant colonies in the Midwest. The story does illustrate the contrast with the traditional authority structures in Dutch immigrant families. However, the growing contact with the marketplace did have repercussions for the family culture. In the Old World, individuals derived their status and authority from land ownership, which determined the division of labor. The more open market for services and land in America influenced authority relations within the family. The opportunities and encouragement to work outside the home strengthened individualism and stimulated private ownership.[24]

Many immigrants believed that they enjoyed more freedom in America than in Europe. For many it had been precisely the promise of more control over their own lives that had prompted them to leave. Immigrants soon noticed that a woman's place in America was different from that in the Netherlands. In five months' time, J.W. de Jong, who settled in the state of Indiana in 1847, had not developed a high opinion of American women: "For every bachelor who wants to emigrate I would think it best if he would first find a wife in Europe, for American women do not want to do much except to sit in a rocking chair and smoke their pipe, and here they have to pay for room and board from 1½ to 2 dollars per week, and on top of that do the washing and mend their own clothes, for that you can certainly keep a wife."[25] It

---

[23]  Dolph Kohnstamm, ed., *"Nog is er geen oorlog." Briefwisseling tussen Max en Philip Kohnstamm, 1938-1939* (Amsterdam: Vossius Pers, 2001), 29-30.

[24]  Suzanne M. Sinke, *Dutch Immigrant Women in the United States, 1880-1920* (Urbana: Univ. of Illinois Press, 2002), 64-65.

[25]  S. Osinga, *Tiental brieven betrekkelijk de reis, aankomst en vestiging naar en in Noord-Amerika, van eenige landverhuizers vertrokken uit De grietenijen Het Bildt en Barradeel in Vriesland* (Franeker: T. Telenga, 1848), 41.

Women in a corn field in Hudsonville, Michigan, ca.
1900. These women did not cultivate the land.
Archives, Calvin College, Grand Rapids, Michigan.

is clear that this De Jong was not about to enter the American marriage market.

In midcentury, Dutch immigrants observed that women in America were treated with greater politeness than in the Netherlands. In 1856 the unmarried Jan George Zahn, who was in his mid-twenties, literally made way for them: "When meeting a woman or a girl on the street a man is supposed to step aside as soon as possible, making sure he allows her to pass on the inside. If a man does not do this and an older person notices, he has the right to give a sound tap or even a slap."[26] He made sure, therefore, to marry a Dutch girl.

In 1873 Dutch immigrants still did not think very positively about American women. The married immigrant Willem Hendrik de Lange from Deventer believed that the American women he met in Grand Rapids thought themselves too good to work. "The Americans idolize their women, so much so that even the richest man would not think of asking his maid to polish his boots. The American woman is lazy, proud, dirty and wasteful. If you acquired one with a $50,000 dowry, she would still be too expensive to keep."[27]

This negative judgment was the result of two misunderstandings. The men looked especially at city women of the better classes who

[26]    Jan George Zahn from Muscatine to family, December 17, 1856, ILC HH. Brinks, *Dutch American Voices*, 399.

[27]    W.H. de Lange from Grand Rapids to H. Houck in Deventer, October 4, 1873, ibid., 414.

could afford to spend much more. Because of the lack of a visible class structure, they failed to see the differences that actually did exist among income brackets. Secondly, they expected their own wives to be productive. Compared to them, American women who did not have to work made a lazy impression. When immigrants forgot that they compared their own farmer's wives or working women with women from the higher classes, their judgment turned out negatively.

A man like farmer Cornelis de Smit from Noord-Beveland, who did compare the same categories with each other, was a definite admirer of the American woman. In 1880 he saw her working in the countryside:

> American women work skillfully and fast; they certainly are not poorly dressed as you see here at times; when they work they move swiftly like swallows. They do not wear wooden shoes by any means; not even when on the farm; it would impede their swift movements too much. They take doing the laundry seriously and treat it totally differently from the way we do. They do not bleach; they boil all their laundry, and in one day they are done with the wash, including the ironing. Their laundry is very clean because they use some sort of white soap, which some produce themselves. They do not know what green soap is. Many of the middle-class women do their own laundry.[28]

The similarity among these observations is that American women appeared much freer and more independent, whether or not this came to expression in recreation or in their enterprising spirit. The only thing that surprised Americans was that Dutch women would skate.[29]

The women themselves shared the expectations of their men as far as work was concerned, as seen in the way Renske de Jong described her situation in South Dakota in 1895:

> Albert does the grain and the corn and the potatoes, he has done about 100 acres, the rest is for me to take care of, that is what the women do here when they do not have children to do it, and we have not got any yet. A farmer's wife has plenty to do here but that is nothing as long as one can do it, but one also has housework of course, keeping the household together, then patching and

---

[28] De Smit, *Naar Amerika?*, 81.

[29] C.L. Streng, "Hollanders at Singapore," (1848) in Lucas, *Dutch Immigrant Memoirs*, 1:121.

mending and making something new. Then I do some needlework for mother and Lykeltje. I have done the cleaning on my own and it was such heavy work that I had to lie down for a day it was too much for me. Fortunately we have not got a very large house, but it is tidy: a parlor, a living room, an attic, and a wood shack, and at the front of the house a porch. I have painted everything myself, three coats for all the floors, the beds and the chairs I varnished because we can not polish them here. I always have to do the churning myself, water the calves, sometimes milking, set the hens, gather the eggs, all these things.[30]

Most Dutch families viewed the position of women in America as progress, because they could find paid work that contributed to the family income. In America more members of the family helped supplement the income than in the Old World, where opportunities to work were often limited for them. Women could work in factories, take piece-work home, or rent out rooms. Daughters earned money as maids, went out doing laundry, or sewed.

A Reformed minister, who had lived in America for five years toward the end of the nineteenth century, confirmed that young women were better off in America than in the Netherlands, where they often had to work in the fields because their husbands did not earn enough money, and besides that they had to keep house in unhealthy homes. The higher earnings in America often enabled women to look after the children at home, a place they could now make comfortable.[31]

Women of the second generation learned to appreciate their own earnings. They found themselves in an in-between phase, because American women as well as women born in the Netherlands stayed home more often. A 1907 survey among women sixteen years and older, whose husbands earned the main income in the furniture industry in Grand Rapids, confirmed this picture. More than 40 percent of second-generation women who were born in America, but who had a Dutch father, worked outside the home, while almost 55 percent worked at home, and 4 percent attended a school. Both the numbers of white American women and of women born in the Netherlands deviated from this: 71 percent of the American women stayed at home and even 94 percent of women born in the Netherlands. As far as the educational level was concerned, the second generation of immigrant women trailed

---

[30]  Renske to Baaije, New Holland, May 13, 1895, in Bakker, *Zuster*, 111.
[31]  Van Hoogen, "Het huiselijk en familieleven," 145.

the Americans at a scant 4 percent against 9.5 percent of the American women.[32]

Women gained more independence by earning wages. Also the fact that women were "in short supply" strengthened their position. According to the American census there were 134.2 (1920), 139.6 (1930), and 139.9 (1940) men respectively for every 100 women born in the Netherlands. This trend was at odds with developments among other nationalities where the ratios became much more balanced.[33] These figures do not indicate that the surplus of men remained high, because only immigrants were counted. The surplus of men grew relatively smaller as the size of the Dutch-American community grew from births.

Women also profited indirectly from the economic rise toward the middle class that many immigrant families experienced because they had more disposable income, even though in every family the father kept a tight rein and would for a long time to come.[34] Robert Schuller remembered this pattern of the early 1930s quite well:

> "Family devotions" were a mealtime tradition too. After plates were cleared Dad would read from a well-worn, leather-bound, Dutch family Bible. If anyone dared allow a snicker to escape... those stern paternal eyes would quickly restore reverence....We had devotions every meal that included potatoes. These were the meals when all of us were gathered around the table. It was said in our county, in Yankee Dutch, "No aardappels, no gebeden," Transalted, this meant, "No potatoes, no prayers." A snack that included no potatoes—boiled, mashed or fried—wasn't a "serious meal" and therefore didn't require a prayer or blessing....So, three times a day, without fail Dad would read and we would try to be good.[35]

---

[32]   Table 2: Activities of women sixteen years and up in households where the head is employed in the furniture industry in Grand Rapids (1907):

|  | total | % domestic | % trade | other work | at home | school |
|---|---|---|---|---|---|---|
| American (white) | 42 | 2.4 | 2.4 | 14.3 | 71.4 | 9.5 |
| U.S.-born with Dutch father | 97 | 5.2 | 5.2 | 30.9 | 54.6 | 4.1 |
| Dutch-born | 117 | 0.9 | 2.6 | 2.6 | 94.0 | 0.0 |

Source: *Reports of the Immigration Commission, Immigrants in Industries*, vol. 15 (Washington: Government Printing Office, 1911), 492 Table 24.

[33]   Hutchinson, *Immigrants and their Children*, 19.

[34]   Sinke, *Dutch Immigrant Women*, 36.

[35]   Robert H. Schuller, *My Journey: From an Iowa Farm to a Cathedral of Dreams* (New York: HarperCollins, 2001), 39-40.

In comparison with the Netherlands, women had more rights in America: they were entitled to own property and also had the right to vote earlier in the various states. However, they did not have equal rights yet; their civil rights were tied to those of their husbands. If the husband was an American citizen, then his wife was one also, automatically. If he died, and she remarried someone who had not been naturalized, she would lose her citizenship.

For an unmarried woman, too, America offered more room than the Netherlands to build an independent life, although not many women made use of this. In 1847 Siebertje Viersen immigrated as a seven-year-old girl with her family to Pella, Iowa.[36] They came via Baltimore, where the Frisian ladies, who were dressed in their regional costumes, attracted a great deal of attention. She experienced the difference in privileges between her and her brothers. They were allowed to hunt to their heart's content and found that they were better off than the nobility in the Netherlands. But she was not allowed to leave the house and felt imprisoned. Saving money with the idea of returning to Friesland kept her going. She earned money by helping a local tailor who had too many customers, thus using the experience she had acquired at home, where she had to sew pants for her father and brothers. Most of the customers could not pay cash and paid with corn and cattle. At first she did not like this, but pretty soon this method of payment proved to be very profitable, because she was able to sell her products at a great profit to gold seekers on their way to California. The pleasure she experienced from earning money proved to be greater than her desire to return to Friesland. Thus, she became an independent woman who remained unmarried but who became quite well-to-do. There is no denying that she was a little eccentric. She would cuddle up in front of her window and whenever she saw somebody pass by who owed her money and had not yet paid her, she would call to him and threaten that she would move in with him until the debt had been paid. This threat worked wonderfully and established her reputation as a woman without a man, but with clout.

## Marriages

The network of Dutch immigrant communities increased the likelihood of finding a Dutch partner with whom to start a family, in which traditions could be passed on. The immigrants' orientation

---

[36] Muriel Byers Kooi, "Siebertje Viersen Speaks," in Wagenaar and Swierenga, *Dutch Enterprise*, 57-62.

toward the future became visible in their high number of marriages. In the Netherlands, one-fifth of the "marriageables" between the ages of thirty and fifty remained single. In America almost everybody got married. Only 6 percent of the men remained unmarried and only 1 percent of the women. The surplus of men among the Dutch immigrants increased the chances for women in America to enter into marriage. The family therefore had an even stronger position in America than in the Netherlands, and because of it women also gained a stronger position.[37] Older men who were bachelors, or men who became single again, looked for a spouse via advertisements in the Dutch-American press or in regional papers in the Netherlands. Within the Dutch community couples found each other in get-togethers of young people, just as in the Netherlands. The influence of America could soon be seen: girls of the second generation were more independent than those of the first generation.[38]

In the pioneer phase of the colonies, young people could even find a partner from the same province. Because of low mobility and the provincial concentrations, such a marriage was quite natural. Eleven of the fifty couples that the Reverend Cornelius Van der Meulen joined in marriage during his first three years in the village of Zeeland were all from the province of Zeeland; the rest found partners from different provinces and thereby established a pattern for the future. The first generation looked for candidates first from their own regions; the second generation had a larger choice from the Dutch-American supply. Because there was a shortage of women, some had no choice but to marry outside their own circle. This remained limited for Protestants: in 1870 only 13 percent married outside the group. Among Catholics this figure was 46 percent, because they lived in less homogenous communities and had fewer objections to marrying someone of the same religious faith from a different nationality.[39]

Mixed marriages also, in those days, ran into prejudice and opposition. Toward the close of the nineteenth century a mother felt compelled to defend her daughter's marriage to a German. After having sung his virtues, she concluded, "In fact, he is good enough to be a Dutchman."[40] The Frisian Jan Tuininga, who as a fourteen-year-old

---

[37]   Sinke, *Dutch Immigrant Women*, 18.
[38]   Ibid., 22-25.
[39]   "Married book from the church of Zeeland, Ottawa Co.," Zeeland Historical Society, Zeeland, Michigan. Swierenga, *Faith and Family*, 163.
[40]   P. Moerdyke, "Chicago Letter," *Christian Intelligencer*, January 9, 1897.

emigrated with his parents' family to Nieuw Amsterdam, Minnesota, in 1853, experienced the reverse. He joined a German Methodist Church that had afternoon services in English. During those services he fell in love with a beautiful British girl. They soon were married, but it was not a harmonious marriage, possibly because an earlier relationship of the girl continued to linger. According to the children, the mother felt that being married to a Dutchman was an embarrassment, which is why she kept her in-laws at a distance. The two parents lived in different worlds, each with his or her family members.[41]

However unsatisfactory this situation may have been, divorce was not a very attractive option. A divorce often led to a break with the Dutch-American community. In fact, both Protestant denominations considered domestic violence an unacceptable reason for a divorce, because only adultery or desertion was considered biblical grounds for divorce. Women or men who wanted to escape bad marriages by way of divorce risked being put under discipline by their church councils and eventually risked rejection by their communities.[42] A newcomer in Kalamazoo bought "a couch for a song" from a divorced woman and found out that divorce there was quite common: "That they split up is nothing new here, we hear it every day. People are not surprised at all."[43]

People entered into matrimony more quickly in America than in the Netherlands. A quick marriage was the first step in the direction of the ideal of owning a farm, which required more than one worker. The American job market was more favorable than the Dutch, so that those who were eager to marry could scrape together starting capital much easier. Formalities were few and giving notice of the intended marriage was not required. As soon as the twenty-three-year-old Reijer van Zwaluwenburg had a need for a household of his own, he asked a girl with the same desire and married her. In his old age he recalled that this desire and a job were sufficient conditions in 1856: "You see, in those days things were not as they are now (1911), that first you must have a good house that is well furnished, before you dared ask a girl to marry you. This was not even discussed. Both of us owned about the same—which was not much."[44]

[41]  Annie Tuininga Brown, "The Life Story of John Tuininga, the Second," manuscript P.T. Moerdyke Collection, Joint Archives, Holland, Mich..

[42]  Sinke, *Dutch Immigrant Women*, 212-16.

[43]  Brechtje Allewijn-Mieras from Kalamazoo to Johanna and Abraham Wisse-Westrate in Zeeland, August 17, 1912. ILC HH.

[44]  Lucas, *Dutch Immigrant Memoirs*, 1:417.

Widows and widowers did not stay single for a long time either. When Katterina Westrate became Jan Grootemaat's widow in 1855 (she had emigrated with him from Kloetinge in Zuid-Beveland to Kalamazoo), she remained single for less than a half a year. She remarried someone from the same area (Pieter Lavooij from Waarde).[45] Jan Jager, a widower from Grand Rapids, heard about the arrival of immigrants from his native area who had a marriageable daughter. He wrote her a letter to arrange a meeting, went to visit her, discussed his plans, and married her the next day. "Time is money," stated an acquaintance who explained this record breaker as being part of the fast pace of life in America.[46]

Religious immigrants easily got over the Dutch objections against remarrying quickly. The Reverend R.T. Kuiper of the Graafschap Christian Reformed Church, who already had been a widower in the Netherlands for two years, married a widow lady within four months of his arrival in 1879. He was not the only one eager to marry. During his ten-year stay in Graafschap he officiated, on average, at one wedding a month in his congregation of 850 members.[47]

Church and family strengthened each other. Whoever wanted to be married by the minister in the village of Zeeland had to have made profession of faith first.[48] In the Christian Reformed Church, ministers made a clear connection between church and family as a "hidden workshop" for the promotion of a "Reformed lifestyle" in America, whose preservation was seen as a divine mandate. Marriages were not individual unions, but a joining of two families. From a social point of view, the church was a safe place to meet members of the opposite gender. In 1910, Aart Plaisier commented that it was not easy for a man to get to meet American girls in Grand Rapids.

Whoever accosted a girl in the street risked a fine of $18 if she called for the police. He protected himself by telling himself that Dutch girls were just as attractive. Only in church could you safely approach someone.[49]

---

[45]  Katterina Grootemaat-Westrate to family, October 25, 1855, and Adriana Grootemaat to family, August 29, 1856, ILC HH, box 27, folders 5 and 6.
[46]  Marten Schoonbeek to his son, April 26, 1874, Brinks, *Dutch American Voices*, 276.
[47]  Marriage Records 1867-1889, Graafschap CRC, Calvin College.
[48]  "Eerste kerkeraadsboek Gereformeerde kerk Zeeland," December 23, 1857, Zeeland Historical Society, Zeeland, MI.
[49]  Van Hoogen, "Het huiselijk en familieleven," 469-74. Brinks, *Dutch American Voices*, 324.

The religious character of a wedding was stronger in America than in the Netherlands, because in America the minister performed the wedding, while in the Netherlands the minister was allowed to solemnize the marriage only after the civil ceremony. The festivities surrounding a wedding in America were an important meeting place for the young. In remote Dakota, weddings were celebrated more lavishly than in the Netherlands, as the De Jong family described in 1902:

> The first day we all attended the wedding with mutual relatives and minister Wijngaarden married Peter and Dina at her parents' house, and in the evening all the young people visited. And the second day mother and I went again to the newlyweds and Tjitske was there nearly three days, as I recall. One hundred and seventy people have been there, all in all a great number of young people, and they enjoyed it very much so. We regret it that you could not be present on account of the distance....A wedding here is better taken care of than in the Netherlands; at such a wedding on the first day one has one or two glasses of wine, and the second day a little whiskey. But besides this, the exquisitely good food for all. And now Pieter and his wife live at Joubert near the store....With all our hearts we commend this new sister-in-law as your own sister, her new brothers and sisters love her as their own child. They received a lot of presents.[50]

These simple ceremonies held at home paved the way for quick weddings in America. Daniël Koppenol met a couple on board ship during his journey in 1910 who were going to get married in America:

> There are a lot of girls who join their boyfriends to give it a try. They are much better off to get married here in America because it costs almost nothing. For instance, you give the minister a dollar or more, whatever you feel like, and you are all set. You may think that is not proper, but I say it is a lot better than in the Netherlands. Because marriage is sacred, and it should be conducted before God by a minister or a priest or somebody.

He himself sent for his girlfriend two years later to get married in America.[51]

---

[50]   L.J. de Jong from New Holland, South Dakota, March 28, 1902. Bakker, *Zuster*, 249.

[51]   L.W. Koppenol, ed., "Het reisverslag van een Hoogvlietse emigrant. Een door Daniel Koppenol geschreven verslag van zijn reis naar Amerika in 1910," *Historisch jaarboek Hoogvliet* 3 (1997): 80.

**Parents and Children**

The prospects for future generations were the most important personal motivation for emigration, although the children themselves, obviously, had no say in the matter. Eight-year-old Gertrude, daughter of the above-mentioned architect Anton Braat of Amsterdam, coming home from school one day, found that the paintings had been removed from the walls and part of the furniture had been packed, with the announcement that the family was moving to America.[52] Her earnest petitions to stay behind with her grandparents or aunts were of no avail. The other children also protested. After a crying spell and promises that they would receive a golden dollar instead of a copper penny for a well-recited Bible verse, the children followed the parents meekly to the Promised Land. A younger brother, however, felt he had to ask his mother if the Israelites on their way to Canaan had forced their children also to carry so much luggage. As second-class passengers their accommodations were fairly pleasant, and during the journey in the spring of 1867 the children amused themselves together and had fun making plans for furnishing their new house, just like their parents.

Once in Minnesota, it became clear how little they knew about their new environment, and how they missed their relatives. They tried to cope with their homesickness by singing Dutch songs with an imported organ or flute-playing, or by using their imagination. They imagined that the lake on which they lived was the ocean, where a ship might dock at any moment to take them back to Amsterdam.[53] This was to remain a dream, however, for Gertrude never returned. The voyage for these middle-class children was not bad at all, but for children of the very poor the voyage in steerage was truly unpleasant. They felt lost in stuffy sleeping quarters, on crowded decks, and among people who spoke all sorts of foreign languages. This was the price exacted from them for their own future.

Children experienced being uprooted by emigration just as much as older people. They had to submit to the collective interest of the family. A better future for posterity may have been an important reason to emigrate; still, families did not revolve around children. The mother played the leading role in establishing a new routine, especially if the father was away from home much of the time. This was less the case with the Dutch; their families usually stayed together, and the father

---

[52]    Gertrude Braat Vandergon, *Our Pioneer Days in Minnesota* (Holland: Holland Letter Service, 1942), 2.
[53]    Ibid., 30.

retained his authority. Italians and Greeks often worked for months on jobs far away from home. In such cases fathers often had difficulty maintaining their authority, and they took their frustrations out on the children.

Children were more flexible and less attached to the Old World, which made it much easier for them to live in a new environment that they took for granted. The different pace between generations in adapting could lead to tensions and conflicts within families. If children imitated their American contemporaries, they were considered impolite and brazen. But precisely those children, who were the first ones to speak English well, were an asset to the family. They formed a bridge between the old and the new culture, a conduit for information about hygiene, fashions, consumption, and useful rights.[54] According to an early observer in 1854, America had known fewer tensions between generations than the Netherlands: "Because of the American principle not to hurt anyone's feelings, there is less friction and fewer quarrels."[55] However, the immigrant first had to discover this easygoing way of personal interaction.

The orientation toward the future helped the first generation of immigrants in the countryside establish a flourishing farm in spite of the drudgery experienced, even though they themselves might never be able to quietly enjoy the fruits of their labor. Sometimes an immigrant hardly had made any financial progress after having slaved away for thirty years. Lieuwe de Jong, at the age of eighty, was financially dependent on his children, who had been able to make a living for themselves in their new country. He had often rented various farms but never acquired property; worse still, his children had to pay off his debts.[56] But as a *pater familias* he did know the riches of a large offspring. His family was already complete when he settled in the Dakotas in 1894, and his children had as many children as their cousins in the Netherlands.[57]

Independent children often formed the vanguard of these pioneer families. In 1847 Sietze Bos was about twenty and had to clear a piece of wooded property together with his brothers in the neighborhood of

---

[54]   Selma Cantor Berrol, *Growing up American: Immigrant Children in America Then and Now* (New York: Twayne, 1995), 80-81 and 92. Klapper, *Small Strangers*, 86.

[55]   E.J. Potgieter, "Landverhuizing naar de Vereenigde Staten. (Een brief uit Pella)," *De Gids* 19 (1855): 523.

[56]   Bakker, *Zuster*, 345.

[57]   Ibid., 482-91.

Zeeland, Michigan. Having finished the job, they built a simple house, after which they went to Grand Rapids, still a village at the time, in order to earn cash by working for 75 cents a day or $10 a month; only once every five weeks they were allowed to go home. From their earnings they bought the necessary household goods. But the people who stayed at home also contributed to furnishing the house, albeit in circumstances that were far from comfortable, "When mother and sister were carrying the stove toward the house, a black bear ran across the path in front of them. But they were not alarmed, since they were unaware that bears could be dangerous."[58]

A half century later this way of life in pioneer settings still had not changed much. A mother from South Dakota wrote to her daughter in Friesland, "It is customary here that the children work for their parents or serve somewhere else till they are 21."[59] It also struck Father G. van den Elsen that children started to work for themselves after their twenty-first birthdays, mostly in the cities, although he believed that Dutch children, more than those of other nationalities, were inclined to continue the parental farm.[60]

The children, having become adults, profited from the investments of their parents after the latter gave up their property. This succession promoted the continuity of the community. For instance, in Wisconsin the descendants of Dutch immigrants were prepared to pay top dollar for land in their neighborhood so they could continue to live and work in their own community.[61] In the northeast corner of Iowa, where many Dutch farmed, this pattern is being continued to this very day. Agriculture there was most intensive. On average, the farms were the smallest in the state and expanded the slowest. These characteristics clearly indicated a strong desire to remain in the area and the community, even when the opportunities for expansion were not very good.[62]

---

[58]   Lucas, *Dutch Immigrant Memoirs*, 1:246, 285. The Dutch did not dare shoot bears that stole their pigs; the "English" had no trouble with it.

[59]   Bakker, *Zuster*, 149 (March 27, 1897).

[60]   G. van den Elsen, *Twintig brieven uit Amerika* (Nederlandsche Christelijke Boerenbond, [1907]), 23.

[61]   Janel M. Curry, "Dutch Reformed Worldview and Agricultural Communities in the Midwest," in Krabbendam and Wagenaar, *Dutch-American Experience*, 71-89.

[62]   Ibid. When agriculture experienced a heavy crisis in the 1980s, the size of the farming population in this area also shrank the least. The high educational level of the population points to a conscious choice to stay there, because alternative careers elsewhere were among the options people had.

The same pattern occurred in the small Catholic community of Verboort in Oregon. Ever since the first purchase of land in 1875, the original families have continued to live in the area. They enlarged their share of available agricultural land gradually from 50 percent in 1907 to 70 percent in 1972.[63] Agricultural land was traded among the members of the community, but not beyond. Thus, the original pioneers were bound together by more than *one* family tie: brothers married sisters from another family, and younger generations had communal grandparents, so that a firm network emerged that kept the local community intact.

The community stimulated this development through social activities. Catholic farmers took turns organizing square-dance evenings, especially in the time before Easter. Lula Vandeheide, for instance, remembered that at the beginning of the twentieth century in one year she had attended such a dance festival in sixteen different area homes.[64] In that way new ties were forged. This custom, which originated in the Netherlands in the area around Boekel and Uden, had been brought over to De Pere, Wisconsin, where the first generation settled, and was repeated in Oregon. When in the early 1950s a local journalist interviewed the matriarch of the family, "Tante Mika," he concluded that she was the richest person in the region, because she had stated," My family is how I measure my wealth." Her family consisted of thirteen children, ninety-eight grandchildren, and sixty great-grandchildren. [65]

This choice for continuity was shared by many other European rural immigrant communities. They viewed the land as building blocks for a family business, while Americans saw their land as negotiable property. American children bought land from their parents but did not hesitate to sell it at a profit, while the children of European immigrants received or bought the land in order to stay in the community to which they had close ties.

The teamwork within the family to build a new life usually strengthened mutual connections, but the opposite could also happen when children decided to go their own way. The technical improvements that consolidated the farm chipped away at the necessity for all the members of the family to be involved in the work. Farm machinery

---

[63]   Irene W. Hecht, "Kinship and Migration: The Making of an Oregon Isolate Community," *Journal of Interdisciplinary History* 8 (1977): 56.

[64]   Scott Vandehey, *Wooden Shoes West: A Saga of John Henry Vandehey* (Times Litho 1979), 238.

[65]   Ibid., 264.

Children helping with the harvest, Atwood, Michigan,
ca. 1910.
Archives, Calvin College, Grand Rapids, Michigan.

and hired workers replaced the children; less personnel was required. Specialization reinforced the modernization process. In principle, this development did not differ much from the way things were done in the Netherlands at that time; the difference was that this development occurred in America much earlier and faster.

If the children were not needed to build up the farm, they went their own way. This is what the children of the well-to-do, freedom loving, and adventurous Frisian farmer Beukma did. They did not appreciate their father's decision to emigrate in 1835, precisely because they had not worked together in the same enterprise. His restlessness and craving to be more than a farmer uprooted his family. After his death in 1860, having spent half of his fortune and leaving the other half to his second wife, they lamented: "O, how much better and certainly how much more profitable it would have been if we had arrived in America 27 years ago without a penny, and if we would have had to support our father with the earnings of our manual labor." The children of this enlightened father started drifting. One son died during a robbery, and another died from an illness in California when they tried their luck during the gold rush of 1849. One son returned to Groningen; the only daughter moved to Illinois. The only contact the children had with each other was via family connections in the old country.[66]

Having children solidified ties with America. A woman would seldom go back to the Netherlands by herself, and for a widow with children the travel expenses for a return were prohibitive.[67] In 1873,

<hr />

[66]   Hilde Bras, "Tussen twee werelden. De migratiemotieven van Klaas Jans Beukma (1789-1860) een Groningse pionier in Amerika," (M.A. thesis, Rijksuniversiteit Groningen, 1993), citation on 73 and 63.

[67]   A rare example was Jantje van de Vliet, who within one year after her immigration and marriage became a widow. She lived temporarily with other families, but after two years returned to the Netherlands to join

Frouwke Pul, who with her husband Marten Schoonbeek had emigrated to Grand Rapids from Nieuwolda, in the province of Groningen, found this out. They had difficulty finding work and a place to live. He earned a little bit of money making and selling wooden shoes and received additional income from their adult daughters who worked as housemaids. A year after their arrival the head of the family fell ill; he died during the economic crisis of 1873. Frouwke was left behind with three underage children, one of whom was mentally handicapped, while her adult daughters would sooner act the role of ladies and marry than support their mother. She soon lapsed into poverty because the municipal poor fund had stopped supporting her after discovering that she had working daughters. Forced by poverty she decided to marry, but her new husband abused her handicapped son and maintained extramarital relationships. The marriage was dissolved eight years later. Her two youngest children then provided an income. Thanks to the kindness of her neighbors, both Dutch and English, she was able to keep her head above water. She would have liked to go back but did not have the money for the journey, certainly not for her children, who had their own agendas. There were a few sparse provisions for immigrants who became needy, but, on the whole, they had to fend for themselves. This suffering on the part of immigrants was certainly not uncommon.[68]

The large size of families helped the Dutch communities grow rapidly, both by way of population surplus as well as through continued immigration. The families of first-generation Dutch immigrants often numbered seven or eight children. American families only had three or four. The more children, the more workers, but also less time and energy for the development of emotional ties between parents and children. In their letters home or to acquaintances, the women would write in the most general terms about their husbands: whether they were reliable and whether they were good providers. The first signs of romantic love emerge in correspondence only after the First World War. At the same time more attention was paid to the lives of the children. The most important facts about the children related to, of course, their

---

her family there. She was able to do so because she had no children to look after. After working for three years as a housekeeper, she married a widower. Frank Verbrugge, ed., *Brieven uit het verleden/Letters from the Past* (Minneapolis: Dept. of Printing and Graphic Arts of the Univ. of Minnesota, 1981), 146-70.

[68]  Brinks, *Dutch American Voices*, 252-82.

birth, their contribution to the family's income, and their schooling, especially their learning to write Dutch.[69]

Emotional bonds certainly existed, even though they were not always expressed. This is shown in the following family story. In 1896 a childless German couple in their forties considered adopting their fourteen-year-old Frisian farmhand, Teake de Jong, so they could leave the farm to him. Teake's parents left the decision up to him, and his sister even encouraged him. Nevertheless, he chose family ties above economic gain. His mother wrote rather matter of factly, "He loves his parents too much, that is also good."[70] His sister Nelly happened to land a job as a nanny in a richer milieu and discovered how children were treated there, how they celebrated birthdays and decorated the Christmas tree.[71] Also, after the turn of the century, women dared to talk much more openly about intimate subjects, such as the desire to have children. Geertje Schuiling, a Baptist, who lived in Manhattan, Montana, wrote to her sister-in-law in February of 1900 in an unusually candid way: "Well, Klaaske, you wrote me that I should write you whether or not it is about time for us to have a little girl. Oh no, no way! There is nothing in the works as yet around here."[72]

In 1914 a marriageable Dutchman in Los Angeles condemned the easy-going lifestyle of American women who took their little children with them everywhere, while in the Netherlands women and small children stayed at home. "Here married women want to enjoy life just the same as when they were still single."[73] For immigrant women being a full-time mother was only natural.

Children did have more mobility and freedom than in the Netherlands. In rural areas this held true for boys as well as for girls. "One could almost say that children in America are born with a sense of freedom." When a seven-year-old boy sees his freedom restricted he starts a fight and, once matters have been settled, he continues to play as if nothing had happened."[74] A Dutch-American mother confirmed this sentiment: "I say sometimes that children are of a different nature.

[69]  Sinke, *Dutch Immigrant Women*, 46-47.
[70]  Bakker, *Zuster*, 129, 143.
[71]  Ibid., 147.
[72]  Sieger Rodenhuis, *Nog zoo gaarne wil ik vanalles van holland weten. Brieven van Klaas Schuiling en verwanten aan de fam. Hoogland 1898-1940* (Hogebeintum: privately printed,1994), 12.
[73]  Letter from Waandert Polder to Cornelia van der Baan, August 10, 1914. ILC HH.
[74]  De Smit, *Naar Amerika*, 83.

It is perhaps something in the western wilderness, they are so much bolder than in the Netherlands."[75]

Children in America had much more freedom of choice. When the Frisian girl Lykeltje did not want to work for her mother any longer because the latter was never satisfied, she apprenticed herself in 1898 to a woman fashion designer and at the same time changed her name to Nellie.[76] She married late, first becoming a schoolteacher at a mission post with the Zuni Indians in New Mexico. On the one hand this gave her more options, because she could return to the Netherlands on her own, but on the other hand she remained responsible for the family and even helped pay off the family debt.[77] Her eight-year-old sister started to behave as an American child already after a year and a half and went out on horseback all by herself, "Tjitske...is a real American. She rides horseback very well. I think you would be surprised to see us."[78] This mobility would even increase, to the dismay of the parents. Her aunt from the Dakotas wrote in 1910, "When he [her sixteen-year-old son] and Bertha [her daughter] drive their buggy with two beautiful four-year-old horses to church on Sundays, he is delighted, but I am in great fear, as the roads are no longer safe these days what with all those motor cars."[79] Maria Verbrugge, who arrived in Leota, Minnesota, in 1904 at the age of twenty-seven, had her own horse within a week, but she postponed riding it for a while.[80]

Older children who were forced by their parents to join them when they migrated could easily leave their families in America. Two teenagers from the Woudenberg family of twelve children left the nest soon after they arrived in order to find work for themselves in Cleveland and Detroit.[81]

For adult children, America provided an opportunity to escape from an oppressive family situation in which they were expected to join in the work without the prospect of a family of their own. In 1908 Marinus Leijnse from Sheboygan warned his brother Simon, who worked on the family farm in Zoutelande, that he had no future working for his father:

[75]    Letter from 1900, Bakker, *Zuster*, 217.
[76]    Ibid., 181.
[77]    Ibid., 195.
[78]    Ibid., 101.
[79]    Ibid., 307.
[80]    Verbrugge, *Brieven*, 52.
[81]    Helen Westra, "'Fear and Hope Jostled.' Dutch Immigrant Life and Death in Paterson, New Jersey," *Origins* 8 (1990): 2-15.

Nevertheless, you surprised me in your letter when you wrote that Bart had been drafted to serve in the military and that Father could really use you. I know that, and I believe it, but if that is the reason for you to stay at home you might as well say goodbye to your girlfriend, for as long as Father is alive he can always use you. But I think that is a poor excuse. I hear you say No, but I am afraid it is. For what would you do once you decided to get married. Don't figure on getting any help from Father, and then to become a farmhand is not all that appealing either. So you stay at home.[82]

Two years later he tried to persuade his father to pay his sons for their contribution to the business, but that fell on deaf ears: "I wrote Father once that he should pay you wages so that you would not have to work for naught all the time, and to give you an opportunity to save a few pennies which might come in handy for you later on. But he replied that he could not pay a fellow who thinks that to work is beneath his dignity, because he did not have a fortune like Mr. Van Leinnen."[83] The son felt that he had a responsibility toward the farm and therefore stayed at home.

What effect did emigration have on the position of children? Most of the time, they had not participated in the decision-making process, unless they had reached an age when they could make their own decisions. They were the ones who glued the family to the new country because their future had weighed heavily in making the decision to emigrate. They saw their status within the family rise thanks to their ability to master English more quickly, which made them "brokers between two cultures." But there were risks as well: a generational gap threatened if the children refused to cooperate in making the goal of the parents come true. Especially in rural areas children were needed for the continuation of the community.

## Material Circumstances of the Families

The higher standard of living in America, which many immigrant families experienced, helped strengthen family ties.[84] The first step was

---

[82]  Letter of March 17, 1908, quoted in Joke M. Blaas-Rademaker, "Van Walcheren naar de Verenigde Staten: Emigratie in de periode 1900-1920," *Nehalennia* 137 (Fall 2002): 39.

[83]  Ibid., 41, October 2, 1910. Mr. Van Leinnen was Baron van Lynden of the Ter Hooghe Estate at Middelburg.

[84]  In chapter six of this book it is argued that the increase in the standard of

Row houses in Roseland, close to Chicago, ca 1905.
Archives, Calvin College, Grand Rapids, Michigan.

the improvement of living conditions in America. Almost everyone who moved to America found it easier to find independent living quarters. Looking back to the 1870s an immigrant from the province of Gelderland recalled how easy it was to own one's own home: "If someone owns a piece of property, he builds himself a house; he cuts down a few trees, hews them into square beams, planes them, fits them together like a square window and smears some clay between them. For the floor and roof he drags a few trees to the lumber mill, of which you usually find quite a few in the woods, have them cut into boards, and thus he builds himself a house for practically nothing. That is the way in which everything is made, even stables and chicken coops."[85] The only limitations those living in the country had were the lack of building materials and manpower. Michigan had an abundance of lumber; in Iowa and the other prairie states the settlers made do with sod. Everywhere newcomers were ready to help each other.

After the pioneer era, housing increased in quantity and quality. Houses could be built quickly and cheaply because land was cheap and there was plenty of lumber available. Compared to the Netherlands, houses offered more living space because of more rooms. Thus, in 1880 a journalist depicted the village of Zeeland as a little paradise: "The well-maintained houses and barns testify to prosperity, and the many

living and the concentration in certain occupations promoted cohesion among the Dutch.
[85] Bloemendaal, *Naar Amerika*, 115-16.

Steketee Department Store in Holland, Michigan.
Hope College Collection of the Joint Archives of Holland, Michigan.

new buildings to progress, yes, it appears to us, blessed is the person who may live here and who may eat the bread of freedom liberally in moderate industriousness! How totally different everything looks here compared to many a village in our old fatherland, where next to the castle of the landowner you see the shabby and dirty shack of the working man."[86]

Even in faraway South Dakota a Frisian family in 1897 could say with pride: "We have a good house: it is large and good looking two sitting rooms and two bedrooms downstairs, and one bedroom upstairs, and all white except for one room, so there is plenty of work, and I just want it so, because that is what I am used to...."[87] Thanks to modernization, the comfort level in many homes improved. Appliances took the work out of women's hands and made it possible to do all the work without the help of a maid. At the same time, much regular housework disappeared as clothing and food began to be inexpensively produced outside the home. The result was that men did not need to do quite as much in the home, while the women's share increased. The saving of time that technology provided was undone by the increasing demands for quality (clothes had to be cleaner, the food had to be more

---

86  *De Grondwet*, May 4, 1880.
87  Bakker, *Zuster*, 167.

varied). Women could raise the standard of living in America without maids, and the result was that they could pay more time and attention to the upbringing of the children. Improved housing also offered the members of the family more individual space.[88]

Immigrants could build up a small fortune in the new country, especially if they had settled in America during the pioneer era. The rule of thumb was that the assets of an immigrant who had arrived before 1850 increased by 10 percent per year, provided they had taken some capital along. The residents of Zeeland Township in western Michigan were all better off in 1860 than ten years earlier. Their assets grew from an average of $219 per household to an amount of $1,159, of which $882 consisted of real estate. The cultivation of undeveloped land resulted quickly in the increase in property values.[89] Prosperity also grew in the cities: almost half of the Dutch in Grand Rapids in 1900 owned their own homes. In the village of Roseland, south of Chicago, no fewer than 75 percent of the residents owned their own homes, against 50 percent in the more centrally located Englewood, but not even 25 percent of the workers on the west side of the city.[90] Roseland, therefore, was the most stable Dutch community, which it remained until 1970.

Financial improvement contributed to the stability of the Dutch community because the need for family members to go out to work decreased. The ample availability of houses in the city did carry the danger with it that families would move frequently because other rental dwellings looked more attractive.[91] This threatened the family's stability. Letters of orthodox Protestant immigrants regularly included the warning not to become self-satisfied in their prosperity. Krijn Goudzwaard from Poortvliet, in his letters to his sister and her family, did not want to elaborate too much about his worldly goods "...that would be more self-exaltation, and I have always been afraid of such

---

[88]  Ruth Schwartz Cowan, *More Work for Mother: The Ironies of Household Technology from the Open Hearth to the Microwave* (New York: Basic Books, 1983), 63-68.

[89]  Hans Krabbendam, "The Unique Crossroads of Pioneer Zeeland," in Robert P. Swierenga and Joel Lefever, eds., *For Food and Faith: Dutch Immigration to Western Michigan, 1846-1960* (Holland: Holland Museum and A.C. Van Raalte Institute, 2000), 55-82. Based on the Holland Township Census of 1860. Look for comparable data on increases in value: Joseph P. Ferrie, "The Wealth Accumulation of Antebellum European Immigrants to the U.S., 1840-1860," *Journal of Economic History* 54 (1994): 1-33.

[90]  David G. Vanderstel, "Neighborhood Development in Grand Rapids, 1850-1900," in Swierenga, *Dutch in America*, 144. Swierenga, *Dutch Chicago*, 148.

[91]  Van Hoogen, "Het huiselijk en familieleven," 150.

things, for the Lord might just want to cause his wind to blow over it. Remember Nebuchadnezzar's 'is not this the great Babylon that I have built,' for what makes us different from anyone else, for it is not from me, or that I should be more worthy than many of my fellow creatures. No, I must say they are all unmerited blessings which the Lord gives us to enjoy on this continent."[92] The financial abundance enabled them to fund churches, schools, periodicals, and societies, which in turn supported the families.

Luxury products came within reach of the immigrants sooner than was true for their compatriots in the old fatherland. In 1847 J.W. de Jong from Indiana saw the advantages of a very sober beginning, "People here do not have much furniture which makes it quite easy for the women, since they have little to scrub and rub or dust."[93] Sixty-five years later the hunger for possessions had replaced simplicity. Mass production brought household goods within reach because of their low price. In 1912 Brechtje Allewijn bought all her furniture in one store for $155, including stoves, tables, lamps, beds, rocking chairs, and pans.[94] Afterwards she discovered that she still had paid too much, but she was happy nevertheless.

Musical instruments, such as organs and pianos, and sewing machines became status symbols of the citizenry. Ministers disapproved of this "ostentation." One of them admonished the people for this outward showing off as follows:

> To furnish part of one's house in such a way that no one may enter there, except those who, like the emissaries of Babel to Hezekiah, enjoy the privilege of seeing the treasures, certainly is a result of the same vanity and folly that affected Hezekiah when he showed them his entire treasury. It is pretty bad when women think they have to put a piano on display, which none of the members of the family is *able* to play nor is *learning* to play, as well as a davenport that is always covered with a cloth on which nobody may sit. But it gets worse when a man gives his wife a surgical instrument which has caught his fancy, though he does not know what it is for, as a present, to put on the mantelpiece....A home is not intended to make the owner shine, but the owner must make the house shine.

92    Grand Rapids, January 6, 1884, ILC HH.
93    Osinga, *Tien Brieven*, 41.
94    Brechtje Allewijn-Mieras from Kalamazoo, April 6, 1912, ILC HH.

Well-stocked table of the Rev. H. Beuker, 1915.
Archives, Calvin College, Grand Rapids, Michigan.

A sewing machine was at least a useful investment. In 1886 Izaak Janse sold a cow for $30 so he could buy his wife a sewing machine for $50.[95] In 1889 one-third of the workers in the furniture industry in Michigan owned sewing machines.[96] Maaike Eringa owned a handy washing machine only half a year after getting married in 1893, and a year later a sewing machine. A few years later she and her husband owned an organ, five chairs, and a number of lamps.[97] This fast accumulation of goods, which of course was reported faithfully to the people back home, strengthened the idea that life in America was good, even in remote places. At the beginning of the twentieth century a lively barter trade existed on the frontier: "We are able to get everything in the same store, you can buy anything there...," a Frisian family from the Dakotas

[95]  Van Hoogen, "Het huiselijk en familieleven," 472. Izaak Janse (Grand Rapids) to F.P. Polderdijk, Nieuwe- en St. Joostland, December 14, 1886, ILC HH.

[96]  *Survey of 5,419 Michigan Furniture Workers, 1889, Reported in the Seventh Annual Report of the Michigan Bureau of Labor and Industrial Statistics,* Table 25. http://eh.net/databases/labor/codebooks/mi07.asc, visited April 3, 2009.

[97]  Beltman, *Dutch Farmer,* 82 and 85.

wrote in 1895.[98] The orientation toward consumer goods was constant. Thirty years later, the Polder family of Montebello, near Los Angeles, commented that life for a working man was a lot better there than in Holland, but that people saved little money, because they bought all kinds of luxury articles, especially washing machines and vacuum cleaners.[99]

Conviviality at home was found between "father's pipe and mother's teapot." Ministers who themselves had immigrated opposed the idea of the Methodists that smoking was a sign of frivolity, since they believed that it certainly increased the pleasant atmosphere in the home and enabled visits to last longer. To them tobacco and cigars even promoted homeliness.[100]

### Food and Clothing

The standard of living of a family depended, to a considerable degree, on what the lady of the house was able to do with the available funds. Food and clothing constituted the most important part.[101] Better meals and new clothes were the most obvious and quickest signs that a family was doing well. In almost all letters, immigrants wrote specifically about these basic necessities of life that stood in sharp contrast to the meager provisions in the Netherlands. There, food had been scarce and monotonous, but people in America had plentiful and varied meals. Although letters from America often had a propagandistic intent to entice the addressees to come over, this information was factually correct: to have meat and vegetables three times a day was manageable even for a small purse, while in the Netherlands meat consumption per capita continued to decrease between 1835 and 1852. The increase in prosperity was shown by an increase of animal products at meals, at the expense of grains and roots.[102] The letters from America were not called "bacon letters" for nothing.

Those proteins were everywhere. Newly arrived Dutch received meat from their neighbors who had just butchered an animal.[103] Even

---

[98]   Bakker, *Zuster*, 101.
[99]   November 30, 1925, Polder correspondence, ILC HH.
[100]  Van Hoogen, "Het huiselijk en familieleven," (May 1899), 147-48.
[101]  Sinke, *Dutch Immigrant Women*, 58.
[102]  Jozien Jobse-Van Putten, *Eenvoudig maar voedzaam. Cultuurgeschiedenis van de dagelijkse maaltijd in Nederland* (Nijmegen: Sun, 1995), 48-49. J.M.M. de Meere, *Economische ontwikkeling en levensstandaard in Nederland gedurende de eerste helft van de negentiende eeuw. Aspecten en trends* (The Hague: Martinus Nijhoff, 1982), 96.
[103]  Verbrugge, *Brieven*, 56 and 60 (1904).

Vegetable display of greengrocer M. Stob, most likely close to Chicago.
Archives, Calvin College, Grand Rapids, Michigan.

the food served in prison was good. The father of Father Verwyst experienced this. In 1848 he joined Father Van den Broek to go to Wisconsin, but he and his family stayed behind in Boston to save up some starting capital first. In the middle of the night the family was startled by the owner of the house, who wanted to evict the occupants. The father chased him out of the house with an axe but was consequently arrested and put in prison where, to his satisfaction, he was fed well and was even able to enjoy more than enough when he also was allowed to eat the portions of two drunks. He felt like a prince in a palace.[104]

Initially, new immigrants were slow to use the variety of American food, such as pumpkins and cucumbers. Everybody had his own vegetable garden in which he grew the vegetables he knew. Immigrants did notice immediately the differences in eating habits, but they usually kept to the tried and true. Thus, the De Jong family in the Dakotas, around the turn of the century, began each day with a meal of pancakes. They reported: "We just planted potatoes, green beans and other beans, green peas and sugar peas, turnips, carrots, onions, cucumbers, pickles, and watermelons; they are like oranges, but they are at least ten times as big and smoother skinned."[105] In 1904 Jacobus Verbrugge wrote from Leota, Minnesota, that the menu was a matter of choice, "It is customary here to have a warm meal three times a day and always with

104  Verwyst, "Reminiscences," 150.
105  Bakker, *Zuster*, 45, 47, and 93.

bread, but I stick to my Dutch customs."[106] "New" products were not avoided when they thrived in the climate, or when they could be grown for the marketplace. Newcomers did have to get used to tomatoes: "We also have tomatoes, but we do not like them. Here they are used quite a bit and we are told that we will have to learn to eat them."[107]

Germans immigrants took the hop plant along to the state of Oregon. It was not only used as an ingredient for beer, but also as a medication and as a source for yeast for baking bread. Every farm had a climbing hop plant next to the kitchen door. This fast-growing plant was soon cultivated for commercial purposes, also by Dutch Catholic immigrants in the Verboort area. By doing so, they continued a Dutch tradition. In Wisconsin the immigrants brewed their own beer in washtubs from a mixture of hop, water, and molasses that did not always turn out too well. The prohibition of the 1920s finally put a stop to this profitable crop.[108]

In the cities the eating habits of the old country could also be continued. The Stob family, who lived among the Dutch in Chicago, was used to eating Dutch food until the First World War: rye bread with lots of cheese and salted herring, kale, and gray peas. Liver was never served, nor spareribs.[109] The availability of plenty of food also meant more work to prepare and store it. In the absence of bakers, people had to bake their own bread and sweet cakes.

In 1852 Geertje van Oosterhout listed what her American neighbors ordinarily ate: "They have breakfast at 6 or 7 o'clock in the morning, and their breakfast consists of potatoes, steak, ham, eggs, bread, butter, cheese, and sometimes more things, and then strong coffee with cream. At 12 noon, the same thing and sometimes jelly covered cake which they bake themselves. In the evening at 6 o'clock, again the same with cookies of all kinds. We stick to our Dutch customs for the most part, because we prefer that." They did not like the American trifles: "We have a cow and a pig. I churn my own butter and bake my own bread, and I also know how to bake cookies. We harvested our lettuce from the garden."[110] This ability to be self-supporting benefited their health.

---

[106]  Verbrugge, *Brieven*, 56 and 60, 1904.

[107]  Brechtje Allewijn-Mieras from Kalamazoo to Johanna and Abraham Wisse-Westrate in Zeeland, August 17, 1912, ILC HH.

[108]  Verwyst, "Reminiscences," 157. Vandehey, *Wooden Shoes West*, 122.

[109]  Henry Stob, *Summoning up Remembrance* (Grand Rapids: Eerdmans, 1995), 39.

[110]  Geertruida van Oosterhout née Frederiks from Madison, Indiana, to Johan S. Frederiks of Middelburg, August 14, 1852, ILC HH.

In dress, the first generation continued to distinguish itself from the Americans, but limited availability of the traditional materials and changes in the function of clothes took care of this tradition after one generation. In rural Dutch-American communities farmers wore wooden shoes, but those who were surrounded by Americans or who lived in the cities bought shoes. Ordinarily, no wooden-shoe makers could be found. The traditional costume that the immigrants wore initially soon lost its social function. Such attire continued to be used longer in homogenous places that were supplied by one geographical center in the Netherlands. In the early 1850s the women in the Catholic church of Hollandtown, Wisconsin, still wore the traditional costume and everybody clomped to church in wooden shoes.[111]

When in 1853 John and Trintzy Tuininga of Petersbierum traveled to America, Trintzy carried a bag containing her lace bonnet and gold buttons. Her mother had strongly urged her never to give up the bonnet because then she would lose her social standing. Unfortunately the bag was stolen during the journey; the financial loss appeared to be greater than the social loss because the use of such a distinguishing mark soon became unnecessary.[112]

Immigrants interpreted the American dress codes as signs of freedom and of a new and higher social status. Thus, as early as 1847 Hendrik Hospers wrote about the dress code of American women in Iowa: "Farmers' wives are all ladies with veils on their hats, and lace on their skirts; whether they look as black as soot makes no difference. All farmers or whatever they may be called, address each other as Sir, that is as gentleman. Everyone rides a horse and in the saddle; when the women visit each other for coffee, they go on horseback; unmarried women wear no hats at all, only married women wear bonnets."[113] An announcement from the same period by Cornelia Van Malsen, née Van de Luijster, from Michigan reads, "Most of the women and girls here go bareheaded; I wear a loose hat, as do many others."[114] The first

---

[111] Verwyst, "*Reminiscences*," 153. "The men and boys sat on one side of the church and the women and girls on the other. The women used to wear those queer Holland-fashioned dresses and some had gold earnings [earrings?]. Nearly all of them came to church in their wooden shoes."

[112] Brown, "Life story of John Tuininga." Cf. also Verbrugge, *Brieven*, 52.

[113] Stellingwerff, *Iowa Letters*, 128, Fall of 1847.

[114] A. van Malsen, *Achttal brieven mijner kinderen uit de kolonie Holland in Amerika, met eenige aanteekeningen en een nagevoegd woord* (Zwijndrecht: J. Boden, 1848), 25. For an English translation see John Yzenbaard, "'America' Letters from Holland, *Michigan History* 32 (March 1948): 59.

generation of immigrants bought modern straw hats from Chicago, and also in the villages there were plenty of customers for this item. Anna Kleis started a clothing store in the village of Zeeland in order to sell the new Chicago fashions. Her store was seen as an asset to the village.[115]

Fashion worked as a leveler, and clothes were inexpensive. The female workers in the cotton factories appeared so well dressed that nobody could tell what kind of work they did. Farmers' wives also, "who, outfitted with parasols and fans against the sun and heat, [were] dressed on the whole according to the latest Parisian fashions," a traveler commented in 1850.[116]

Renske de Jong wrote in 1894 about the simplicity and functionality of clothes in the Dakotas: "Men wear only trousers and a smock. Women wear shirts and bright dresses; no jackets, they do not have these here. The little boy has a short, flannel shirt with short sleeves, a very thin nighty, I could say (it is not exactly a dress), and socks."[117]

Since 1880, catalogues of mail order businesses brought American consumer goods within reach of every family. Twenty years later this way of shopping received an extra boost by the regulation that postal matter could be delivered free in rural areas. During the First World War, advertisements in the Dutch-language press changed from traditional dresses to American fashions.[118] After that time, external differences with the Americans were no longer conspicuous. Historian Jacob van Hinte noticed in the summer of 1921 in the Reformed Church of Paterson "especially among the girls, typically American figures."[119]

### Child and Women's Labor

During the pioneer phase, children were an almost indispensable source of income. In an environment in which little money circulated, every dollar counted. From the beginning, children between fourteen and eighteen years of age were sent out to work independently. They were too young for the heavy work of uprooting trees and walked twenty-five miles from Graafschap to Kalamazoo in order to earn cash

[115]  Ibid., *De Grondwet*, September 25, 1888.
[116]  C. Borgman, *Bezoek in de Verenigde Staten van Noord-Amerika in het jaar 1850* (Groningen: n.p., 1854), 52.
[117]  Bakker, *Zuster*, 61.
[118]  Sinke, *Dutch American Women*, 79.
[119]  Dagboek "Naar Amerika" (24 July 1921), Van Hinte Collectie, Historisch Documentatiecentrum voor het Nederlands Protestantisme, Vrije Universiteit, Amsterdam.

as manual workers or as maids. They were not altogether by themselves there; among these young workers a youth culture developed, as Rieks Bouws recalls: "What a joy and what a pleasure it was when we met a Dutch boy, as happened sometimes when someone came down the road, or if on Sundays two or more of us would get together. We felt like brothers and sisters at times like that." The mutual bond was strong, because these young people were allowed to go home only once every five months. In that way, during the first years of their life in America, they actually helped build a new existence. "Parents acquired possession of oxen and cows due to the industry and thrift of their children, who believed that they were obliged to do this for their parents, and so both worked together for the common advantage."[120]

Toward the end of the nineteenth century the Netherlands had the lowest percentage of women working for wages in Western Europe. This held for single and even more so for married women.[121] Women were not drawn to America for jobs outside the home. Actually, they had plenty of work to do. Together with their children, women made an indispensable contribution to work on the farm, even though they usually did not work in the fields, with the exception of the pioneer phase when everybody was used in clearing the land. Once the husband had plowed, the wife and children smashed the coarse clods with axes and knives. Boys just eight years old were considered fit to plow. Children had to do the weeding and harvesting and especially had to look after the vegetable garden.[122] The boys in the Heusinkveld family, who came from the Achterhoek and settled in Alto, Wisconsin, in 1855, were hired out as workers at the age of nine, and the girls when they were about twelve years old. One of them got married at the age of sixteen.[123] On the prairies, children of five were already given small jobs to do: bringing food to the workers, or delivering a message to

---

[120]  Lucas, *Dutch Immigrant Memoirs*, 1:108-09.

[121]  Corrie van Eijl, *Het werkzame verschil. Vrouwen in de slag om arbeid, 1898-1940* (Utrecht: Verloren, 1994), 369-78. Jan de Vries, *The Industrious Revolution: Consumer Behavior and the Household Economy, 1650-Present* (Cambridge: Cambridge Univ. Press, 2008), 224. In the Netherlands the percentage of women in the professions hovered around 23 percent, over against 30 percent in England, 35 in Germany, and 37 in France. Only 5 percent of married women in the Netherlands were part of the professional workforce.

[122]  Elliott West, "*Children on the Plains Frontier*," in Elliott West and Paula Petrik, eds., *Small Worlds: Children and Adolescents in America, 1850-1950* (Lawrence: Univ. Press of Kansas, 1992), 26-41.

[123]  Hannah Bruins Vandervelde, ed., *Bruins' Genealogy and Early History Heusinkveld Genealogy* (Waupun: n.p., 1941), 22, 27.

Children of the
Van Kampen
family in Shelby,
Michigan,with
horses, 1912.

Archives, Calvin
College, Grand Rapids,
Michigan.

the neighbors. Although the days were long and the work heavy, these children often had more freedom than their contemporaries in the city. In 1856, in the city of Sheboygan, children attended school on average ten months out of the year, against almost seven months in Holland County, Wisconsin.[124]

Around the turn of the century, children in the state of Oregon drove the horses while their father scattered seed from the back of the wagon, and a brother or sister followed with a harrow to plow the seed under.[125] Children were also put to work in factories or in home industries to make products such as purses or hats, especially when they were a little older when they arrived in the U.S. Laws against child labor were ineffective; only higher wages for the workers were effective in getting children out of the factories and into the schools. If the family was truly needy, the children would hand over the money they had earned. Around 1920 this attitude changed so that children were allowed to keep part of their earnings.[126] The realization that it was important for children to have time to play only grew after the First World War.

The workplace appeared to be a good school in which to learn American customs. It did not take Brechtje Allewijn long to realize that the pace of work in America was much faster than she was used to.

---

[124] Van der Pol, *Reservation*, 163: Marylin Irvin Holt, *Children of the Western Plains: The Nineteenth-Century Experience*, (Chicago: Ivan R. Dee, 2003). A. Constantine Barry, et al., *Annual Report of Superintendent of Public Instruction for 1856* (1857), 171.

[125] Vandehey, *Wooden Shoes West*, 239.

[126] Berrol, *Growing up American*, 63.

As long as her husband had work as a carpenter, she preferred to stay home:

> I do not think I would find it easy to go and work out. I am still used to the way Dutch people work, and here everything has to be done in such a hurry. For instance, they do the main laundry in just a couple of hours, hang it to dry and so on. They boil nearly all of it, and after it has been washed, it is dried immediately. Here, they wear only underwear made of woven fabrics which cleans easily, but we, with our Dutch fabric, have difficulty cleaning it that way.

But after a few months Brechtje did go housecleaning for other people. At first she took her own tools along, but soon she adopted the American working method: you do not shimmy, but sponge, you do not swab, but you mop (with a mop on a handle).[127]

In America the wages of domestic helpers were at least three times higher than in the Netherlands. In America it was also difficult to get good help. For maids who went to America, life improved noticeably. They did not need to perform heavy household work, had to scrub less, and, besides housekeeping, they did not have to work in the field. "A maid is on the same level as a daughter," Klaas Schuiling wrote in 1900.[128]

Adriana Grootemaat described her duties as a maid in 1856: "I earn sixty cents short of five guilders a week [almost two dollars], including board, and then we do not have to work nearly as hard as you do, because we do not do any outside work. People would think it a disgrace if someone would order the maid to dig up a mess of potatoes." More than 80 percent of the maids in Michigan earned between one and two dollars a day in 1895; 84 percent of them were between sixteen and twenty years old.[129] In 1910, a maid in rural South Dakota earned three dollars a week; in Chicago her salary would easily be six.[130]

---

[127] Brechtje Allewijn-Mieras from Kalamazoo to Johanna and Abraham Wisse-Westrate in Waarde, March 11, and July 13, ILC HH.

[128] Sinke, *Dutch Immigrant Women*, 100-108. ILC HH, box 27, Klaas Schuiling, 1900-1913 (p. 14 in the published letters).

[129] Adriana Grootemaat to family, August 29, 1856, ILC HH, box 27, folder 6. *Survey of 2,300 Female Domestics in Michigan Agriculture, 1895, Michigan Bureau of Labor and Industrial Statistics, Twelfth Annual Report, Year Ending February 1, 1895* (Lansing: Robert Smith., 1895), table 8, Average Wages by Week and table 4, Wages by Age. Approximately 7 percent of foreign-born girls who worked in Michigan as domestics came from the Netherlands.

[130] Bakker, *Zuster*, 308. Anna Kuijt to her uncle and Cato, Chicago, August 12, 1911, in Brinks, *Dutch American Voices*, 448.

Improvement in status depended in part on the type of work done in the region of origin. Thus, work in the dairy industry merited higher status for women than field work, because farmers' wives who made cheese and butter supplied a marketable product and in that way contributed to the prosperity of the family. Women from the province of Zeeland who had been farm workers in agriculture experienced this improvement relatively more often than farmers' wives from the province of Groningen who had made cheese and butter.[131]

To work in factories was something new; for women in the Netherlands this was still a rarity. Only 15 percent of the women who had a job worked in a branch of industry. In the nineteenth century, no more than 10 percent of married women of immigrant families worked outside the home, and as soon as the income was adequate, they withdrew from the job market. In this respect they did not differ much from their behavior in Europe.[132] In the twentieth century, girls preferred to work in a factory rather than in a household, because the wages were higher and the hours more agreeable. In 1920 the elder Cornelis Verplanke told his family in Waarde, in the province of Zeeland, that it was customary among the Dutch immigrants for the girls to work also in relatively small-scale industry: "Janna, the youngest, 26, is also at home, but three or four times a week she works in Zeeland about one mile from here in the factory of Piet Verplanke, a son of my brother Frans. She earns 20 cents an hour. Piet manages that factory. It makes handles for coffins and fabric covers and things like that. A lot of girls work in factories, which they prefer to serving as a maid, in fact most people cannot get a maid, not even when they pay well."[133] In these ethnic centers the employees often knew their bosses personally, so that the atmosphere was rather congenial.

A Dutch factory worker earned not enough to support a family of two children in the years between 1840 and 1880; for this he needed at least five hundred dollars per year. In order to keep his head above water his wife and children had to lend a hand most of the time.[134] The average annual income of a schooled Dutch-American worker's family in Grand Rapids amounted to $758 around 1910. Twenty percent

---

[131] Maritha Jansen, "Vrouwenarbeid in de landbouw in Groningen en Zeeland rond 1850: een vergelijking," (M.A. thesis, Katholieke Universiteit Nijmegen, 1984), 88.

[132] Degler, At Odds, 140.

[133] Cornelis Verplanke to family, 1920, ILC HH.

[134] Oscar Handlin, Boston Immigrants: A Study in Acculturation, rev. ed. (New York: Antheneum, 1975), 85.

of those families in fact had more than a thousand dollars at their disposal. Children on average contributed a quarter to the family's income. Of the 120 families that participated in this research only one mother worked.[135] Compared to Polish and Swedish immigrant families in the city, few Dutch rented out rooms. Only 1 percent of the family income came from boarders, while the other nationalities earned 7.5 percent of their income that way. It seemed to be an emergency measure for those families, which seldom proved to be necessary.

After 1900 it became easier for Dutch immigrant families to function. They had more family members in the area and were able to visit them for birthdays and New Year's Day. In the twentieth century, families already organized reunions, which even members from the old country attended.

## Families as Pillars

Families formed a rock-solid basis for the Dutch community and provided stability, prosperity, and continuity. The marriage market in the United States was more favorable than in the Netherlands. Men could sooner earn an income that would support a family. Women were in the minority and had a better chance to marry because there were more (young) men around. Besides, women in the United States could get a better start, since they had more opportunities to earn incomes of their own in a growing economy that demanded a greater labor force. To get married was easy and inexpensive. To be married became the norm, and the children contributed to the recovery or the improvement of the family's income. The person who during the pioneer phase was able to have the members of his family join in the work had an advantage. Creating opportunities for the next generation was, after all, the main impetus for emigration. What sense did it make to build up a farm without offspring? An increase in prosperity provided more elbow room for the present and more certainty for the future. Owning a home stabilized families and increased consumption. Patterns of eating and dressing changed only slowly.

Naturally, families were exposed to the same problems as in the Netherlands, and they were vulnerable as a result of losing supporting networks, but these were replaced by new ones. Having large families provided many building blocks for the subculture. A strong community, in turn, was able to compensate for the loss of family members. After one generation, thanks to families, relationships between grandparents

---

[135] *Immigrant Commission*, vol. 15, 499, table 33 and 504, table 39.

and grandchildren re-emerged, not necessarily within one household but certainly in the same region. If, besides parents and children, grandparents also came along, stability and permanence were strengthened even more.

Initially, not much changed in the mutual relationships among the family members. Children certainly noticed that there was also more freedom for them, especially in the countryside. They occupied a more important place in the family than in the Netherlands. Some of them left for the United States first, in order to prepare for the rest of the family to come over later. Young children also received more status by quickly picking up the language and by contributing to the family income. Only in remote areas did family members have to put up with each other, but this was determined more by geography and demographics than by ethnicity or ideology. There was no prohibition against associating with others, and they could participate in available recreational activities, insofar as (church) mores permitted.

Many American developments, such as suffrage, the temperance movement, and the beginning of the building-up of a social system, ran parallel to those in the Netherlands. Education and child care offered women opportunities for careers of their own. Their place did not change radically in comparison to the Netherlands. Raising a family remained the norm, but access to American society lay open and offered women more independence. The active participation of children and women in the production process had a twofold effect: on the one hand, participation in this process strengthened their integration and, on the other hand, it strengthened their own community. Providing services or products oriented families more toward the outside world, which, after all, had to be convinced of their abilities and value.

The ample presence of children provided an economic and social basis for community building and an agenda for the subculture. The future of the children bound the parents to America. Schools were built for them and libraries established. For their sake and by them the Dutch language was exchanged for English. Communication within the subculture was driven to a large degree by the children's interests.

# CHAPTER 6

# Work and Prosperity

At a meeting of representatives of the Dutch immigrant churches in Michigan held May 25, 1853, the president read the seventh chapter of the Bible's book of 2 Kings. The passage records the story of four lepers who, during a siege of Jerusalem, decided to go to the enemy's camp to see if they could get something to eat, since there was a great famine in the city. When they arrived at the army camp, they noticed that the enemy had fled. After having eaten their fill, and having hid part of their booty, their consciences began to act up and they returned to the city to share the good news. The church representatives applied this story to their situation: they too had found an unexpected treasure. In response, they decided to take up a collection twice a year for a fund that was to help destitute Dutch families and individuals to emigrate. The first rounds produced amounts of $127 and $253. Each congregation and every person who had contributed a minimum of $3 could suggest someone whose crossing would be financed if the lot fell on them. This form of financing in advance (the travel expenses were to be refunded) only helped a handful of people make the crossing, but it did show that the community in America felt responsible for compatriots who wished to come also. However, it soon became evident that it was much better to arrange this informally, since the cycle of the American economy determined the success rate.[1]

The "exodus" of 1846-1847 took place when the American economy had recovered from the depression that had begun a decade earlier. The same pattern could be seen in the years after the American Civil War until the mid-1870s, and in the period between 1878 and 1893, when another crisis developed that lasted four years. The last wave ran with a few fluctuations from 1900 until the beginning of the First World War.

Emigration always entails a change of employment. But such a change need not always be radical. In both countries a process of economic modernization had gotten underway, albeit it moved at a slower pace in the Netherlands. The results of this process were different for each occupational category. Agricultural workers were more likely to get ahead than independent farmers, who stood to lose more. Industrial workers and people employed in the service sector did not escape change either. Thus, in the nineteenth century roughly two-thirds of the Dutch immigrants changed jobs: agricultural workers went to work in factories, craftsmen and laborers landed jobs in agriculture. The latter category held the best chance to move ahead economically.[2] Employment opportunities provided a strong economic basis for communities, while a concentration of occupations promoted group cohesion even more. Increased prosperity strengthened the mutual bond of the first generations of Dutch immigrants, which weakened later on.[3]

---

[1]   *Classis Holland, Minutes 1848-1858* (Grand Rapids: Eerdmans, 1950), 139-40, 148-52, 165, 168-69, 177-78, 218, 255. David W. Vanderstel, "The Dutch of Grand Rapids, Michigan, 1848-1900: Immigrant Neighborhood and Community Development in a Nineteenth Century City" (Ph. D. diss., Kent State University, 1986), 493.

[2]   This held true in the case of the model colony of Holland, Michigan; cf. Gordon W. Kirk, Jr., *The Promise of American Life: Social Mobility in a Nineteenth Century Immigrant Community, Holland, Michigan 1847-1894* (Philadelphia: American Philosophical Society, 1978). Annemieke Galema, *With the Baggage of the Fatherland: Frisians to America, 1880-1914* (Detroit/Groningen: Wayne State Univ. Press and Regio Projekt Groningen, 1996), 137-40, confirms these numbers for Frisian immigrants between 1880 and 1920. Of the 295 Frisian agricultural workers, only 38 men had the same occupation in America. Of the 8 Frisian bakers, only 3 baked bread in the United States.

[3]   Joseph P. Ferrie, "The Wealth Accumulation of Antebellum European Immigrants to the U.S., 1840-1860," *Journal of Economic History* 54 (1994): 6, 25.

## Farmers

The most important attraction of America during the entire nineteenth century was the availability of farm land, which was so cheap that even limited monetary reserves or sufficient credit was sufficient to start a farm. In the village of Zeeland, the proportion of farmers to farmhands was seven to three in 1850. Ten years later 95 percent of all heads of households in agriculture had themselves registered as farmers with only 5 percent listed as farmhands.[4]

Until 1880, 80 percent of the Dutch immigrants came from the countryside. After that, city dwellers gradually assumed a larger share in immigration. As of the middle of the nineteenth century, farmers in the Netherlands began to modernize their farms. This process could be observed in the case of farmers in the province of Zeeland: they began to use fertilizer, which gradually became less expensive and of better quality, and they began to drain their land. Starting in 1860 they began to use row-cultivation machines and cutting and threshing machines. After 1880, cultivators and mowing machines took over part of the heavy work on the most progressive farms. Farmers experimented with seed improvement and crossbreeding of cattle. To that end products from abroad were used. Cheap American grain that flooded Europe after the Civil War stimulated this modernizing trend and led to an oversupply of farm workers. Low grain prices led to the testing and growing of new products, such as sugar beets.[5] The agricultural crisis in Europe of the 1880s and 1890s added to the oversupply of Dutch farmhands and encouraged their emigration. But for them the modernization in America was not completely new either; only here they became participants in the competition, instead of its victims.

Compared with other (eastern and southern) European countries, Dutch agriculture was already market-oriented and intensive. However, in the United States the emigrants arrived in a much more dynamic environment. Large nature reserves were cultivated, Indians were driven away or bought out, transport routes were built, and ever stronger ties

[4]   J.L. van Zanden, ed., *"Den Zedelijken en materiëlen toestand der arbeidende bevolking ten platten lande." Een reeks rapporten uit 1851* (Groningen: Nederlands Agronomisch-Historisch Instituut, 1991). J.L. Krabbendam, "Van Zeeland naar Zeeland. De ontwikkeling van het dorp Zeeland in Michigan, 1847-1860," *Nehalennia* 114 (September 1997): 42.

[5]   Stasja Franken, "De Transformatie van de Zeeuwse landbouw in de tweede helft van de negentiende eeuw" (Goes: Archiefdienst, 1992), 65-67. Peter R. Priester, *Geschiedenis van de Zeeuwse landbouw circa 1600-1910* ('t Goy-Houten: HES Uitgevers, 1998), 397.

were forged, first with a national and subsequently with an international market. Farmers started growing more diverse crops and switched over more and more to mixed farming.[6]

In America they got acquainted with different practices and methods. After Boudewijn Nieuwenhuise had lived in Franklin, Wisconsin, for two years, he wrote to people in Kloetinge in Zeeland November 8, 1853:

> that this year he [had] somewhat followed the American way of growing and processing [potatoes], (namely) by planting them on top of the soil, barely covered, 3 square feet apart. Some people plant them 4 feet apart from each other; they take big potatoes, cut them into 3 or 4 pieces, and then throw the whole potato into a small hole, usually in squares. When they are big enough, they drive through them with a plow straight and crosswise. As much soil as possible is piled up against every bush, and the job is finished. In the fall people come with a hoe, the piles are overturned and the potato is pulled up.

Other operations he still did the old way, "I also take as much manure to the land as I can produce." Many Americans threshed on the land and burned the straw, but he did not. He took the straw home for the cattle. "The practice of many Americans is to sow and mow as much as will grow, but they do not like to work their land much."[7]

Thirty years later, farmer Cornelis de Smit from Noord-Beveland, who made a fact-finding trip to the Dutch settlements in the Midwest in 1881, also noticed it right away: "Once you get to know the American farmer, you conclude immediately that he cares very little about tidiness on his farm, but that he is much more interested in making a lot of dollars."[8]

The Frisian Pieter de Jong, who in 1895 had found work in South Dakota for two years, determined to his surprise that in America even animals had more freedom: "The animals walk freely here all through the winter and are in the shed at night. Some farmers leave them outside and the animals themselves prefer to walk about freely instead of being stabled. The straw bales just lie in the field for the cattle to help themselves. The grain is simply threshed in the field and is left where it

---

[6]     Jon Gjerde, *The Minds of the West: Ethnocultural Evolution in the Rural Middle West, 1830-1917* (Chapel Hill: Univ. of North Carolina Press, 1997), 138.

[7]     Letter of December 4, 1855, ILC HH.

[8]     De Smit, *Naar Amerika?*, 24.

Dairy in Harrison, South Dakota.
Archives, Calvin College, Grand Rapids, Michigan.

is."[9] About the same time, the Staphorst farmer Kier Coster, who sold his farm in 1893 in order to go to Colorado, confirmed that Americans looked after their cattle poorly. His first impression during the train trip was: "Cows and horses are kept outdoors all over America, insofar as we have seen. We saw them by the hundreds. The cows are mostly red, the horses mostly brown, and the pigs black. They do not receive the fine care you give your animals. If I were a horse or a cow, I would rather live in the Netherlands....Nevertheless there are plenty among them that are good animals for slaughter. Which goes to show that there must be more nutrients in that dead grass than meets the eye."[10]

While the Dutch may have viewed the American farmers as too relaxed, on the other hand, farmers who had adjusted themselves to the new circumstances considered the Dutch farmers slow, conservative, and apt to work unnecessarily hard: "[he] works himself to death exerting himself with the hardest work, yet the American accomplishes more because he is always intent on saving time and energy." A poor American farmer would rent machines to do his threshing or haying, while a Dutch farmer would make do "with the most simple and inadequate equipment, and from ancestral habit he grabs a flail in order to work himself to death for a number of months." Apart from

9   Letter to Baaye Bakker, February 17, 1895, Bakker, *Zuster*, 83.
10   Letter of March 11, 1893, published in "Staphorsters in Noord-Amerika. Kier Costers aankomst in de nieuwe wereld 1," *'t Olde Stapperst* (December 1989): 90.

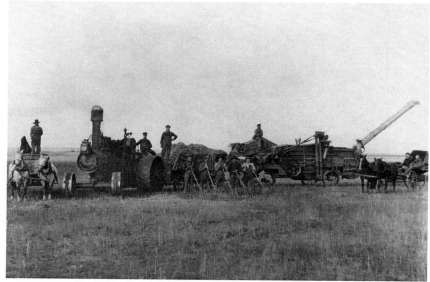

Farm machinery in Hague, North Dakota.
Archives, Calvin College, Grand Rapids, Michigan.

faster use of tools, the Dutch farmer also had to learn to fire workers who performed poorly and to confer more with merchants in order to get insight into the market.[11]

This reticence was more characteristic of the small farmer than of the agricultural entrepreneur. Farmer Bloemendaal from Gelderland sang the praises of the mowing machine that could do the work of fifteen farmhands: "I cannot praise this machine enough. It is a piece of art, a jewel! It makes the farmer rich, populates the country, it loads railroad cars with freight, makes wheat affordable, and provides the poor with bread."[12]

Recent research shows that a high measure of individualism on the part of a farmer went hand in hand with a more capitalistic and commercial approach to farming, while farmers who cherished stronger community values aimed more at a durable operation.[13] The first impressions of Dutch farmers indicate that they noticed this difference immediately, and that they did not have much use for this American individualism. Although all of them were acquainted with production for the market, their pattern of expectations was shaped

[11]  *De Wereldburger,* December 20, 1888
[12]  E.J.G. Bloemendaal, *Naar Amerika* (Arnhem: Arnhemsche Drukkerij en Uitgeverij, 1911),143.
[13]  Swierenga, "Little White Church," *Agricultural History* 71 (1997): 427-28.

by how they functioned in a community. Aside from the indispensable role of a community in the first phase of immigration (1846-1860), when mutual help was essential and produced a firm mutual bond, this sense of community remained of paramount importance, also later.

Dutch farmers in the Midwest sought to balance the pursuit of profit and the preservation of the community. Social-geographer Janel Curry discovered that three Dutch agricultural communities in Minnesota and Iowa owned the land for a century and a half, not always within their own families, but nevertheless within their own rural community. The development of land prices and the proceeds did not differ from those elsewhere in these states. By expanding the boundaries of the community, the younger generation could find employment within its own group. The Dutchmen of Hull in northwest Iowa preferred to keep their land for agricultural purposes rather than sell it to developers for a lot of money. Their response to economic pressure was to buy extra land in the vicinity of their town in order to assure the future of farms. Besides expansion of agricultural land, they also launched new economic activities to create jobs for the next generation.[14]

Clever farmers with a talent for entrepreneurship were able to combine profitability with preserving the community. Derk Bruins from Alto, Wisconsin, was such a person. Being responsible for nine children, he did not want to take excessively big risks in business. After he had inherited the farm from his father as the youngest son, he turned it into a profitable business; with the proceeds he bought adjacent land and there he placed his best farmhands, who were at the point of starting a family. He himself experimented with improvement of his cattle and with cattle feed.[15]

The cattle breeders soon noticed that they were part of a national economy. Meat and cattle prices were lower than in Europe, due to the large supply. Izaak Janse, who emigrated from the island of Walcheren to Grand Rapids in 1880, described the difficulty farmers had to get a good price for their cattle:

---

[14]   Janel M. Curry, "Dutch Reformed Worldview and Agricultural Communities in the Midwest," in Krabbendam and Wagenaar, *Dutch-American Experience*, 71-89. Cf. also Sonya Salamon, who in her book *Prairie Patrimon: Family, Farming and Community in the Midwest* (Chapel Hill: Univ. of North Carolina Press, 1992) shows the same practices among German immigrants.

[15]   Minnie Bruins Cole, "Derk Bruins Family History 1890-1915," in Hanna Bruins Vandervelde, ed., *Bruins' Genealogy and Early History Heusinkveld Genealogy* (Waupun: privately printed, 1941), 33-34.

Hay is 13 dollar per ton (2,000 pounds), meat on average is 4 cents [per pound]. A farmer cannot command more, 5 cents at the most, and thus an animal that is 3 years old can eat more hay in one winter than it is worth altogether. You ask perhaps where the animals come from. Oh, there are plenty of them. For instance, in other states, such as Texas, Dakota, Minnesota and other places. They are nothing but one big pasture where people have countless herds, where animals are counted by the thousands; for example, Dakota is a state that is as big as England, Scotland and Ireland combined. It is all pasture with few people living there as yet; these herds belong to companies, and are driven by a large number of herdsmen on horseback. These are often the roughest and most indifferent young men who care little about their own life, and who often come to blows with the wild tribes of America who are out to get their herds. It is a job that is a lot more dangerous than being a shepherd in your Nieuwland. But these fellows certainly would not feel at home tending a peaceful flock of sheep.[16]

Immigrant agricultural workers fostered hopes of owning their own farms. For them the change was the greatest: they became owners who were responsible for a business, and employers instead of employees. This transition usually happened gradually: first they worked in the city or on somebody else's farm, then they bought land, developed it, and established their own farming businesses.

The contrast between the requirements of owning a farm in the Netherlands and in America was enormous. In the Netherlands an independent renter needed the equivalent of four hundred dollars to rent a small farm of ten hectares. A farm worker needed at least four annual salaries just to get started. Such an amount was an insurmountable obstacle, since he could hardly save from his meager income.[17] In the United States, on the other hand, he could acquire just as much land for fifty dollars, although he would have to work very hard at cultivating it.

Estimates for Holland, Michigan, show that more than 90 percent of agricultural workers from 1850 had improved themselves thirty years later, 86 percent by actually becoming farmers themselves, and 6 percent by finding work in the service sector.[18]

---

[16]  Izaak Janse (Grand Rapids) to F.P. Polderdijk, Nieuw- en St. Joostland, February 17, 1886, ILC HH.

[17]  J.L. van Zanden, *The Transformation of European Agriculture in the 19th Century: The Case of the Netherlands* (VU Univ. Press, 1994).

[18]  Kirk, *Promise*, 81.

Green grocers Schut on their way to the market, ca 1900.
Archives, Calvin College, Grand Rapids, Michigan.

In Pella many of the first wave had arrived as farmers. By 1870 available land was gone, without many new economic initiatives being developed, resulting in the community becoming more and more dependent on agriculture for the next thirty years. It was not until the twentieth century that it became more economically diversified. The result was that per generation the chance for social advancement decreased. This did not make Pella attractive to new immigrants, who after 1880 escaped the agrarian crisis in the Netherlands. Even more so, for the second and third generation of farmers there was no future in Pella either, and only 28 percent of grandsons inherited farms from their grandparents.[19]

The Dutch vice-consul, N. Anslyn from Keokuk, Iowa, reported on the year 1864:

> With only very few exceptions the majority of Dutch immigrants from the Netherlands consists of day laborers and farmers, and since they are ordinarily very thrifty and hard working, they soon

[19]   Doyle, "Socio-Economic Mobility," 246, 247, and 257.

advance to the point that they buy a small piece of land, partly on credit, and often a team of horses and a wagon, which they use to work the small farms they have rented, and for the rest they haul freight. Since these people are usually very regular in making their payments, they establish a credit record. There are many people in this state who arrived here without resources, yes even with debts, who are well off now. The first requirement to succeed as an immigrant is a sound mind, courage to meet disappointments, a strong constitution to be able to cope with the climate, and a strong body to be able to do and carry out the hard work that awaits them here.[20]

Truck farmers, who found a means of support especially around Chicago, formed a category between workers and farmers; they drained the wet, and, to Americans, unattractive peat soil on the edge of Lake Calumet and used the fertile soil for intensive crop farming. Poor Dutch workers found their way to the Windy City especially after 1880. When, after having worked in the city for a while, they had gained some financial reserves, they bought a horse and wagon, rented a piece of land in the southwest, for example, in places that were first named High and Low Prairie and later Roseland and South Holland, where they grew vegetables that they themselves sold at the central market in the city. There was great demand for their products, such as potatoes, asparagus, cucumbers, cabbage, corn, melons, tomatoes, and onions. During the Civil War, Roseland earned the nickname "Onion Town" because of its vast onion fields.[21] During economic crises green vegetables especially seemed to produce stable prices.

The community of High Prairie (Roseland) formed the background of Edna Ferber's 1923 book, *So Big*, which was already turned into a movie before the book received a Pulitzer Price in 1925. In it, the Dutch community is pictured as consisting of ignorant truck farmers without culture who had no eye for the higher ideals of schoolmarm Selina Peake, but who worked brutally hard.[22]

---

[20]    *Verzameling van consulaire en andere verslagen en berichten over nijverheid, handel en scheepvaart* (The Hague: Ministerie van Landbouw, Handel en Nijverheid, 1865), 1411.

[21]    Swierenga, *Dutch Chicago*, 551-64. Marie K. Rowlands, *Down an Indian Trail in 1849: The Story of Roseland* (repr. Palos Heights: Dutch Heritage Center, 1987), 59.

[22]    It appeared in a Dutch translation under the title *Moeder's Jongen* (Amsterdam: Querido, 1924). After the first filming of 1924, two more remakes appeared in 1932 and 1953. It is possible that Ferber obtained the

In other places in America (and later in Canada), the Dutch bought up similar muck lands and, thanks to intensive cultivation, built flourishing farms. Such was also the case in Pultneyville and Eastmanville in New York, in Celeryville in Ohio, in Hudsonville and Kalamazoo in Michigan, in Highland and Munster in Indiana, and in Hollandale, Minnesota. These truck farmers were able to buy inexpensive land in swampy areas; they were not dependent on railway contracts and could employ their usually sizeable families to do the work. Families of ten children were no exception, and a baby was welcomed as "another weed puller." The truck farmers were able to sell their products on contract to the many processing factories that provided the growing population centers with durable food, but also at markets and to individual clients who had specific preferences.[23] In the region around Chicago the city expanded, and the truck farmers sold their land in the 1950s. This caused the community to move ever farther into the suburbs.

One could expect that bulb growing was also a direct transplant from the Netherlands, but the Dutch entered this sector in the U.S. relatively late. In the state of Washington a bulb industry came into being that employed more and more Dutch, especially around the town of Lynden. The founder of this sector was the Englishman George Gibbs, whose hobby was plant improvement and who proved the Dutch bulb growers wrong who claimed that he had too little experience. In 1898 a delegation of Dutch bulb farmers visited his nursery and was impressed by the possibilities. An experimental station of the American Ministry of Agriculture confirmed the excellent conditions for the bulb-growing business in America. Soon after, Dutch farmers and workers in the lumber industry came from other western states and from the West Coast to Lynden, where they established a Christian Reformed and a Reformed church as a matter of course. Although most Dutch were cattle farmers, bulb growing offered a good alternative because selling them offered cash.[24] After 1926 America closed its borders to

ingredients from her experiences as a youngster with Dutch immigrants in Kalamazoo, where she was born in a Jewish family, but especially in Appleton, Wisconsin, where she began her journalistic career. She herself claimed that it was based completely on fantasy, although carefully prepared and researched. Edna Ferber, *A Peculiar Treasure* (1938: reprint, Cleveland, The World Publishing Co., 1947), 97, 276-82.

23   David L. Zandstra, "In the City, but not of the City: Dutch Truck Farmers in the Calumet Region," in Swierenga, Sinnema, and Krabbendam, *Dutch in Urban America*, 118-27.

24   Arnold Brink, "Lynden," *Origins* 4.2 (1986): 34. Howard Spaan, "Lynden is Not Another Pella," *Origins* 12.2 (1994): 22-29.

narcissuses and other bulbs for ten years to prevent plant diseases. These restrictive measures only stimulated the emigration of Dutch bulb growers who had an important share in this flourishing industry. In the 1920s the northwest corner of the state of Washington was the scene of the first tulip festival for the promotion of that flower. As the result of a combination of the economic crisis and harsh winters some festivals in the 1930s were canceled, while others survived that period and are still being held.[25]

The prototype of the Dutch agriculturalist was the farmer in the Midwest, where the price of grain in the nineteenth century was so high that some farmers did not even practice crop rotation. In Iowa, wheat was also an important product until the 1880s, when growing corn appeared to suit the soil better. Vast wheat fields could be found farther west in the Dakotas and Minnesota. But grain was not the only product. Fruit growing seemed to bring good results in Michigan, and after the turn of the century also in California.

For most of the farmers cattle breeding was a sideline, but Frisian immigrants in Massachusetts and especially in California made it their principal livelihood. There, these immigrants modernized the dairy industry in the 1920s. Thanks to this specialization they were able to build a supportive network of relationships with a relatively small number of families.[26] They moved to the West Coast when railway connections had made this region easily accessible to immigrants. At the same time trucks made it possible to buy inexpensive land at a considerable distance from the railroads and cities and to bring perishable dairy products quickly to markets.

California appeared to be an excellent alternative to Friesland, where not enough land was available for the further expansion of cattle farms, while competition from countries such as Denmark and products such as margarine increased. In response to this, the Frisians formed cooperatives that jointly bought cattle feed and built dairy factories. They intensified the feeding patterns and the quality of their cattle and increased hay production with fertilizers and drainage.

---

[25]   Charles J. Gould, *History of the Flower Bulb Industry in Washington State* (Mount Vernon: Northwest Bulb Growers Association, 1993), 4-11,195-205. A comparable settling of bulb growers took place in Terra Ceia, North Carolina: see John Yzenbaard, "A Dutch Settlement in North Carolina," *Origins* 4.2 (1986): 40-43.

[26]   Based on the research of Trudy Vermeer Selleck, "'Land of Dreams and Profits:' Social Networks and Economic Success among Dutch Immigrants in Southern California's Dairy Industry, 1920-1960" (Ph.D. diss., Univ. of California, Riverside, 1995).

Map 10: Frisian dairy settlements in California.
Courtesy Trudy Selleck.

However, this growth was insufficient to offer everyone a livelihood. In addition, the price of land in Friesland tripled in the first two decades of the twentieth century. These Frisians sought another destination and found it in California, where they could apply their experience in cattle farming without pastures in the cattle farms around Los Angeles. This innovation created a new model for milk production, which was imitated in the entire state. Together with Portuguese, Swiss, and Danish cattle farmers they provided the fast-growing population of California with dairy products. In the meantime, as of 1920 California also attracted Dutch Americans from the Midwest for economic reasons or because of the climate.[27]

[27]   Galema, *Frisians to America*, 40-42, 60.

The high wages in this industry for experienced milkers and the capital they had brought along enabled the Frisians to establish their own farms. These farmers did not form an exclusive company but certainly did form a tight community that dominated the industry. They owned half the cows in the area around Artesia and Bellflower. Because of this, the Dutch community was able to grow to twelve thousand between 1920 and 1950.

The uniqueness of this situation did not only apply to the beginning phase, but also to the continuation of the community in spite of economic pressures. In other parts of America the rapid growth of cities had forced farmers to move to other areas and had scattered the farms. The same thing threatened to happen in southern California, but the milk-producing farmers always knew how to move jointly to an area farther away. In Artesia and Bellflower these cattle farmers made use of new legislation to obtain local autonomy. That is how they could prevent their farms to be bought one at a time by developers, which would have fragmented the community. With foresight they bought inexpensive land in areas farther away around Chino, where they moved in the 1960s when urbanization advanced farther. Only in this way were the Dutch immigrants able to participate fully in the economic modernization without losing their territorial connection. Mobility was after all one of the most attractive aspects of America.

**Risks**

People at the bottom of the ladder, such as agricultural workers, could move up, but those higher up could be disappointed. Not all immigrants prospered at farming, and some lost all they had. Of those in Holland, Michigan, who had their own farms in 1850, 16 percent had become agricultural workers and 12 percent laborers twenty years later.[28] That is how, for example, two farmers from different parts of the Netherlands experienced this development. The Groninger farmer Klaas Jans Beukma from Zuurdijk emigrated to Lafayette, Indiana, in 1835, and later moved on to Plainfield, New Jersey. In the meantime he lost his privileged position. He had emigrated especially in order to realize an ideal of freedom, which had proven to be impossible in the Netherlands because of political and economic restrictions, and to secure a better future for his children. He had a mixed farm in Groningen, and in Indiana he grew primarily vegetables and fruit because he had discovered that there was a demand. His farmhand became his business

---

[28]    Kirk, *Promise*, 78.

partner. In 1849 he moved to the East Coast, because he languished culturally in the West. After his frontier adventure he yearned for his former lifestyle. The land that he subsequently bought was much poorer than he was accustomed to, but by working it intensively and through mechanization he was nevertheless able to make a living. Via his relatives in Groningen, whom he provided with information and who came to visit him, more modern plows found their way from America to the Netherlands.[29] He used up his resources and could not be called a success as an investor.

Jannes van de Luijster from Zeeland went down in social status, relatively speaking, because his former farmhands in the Netherlands became his equals in the United States. This well-to-do gentleman farmer had a farmhand drive him in Zuid-Beveland, but in Michigan he had to drive his own horse. He did retain his influence in the church that he financed, but that did not keep his fellow church members from calling him to account when they disagreed with his decisions.[30] He invested more in the community than in his own farm and gained the recognition of the people in the area, who honored him by naming the town's central park after him. He did not die a poor man, because he gave each of his children 80 acres, which made a person a well-to-do farmer; a farm of 120 acres made the owner wealthy.[31]

Without an agricultural background, making a living in agriculture was risky. The Huijser family, who emigrated with four children from Barendrecht to Winnie in Texas, experienced this.[32] This prosperous shopkeeper sold his business in order to fulfill a boyhood dream of going to America. Via relatives in Chicago they arrived in Orange City, where they were extremely unhappy, as the eldest daughter recalled:

> It [the house] could not possibly be compared to our house in the Netherlands. No one to help Mother, to serve us or look after us children—what a change. What a different world we had entered. The customs, the language barrier, and the living standard influenced us greatly. Sometimes our parents were overwhelmed by fear and tension....How humiliating. The taunts and the

---

29  Hilde Bras, "Tussen twee werelden. De migratiemotieven van Klaas Jan Beukma (1789-1860) een Groningse pionier in Amerika" (M.A. thesis, Rijksuniversiteit Groningen, 1993), 51-53.
30  Krabbendam, "Forgotten Founding Father," 1-23.
31  Verhage, "Grandfather Remembers These," 8. De Smit, *Naar Amerika*, 51.
32  "Janet Huyser's Recollections," *Origins* 16.2 (1998): 2-10.

ridiculing by classmates. The scorn and the giggling cut through my soul. How I hated Orange City. I despised their farmers, their unmannered attitude. No culture....

But life would get even worse when father Huijser bought forty acres in Texas hoping to change them magically into a citrus orchard. He planted sugarcane, corn, and fig and orange trees, but he saw the harvest trampled time and again by loose running cows, devastated by storms, and flooded by downpours; the family survived only through work on a rice plantation. A fine of thirty-five dollars for shooting a dangerous bull was the deciding factor in abandoning the project. The family left Texas ruined but stayed in America: lack of agricultural experience, unrealistic expectations, and unanticipated setbacks ended this dream, but they remained part of the Dutch network.

Working the land required physical effort on the part of the pioneers and demanded a concerned, continuous, persistent commitment. But developing a farm also included a moral dimension. The person who wrested prosperity from the wilderness could claim rights to the land, which is why squatters who took and worked a piece of land they did not own could lay claim to it by common law. In fact, the Homestead Act of 1862 legalized and regulated this practice. The division into separate parcels that were sold to individuals left no room for communal pastures or farmland.[33] This construct threw the developer back upon his own resources and upon his voluntarily assumed relationships.

That moral and community motives were stubborn is proven by Dykstra, the editor-in-chief of the influential weekly *De Volksvriend*. Dykstra had been a part-time farmer himself in the Dakotas when he was a minister there. Up till the early 1930s he admonished farmers for putting forth too much effort at getting a reasonable price, because he found the joy of farming more important than financial gain.[34] From the perspective of taking pleasure in a farmer's life he resisted fixation on mechanization, reliance on subsidies from the federal government, and labor unions for farmers that pleaded for radical measures in the days of the Great Depression. He feared that farmers would lose their independence. With these opinions it was no wonder that he objected to Franklin D. Roosevelt's New Deal. Most of the Dutch in the West did not vote for their kinsman.

---

[33]    Vancius, *Health of the Country*, 191-208.
[34]    Dykstra, "B.D.," 130-35.

## Laborers and Wage Earners

In the cities it was more difficult than in the country to obtain an independent position. R.T. Kuiper, the Christian Reformed minister of the village of Graafschap, to the east of Holland, Michigan, thought it necessary in 1882 to temper the high expectations of being one's own boss, in his advice to potential emigrants: "But in contrast to a hundred people who have a somewhat independent position, there are a thousand who seek a subordinate position in factories, mills, and stores, or other employers."[35]

Kuiper's observation about the shift of the position of the worker from being self-employed to having a subordinate position was correct for the area he surveyed. In the preceding decade the center of gravity of the local economy in Holland had shifted from agriculture to industry. Until 1870 agriculture had been responsible for the greatest growth by developing new areas and by perfecting operational management. Between 1854 and 1874 the production of corn increased 350 percent, wheat 800 percent, and hay 1900 percent, while the population quadrupled. After this, the yield stabilized. Toward 1870, Holland had become quite accessible because of shipping connections to the west via Lake Michigan, and by railroads that ran in other directions. This caused the industrial production of raw materials (saw mills, corn mills, tanneries) to be shifted to places where clothing, saddles, wagons, furniture, and pumps were produced.[36]

The flow of Dutch emigrants to the cities after 1880 required new connections for the emigrants to find out where workers were needed in harbors, markets, or factories, and where public works were carried out. In addition, one could obtain information in cafés, hotels, and boardinghouses, or through the more official channels of immigration agencies and immigrant societies. The official reports that the Dutch consuls composed about opportunities for immigrants were often too general to be useful for an individual person.[37]

Emigration to the cities almost always entailed a change of work. This held true even for skilled trades which were much less specialized in America: carpenters had to draw plans, and glaziers also had to

---

[35]  R.T. Kuiper, *A Voice from America about America* (Grand Rapids; Eerdmans, 1970; orig. Dutch edition 1882), 67.

[36]  Kirk, *Promise*, 21-39.

[37]  John J. Dahm, Sr., "Christian Seamen's Home in Hoboken," *Origins* 6.2 (1988): 28-32.

install window frames. Mechanization made old skills economically unrewarding.[38]

The largest concentration of Dutch in one sector was in the furniture industry of Grand Rapids, Michigan. Grand Rapids found itself in a favorable location between two fast-growing population centers in the Midwest, Chicago and Detroit. Thanks to the waterways that produced hydropower, lumber could be supplied easily and the finished product could be transported elsewhere without difficulty. Machine factories supplied tools, furniture makers from the eastern states provided the knowledge and the capital for establishing this branch of industry. The city grew rapidly. In 1858 the first railway connection came to the city, which enlarged the trading area, with a greater expansion to follow ten years later when three more railroad lines were added. In 1850, 10 percent of the 2,686 inhabitants originated in the Netherlands. Until 1870 these were mainly young Dutch who sought temporary work, but who afterwards established themselves there permanently. Until 1890 the population of the city doubled every decade, and afterwards the growth continued as well.[39]

The growth began after the American Civil War. The number of people who found work in the furniture sector increased from 281 in 1870 to 2,279 ten years later, and to more than 6,000 at the end of the century. In the beginning of the 1880s a workman wrote his former boss in Zeeland that he could walk from one side of the Grand River to the other side across logs.[40] The heyday of the furniture industry in the late 1920s offered work to twelve thousand people, who together produced half the industrial output of the city.[41] Characteristic of the furniture industry of Grand Rapids was that the factories had first been shops that later in the twentieth century had merged into large factories.

The concentration of fellow countrymen in one branch of industry strengthened the network, but it could result in established Americans labeling immigrants and judging them accordingly. For

---

[38]   Brinks, *Dutch American Voices*, 265. Van Pernis, *According to Thy Heart*, 34, describes the differences in construction methods. In America, builders used different measures, used cheaper materials, and strove to standardize. For experienced workmen the transition was more difficult than for the younger ones.

[39]   Vanderstel, "Dutch."

[40]   Izaak Janse in Grand Rapids to F.P. Polderdijk in Nieuw- en St. Joosland (between 1881 and 1893), ILC HH.

[41]   Frank Edward Ranson, *The City Built on Wood: A History of the Furniture Industry in Grand Rapids, Michigan, 1850-1950* (Ann Arbor: n.p., 1955), 13, 52-53.

**Furniture factory in Grand Rapids, ca. 1900.**

Archives, Calvin College, Grand Rapids, Michigan.

instance, a journalist observed about Grand Rapids that the city had a population of "ten thousand people, and ninety thousand Dutchmen."[42] In the furniture industry the Dutch formed the largest group of immigrants and made up nearly half of the labor force.[43] Carpenters and woodworkers had excellent prospects in Grand Rapids. The Dutch formed the work force and were not the proprietors. They had a reasonable income compared to the average situation in America. In 1910 a worker earned $538 annually; this was $50 more than the average wage in America. However, they had to work hard for it. A strike in the summer of 1911 did not result in a direct improvement, in part because the law-abiding Protestant Dutch were not members of a labor union, which they considered to be an objectionable secret society. Only 2 percent of the Dutch who earned their living in industry and mining joined unions. The average worker either landed in a church community that barred union membership or he worked hard at reaching middle-class status, which resulted in him losing interest in class warfare.[44] In

---

[42]  Cited in ibid., 41.
[43]  *Reports of the Immigration Commission, Immigrants in Industries*, vol. 15 (Washington, D.C.: Government Printing Office, 1911), 470 table 5.
[44]  *Reports of Immigration Commission*, vol. 1, 419: compared with 4.6 percent

the ensuing years the standard nine-hour day was introduced and the annual income rose to $1,500 in 1920.[45] Furthermore, Grand Rapids numbered salt, copper, and shoe factories, as well as gypsum mines and flour mills, which made for a diverse economy.

The city of Grand Rapids was small enough for workers to be able to live outside the city and there to have a sideline. Izaak Janse lived a forty-minute walk from his factory. At home he had fruit trees, kept a couple of pigs and fifteen chickens, and he hoped to buy a few cows. He also harvested sufficient wheat for his own use and for sale.[46]

Three-quarters of the emigrants from the clay provinces of Zeeland and Groningen were unskilled and had to experience the transition to a factory job. Gradually the share of skilled workers in the city of Grand Rapids rose from 30 to 41 percent, while the share of the unskilled went down from 61 to 23 percent; the share of the semiskilled tripled from 4.2 to 13.8 percent between 1850 and 1900. The middle class also grew, especially the number of grocers, teachers, and ministers. In the communities one could always find a variety of occupations. There were even districts where a rich Dutch upper class lived.[47]

Paterson, New Jersey, also gained a reputation for its working-class milieu. Factories for building machinery and locomotives and for producing clothes and silk offered many employment opportunities. In this sector ample investments were made. The proximity of arrival terminals of the immigrants in Hoboken made this area attractive to immigrants who were without financial resources, because they could get work immediately without having to travel far. The silk factories attracted immigrants from Europe who had experience and who were able to make the highly valued products. Paterson enjoyed the reputation that workers had good prospects for improvement, although in reality the step from worker to entrepreneur was too wide; only a small group of 3 percent could make it.[48] Willem Woudenberg, a

---

of Germans, 9.3 of Swedes, 14.8 of Irishmen, 16.6 of Englishmen, 17.6 of Scotchmen, 39.0 of Welshmen, and 39.0 of North Italians. Pieter Stokvis, "Socialist Immigrants and the American Dream," in Krabbendam and Wagenaar, *Dutch-American Experience*, 91-101.

45    Ranson, *City*, 66-67.
46    Izaak Janse (Grand Rapids) to F.P. Polderdijk, Nieuw- en St. Joosland, March 22, 1883, ILC HH.
47    Vanderstel, "Dutch," 324-25.
48    Richard D. Margrave, "Technology Diffusion and the Transfer of Skills: Nineteenth-Century English Silk Migration to Paterson," in Philip B. Scranton, ed., *Silk City: Studies on the Patterson Silk Industry, 1860-1940* (Newark: New Jersey Historical Society, 1985), 9-34, esp. 18.

Silk factory in Paterson, New Jersey.
Archives, Calvin College, Grand Rapids, Michigan.

fifty-two-year-old man who with his wife and twelve children emigrated from Amersfoort to Paterson in 1910, did not make much headway as far as work was concerned. From a proper butcher shop in Amersfoort to a smelly silk factory was no advancement.[49] A hard twelve-hour workday that paid a weekly wage of ten to twelve dollars was the only option for someone who did not have a command of English.

In other places Dutch immigrants found work in factories as well. De Pere, Wisconsin, offered hundreds of immigrants work in iron foundries and coach builder's shops, which began to thrive in the 1870s.[50] In Pullman, the Frisian emigrant Pieter Groustra found work building railroad coaches under the supervision of a Dutch foreman. He arrived in 1881and worked thirty-three years for the same boss. He kept in close touch with Frisian colleagues, even though he noticed rather quickly that workers who had a grasp of English earned a dollar a day more.[51]

[49]   Westra, "'Fear and Hope Jostled,'" *Origins* 8 (1990): 2-15.
[50]   Vandehey, *Wooden Shoes West*, 90-91.
[51]   Annemieke Galema, "A Frisian in the American City: The Letters of Pieter Ypes Groustra and His Family from Chicago, 1881-1946," in Krabbendam and Wagenaar, *Dutch-American Experience*, 267.

## Entrepreneurs

Toward the end of the nineteenth century, the Dutch in the cities began to establish their own businesses. Jan ter Braak, from Eibergen in Gelderland, opened his own shop in 1873 in southwest Grand Rapids to make wooden shoes. Fifteen years later he owned a large factory where he produced twelve thousand pairs annually, which he sold throughout America as safety footwear for factories.[52]

The members of the First Reformed Church in Detroit worked together for contractors, printing establishments, and transport companies, before a large number of them found work in the automobile industry.[53] The most remarkable group of ethnic entrepreneurs lived in Chicago. There the small independent waste-processing collectors and carriers used their network efficiently to build up their industry.[54] Collecting garbage was tough work, but it offered a few important advantages for immigrants with few resources other than their ability to work. Garbage was ever growing in a booming city. In contrast to the inner city, which was served by the city sanitation department, the surrounding suburbs constituted a free market where people could operate independently. This way the immigrants did not run the risk of being laid off in bad economic times. With only a small investment one could buy a horse and wagon, later a truck, and begin a transport business. Most workers were comfortable with horses thanks to their practical experience in the Netherlands, and they did not need to know much English.

Thanks to churches and schools, many families were interrelated; they knew who was trustworthy, they helped each other find work, and they could rely on informal agreements. This network of 450 small Dutch family businesses had its own organization that regulated mutual relationships, rented or bought dump sites jointly, and went to war against aggressive competitors, mostly Italians or Irishmen and unwanted labor unions. In the 1950s larger businesses that were able to invest in greater mechanization came into being through marriages and takeovers, and eventually these blossomed out into an international enterprise, Waste Management. This company bought out many others, which made the Dutch prosperous.

---

[52]   Vanderstel, "Dutch," 367-68.
[53]   James Evenhuis, "Detroit's Motor City," in Swierenga, *Dutch in Urban America*, 21-22.
[54]   Swierenga, *Dutch Chicago*, 576-649.

Hekman's Cookie factory in Grand Rapids, ca. 1915.
Grand Rapids History & Special Collections Center, Archives,
Grand Rapids Public Library, Grand Rapids, Michigan.

"Dutch Chicago," a community of tens of thousands, because of its size was able to provide a counterbalance to *the* dominant center of Dutch-Americanism, Grand Rapids. The Dutch in Chicago did not let themselves be bullied by the intellectuals in Michigan, even though they did not differ much from them. With a few exceptions, they were solidly Republican. They shied away from publicly displaying their acquired prosperity, but they were in all things first and foremost "Chicagoans": energetic, enterprising, and practical. The feeling that they could be autonomous encouraged their entrepreneurial spirit.[55]

The Dutch in the old country made surprisingly little use of "their" immigrant network to find new markets in America. Conversely, only a few Dutch immigrants engaged in direct trade with the Netherlands. Only in 1903 did Dutch and American businessmen establish a Dutch-American Chamber of Commerce at the initiative of the Dutch envoy, G.A.W. Baron Gevers. They were active especially in shipping, banking, and import in America and concentrated on the East Coast.[56]

---

[55] Van Hinte observed a lack of entrepreneurial spirit among the Zeeland communities around Rochester in the state of New York, *Netherlanders in America*, 804-07. His explanation for this is a lack of religious leaders and of schools of their own, and a lower educational level.

[56] Walter H. Salzmann, *Bedrijfsleven, overhead en handelsbevordering. The Netherlands Chamber of Commerce in the United States, Inc. 1903-1987* (Ph.D. diss., Universiteit Leiden, 1994), 8-58. Hans Krabbendam, "Capital

In most Dutch settlements the retail business was in the hands of fellow countrymen. The "Hollanders" in Muskegon were a good example of the middle class that was strongly represented in this city.[57] After the first Dutch had found work in the saw mills around 1856, more compatriots settled in this city, so that in 1859 the first Reformed church opened its doors, followed by a Christian Reformed church in 1867 and other churches. Hope College students earned their tuition fees in the harbor, or in one of the more than thirty lumber yards. Two brothers, Johannes and Adriaan Mulder, opened a grocery store with the money they had first earned in a factory that produced wooden slats. Others followed in their footsteps, and until 1947 it was possible to make a long list of stores with Dutch owners: twenty-four grocers, ten butchers, two pharmacists, three grocery businesses, three shoe stores, two hardware stores, one clothing store, an insurance office, three furniture stores, three barbers, flour and food supply stores, one mill and four bakers, a store for ladies' articles, a bookstore of Henry Baker, a book bindery, a printing and publishing business, a box factory, and four physicians. Some ten Dutchmen held public office. The history of the city mentions three Dutchmen who had been mayor. In 1898 two Dutchmen had even opposed each other in the battle for this post.[58]

Store keepers in Grand Rapids and Chicago had a sizeable Dutch customer base. Especially their own medical doctors, insurance agents, and store keepers knew how to hold on to their compatriots for necessary services and their daily shopping needs. For clothes and household articles people had to go to others. Nevertheless, one or two individuals succeeded in establishing a reputation in this industry. Gerrit Roelofs emigrated from Zwolle to Grand Rapids in 1872 and found work in a business of household articles, a job similar to the one he had had in Zwolle in his father's store. He took the initiative to approach Dutch manufacturers of earthenware for samples.[59] Typically Dutch products such as chocolate (from Van Houten), cigars, and silver objects remained popular with the immigrants.

Diplomacy: Consular Activity in Amsterdam and New York, 1800-1940, in Harinck and Krabbendam, *Amsterdam-New York*, 167-81 and Krabbendam, "Consuls and Citizens," in Swierenga, *Dutch in Urban America*, 59-76.

[57] Cornelius Steketee, "Hollanders in Muskegon, 1850-97," *Michigan History* 31.4 (1947): 382-87.

[58] Benjamin H. Telman, "Hollanders in Muskegon Politics: 1872-1914," *Michigan History* 31.4 (1947): 387-92.

[59] Cora Helen Roelofs Verbrugge, *The Life of a Dutch American George Roelofs (1853-1919) of Zwolle, the Netherlands and Grand Rapids, Michigan* (n.p., privately printed 1994), 57-64.

Frans van Driele's Flour
Business in Grand
Rapids, 1876.

Archives, Calvin College,
Grand Rapids, Michigan.

In the Far West, immigrants could survive only if they combined a number of different functions. A case in point: Frank van Domelen, born in Little Chute, Wisconsin, in 1871, had already seen quite a bit of the United States when he opened a store in Banks, Washington County, Oregon. He had already lived in Nebraska and in Gaston and Greenville, Oregon, where he combined mail delivery with the manufacturing of baskets. When the railroad came to the area where he lived, he moved to Banks, where the station was built, and opened a shoemaker's shop. In the meantime he kept delivering the mail faithfully and provided violin lessons, until eventually he rented a farm. Henry Vanderhey managed the "general store" in Banks, which opened every morning at seven to supply farmers with sugar, flour, yeast, coffee, candy, fabrics, and tools and stayed open until ten o'clock in the evening. In the meantime the shopkeeper delivered groceries that had been ordered. Also, after mass on Sunday the store was open for the churchgoers who came from the surrounding area. The Catholics were willing to do much for their church, and mass was read daily. During the Prohibition years, between 1919 and 1933, many people distilled whiskey illegally to supplement their meager family incomes. Hidden among egg cartons the whiskey, which yielded about $10 per gallon, was transported to the buyers with the approval of Father McDevitt, himself a regular customer.[60]

Only 3 percent of the thousands of Dutch households in Grand Rapids could be categorized as belonging to the well-to-do class. Most entrepreneurs had a grocery business or were in street trading.[61] The most successful family was the Steketees of Grand Rapids. Father Jan Steketee, one of the leaders of the emigration from Zeeland who made the journey to west Michigan in 1847, built up a lumber business. Four of his six sons followed in his footsteps as entrepreneur: Cornelis took over his father's business, Paul started the first warehouse in Grand Rapids in 1862 (which was closed in 1998), Jan started out as a farmer but ended up as a realtor and Dutch consul, and his brother George was the first Dutch mayor of Grand Rapids. Even more impressive was the fortune of the Frisian Baptist Folkert H. Kuipers, soon known as Frank Cooper, the first one to set up a warehouse in Chicago together with a German partner, Siegel-Cooper, where Dutch immigrants easily found jobs.[62]

In the midst of the depression years of the 1930s, barber Hendrik Meijer, an immigrant from a socialist family in Hengelo, was forced to close his business because his customers had family members cut their hair in order to save money. In the meantime he had started a dairy farm and sold his milk door to door. At the same time he had arranged to put up an industrial building in Cedarville, Michigan, which he rented out. When he could not find a tenant in 1933, he took control himself and opened a grocery store.[63] The success of his undertaking was due to the cheap labor of his own family members and to the early move to self-service. He doubled the space of his store, learned from his competitors, and did whatever he could to keep prices low. He was a great believer in advertising and let himself be inspired by the new trend in supermarkets to build more stores until he could set up a chain of stores. He stayed outside the religious Dutch network but did give his enterprise a Dutch logo in the form of a typical Dutch boy with the name "Thrifty." To open his stores on Sundays went against the grain of the churchgoing Dutch and other believers, but Meijer remained unconcerned. His Dutch customers acted likewise: they bought where prices were best, throughout the week.[64]

---

[60]  Vanderhey, *Wooden Shoes West*, 98-101, 103, 107-08.
[61]  Vanderstel, "Dutch of Grand Rapids," 377.
[62]  Swierenga, *Dutch Chicago*, 663-64. Van Hinte, *Netherlanders*, 957.
[63]  Hendrik G. Meijer, *Thrifty Years: The Life of Hendrik Meijer* (Grand Rapids: Eerdmans, 1984), 99-116.
[64]  Swierenga, *Dutch Chicago*, 650.

## White Collars

Proportionally fewer Dutch worked in offices or stores than the rest of the immigrants.[65] Brochures for immigrants consistently discouraged office personnel to come to America with high expectations, because offices did not hire staff that spoke poor English. Teachers did not have easy access either to their particular field: many were hired seasonally, and in rural areas school was conducted only during the winter months.

Willem Hidde Bok, an "economic refugee" who had escaped from the creditors of his notary public practice in Helder in 1870, was an exception; thanks to his knowledge of foreign languages he found work as a translator at the office of the Western Union Telegraph Company in New York, after his efforts in business as a merchant in patents had proven to be unsuccessful. He could not find any other work, missed the support of an immigrant network, and was not able to use his European professional skills. His son Edward, who had emigrated with him as a seven-year-old boy, got acquainted with the American business world through his office jobs and built up a network of contacts that he exploited cleverly in his journalistic enterprise. Because of his persistence and sharp eye for what the public wanted to read in a growing market of specialized consumer magazines, he was able to climb to the top as editor-in-chief of the *Ladies' Home Journal* in Philadelphia, where he held sway for thirty years.

Edward Bok was an example from the second generation, who mastered the language. The generation that followed could take advantage of advanced education, which taught them business skills and trained them as service providers. This preparation enabled them to continue to climb the social ladder.[66]

Whoever received an education in America had good prospects, especially in the cities. A good example is the experience of the family of the Reverend De Beij of Chicago; the De Beijs established a new life for themselves in the city at the same time as the Bok family. In 1870 De Beij described the opportunities the city offered:

> My wife's youth has been renewed like the eagle's and she is happy. [Son] Willem intends to become a doctor. He is doing

---

[65]  Hutchinson, *Immigrants*, 244-45.
[66]  Hans Krabbendam, *The Model Man: A Life of Edward Bok, 1863-1930* (Amsterdam: Rodopi, 2001).

Wezeman Grocery Store in Grand Rapids, 1909.
Archives, Calvin College, Grand Rapids, Michigan.

well. He plans to come home in June and complete his studies in Chicago. An American professor, who does not charge us, has accepted him as a student. The other children are healthy, they learn well and among themselves speak only English. You would be surprised if you were here. Are you so afraid of the Ocean? Ah, for a cabin passenger there is nothing to it. I have forgotten how many thousands of Americans visited Europe for pleasure in 1869. You don't have to miss it for the sake of money, provided of course that you are not too much in love with it. Our financial situation also is much better here than in the Netherlands. We receive 10 % more, which really adds up. I bought $800.00 worth of homesteads, which will easily give me a profit of 25 percent. Anyone coming here with nothing can certainly make a go of it. Whoever has a lot of money can accomplish a lot. If people like you lived here, you could be rich within a few short years. It is like this, once you have grown accustomed to being here, you will find a land here of unspeakably many prospects and enjoyment. To be afraid all the time is an attitude that is simply unknown here.[67]

---

[67]    Letter from Rev. Bernardus De Beij from Chicago to P.A. Lanting in Middelstum, April 1, 1870. ILC HH.

**Evidence of progress: the metamorphosis of a farmhouse.**
Hope College Collection of the Joint Archives of Holland, Michigan.

## Prosperity

Advancement was possible for each generation. But its success depended on the economic circumstances in America, the skills acquired in the old country, ambition (some preferred a lower, steady income to a better-paid but uncertain job), and the time of arrival. However, before 1870 a greater opportunity for social advancement existed than afterwards, when land became more expensive, and the chance of a decline was smaller because labor (mostly unskilled) was worth more.[68]

Whoever took the risk to decide quickly and to develop a new territory as the first one stood to earn a high return on his investment. In newly opened areas the most fertile and the easiest accessible pieces of land were the first to be sold. The value of this land increased the fastest, and the yields were the highest. The rest of the area was developed only when the expectations for prices of the cultivated products appeared to be stable in the long run, the average proceeds increased, and the cost of transportation (by railroad) became less. Especially after the turn of the century this last factor determined half of the decisions whether to develop or not.[69]

The history of Pella, Iowa, illustrates that the rise in prosperity was greatest in the first period. The increase was nearly 13 percent annually in the years 1853-1860, while the population grew by almost

[68]   Kirk, *Promise of American Life*, 134.
[69]   Frank D. Lewis, "Farm Settlement on the Canadian Prairies, 1898 to 1911," *The Journal of Economic History* 41 (September 1981): 517-35, and "Farm Settlement with Imperfect Capital Markets: A Life-Cycle Application to Upper Canada, 1826-1851," *Canadian Journal of Economics* 24 (2001): 174-1965. The same patterns prevailed for the American prairies.

7 percent. Between 1871 and 1890 the value of people's assets increased more than 4 percent, but afterwards growth stagnated until 1925.[70] In the same time frame prosperity across the population spread more evenly, which was evident from the high level of home ownership on the part of 79 percent of the population. The average income quadrupled from $289 in 1853 to $1,183 in 1925 (corrected for inflation).[71] The Dutch succeeded in increasing their assets faster than other groups in Pella.

Many immigrants aspired to the higher status of Anglo-Americans and adjusted their conduct to promote their social climb.[72] More often this process happened unconsciously, since normal economic transactions, such as the purchase of farm equipment, resulted in changes. House interiors were already American because immigrants could not take their furniture along, at the most a feather bed. When the Reformed minister Henry Dosker arrived in Grand Rapids in June 1873 he described with excitement the delightful furniture in his spacious parsonage in a letter to his "unforgettable friend," Herman Bavinck:

> When we arrived here in Grand Rapids, a large crowd of people was waiting for us; a wagon and an omnibus stood ready to take us and as many as could be seated in it to our new home which turned out to be a large wooden structure with 10 rooms, a large brick walled cellar, a shed, 2 horses and a nice garden; the parsonage was furnished for the greater part, there were 4 tables, which one can make as large as desired—American style—5 American beds with mattresses, of which one with springs, a wash stand with cabinet and appurtenances. 24 chairs, a beautiful oven and cooking stove, a runner on the stairs, American wallpaper in the hallways, 12 beer glasses, 12 wine glasses, 12 sets of plates, and all kinds of kitchen utensils, cups, knives, forks, crystal cake plates, etc., etc.[73]

Another indication of the prosperity of the Dutch immigrant was the direction of the flow of money. Until 1887 more money flowed from

---

[70]  Doyle, "Pella," 274.
[71]  Ibid., 287, 293, 310.
[72]  Gjerde, *Mind of the West*, 230.
[73]  Henry E. Dosker to Herman Bavinck, Grand Rapids, June 2 [1873], Historisch Documentatiecentrum voor het Nederlands Protestantisme, Vrije Universiteit Amsterdam, Archives of H. Bavinck. With thanks to Dr. George Harinck.

the Netherlands to America than in the opposite direction. By way of postal money orders, amounts of up to two hundred dollars could be remitted. After 1880 this was used much more often, although small amounts were also sent in paper currency or by way of bank checks. Lack of trust in American banks and poor accessibility made the post office the most important money intermediary. The average amount from the Netherlands decreased slowly from twenty-two dollars around 1880 to less than sixteen dollars at the outbreak of the First World War. The average amounts that came from America per postal order was just below twelve dollars. After 1888 the direction of the money flow was reversed, when the Netherlands received more money on balance from America than it sent. In the first decades of the twentieth century, this increased to five times the volume of the total sums the Dutch sent to America. This was the result of the rise in prosperity on the part of the immigrants and of repayment of loans for the journey. The Dutch transferred more than two million dollars to America between 1870 and 1920, while their countrymen sent back six million. Thus, the stream of money between the Netherlands and America kept pace with the general trend.[74]

A well-informed weekly reported how the prosperity in America made it possible for many people without means to pay for the ocean voyage, "...that relatives and friends who already went to America earlier and did very well, were able to buy free passage for their next of kin, and have them come over."[75] This financing in advance also contributed to the image that America was the fountain of prosperity.

## Advancement

The American economy offered Dutch immigrants sufficient opportunities to get jobs. The best chances were found in agriculture, especially in the nineteenth century. There, people of little means could build up their own businesses with grit and determination. In the cities there were, besides a great variety of unskilled work, also concentrations

[74]  These surveys appeared annually in series whose name changed after the change of a head of state and the description of the service: *Verslagen aan de Koning betrekkelijk den Dienst der Posterijen, der Rijks-Postspaarbank en der Telegrafen in Nederland* (1878-1892), *...aan de Koningin-Weduwe/Koningin betrekkelijk den Dienst der Posterijen en der Telegraphie in Nederland* (1893-1904), and *Verslag aan de Koningin betrekkelijk den Dienst der Posterijen, der Telegrafie en der Telefonie in Nederland* (1905-1919). *Reports of the Immigration Commission*, vol. 37, 275-76, 280.

[75]  *De Wereldburger*, May 17, 1888.

in certain sectors. This combination bound the communities closer together because it provided contacts for newcomers. At the same time this labor situation established a connection between the community and American structures: many learned the tricks of the trade from Americans and adjusted to their way of working. Labor conflicts were not used to force changes, because only 2 percent of the Dutch workers joined a union. In between the farmers and workers and a few employers a growing middle group existed: people who with their stores created a place of their own. The second generation profited from the growing educational opportunities to find work in all kinds of service-related occupations. The later an immigrant arrived in the city of Grand Rapids, the greater the chance that he would stay. Of the Dutch who lived in the city in 1850 only a quarter could be located ten years later, while half of those living there in 1880 still lived there twenty years later, especially skilled workers. Better jobs made for a stronger community.[76]

The chances for advancement diminished somewhat but were still considerable compared to the stagnating economy in the old country. Especially those who arrived in America with useful skills, such as in construction, were able to secure fast economic progress for themselves. Work that did not depend on physical strength produced more riches in the long run. The agricultural workers reached their (lower) financial peak earlier.[77] The time of arrival, concentration in a few sectors besides dispersion across cities and villages, educational level, and moderate mobility contributed to a prosperous community of Dutch immigrants.

[76]   *Reports of the Immigration Commission.* vol 1, *Summary,* 419: The percentage of Dutch in industry and mines was the lowest compared to other Europeans: Germans 4.6 percent, Swedes 9.3 percent, English 16.6 percent, and North Italians 39.8 percent. Vanderstel, "Dutch," 415.

[77]   Ferrie, "Wealth Accumulation," *Journal of Economic History* 54 (1994): 15, 27.

# CHAPTER 7

# Transfer: Language and Education

Indispensable for establishing and maintaining a subculture was a set of communication channels among the members mutually, both with the world they had left and with the new environment that surrounded them. The primary means of communication was the Dutch language, which the immigrants spoke among themselves, through which they maintained contact with their relatives in the homeland, and which was used in the newspapers that enterprising compatriots published. Education was the preeminent sphere through which identity was transferred to the next generation. The pragmatic use of the Dutch language and an alternative education system contributed to a new Dutch-American identity.

## Which Language?

Most immigrants from the Netherlands who landed in New York did not speak standard Dutch, but a dialect.[1] Only well-educated

[1] Jaap van Marle and Caroline Smits, "De ontwikkeling van het Amerikaans-Nederlands: een schets," in J.B. Berns and J. van Marle, eds., *Overzees*

emigrants used standard Dutch, and they were also the ones who were able to express themselves sooner and more easily in English. Toward the end of the nineteenth century, the standard language had penetrated much farther into the Netherlands at the expense of dialects. Emigrants left with, at the most, a list of Dutch-English words for practical use to conduct business, buy food, look for work, and find a place to live. A popular manual "to learn to read, write and speak English in a very short time without a teacher," was *De Vlugge Engelschman*. In barely one hundred pages the book presented English as a simple language of which only the pronunciation was difficult. The reader was served up rows of nouns and verbs in a simple phonetic script with a few sample sentences that conveyed practical travel information and some features about American society. In this way the traveler learned right away something about American railroads with the pronunciation exercise: "In emèr'ikee theer aar oon-li toe klaasses."[2]

In the nineteenth century hardly anyone had a command of written English. This ability was so time consuming that "to write an English letter" became an expression for taking a nap.[3] Within the homogeneous and stable Dutch settlements, new arrivals were able to manage with Dutch for daily use until the Second World War, since there were enough go-betweens to translate for them. But the Dutch language in the settlements in America underwent a development of its own. Improvising conversations with neighbors who spoke a different language led, as a result of the dominance of English, to an American variant of the Dutch language containing English elements and parts of various dialects. None of the Dutch dialects could develop into the dominant language. Thus, an American variant of the Dutch could function as the *lingua franca*. This blend was spoken by people who wanted to hold fast to Dutch. Immigrants who wanted to transition quickly to English, but whose education was too limited, invented "Yankee Dutch," which used English words with Dutch grammar and phonology. These speakers thought that they spoke real English and

*Nederlands* (Amsterdam: Meertens Instituut, 2000), 63-83.

2    (Kampen: Ph. Zalsman, 1910), 90. Published since 1863, it was five times reprinted. Every language group had instructional methods like this; see Van Pernis, *According to Thy Heart*, 30. The first manual of H. Picard, *The Little American. Handleiding om in korten tijd zoo veel van de Engelsche taal te leeren als noodig is, om zich verstaanbaar uit te drukken* (Amsterdam: Hoogkamer, 1847), saw its fourth printing in 1854.

3    A.J. Barnouw, *Monthly Letters on the Culture and History of the Netherlands* (Assen: Van Gorcum, 1969), 5.

understood America. This resulted in all kinds of misunderstandings, which the more educated poked fun at. In everyday life "Yankee Dutch" functioned next to English and Dutch as a spoken language.[4]

The first generation used its own dialect, certainly in the home. Language and pronunciation betrayed region, social status, and occupation.[5] Even though immigrants might have a preference for people from the same area who spoke a recognizable dialect, their community obviously also included those from areas where a different dialect was spoken. To facilitate social intercourse, they had to choose between standard Dutch and English as the common language. Jacob den Herder, a pioneer from Zeeland, Michigan, recalled that his aged mother was only able to speak the dialect of the province of Zeeland, and for that reason had difficulty understanding her neighbor lady from the province of Drenthe. This confusion of tongues promoted, according to Den Herder, the use of English to bridge regional differences, but in the meantime standard Dutch continued to be used as well, especially because it had more prestige than a dialect. Dialects from the province of Zeeland were dominant in the village of Zeeland but did not monopolize everyday speech because the immigrants who had come from the province of Zeeland came from areas with very different dialects. Moreover, each immigrant village, such as Holland, had a regional function for the Dutch living in the area, so that in the course of the century a standard language, American style, developed.[6]

The regional Frisian language also had to make room for English because of its low domestic status and the lack of support by institutions, such as churches and societies. In addition, Frisian was a spoken, not a written, language. Only when Frisians took advantage of their numeric majority in a community did Frisian, as a language, stand a chance. This situation presented itself only in Friesland, Wisconsin. After the first pioneers had resold their farms around 1900, Frisians decided consciously to maintain their communal identity and their language.[7]

---

[4]    Dirk Nieland recorded this spoken language, which disappeared around 1910, in 'n Fonnie Bisnis (Grand Rapids: Eerdmans, 1929).

[5]    Hans Knippenberg and Ben de Pater, De eenwording van Nederland. Schaalvergroting en integratie sinds 1800, 3rd ed. (Nijmegen: SUN, 1992), 169-77.

[6]    Lucas, Dutch Immigrant Memoirs, 1:215. Jaap van Marle, "Waarom er geen Amerikaans Zeeuws bestaat," Nehalennia 114 (1997): 47-56.

[7]    Jaap van Marle, "Het Fries in Amerika," Philologica Frisica (Ljouwert [Leeuwarden]: Fryske Akademy, 2000), 164-79.

The mentality of the immigrants determined the speed with which English replaced Dutch or a dialect. The "better citizens" who settled in Iowa had prepared themselves for their new environment by learning English while still in the Netherlands. Besides, immigrant leader Scholte was a proponent of a swift transition to English.[8] The later immigrants did not wish to give up Dutch and therefore chose a colony where they were able to continue their Dutch way of life. In stable and fairly isolated Pella, Dutch remained in use until after the Second World War. The attachment to Dutch was so strong that this language survived the curtailing of foreign languages during the First World War. Americanization promoted English to protect national security and discouraged the use of German and the related Dutch language. In 1919 the congregations in Iowa reversed the language of their worship services back to Dutch. While the Reformed Church, in comparably isolated places in Wisconsin, changed between 1925 and 1938 to English worship services, Pella continued to use Dutch until the 1950s. It was not until a shortage of Dutch-speaking ministers arose and the postwar immigrants quickly adjusted to English that Dutch disappeared in public, although at home it continued to be used until the end of the 1980s.[9]

A strong desire to cling to one's own identity put the brakes on the use of English but did not resist its influence. Even older people who lived in the privacy of their own family did not escape borrowing words from English. Cornelia Polder, who moved with her husband and two daughters from Loosduinen to Los Angeles in 1914 at the age of fifty-six to join her adult children, continued to speak Dutch the rest of her life. She adopted only a few words from English for daily use, such as paper, store, driver, Krismis, dress, zwemmingpoel, dinner, supper, gasoline, and money.[10]

[8]    English lessons: in 1848 prospective emigrant Jan Hospers of Hoogblokland read regularly in an English Bible in preparation for his departure and received English lessons every week from teacher H. Picard, who was, however, better at reading than speaking it. Stellingwerff, Iowa *Letters*, 131 and 192. Jan Hospers wrote in September 1848 from the Netherlands in English: "When I shall be in Pella, I shall always speak English, and at this manner I shall learn very well" (Hospers letter 48), Philip E. Webber, "Language and the Church: Case Studies from Pella, Iowa," in *The Dutch and Their Faith* (Holland: Joint Archives, 1991), 65-69.

[9]    Janice Hildebrand, ed., *The Heart of Sheboygan County: Sheboygan Falls, Plymouth, Lima and Lyndon Townships* (Curtis Media Corp., 1992), 18-21.

[10]   Letters of Cornelia Mulder to Cor and Anton van der Baan, January 11, 1919, December 16, 1930, August 25, 1931, March 10, 1941, ILC HH.

The second generation learned English either formally in school or informally at work, which put both languages on an equal footing. In the next phase, Dutch lost ground and fell into disuse until only words such as *vies* (dirty), *flauw* (bland), and the *dominie* (minister) were still used. The generation that retired in the 1960s had still learned Dutch at home but over the years had lost the proper sentence structure. In spoken Dutch it was not so much English nouns and verbs that were adopted, but especially interjections such as "You know," and "see," and conjunctions such as "but" and "and." Linguists observed that Dutch-speaking people borrowed surprisingly few nouns from English compared to other immigrant groups, such as the Swedes, Norwegians, and the French. From this they concluded that Dutch immigrants put forth a real effort to keep their own language pure by avoiding borrowed words, but that they were not able to get away from the influence of the manner of speech, which explains the remarkable number of English interjections.[11] Immigrants chose to use Dutch, English, or a mixture for specific reasons; for instance, in order not to lose contact with grandparents, to distinguish themselves from others (the "English"), or simply to reduce the difference with others. Thus, it could happen that in a few isolated places immigrants of the fourth generation still had some command of the Dutch language, even though it was not perfect. In their youth these speakers often had had a very close relationship with the older generation, which had stimulated their curiosity of Dutch. With that, they formed an exception to the rule that an original language in a foreign environment disappears after three generations.[12]

All these possibilities show that language use underwent a development that seems to have gone too slowly to be noticed by the parties involved, but which inevitably led to full adoption of English. The composition of the colony determined to a large extent the pace of change. The most important factors were the size and concentration of the community and its isolation. The larger the group, the stronger the position of Dutch; the farther removed from other groups, the stronger

[11]  Jaap van Marle and Caroline Smits, "Deviant Patterns of Lexical Transfer: English-Origin Words in American Dutch," in Jetske Klatter-Folmer and Sjaak Kroon, eds., *Dutch Overseas Studies in Maintenance and Loss of Dutch as an Immigrant Language* (Tilburg: Tilburg Univ. Press, 1997), 255-72. In 1966, 3.7 percent of words used by Dutch-speaking people in the Midwest consisted of words borrowed from English, especially "yes and "no," interjections such as "you know," and nouns.

[12]  Philip E. Webber, *Pella Dutch: The Portrait of Language and Its Use in One of Iowa's Ethnic Communities* (Ames: Iowa State Univ., 1988), 74-76.

their own language. For that reason the transition to English began in the cities. The loss of local autonomy after 1950 signaled the end of the old language in the rural areas as well.

## Function of the Dutch in Various Spheres

The strong position of the family in the Dutch subculture increased the need for the use of Dutch, especially when few marriages with foreigners took place. A stimulus for Dutch was the presence of grandparents who wished to be able to talk with their grandchildren. Wherever three generations lived within visiting distance, Dutch was needed longer, but even then the chance of success was greatest when it took place in a homogeneous community. In a place that was surrounded by other nationalities, the will to retain Dutch was certainly present but insufficient to have the younger people also speak real Dutch. The older generation did try to learn English and was proud of its progress but remained trapped in the first phase. Thus, Dirk and Cornelia Polder wrote to the Netherlands from California on October 25, 1914: "This evening I was quite proud that I was able to respond in English to the 'Good evening' greeting of two Japanese, and in the morning to offer a morning greeting to various people, and during the day to say 'koebai' [goodbye], and to know that it is English." A few years later these older immigrants had made little progress in spite of the efforts of their children to pass on at home the lessons they had learned in school. The children tried to teach the grandchildren some basic Dutch. They kept it up for ten years. One son decided intentionally to teach his children only English, to the annoyance of the grandparents who were not able to converse with them. Of the grandchildren who were born toward the end of the 1920s, no one spoke Dutch anymore.[13]

Access to learning English was more difficult for women than for men, and as educators of their children they were especially responsible for teaching the children the old language. Statistics from 1910 reveal that only 34 percent of the Dutch immigrant women who were older than fourteen mastered English, over against 80 percent of the men. On the one hand, these women had an interest in maintaining Dutch, while on the other hand they very much encouraged their children to learn English, which would help them get ahead in life. After the community had shifted to English, it was of all people men who cultivated Dutch as a component of their male culture. They spoke the old language

[13]  Polderbrieven, December 29, 1917; May 21, 1920; May 19, 1928; and January 13, 1935. ILC HH.

at work, and especially at the informal breakfast meetings that they arranged after the Second World War.[14]

After 1880, the waves of immigration brought ever more people from cities who spoke standard Dutch and elbowed out the use of dialects. Also, the need to maintain contact with the Netherlands by way of letters strengthened standard Dutch.

Izaak Janse of Grand Rapids, an immigrant from the province of Zeeland, saw to it that his children attended school until the age of fourteen and had them take private tutoring in Dutch, which cost him one hundred dollars per season. Thus, his children were able to keep in touch with relatives in the Netherlands. Until 1916, parents taught their children to write in Dutch at home. What is more, they were able to use the linguistic methods publishers in Grand Rapids and Holland, Michigan, produced until 1944.[15]

Until 1900 an article written in standard Dutch would reach the majority of the Dutch in America. Even though in everyday life English replaced Dutch more and more, the latter proved to have a long life nevertheless, witness the publication of *De Wachter*, a weekly (biweekly after 1967) publication of the Christian Reformed Church that began in 1868 and remained in existence for 118 years until 1985. The *Pella Weekblad* finally disappeared in 1942 because there were no qualified typesetters left who could lay out a paper in Dutch. In Orange City the newspaper *De Volksvriend*, which for decades had served as the clearing house for all kinds of information for Dutch communities, kept publishing in the old language until 1951. At that time the local Dutch church services of the Reformed Church (1952) had also ceased; those of the Christian Reformed Church followed three years later.[16]

14    Jaap van Marle, "The Acculturation of Dutch Immigrants in the USA: A Linguist's View," in Richard H. Harms, ed., *The Dutch Adapting in North America: Papers Presented at the Thirteenth Biennial Conference for the Association for the Advancement of Dutch-American Studies* (Grand Rapids: Calvin College, 2001), 22. Sinke, *Dutch Immigrant Women*, 183-85.

15    Izaak Janse (Grand Rapids) to F.P. Polderdijk, Nieuw- en St. Joosland, January 25, 1905, ILC HH. Frank Verbrugge, ed., *Brieven uit het verleden/ Letters from the Past* (Minneapolis: Dept. of Printing and Graphic Arts of the Univ. of Minnesota, 1981), 220. Herman J. DeVries, Jr., "Henry Van Andel: Dutch Grammar Books and the Language Problem," in Robert P. Swierenga, Jack Nyenhuis and Nella Kennedy, eds., *Dutch American Arts and Letters in Historical Perspective* (Holland, Mich.: Van Raalte Press, 2008), 81-92.

16    Gerald F. De Jong, "Four Generations of a Dutch American Community," in Herman Ganzevoort and Mark Boekelman, eds., *Dutch Immigration in North America* (Toronto: Multicultural Society of Ontario, 1983), 230-31.

In the homogeneous communities in Wisconsin with Roman Catholic people from Brabant, little standard Dutch was spoken. The residents of Little Chute and Hollandtown did not need a bridging language because they spoke the same dialect. Standard Dutch was not used in their church services, because mass and the hymns were in Latin. Moreover, the national leadership of the Catholic Church stimulated the use of English for the promotion of the unity of the church. The ease with which Catholics entered into marriage with non-Dutch speakers meant a further erosion of Dutch.

Initially only the Protestant churches promoted the retention of Dutch. The birth of the Christian Reformed Church in 1857 strengthened the use of Dutch through a combination of factors based on principle and practice. After all, Dutch was, simultaneously, both symbol and instrument in the battle against Anglo-Saxon ideas and practices in the church. The old language received an extra boost from the fact that the CRC remained dependent for quite some time on ministers from the Netherlands. In 1915 only 17 of the 223 CRC congregations conducted services in English; in 1929 the majority of the services were in English: 1,143 against 912, and in 1943 only one-fifth of the services in Iowa, where conditions for Dutch were most favorable, were conducted in the old mother tongue.[17] As a result, new waves of immigrants preferred the CRC just because it kept up the connection with the Netherlands.[18]

The second generation determined which language would dominate; its loss of proficiency in speaking correct Dutch discouraged its use and caused a generation gap, since for these people Dutch was no longer a means of communication but a sign of conservatism. The first generation attached a moral condemnation to the use of English, as Christian Reformed minister J.R. Brink observed when in 1919 he heard a mother reprimand her child with the words, "Shame on you for speaking English, and that on Sunday!"[19] English lacked the Dutch

[17] Stob, *Summoning Up Remembrance*, 29. Walter Lagerwey, "Americanization and Language Conflict," *Origins* 17.1 (1999): 44-48. Ralph Bronkema, "The Christian Reformed Church in Iowa" (unpublished report, 1943), 43, in Bronkema Papers, Heritage Hall, box 1, folder 4. Annually CRC churches conducted 4,472 services in Iowa: 3,529 in English, 919 in Dutch, and 24 in German.

[18] L.J. Hulst, *Drie-en-zestig jaren prediker* (Kampen: Kok, 1913), 152-54. See James D. Bratt, "Lammert J. Hulst: The Pastor as Leader in an Immigrant Community," in Krabbendam and Wagenaar, *Dutch-American Experience*, 209-21.

[19] John Knight, *Echoes of Mercy, Whispers of Love: A Century of Community Outreach by the Christian Reformed Churches in the Greater Grand Rapids Area* (Grand Rapids: Grand Rapids Area Ministries, 1989), 17.

nuances for authority relations. The new language suggested more equality because the distinction between the informal and the formal "you" disappeared.[20] The decision of the Christian Reformed Church to begin the work of evangelism in the cities hastened the use of English, because outsiders could be reached only in that language.

The same motive, to attract newcomers to the church, was the underlying reason for the remarkable substitution of standard Dutch for German in the Christian Reformed Ostfrisian congregations in Iowa and Minnesota toward the end of the nineteenth century. There were two more reasons for this noteworthy reversal. The first was that in Germany itself Frisian was replaced by German (and ministers for the American Ostfrisians often came from Germany), and the second, more pragmatic reason was the fact that many more German than Dutch immigrants entered the country. Standard Dutch gradually made room for German, to be replaced by English in the 1930s.[21]

Even conservative church leaders in the nineteen thirties began to realize that without a countermove Dutch would disappear soon. They pleaded to retain the language in the schools in order not to lose contact with the Netherlands. The fate of Dutch was in the hands of the schools.

## The "Dutch" or Christian School

Dutch immigrants had three reasons to establish their own schools: to learn basic skills in order to be able to function in America, to maintain Dutch as long as it was meaningful, and to offer ideological training. Education played a double role in America in molding the Dutch subculture. At first, education strengthened the cohesion of the ethnic group, but later it undermined it.

The move west made parents themselves responsible for the education of their children, because the frontier still lacked schools. Thus, immigrants could educate their children in their own language. After the pioneer phase the quality requirements became stricter, which led to a consolidation of schools; this meant that the direct influence of the parents decreased. In thinly populated areas continued education actually was a luxury anyway. In the Far West, which was populated around 1900, the availability of education was so limited that Frisians in the Dakotas were still not able to speak English thirty-four years

[20]  Sinke, *Dutch Immigrant Women*, 181.
[21]  Herbert J. Brinks, "Ostfrisians in Two Worlds," in De Klerk and De Ridder, *Perpectives*, 22-29.

after their arrival.[22] Dutch was spoken there for want of something better, but it was not a deliberate choice.

However, in populous communities people could make this choice. Krijn Goudzwaard, who in 1866, at the age of thirty-four, had immigrated with his wife and five children from Poortvliet to Grand Rapids, made such a choice. He took his children out of the English school so that they could learn to read good Dutch, something which he reported proudly to his family in the Netherlands: "Kornelis is the eldest of the three. He has attended the [Dutch] school now for four weeks and already has begun to read the Bible, but you have to know that he is a very quick learner. He was not able to read a word of Dutch, but now he reads exceptionally well without hesitation." This mastering of the language also had a practical benefit, because his home functioned as a way station for newly arrived relatives.[23] In his old age he wrote about the state of affairs in 1898:

> ...we have many acquaintances here including the ones we came to know in the 32 years that we have lived here; there are some twenty thousand Dutchmen in this city...everything is in English here. We do have Dutch schools. They are established by congregations in order to get the Dutch language and sound biblical principles firmly into the children's heads. We also have a Dutch Academy in this city with five or six professors and more than 50 students. Their studies are in English as well as in Dutch, and we have 15 or 16 congregations where Dutch is preached, and also three congregations of Dutch people where the preaching is in English, and those congregations are not small....As far as we are concerned, we speak Dutch and our boys also; the latter are also able to read the Dutch Bible, but they cannot write letters in Dutch because they do not know how to spell it.[24]

Education was a crucial theme in American politics of the nineteenth century. Especially with immigrants in mind, schools were used as instruments to teach desired political behavior (as American citizens), and an economic mindset (functioning in a free-market economy), and to discourage undesirable isolation. Immigrant groups had different ideas about the importance of schooling. Italian immigrants were more interested in practical training than in academic

---

22   Pake in Bakker, *Zuster*, 377.
23   November 30, 1873, ILC HH.
24   March 15, 1898, ILC HH.

Lucas Public school, Michigan, 1908.
Archives, Calvin College, Grand Rapids, Michigan.

learning, and education for girls was considered unnecessary. This held for most of the south and east Europeans. Also, the popularity of return migration determined how people looked at education. Ethnic groups such as the Greeks and Italians, who intended to work only a few years in the United States in order to start businesses or farms back in their own countries with the money they had earned, saw the time spent on education as loss of income for their children. The setting of the Dutch immigration was different. The Dutch came in order to stay, and in addition were used to a proper and elaborate educational system. If the income of the children was necessary to support the family, education was postponed, or the mother had to work instead of the children. In general, the prosperity of the Dutch rose fast enough to be able to pay for education. Mutual assistance prevented economic setbacks from leading to a lack of education.[25]

The strong orientation on the future of the children as motivation for emigration encouraged schooling. This was evident from the arrangements already made before leaving. Before departing, the emigrant societies made agreements to build a school "so that after having arrived the children could be kept busy as soon as possible," as the Utrecht bylaws promised. According to these bylaws, homes for a teacher and a doctor would have to be built quickly, which shows that the provision as such was more important than a specific Christian interpretation of education. The board stated explicitly that it left each family free to decide how to educate its children. The bylaws of Zeeland

[25] Selma Cantor Berrol, *Growing Up American: Immigrant Children in America, Then and Now* (New York: Twayne, 1995), 31-59.

were more specific by pointing out the lack of religious freedom as the cause for emigration, but they established more practical matters instead of matters of principle. The board was to provide teachers "both in the Dutch as well as in the English language," who would be paid from the general fund and contributions from parents.[26] As early as 1849, one of the two Americans in the village of Holland, postal agent and shopkeeper Henry Post, hired Elvira Langdon, a British "schoolmarm," to teach children to speak English.[27] She did this in the orphanage, which proved to be superfluous when it appeared that orphans were taken in by other families in the community. Societies on the East Coast of the United States paid her salary.

Initially, church and school overlapped each other: during the pioneer phase the church building was used as a school and vice versa. The first teachers had come with the group of emigrants or followed soon after. In America, immigrants received the freedom to design "public" education that suited their own taste. In the village of Zeeland Robbertus de Bruyn provided sound Christian education according to expectation: "Neither the Bible nor religion were banned from our school, nor ignored under the faithful leadership of the esteemed teacher Robbertus M. de Bruyn; but also, at the same time, not in such a way that day after day the school was a catechism class, but the spirit and character of religion was always present."[28] These reassuring words spoken at the fiftieth anniversary of Zeeland in 1897 not only served as a description of education, but also as a plea for the public school, which at that time was beginning to receive competition from Christian schools.

The citizens of Pella wanted the same combination of Christian instruction and training in English. There James Muntingh and Isaac Overkamp, both experienced teachers (the first one had been head of a teachers' training school and the second one mastered English), started a similar program replete with Christian elements as a result of which no need was felt for a separate Christian school.

In 1857 Albertus Van Raalte founded the first Christian school in Holland, Michigan. In the years that followed he campaigned for similar initiatives to get off the ground in other settlements. These efforts foundered after five years because the difference with the public

---

[26]   See the rules of the original emigration associations of Zeeland (art. 9 and 13) and Utrecht (14 and 17). Van Raalte had made no provisions beforehand regarding the arrangement of education.

[27]   Lucas, *Dutch Immigrant* Memoirs, 1:395.

[28]   Ibid., 1:214.

school, as far as both content and pedagogy were concerned, was too insignificant. The most important impetus for explicitly Christian grade schools next to the public school was the split of the True Holland Reformed Church (the later CRC) from the RCA in 1857. The first minister of this new denomination had himself been a teacher in a clandestine Christian school in the Netherlands, and he pushed for their own Christian school. The most important reason for organizing their own church was the desire to retain the orthodox-church style as it had developed in the Netherlands. This orthodoxy could be passed on only in Dutch, because it assumed a close connection between school, church, and family. This increased the value of Dutch. The fear of foreign influences that might penetrate into the "True Church" via the English language heightened the pressure to maintain Dutch. After all, the next generation had to be tied closely to family and church.

The first Dutch school in Grand Rapids opened its doors in 1855. Adriaan Pleune gave lessons in the Second Reformed Church (the first Dutch-language church in the city) for a whole year, and not just for a few months as was done in the "Colony." Less than two years later the school joined the group that left the RCA for the CRC. In the beginning phase, the Dutch churches in Chicago also established their own schools, the Reformed in 1866 and the Christian Reformed in 1871. In the cities the lifestyle of Dutch immigrants came under heavy pressure, and the public school was stripped of its Protestant-Christian character sooner, which moved the immigrants to establish their own schools earlier.[29] However, these parochial schools went downhill fairly quickly because the negative arguments were not strong enough to maintain an alternate educational system. Therefore the Christian Reformed Synod declared in 1873 that church councils ought to put forth more efforts in starting Christian schools. Initially, this movement had little success because many new immigrants did not earn enough money to help pay for a parallel educational system. Besides, they did not see a compelling reason for an alternate school as long as the public school showed no hostility toward the Christian faith. In addition to reading, writing, and arithmetic, children learned psalm verses and biblical history. Only in Grand Rapids, which became more and more the center of the CRC and where there was much more diversity than in the agrarian communities surrounding it, were the means and motives for setting up parallel schools adequate. In the summer of 1873, W.H. de Lange received a contract from the church council of the True Reformed Church of

---

[29]   Swierenga, *Dutch Chicago*, 353.

Grand Rapids to teach a hundred children how to learn to read and write Dutch for $10 per week, five days from 9 in the morning until 4 in the afternoon. It was no easy task, judging from his sigh: "Even so these 'Yankees' are uncivilized rascals and not easy to control."[30]

The pressure of English and changes in the community increased the need for Dutch grade schools. This held true especially in the cities. English was added to the schedule to enable the children to function in their surroundings, but Dutch did not disappear as long as new immigrants came. When the immigration door was nearly closed after the emigration laws of 1921 and 1924 were enacted, and the economic climate also worsened in the 1930s, the necessity to learn Dutch disappeared.[31]

Until 1890, people's main reason for establishing their own Christian schools was to retain the religious Dutch character. Not much attention was paid to the development of educational methods, as long as the Bible and the catechism were read and learned, and the teachers set an example by living a Christian lifestyle. This defensive objective resulted in the Dutch language getting a central place, because transferring cultural practices could best be done in the old language. Until that time Christian schools were therefore called "Dutch Schools."[32] After 1890, Protestant immigrants who, having been influenced by the ideas of Abraham Kuyper, believed in a cultural offensive, streamed into America *en masse*. They were motivated to strike a note of their own and promoted the use of English, because they realized that without knowledge of that language they could not make an impact upon the culture. After 1930 this movement again changed education into a defensive instrument against modernizing influences from the outside. The Christian school played a prominent role in this because in 1920 more than half of all Christian Reformed children enjoyed a Christian education. The number of Christian schools increased from six in 1881 to seventeen in 1900, thirty-five in 1910, and eighty in 1920. The growth stagnated as a result of the economic crisis of 1929. At that time fourteen thousand Dutch-American children

---

[30]    Letter, October 4, 1873. Brinks, *Dutch American Voices*, 413.

[31]    Harro Van Brummelen, *Telling the Next Generation: Educational Development in North American Christian Schools* (Lanham: Univ. Press of America, 1986), 55.

[32]    Ibid., 6. The Ostfrisian emigrants who joined the CRC did not see the need for schools of their own because education in Germany and the U.S. resembled each other as far as attention to Christian values was concerned.

enjoyed Christian education in eighty-nine schools spread over fifteen states.[33] Because the church councils handed over the government of the schools to parents, the involvement of the families with the schools increased.

Already in the Netherlands these parents had understood the importance of a good education. On January 1, 1901, a compulsory education law further reduced illiteracy, which stood at 10 percent. In the same year, more than 90 percent of the Dutch children of ten and eleven years attended school in Chicago. The customary pattern was to start school at six, to be followed by eight years of education. The result of this attitude was that 95 percent of the Dutch immigrants were able to read and write.[34]

A second Dutch trend that was continued in America was the growth of special, confessional education. Between 1865 and 1900 the number of students in Christian day schools in the Netherlands rose from 20 to 31 percent.[35] This stimulus to change the content of education from that of the public school came exactly on time, because the old *raison d'être*, Dutch, was quickly losing ground. Even though the organizers did not fully grasp Kuyper's ideals, and did not implement his suggestions to transform society into a Christian society nearly as far as in the old country, they did subscribe to his idea that principles were crucial, and they let themselves be inspired by his organizational strategy.

Under the direction of the passionate principal, B.J. Bennink, the Christian schools in west Michigan between 1890 and 1920 became quite successful in quality and therefore in quantity. Better trained teachers immigrated to the United States after 1890. They could actually offer a different form of education instead of the usual three Rs (Reading, wRiting, and aRithmetic), one rounded out with religious doctrine and Bible knowledge. An annual program helped teachers with training and lesson methods, and with the use of English. The emphasis on language increased, because new teachers themselves

---

[33]  Ibid., 72. *Year Book – Convention book* (Chicago: National Union of Christian Schools, 1929-1930), 34. The greatest concentration was in the state of Michigan, where half of the number of students and teachers belonging to the National Union of Christian Schools were found in twenty-eight, often large, schools.

[34]  Swierenga, *Dutch Chicago*, 351-52.

[35]  Hans Knippenberg, "Deelname aan het lager onderwijs in Nederland gedurende de negentiende eeuw" (Ph.D. diss., Universiteit van Amsterdam, 1986), 77-78, 91. This increase was noticeable especially in Catholic regions.

School building in New Groningen, Michigan, ca. 1880.
Archives, Calvin College, Grand Rapids, Michigan.

spoke Dutch less often, and their students heard the old language less often in their surroundings. The effort to teach the youngest children Dutch foundered eventually around 1914, because coordination with the rest of the classes proved to be an uphill battle. Instead of teaching Bible in Dutch, Dutch became an option.[36]

During and after the First World War, American patriotism entered the Christian schools, and training to be good citizens became a priority. The change of language opened the door to America wider, and it became difficult to fundamentally criticize a society that was depicted positively, except for matters such as alcohol abuse and child labor. Because the schools hardly followed any teaching methods of their own, their own character remained limited to doctrinal and moral instruction. The creation of an umbrella organization in 1920, which through inspections was to improve the quality of Christian education, did little good, because this organization paid more attention to fundraising and public relations than to encouraging pedagogical reflection and the development of Christian curricula.

In contrast to the Christian Reformed Church, the Reformed Church sided officially with the public school system. The East Coast had little use for sectarian education and put broad social interest in

[36]  Van Brummelen, *Telling the Next Generation*, 87.

integration and quality first. The churches themselves had to take care of any supplementary education in the Christian tradition. This happened indeed, even in far-away areas. The Reformed Church in Alto, Wisconsin, provided Bible teaching in its own church building until the 1890s, with the tried and tested catechism method of Jacobus Borstius. Some children quickly memorized the answers but did not have the slightest idea what the lessons were all about. The distance between everyday Dutch and the language of the church made the transition to English necessary.[37]

The Christian Reformed Church felt the pressure on the Dutch language forty years later. In 1903, the progressive Johannes Groen, minister of the Eastern Ave Christian Reformed Church in Grand Rapids, argued the case for a combination of English and Dutch in Christian schools. He preferred English because otherwise the English-speaking churches would be excluded, but he did not want to give up Dutch completely, since the language had emotional value, offered access to the Dutch Calvinistic heritage, preserved contact between the generations, and had character-forming value: "Our beautiful, and dynamic Dutch language that is so rich in words, maintains a certain pride of character and precision in the way it expresses thoughts."[38] Furthermore, he was mindful of the difference in prestige the language had. If Dutch were only taught in the lower grades the older children would be less kindly disposed toward it.

Besides having a uniting effect among the proponents of the Christian school, this campaign also caused division. When two CRC ministers caused a stir in the village of Zeeland with a campaign for the Christian school, a part of their congregation left for the RCA. They saw too little difference between a separate Christian school and their public school. There, Christian teachers prayed and gave Bible instruction just as well as in a Christian institution. Students received a Bible as a graduation present, and the school board consisted of members of Reformed churches. In Holland, the municipal Board of Education began its meetings with prayer, and every school day in the

---

[37]   Cole, "Derk Bruins Family," in Vandervelde, *Bruins' Genealogy*, 35-37. Borstius Primer: William Schrier, *Gerrit J. Diekema, Orator: A Rhetorical Study of the Political and Occasional Addresses of Gerrit J. Diekema* (Grand Rapids: Eerdmans, 1950), 201-02.

[38]   Cited in Walter Lagerwey, *Neen, Nederland 'k vergeet u niet. Een beeld van het immigrantenleven in Amerika tussen 1846 en 1945 in verhalen, schetsen en gedichten* (Baarn: Bosch en Keuning, 1982), 87.

public school started with Bible reading and prayer until the Second World War.[39]

The Reverend Peter Moerdyke, a progressive spokesman of the Reformed Church in the West, lamented shortly after the turn of the century that it was taking way too long before the churches, especially in the big cities, finally began to see the needs of the second and third generations and gave priority to services in English. He praised the courage of the Third Reformed Church in Holland, Michigan, which changed to English church services altogether. He considered it an excellent move that those who wanted to keep Dutch left to form their own church. The Third Reformed Church in Roseland had also established a new congregation for those who spoke English. Even more so than his Christian Reformed colleague in Grand Rapids, Moerdyke was convinced that this development could not be stopped and that the Reformed Church had to adjust.[40]

## Higher Education

Interest in advanced education was of great importance to the immigrants, especially as a provision for educating their own ministers, but also to attract the community. In 1853 Henry Scholte, together with a number of Baptists, founded a Christian college: Central University opened its doors the following year with thirty-seven students. It was not until 1916 that a reorganized Central College became officially associated with the Reformed Church in America.

When Van Raalte noticed that he received little support for his Christian grade schools, he turned successfully to the founding of a school for continued education in 1851; it was first baptized the Pioneer School and has been known officially since 1857 as the Holland Academy. In 1862 the academy began to offer college-level classes, initially as preparatory training for the New Brunswick Theological Seminary in New Jersey. Because the government did not fund higher education, the citizens had to assume this task themselves. In this way the community received extra recognition and strengthened its own identity. This educational institution provided leaders for the Dutch community, but at the same time it linked the community to the norms that prevailed in America, since the colleges did not become

---

[39]  Lester De Koster, "Raised in Zeeland 1915-1929," *Origins* 9 (1919): 31-36.
[40]  Peter Moerdyke, "Chicago Letter," *Christian Intelligencer*, February 26, 1902.

full-fledged universities. In 1866 the institution was given the name of Hope College, and its name was officially established.[41]

These colleges became the incentive for creating a level between grade school and higher education, namely the high school. The first Christian high schools were founded after 1910, and only in communities with sufficient members. The stimulus for these secondary schools came from the institutions of higher learning rather than from the grade schools. In order to flourish, colleges needed well-prepared students. The Christian colleges launched and supported initiatives to recruit future students. In 1882, Dutch immigrants in Orange City, Iowa, founded the Northwestern Classical Academy that prepared students to study at Hope College, until Northwestern in 1928 became a junior college itself and developed into a four-year college in 1961.

In 1901, Hope President Gerrit Kollen was successful in mobilizing the Reformed churches in Cedar Grove, Wisconsin, and its surrounding area to found a Memorial Academy that prepared students for Hope College. This school remained under the supervision of the Reformed Church until 1937, to be merged later into the first public high school.[42]

In Harrison, South Dakota, the Harrison Classical Academy was established in 1902. "Classical" did not refer to the classics, although the curriculum did pay a great deal of attention to Latin and Greek, but to the ecclesiastical organization of the classis which, just as with Northwestern, was in charge of the school, and which of course also had to raise funds for the school. For the first four years this school was a one-man affair. B.D. Dykstra, a well-trained part-time minister from neighboring Platte, instructed a group of twenty students for a period of four years, without admitting first- or second-year students.[43] "We also have a Christian school in our municipality [Harrison, South Dakota]," the residents wrote home proudly, and they praised the growth of Christian education.[44]

In 1916 the Ostfrisian Reformed founded their own educational center, Grundy College in Grundy Center, Iowa, which drew many Dutch

---

[41]  Elton J. Bruins, "The Early Hope College History as Reflected in the Correspondence of Rev. Albertus C. Van Raalte to Rev. Philip Phelps Jr., 1857-1875," in Harms, *Dutch Adapting*, 1-8.

[42]  Richard Dykstra and Patricia Premo, eds., *Cedar Grove, Wisconsin: 150 Years of Dutch-American Tradition* (Cedar Grove: Standard Printing, 1997), 59-63.

[43]  D. Ivan Dykstra, "The Harrison Academy," *Proceedings of the Association for the Advancement of Dutch-American Studies* (1985), 35-48. Dykstra, *B.D.*, 42-63.

[44]  Bakker, *Zuster*, 275 and 339 (1908).

students. This project was the darling child of the leading minister, Dr. W. Bode, who hailed from Germany, belonged to the tradition of the Secession, and who joined the Christian Reformed Church in a separate classis in 1896. The lack of education in the German language at Calvin Seminary compelled Bode to found a separate college where German-speaking candidates could receive their training. Just before the First World War they had become more conscious of their German identity, which came to expression, for instance, in 1912 when they changed the Dutch name of their church periodical from the *Grensbode* to *Der Grenzbote*.[45] His dream evaporated in the 1930s when the financial elbowroom became too constricted. When in 1934 the school was no longer able to meet its expenses, it had to close its doors. In the meantime the Ostfrisians had given the CRC an injection of intellectual reflection and missionary zeal.

An effort in 1919 to establish a Christian Reformed counterpart to the Northwestern Classical Academy in Hull, Iowa, called Western College, also foundered. These initiatives failed because they were not able to generate sufficient income in economically hard times, did not have enough backers, and lost in the competition with the larger institutions, which could offer more quality and "buy" the better professors. Still, these efforts in the West were significant. Apart from the handful of students who received training there, these schools testified to the high expectations of the western settlements, to their self-consciousness, and to the great value they attributed to education.[46]

In the cities, educational institutions were more likely to succeed because the recruiting area was larger. In 1911 children in the suburbs of Douglas Park and Cicero in Chicago could attend Timothy Christian High School, an initiative of the local Christian Reformed church. A second high school, named Chicago Christian High School, followed seven years later; it was the first school of parents who came from different churches. It began with twenty-eight students. The motive behind this school was mainly to enable the new generation to obtain a diploma responsibly, thus giving them access to jobs in offices and the professions. These Chicago residents had, besides their philosophical

---

[45]    Brinks, "Ostfrisians in Two Worlds," De Klerk and De Ridder, *Perspectives*, 21-34.

[46]    Henry Zwaanstra, "Grundy College: 1916-1934," in De Klerk and De Ridder, *Perspectives*, 109-50. In 1955 the CRC did succeed in establishing its own college in Northwestern Iowa: Dordt College in Sioux Center.

Students of Eastern Christian High School
in Paterson, New Jersey, 1920.

Archives, Calvin College, Grand Rapids, Michigan.

ideals, educational goals as well. They demonstrated a fairly pragmatic attitude by attracting teachers from outside the Dutch Protestant community in order to guarantee sufficient quality. The curriculum was focused on preparation for jobs in commerce, which was also the driving force behind the school in Paterson, New Jersey.[47] In 1920, prominent members of the Christian Reformed Church in Grand Rapids also took the initiative to establish an independent Christian high school when it became known that Calvin College was seriously planning to become a regular four-year college and wanted to divest itself of the preparatory route. The school was able to get off the ground with more than two hundred students.

The result of these efforts on behalf of their own educational institutions was that in the 1920s a complete course of Christian education was established from grade school through college. Once this possibility had been created it had to be used and expanded, since many immigrants had reached a reasonable standard of living. In 1930, a principled foundation had been laid to justify this program by the editor-in-chief of the *Banner*, H.J. Kuiper, and other Christian Reformed

[47]  Swierenga, *Dutch Chicago*, 383-407.

leaders. Others wanted to keep their Reformed children separated from others for practical reasons. They wished to keep their children from nonbelievers, of course, but also from other non-Reformed young people, in order to encourage primary relationships (through marriage and friendship) within their own circle. They gave priority to the unadulterated continuation of the tradition. The Reformed Church, on the other hand, believed itself to be more responsible for the public well-being.[48]

Even though the actual school curriculum was not always convincingly different, the social consequences of having a separate education were great. It is true that Christian schools were not able to maintain Dutch, but without their efforts Dutch would have passed out of use even faster. Jacob van Hinte observed in the 1920s that the best Dutch was published in the most conservative periodicals and newspapers that appeared in northwest Iowa.

Christian Reformed churches exerted pressure on the schools to teach Dutch so that preaching in Dutch could be maintained longer. They admonished parents to send their children to the Christian school and, thus, to fulfill their baptismal promise to give their children a Christian upbringing. Friendships established in these schools, and especially in the secondary schools, could lead to marriages that supported the continuity of the subculture. The high schools drew students from various communities in the area, thus promoting mutual connections.

The financial sacrifices of the proponents of Christian education (in fact, they paid double since they also paid taxes for the maintenance of public schools) brought the Christian Reformed community even closer together.[49] The possibility of marrying someone within the subculture with a comparable education, and the regular reunions, strengthened the mutual ties. The various viewpoints among Dutch Protestants regarding the choice between public and Christian schools reflected a greater or smaller trust in America. Determining factors in making a choice were loyalty to traditions in the Netherlands and in America. The first generation of immigrants had certainly put forth efforts to establish Christian schools, but it was not overly concerned when this was not successful, since local autonomy was strong enough

---

[48]   James A. DeJong, *Henry J. Kuiper: Shaping the Christian Reformed Church, 1907-1962* (Grand Rapids: Eerdmans, 2007), 91-110.

[49]   Gary D. Bouma, *How the Saints Persevere: Social Factors in the Vitality of the Christian Reformed Church* (Clayton, Victoria, Australia: Dept. of Anthropology and Sociology, Monash Univ., 1984), 58, 71-73.

Funeral of Gerrit E. Boer passing
the Calvin College Campus in 1904.
Archives, Calvin College, Grand Rapids, Michigan.

to keep a grip on education. In the course of the century, however, this concern grew, especially in the cities.

The Reformed Church accepted public education and invested in higher education that provided leaders for their churches. The Christian Reformed Church was more focused on primary education.[50] This difference in approach was determined in part by ideology, fed by the campaign for Christian education in the Netherlands, and resulted partly from a practical choice. Until 1920, the CRC counted a great number of new immigrants who preferred to make money quickly. They considered investing in higher education not yet necessary. In 1900, only 5 percent of the Dutch-American children in Chicago (which had attracted many immigrants since 1880) had high school diplomas. The influx of immigrants determined the choices, which were easily made in favor of the grade schools. It was not until this wave was ready for continued education and also had the financial means for it that advanced education was considered.[51]

New immigrants from the Netherlands imported educational experiences from the home country. The first group claimed lack of educational freedom as the reason for their leaving, but they were satisfied in America with the financial autonomy of their communities

---

[50]    Norman Kansfield, "Education," in James W. Van Hoeven, ed., *Piety and Patriotism: Bicentennial Studies of the Reformed Church in America, 1776-1976*, Historical Series of the Reformed Church in America, no. 4 (Grand Rapids: Eerdmans, 1976), 147-48.
[51]    Swierenga, *Dutch Chicago*, 352.

and their ability to control appointment policies. Progress in acquiring equal rights for their own schools in the Netherlands made a new batch of immigrants look at America more critically. Later in the century the fight in the Netherlands for equal school funding for public and parochial schools became an issue in America. Especially the segment of the immigrants that chose for the CRC propagated Christian education, even though this meant abandoning the Dutch language.

Public schools had their disadvantages. New children were often pestered because they smelled, wore weird clothes, and ate strange food. In 1901, half of the students in the big cities had been born abroad. Until the First World War it was customary to have all children who had just arrived start at the beginner's level with lessons in English. After an initial language course, they were placed with their peers. But those circumstances were no reason to take children out of school. Many children attended school irregularly and not the whole year around. Between 1911 and 1915 on average only 40 percent of the children in Chicago actually attended school. The compulsory education laws that were adopted in the various states around the turn of the century to protect children against child labor had little effect on school attendance because enforcement proved difficult. While around the First World War 40 percent of children with parents born in America enjoyed a high school education, only 5 to 10 percent of immigrant children went to high school. This level was higher for Dutch children, although it was not until the Second World War that they went to college in large numbers. In 1941 it became possible to publish a commemorative book full of illustrious kinsmen in America who had earned diplomas and who filled scores of professorships.[52]

Even though there were only a few Dutch-American colleges, they did reinforce each other through mutual exchanges. Hope College provided professors for Northwestern, and temporarily for Harrison. After the Second World War, Calvin provided professors for Trinity Christian College in Chicago and for Dordt College in Iowa. Girls attended college by way of exception, mainly because of a lack of opportunity in the professions, and it was not until the twentieth century that high school attendance became normal for them, thus enabling them to continue their studies.[53]

---

[52]  H.M. Vlekke and Henry Beets, *Hollanders Who Helped Build America* (New York: n.p., 1942).
[53]  Cole, "Derk Bruins Family," 39-42.

## Catholic Education

Whereas some of the Protestants deemed the Christian character of the public schools inadequate, many Catholics on the other hand found them too explicitly Protestant because they used the Protestant King James Bible translation. For these Catholics, keeping the faith was more important than keeping their native tongue. They harbored a deep-seated fear of Protestant proselytizing, which in their view would inevitably lead to a total loss of faith.[54]

When the state of Wisconsin introduced English as the official language in 1854 and required a test of teachers that consisted of a math problem, a spelling test, reading, and grammar, Dutch Catholic immigrants did not find this insurmountable.[55] They also founded parochial schools, although Dutch was used much less there than among the Protestants. The first Catholic immigrants who settled in Little Chute in 1844 started a small school that was funded by missionary Van den Broek, where mainly children of the Menominee tribe received an education. This school was very basic and was closed after the Menominee left. Subsequently, sisters of a monastery in Fond du Lac took over the instruction in Little Chute. They were paid by the school district. In 1884, Bishop Krautbauer began to promote plans to establish a parochial school, encouraged by the hierarchy of the church that wanted to set up a Catholic educational system. The immigrants doubted the feasibility of the plan to entrust the education of boys to nuns, but the episcopate persisted and the school opened its doors in 1890. The nuns of Notre Dame also gave instruction in the public school until a new school superintendent put a stop to that in 1895, because he deemed the presence of nuns incompatible with the aims of the public school. The parochial school continued to grow and new buildings were added. In 1940, the school in Little Chute numbered 745 students, with another 235 students in continued education. In fact, it was so successful that the public high school remained closed from 1930 to 1966 because too few students were left who did not attend the Catholic school.[56]

---

[54]    Van Brummelen, *Telling the next Generation*, 277-78. Cf. Degler, *At Odds*, 141-42.

[55]    Vandehey, *Wooden Shoes West*, 49.

[56]    *Sesquicentennial of St. John Nepomucene, Little Chute, Wisconsin 1836-1986* (St. John's Parish, 1986), 64-69. *Little Chute. A Century of Progress 1899-1999* (Little Chute: Village of Little Chute Centennial Committee, 1999), 240-52. When the public school reopened the roles reversed, and the Catholic high school had to close in 1972 because the costs were too high for the community, and neighboring parishes refused to lend their support.

Winners of a typing contest at
Grand Rapids Christian High School, ca. 1920.

Archives, Calvin College, Grand Rapids, Michigan.

The rural public schools around Green Bay were on the whole still independent undertakings in 1894, led by their own school societies. Young ladies who had passed an examination, including special attention to the pronunciation of English, taught for $300 per season. Under those conditions, Catholics could get nuns appointed without any problems.[57]

Founding Dutch Catholic colleges proved less successful. In Baker City in the eastern part of the State of Oregon, Father Peter de Roo had managed to keep a Catholic college running for a few years in the 1880s with money from an inheritance, but he had to give up this initiative due to lack of support. He became the pastor in Verboort in the western part of the state in 1894, as successor to a Belgian priest who had arrived there in 1889 and who returned to Belgium five years later.[58]

The Norbertine fathers who arrived in Wisconsin in 1893 used French to converse with Walloons and the French. They learned

---

[57]  Lagerwey, *Letters Written in Good Faith*, 86-87 (letter by Pennings written to his fellow brothers from Delwich, Wisconsin, January 10, 1894).

[58]  Ibid., 144.

English in the meantime, but among themselves spoke only Dutch. Only a few parishes asked for sermons in Dutch.[59] In October 1898 Father Bernard Pennings began tutoring a couple of boys in Latin, intending to prepare them for the priesthood. His lessons expanded into an advanced training course, which became St. Norbert's College. The college offered a four-year program to male students of the Green Bay area who wanted to secure better jobs through advanced schooling. In 1952, girls also were admitted. But St. Norbert did not develop into a school that was focused on the Dutch community and did not become a mainstay of the Dutch Catholic identity.

## Religion and Language

The transfer of the Dutch language and the Dutch cultural heritage was not the highest priority for Dutch immigrants. The first generation certainly cherished the ideal of cultural continuity but did not cling to the Dutch language. It wanted to use English for practical reasons. It was actually the second wave of immigrants, who settled in isolated areas and who found the pace of adaptation too fast, that devoted itself to keeping Dutch.[60] But this objective was also temporary. Language is first of all an instrument for communication with one another and the outside world. When English was better at fulfilling this role, Dutch was sacrificed. Attachment to the Dutch traditions of faith did slow down this transition but could not block it. Passing on the contents of faith was most important, and to that effect the Dutch language was used as long as possible.

The Dutch immigrants looked for places where they could live together, but they did not develop a conscious strategy of total isolation. They did not follow the example of the Amish.[61] Although

---

[59]  Ibid., 97.

[60]  Jaap van Marle, "Over de rol van godsdienst bij taalbehoud," *Streven* (June 2003): 512-22. Berns and Van Marle, *Overzees Nederlands*.

[61]  The Amish divided the world into two parts: insiders and outsiders. The boundaries were strictly observed at the cost of the development of the individual members. Clear rules of conduct prevented contact with the surrounding world: no modern means of communication, such as the telephone, radio, TV, and vehicles such as the automobile, which would disrupt the geographical relationship. Their press brought mostly their own news. They did not have any organizations either that could give guidance in the process of change, which therefore caused homogeneity to be maintained. Thanks to their own provisions, they did not become dependent on the outside world as far as education, healthcare, and social security were concerned. See Peter Ester, *De stillen op het land. Portret van de*

the Protestant Dutch were inclined to isolation in their Reformed tradition, it did not translate into a total isolation because they were also convinced of their missionary mandate in this world. For that reason they always consciously looked for points of contact with the outside world and thought about ways to change it. Thus, the Dutch soon overcame resistance to modern means of communication and accepted radio and TV. They did distance themselves from amusements and entertainment, dancing and the movie theater, because these forms of recreation diverted them from their goal, but in this respect they were not the only ones; other Americans also wanted to shield themselves and their children from them. For the Amish, having their own grade school was essential in binding the next generation to the community, but continued education was discouraged. The Dutch had a much stronger need for continued education and university training. This attitude led to debate, and periodically to conflicts, between innovators and representatives of strong authority institutions, such as church councils and synods. Opinion leaders directed that debate but were not able to prevent reflection about change, which was innate, as it were.

In summary: education in the Dutch language strengthened, temporarily, one's own community, but also caused division. It hardly played a role in the passing on of the Dutch cultural tradition. Until 1920 education in the Dutch language was especially a matter of secondary, practical importance. The function of strengthening one's own identity then shifted from the study of the language to Christian education, which had viability only in areas with a concentration of Dutch families.

When the new Dutch envoy in Washington, Jonkheer John Loudon, received an invitation for a working visit to western Michigan in 1911, his predecessor advised him to respond as he saw fit:

> It also seems to me that it is hardly necessary to visit Michigan; as far as I am concerned, for an envoy to pay a visit there once every 10 years is sufficient. But if it looks good to you, it is fine by me that you go to Hope College, for instance, to the so-called commencement day (in June, I believe). We also should not forget that this college loses more of its Dutch character every five years and that it, in fact, has become a regular American school. But, suit yourself.

*Amish-gemeenschap in Amerika*, 3rd printing (Kampen: Agora, 2001), 74-75. For a comparable title in English, see Donald B. Kraybill, *The Riddle of Amish Culture* (Baltimore: John Hopkins Univ. Press, 2001).

When Loudon traveled to Grand Rapids the next year he was happily surprised nevertheless, and reported back: "Everyone I met spoke Dutch, even the children who, when they came out of school, ran after our horse-sleigh, and answered me in Dutch as soon as I called out something to them."[62] Dutch diplomatic representatives seldom visited the Midwest and only used such contacts when the reputation of the Netherlands was being criticized. Fortunately, the immigrants were not dependent on diplomats. They took care of their own contacts.

[62]  National Archives The Hague, inv. 2.21.205.37 Collection John Loudon, inv. 3: correspondence with De Marees van Swinderen, letter of the Minister of Foreign Affairs to Loudon, February 23, 1911; inv. 2.05.13 Embassy US, file 1116, service trips Michigan, J. Loudon to Minister of Foreign Affairs, February 20, 1912.

# CHAPTER 8

# Contact: Letters and Newspapers

On September 23, 1912, Brechtje Allewijn sent a birthday card from Kalamazoo, Michigan, to her sister Jacoba in Yerseke, Zeeland. She used the occasion to take out a subscription to the weekly, *De Vriend van Oud en Jong* (the *Friend of Old and Young*), which could be sent monthly, bundled, to America for seven and a half cents. This magazine was a welcome supplement to *De Zeeuw*, the Christian newspaper for Zeeland that her in-laws mailed to her husband weekly.[1] This way, she kept up to date on regional news, apart from news about relatives.

Brechtje did nothing unusual. Just like other immigrants she tapped new information sources in order to stay abreast of the ups and downs in her old neighborhood. By doing so she profited from the agreements that since 1875 had streamlined international postal traffic and had made it affordable. Through correspondence and by sending periodicals, immigrants and those who had stayed behind remained part of a subculture. This exchange maintained a strong immigration tradition. Publications in America itself strengthened the local

---

[1] Brechtje Allewijn-Mieras of Kalamazoo to Jacoba Mieras in Yerseke, September 23, 1912, ILC HH.

communities and connected the dispersed immigrants. Besides their informational and commercial functions, these papers also fulfilled a social role as forums for determining positions in the new situation. Like paper watchtowers they looked out across the ocean to become aware of developments in the old country, and at the same time kept an eye on news in America.

Thus, the Dutch-American immigration culture was fed from three sources: from the Netherlands as the cradle of its identity, from America as its alternate identity, and from the personal experiences of all sorts of Dutch Americans. These three sources interacted directly through regular contacts and incidental visits back and forth, partly in writing through private correspondence and publications (newspapers, periodicals, and books), and indirectly through financial transactions and the exchange of goods. The massive emigration between 1840 and 1920 coincided with a revolution in communications. Thanks to all kinds of innovations in transport, postal traffic, and technology, the immigrants of the nineteenth century were able to keep in closer contact with their old homeland as well as with the new.

## Postal Traffic

Although thousands of letters have been saved, they constitute only a small portion of the millions that were sent. The streams of letters to and from America stayed reasonably balanced, with a small surplus of letters from the Netherlands. Although many immigrants complained in their letters about a lack of response, those who remained behind were more justified in doing so. Between 1871 and 1919, the Dutch sent twenty-three million letters to America, and twenty-two million were sent in return. The volume doubled every ten years, with a few variations that were caused by slumps in the economy. Worsening economic prospects in America encouraged immigrants to advise their friends and acquaintances to postpone their coming.[2]

The exponential growth of letter traffic between 1871 and 1919 was possible thanks to the high literacy rate in the Netherlands and

[2]   The business mail was small. On average some 22,500 specimen and samples were sent to America between 1887 and 1914, while annually 15,400 articles came from America. If these shipments were accompanied by a letter, they would have constituted a fifteenth part of the total letter exchange. About the nature of immigrant letters, see my: "Avant La Lettre: The Use of Dutch Immigrant Letters in Historical Research," in Harms, *Dutch Adapting*, 34-43. In the years 1874, 1875, 1887, 1892, 1893, 1897-1905 (1899 excepted), 1908, and especially in 1909, more letters were sent from America than came from the Netherlands.

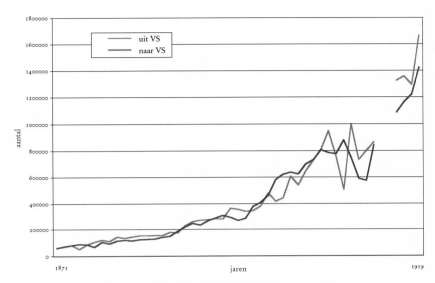

Graph 1: Number of Dutch letters sent to
and from the United States, 1871-1919.

the breakthrough in international postal traffic in 1875. That year, a number of countries signed a treaty for a worldwide system with uniform rates and reciprocal services. The postage for a letter to America decreased from 44 dollar cents in 1843 to 40 cents in 1849, when America and England signed a postal treaty; to 16 cents in 1868, when the Netherlands and America signed their first postal treaty; to 5 cents between 1875 and 1920, while printed matter up to 50 grams could be sent for 1 cent, and a postcard needed 2.[3] Variety in the kinds of communication for short and elaborate messages strengthened the ties even further. Letters could be mailed prepaid or postage paid, postcards with a single question or message could be accompanied by a prepaid option to respond. The reliability of delivery also improved, thanks to the option of registered mail. After 1908 private parties could easily ship goods by parcel post.

The frequency of delivery shot upwards. Already in 1881 thirteen mail boats each month left a Dutch port to deliver their cargo via

---

[3]    The exchange rate is kept at forty dollar cents to one Dutch guilder. Between 1879 and 1892 two cents extra was added for overseas surface mail. See J. Giphart and C. Muys, "Tweehonderd jaren postverbinding Nederland-Verenigde Staten van Amerika," in *Catalogus 4e NVPH (Nederlandse Vereeniging van Postzegelhandelaren) Show* (The Hague: n.p., 1982), 37-93.

England or France to America. Every Saturday a ship left directly for New York, alternately from Rotterdam and Amsterdam. The time involved in delivering mail shrank from three months to two weeks. In the 1920s it became possible to send short messages quickly by telegram. The number of cable telegrams grew from 350,000 in 1921 to more than 600,000 in 1929, without replacing handwritten letters. Mail messages diversified for various functions: birth and death announcements came by telegram, congratulations by postcard, reports by letter, money by postal order, and presents by parcel.[4]

Immigrant Krijn Goudzwaard in Grand Rapids used all of these means. He read Zeeland newspapers regularly and received packages and personal communications from the many acquaintances who emigrated. In 1881 he wrote, "...today many people come to America, not a day passes as it were without people arriving in this city, now people from Oudvossemeer are on the way...." In the fifteen years that he had been in America he had begun to believe that life here was so different from that in the Netherlands that he did not think it a good idea to write about the new country "...which you people would not understand anyway."[5]

Many contacts had both business and emotional sides. The business side concerned arrangements with family members who stayed behind, who often had lent money, and who at a certain point desired repayment. Because the immigrants needed a few years to save up a surplus, they had to keep their backers informed of their economic ups and especially downs. Delays in repayments needed an explanation. Family members who had stayed behind sent money to meet setbacks in America. Klaas Schuiling, for instance, postponed payment of his loan to his family in Friesland year after year in order to make necessary investments and to be able to pay off the mortgage on his farm in Montana. Ten years after his immigration in 1898, he still owed debts in the old country. This kept the flow of letters going.[6]

The business aspect of the letters could be far-reaching. In the span of twenty years, the Reverend Bernardus de Beij of Chicago

---

[4]    W.S. da Costa, *Binnenlandse en Internationale Posttarieven van Nederland 1850-1990* (Assen: Nederlandse Vereniging van Poststukken en poststempelverzamelaars, 1990), 140. *Verslagen aan de Koning betrekkelijk de diensten der posterijen ...1881*, 3. *Verslag aan de Koningin betrekkelijk de diensten der posterijen ... 1930*, appendix 76. The total number of telegrams included both telegrams received and sent.

[5]    April 22, 1881, ILC HH.

[6]    Rodenhuis, *Nog zoo gaarne wil ik vanalles van Holland weten*, 25.

received more than a hundred letters from the Netherlands with requests for information, and he faithfully answered them, while Albert Kuipers, the founder of Platte, South Dakota, claimed that he had answered more than two hundred letters in one year.[7] Gerard van Pernis believed that the reports of his successful emigration as a seventeen-year-old in 1907 to Holland, Michigan, had made hundreds of people from the same area decide to follow his example.[8] Van Pernis may well have overestimated his influence, but it is true that reliable, private information stimulated emigration. Potential emigrants, before leaving, asked their American relations about the prospects and how to organize the journey. Once at their destination, the tie with those who had remained behind grew gradually weaker, while the immigrants looked for compensation from other immigrants for the gaps that had been created in their network. After all, most emigrants had been torn from their daily contacts with family, friends, fellow believers, and fellow citizens. Many immigrants walked around with guilt feelings toward the family they had left behind and tried by way of letters to rescue something of the family culture. This turned the correspondence into a highly emotional experience. In the letters the immigrants reported their initial experiences and interpreted them. By mentioning what was strange and threatening, and what was fresh and attractive, they worked at building their new identities at the same time.[9]

The emotional side of the correspondence was strengthened by the possibility of sending portraits along. In the 1880s photo studios that could make official portraits also became part of rural communities in America, while in the twentieth century hand cameras and inexpensive prints made it possible to send many informal photos along in the mail. Once received, the portraits were given a prominent place, were talked to, and were treated as if people were having an actual visit. Cornelia Polder wrote in February 1917 to her daughter in Roosendaal:

> ...and look, it is hard to believe, but birthday girl Corritje and her sisters arrived here this afternoon, and they sat on the table when

---

7    *De Wereldburger* (March 8 1888), 10 and (January 10, 1890), 639.
8    Van Pernis, *According to Thy Heart*, 37, 58-59.
9    Kathleen Anne DeHaan, "'He Looks Like a Yankee in His New Suit' Immigrant Rhetoric: Dutch Immigrant Letters as Forums for Shifting Immigrant Identities" (Ph.D. diss., Northwestern Univ., 1998), 237, 247, 267-72. Pieter Stokvis, "Nederland en de internationale migratie, 1815-1960," in F.L. van Holthoon, *De Nederlandse samenleving sinds 1815. Wording en samenhang* (Assen: Van Gorcum, 1985), 71-92.

we had our tea; I could not keep my eyes from them, and now they sit in our bedroom. When I do my hair in the morning they look at me; that cupboard on which they sit is the cupboard with the mirror, with more portraits on it, and as often as I have to be in that cupboard I can see all those faces, how sweet they look. O, how I would love to see them in person.

In the Netherlands the American photos circulated as concrete evidence of the immigrants' lives and as a visible advertisement for a better future.[10]

The letter writer was the person who represented the family, which meant the husband more often than the wife, although this division of tasks was not exclusive. The writers were the ones who had time and energy to write. In the busy period in which all energy was taken up with survival, writing was often postponed until more time was available. Izaak Janse wrote a letter to his former employer in Zeeland once a year, in the winter.[11] The time of writing was often during the weekend and especially on Sundays. Most letters were written in the quiet atmosphere of the home. In the introductory paragraphs, the authors used predictable opening words such as, "Because of God's goodness, we are healthy and well." As the correspondence became more regular and personal, descriptions were given of the immediate surroundings in which the letters were written, often with a complete listing of the whereabouts of family members, the weather conditions, and the time. This composition suggested nearness, immediacy, recognition, and protection. These elements strengthened the intimate (family) ties that were felt on birthdays and visits, during which the person in question was talked about. The expectation to see each other again stimulated the correspondence. The subjects treated in the letters dealt especially with family events. Of course, other subjects were mentioned as well, such as disasters and fires, but usually only when they touched upon one's own livelihood, or when the newspapers reported them widely.[12]

---

[10]   Polder letters ICL HH. Rob Kroes, "Migrating Images: The Role of Photography in Immigrant Writing," in David E. Nye and Mick Gidley, eds., *American Photographs in Europe* (Amsterdam: VU Univ. Press, 1994), 189-204.

[11]   Izaak Janse (Grand Rapids) to F.P. Polderdijk, Nieuw- en St. Joosland, December 14, 1886; February 22, 1887; and January 25, 1905, ILC H H.

[12]   Examples of letters may be found in Brinks, *Dutch American Voices*, and titles in the bibliography.

## Newspapers and Magazines

The hunger for information about the old country was insatiable. As early as 1855, E.J. Potgieter was able to report about Pella, "American and Dutch papers keep us posted quite adequately about news from home and abroad; whatever Pella may be, it is not Patmos."[13] The author referred to the isolated island of Patmos, where the apostle John received and wrote down his visions.

Because American newspapers hardly ever wrote anything about the Netherlands, Dutch newspapers found their way across the ocean. Many periodicals were also sent to America; these were usually not subscriptions but single issues. In the ten years between 1876 and 1885, the only period in which this sort of printed matter was counted, the number of newspapers and magazines that Dutch Americans received grew from 25,000 to 57,000, an average of 47,000 mailings a year. The reverse stream was a quarter less, although still surprisingly high. Annually, the Dutch received around 35,000 periodicals from America with news about the settlements there. Because newspapers were often sent bundled, multiples of these numbers must have arrived. Calculated over the number of Dutch immigrants in America these data mean that every immigrant received at least one newspaper annually.[14]

In 1890, in the new colony of Platte, South Dakota, at least one newspaper a day arrived from the Netherlands: Albert Kuipers counted five: the *Asser Courant*, the *Leeuwarder*, the *Nieuws van den Dag*, the *Oprechte Steenwijker*, and the *Balkster Courant*, next to the other local papers and the Dutch-American periodicals: *De Grondwet*, *de Wachter*, *De Volksvriend*, *de Hope*, and the *Nederlander*. Those papers were read immediately in the post office adjoining the "Dutch store" and exchanged.[15]

When after the turn of the century illustrated magazines appeared in the Netherlands, they were mailed overseas as well. The Polder family, which left for New York on the last ship from the Netherlands just before the outbreak of the First World War in August 1914, was kept informed of the developments in Dutch society by

[13]   Potgieter, "Landverhuizing," *De Gids* 19 (1855): 514.
[14]   In the decade between 1876 and 1885, newspapers, magazines, and periodicals were counted separately. During this period two-thirds of all printed matter consisted of newspapers and periodicals, regardless of whether they were sent to America or came from America. After 1885 this distinction was dropped. During the half century of these counts it is estimated that 15.25 million pieces of printed matter were sent to the U.S., and 13.75 million were received from there.
[15]   *De Wereldburger* (January 17, 1890), 653.

South Holland Post Office, Illinois.
Archives, Calvin College, Grand Rapids, Michigan.

having the *Schouwvenster* (the *Show Case*) mailed to them. If on occasion a copy got lost in the mail, the recipients complained that they missed a segment of the serial story. "I look forward to the *Schouwvenster* every day," Cornelia Polder wrote to her daughter Cor, who mailed her this illustrated weekly for the Christian family. It was considered a family friend.[16]

In the period between 1871 and 1919, seven and a half million periodicals came to America and an estimated six and a half million found their way to the Netherlands from America. Bernardus de Beij kept abreast of news in the Netherlands by way of subscriptions to church papers and the *Provincial Groninger Courant* (*Provincial Newspaper of Groningen*). As an important person among the Dutch in Chicago, he undoubtedly passed on this news to many compatriots. As a supplement to personal letters, newspapers therefore brought varied Dutch information to the immigrants. But the reverse was also true: until the 1920s Dutch newspapers liked to print letters from emigrants because their readers were hungry for news about real life in America.[17]

[16]  Letter of November 30, 1931. She had been reading the paper since 1925, which at that time was in its eighteenth year of publication, letter of April 24, 1934, RSC.

[17]  Herman Ganzevoort, "My hands will be my capital," in Bruins, *Dutch in America*, 62-82, Frans van Waterstadt of Leeuwarden wrote many letters

The newspapers printed these firsthand experiences to counterbalance the biased information of the recruiting folders put out by the railway and shipping companies.

## Personal Contacts

Until the last quarter of the nineteenth century only someone with ample time and money could afford to make a trip across the Atlantic Ocean just for pleasure.[18] Business contacts or journalistic curiosity brought only one or two people from the Netherlands to the other side. Regular tourism did not take off until the steamship companies provided scheduled departures in the 1870s.

It seemed reasonable to expect that institutional contacts, for instance between churches, would also lead to an exchange of people. The average Dutch citizen, however, heard only little about the adventures of his kinsmen. Personal visits by prominent personalities evoked a wide interest in American church and social developments. After the well-known minister Marinus Cohen Stuart had attended an international conference of the Evangelical Alliance in New York and traveled around the country for six months, he published a two-part account of his experiences. In 1881 the Reformed orphanage director J. van 't Lindenhout did the same with his travel account of a six-week stay in America whose purpose it was to find support and places to work for his orphans. Thus, enterprising people were the driving force behind attention for America.[19]

The Reformed Church was indeed interested in what was happening in the Netherlands; however, the Dutch churches showed little real interest in their American sister churches. This lack of interest was in keeping with an attitude of superiority. The Dutch Christian periodicals considered the RCA a daughter of the Reformed Church in the Netherlands and did not have an eye for its independent

between April 14, 1927, and May 11, 1929, about his experiences in Canada for the *Leeuwarder Courant*. He himself had also sifted through newspapers for news about real life in Canada.

[18]   Pien Steringa, *Nederlanders op reis in Amerika 1812-1860. Reisverhalen als bron voor negentiende-eeuwse mentaliteit* (Utrecht: Vakgroep Geschiedenis, 1997), 8.

[19]   M. Cohen Stuart, *Zes maanden in Amerika* (Haarlem: Tjeenk Willink, 1875). J. van 't Lindenhout, *Zes weken tussen de wielen of De Hollanders in Amerika* (Nijmegen: n.p., n.d. [1886]). For other examples of journalists and scientists, see: A. Lammers, *Uncle Sam en Jan Salie. Hoe Nederland Amerika ontdekte* (Amsterdam: Balans, 1989).

development.[20] Personal letters to church weeklies in the Netherlands were dealt with cautiously when they contained criticism of the Reformed Church. Visits of authoritative ministers such as Van Raalte in 1866 and Van der Meulen in 1869 to synods of their Dutch mother church helped strengthen the reputation of the Reformed Church but did not lead to real cooperation. Both leaders made the journey for personal therapeutic reasons. Van Raalte's wife, Christina, was in poor health and sought relief in the Netherlands. Van Raalte himself hoped that this visit might lead to common missionary projects, but he did not succeed in this respect. Within a year after his return he retired. Three years later, Cornelius Van der Meulen was sent to the synod of the Christian Secessionist Churches in Middelburg as an official delegate, as a reward for his faithful service and in order to recuperate from the emotional blow he had received as a result of his wife's death. The old minister felt at home at the synod and cherished the attention he received from the other delegates. He confirmed the similarities in doctrine and organization between the churches in America and their sister churches in the Netherlands and challenged rumors that the RCA had become liberal.[21]

In the 1880s, religious periodicals offered specific information about the level of suitability of various regions, coupled with the advice not to remain in the big cities on the East Coast but to move west, but they hardly offered any information about churches and faith. Only the issue of Freemasonry stirred people to write. The presence of Freemasonry showed the RCA in a bad light because it took firmer measures against the critics of Freemasonry than against the Freemasons themselves. This strongly reminded some readers of the oppression by the Reformed Church in the Netherlands.[22] During this period representatives of the Christian Reformed Church traveled to the Netherlands to defend the reputation of their denomination. True interest by Dutch church leaders did not occur until the twentieth century, in the footsteps of Abraham Kuyper, who traveled all over America in the summer of 1898 to deliver his now famous Stone

---

20  Piet Hein Burmanje, "Trouble in Paradise: The Dutch Reformed Press and Its Views on Calvinist Emigration," in Rob Kroes, and Henk-Otto Neuschäfer, eds., *The Dutch in North America: Their Immigration and Cultural Continuity* (Amsterdam: VU Uitgeverij, 1991), 25-33.

21  *De Bazuin*, August 27, 1869. *Handelingen en verslagen*, 986, 1021. It is remarkable that Scholte never went back, although he did try to be appointed ambassador to Europe, preferably the Netherlands.

22  Burmanje, " Trouble."

Lectures at Princeton University. The result of his appearance was that more Dutch theologians went to America to look around critically, be inspired, and learn to appreciate Europe again.[23]

Successful immigrants returned to show their achievements and attracted a lot of attention from the press. Such an honor was conferred on Edward W. Bok in 1921. This successful businessman returned to the Netherlands upon his retirement as editor-in-chief of the leading ladies' magazine, the *Ladies' Home Journal*. His arrival was preceded by the publication of his life's story (which he had just published in the United States) in serial form in the liberal newspaper *Het Vaderland* in The Hague. The national press hailed the author as an example of someone who had the ability to do things independently and praised his Dutch qualities that had stood him in good stead in America.[24]

All these travelers belonged to the elite. The ordinary man or woman was less able to afford the voyage, although there was quite a bit of travel back and forth. Unmarried young men would return to the old country from time to time. John Broeren was twenty-eight years old when he sought work in Wisconsin in 1857 as a wooden shoe maker and carpenter. When he lost his job in the fall of 1860, he returned to the Netherlands and went back to Green Bay the next spring. Lambert Wellens followed a similar pattern: he emigrated in 1856 as a twenty-year-old, tried his luck in the mines of California, returned to the Netherlands in 1867, found a wife in the area where he was born, started a family, and decided in 1883 to go back to De Pere, Wisconsin. He subsequently went back to the old country three more times.[25]

After 1890, regular departures and affordable tickets continued to make travel back and forth easier. In the fall of 1890, the Netherlands

---

[23] James D. Bratt, "Abraham Kuyper, American History, and the Tensions of Neo-Calvinism," and George Harinck, "Valentijn Hepp in America: Attempts at International Exchange in the 1920s," both in George Harinck and Hans Krabbendam, eds., *Sharing the Reformed Tradition: The Dutch-North American Exchange, 1846-1996* (Amsterdam: VU Univ. Press, 1996), 97-114, and 115-38. George Harinck, "Drie theologen zien Amerika," *Transparant* 6.4 (November 1995): 34-42. Lammers, *Uncle Sam*, 25-28.

[24] Krabbendam, *The Model Man*, 166.

[25] *Commemorative Biographical Record of the Fox River Valley Counties of Brown, Outagamie and Winnebago* (Chicago: J.H. Beers, 1895), 326. See also the biographical sketches of Martin van Beek (41) and Lambert Wellens (335-36). Hermann Raymakers followed the same path, emigrated in 1847, worked as a carpenter, returned to Venray in 1856, married, started a family, and returned to Wisconsin, with one more trip to his old fatherland (368-70).

American Steamship Company (NASM) announced a "Dutch Excursion" at heavily discounted prices.[26] Of the 447 adults who exchanged Walcheren for America between 1900 and 1920, 45 returned, sometimes to venture to America years later to try their luck once more. The largest part of this group consisted of unmarried emigrants who were flexible and had fewer responsibilities for others, but sometimes families traveled back and forth as well. Families that had stayed behind were encouraged to come to America for a few months' trial to see if they might like it. The travel costs often were advanced.[27]

The return of successful emigrants had great advertising potential. The case of Gerrit Lammers is a good example; he had arrived in Gibbsville, Wisconsin, at the age of eight in 1854; in 1868 he made a trip to Aalten, the area he came from, and on that occasion he spoke so highly of the opportunities America offered that he returned to Wisconsin in the company of 132 people from the Aalten area, and in the following year he took with him another 341 people from the same region.[28]

After the turn of the century, return trips became more common. Before 1909, 40 of the 578 Dutch workers in the furniture industry in Grand Rapids had been back to the Netherlands once or several times. Among the group that had lived in America between five and nine years, this percentage was twice as high as among those who had been in the United States less than five or more than ten years. Starters did not have enough money for travel and heads of families had other responsibilities. Compared to their fellow immigrants from other European countries, the Dutch were only half as keen on traveling.[29]

[26]  *De Volksstem* (De Pere), September 3, 1890.
[27]  Joke M. Blaas-Rademaker, "Van Walcheren naar de Verenigde Staten: Emigratie in de periode 1900-1920," *Nehalennia* 137 (2002): 37-46.
[28]  *History of Sheboygan County Wisconsin: Past and present.* 2 vols. (Chicago: S.J. Clark 1912), 2:568.
[29]  Table 3: Visits abroad by male workers born abroad, subdivided by period.

|  | <5 years in the US | 5-9 years in the US | >10 years in the US | Total |
|---|---|---|---|---|
| Dutchmen | 68 | 52 | 458 | 578 |
| Returned | 4 (5.9%) | 6 (11.5%) | 30 (6.6%) | 40 (6.9%) |
| Swedes | 77 | 96 | 329 | 502 |
| Returned | 5 (6.5%) | 26 (27.1%) | 64 (19.5%) | 95 (18.9%) |
| all in survey | 411 | 355 | 1171 | 1937 |
|  | 25 (6.1%) | 61 (17.2%) | 153 (13.1%0 | 239 (12.3%) |

The regular stream of immigrants from the Netherlands to the settlements in America continued to bring a fresh supply of news and goods from the old neighborhood. Seventeen-year-old Gerard van Pernis was given two boxes of presents that he had to take along and deliver to an acquaintance in Boston.[30] An example of the thirst for information was the effort of Izaak Janse from Grand Rapids; he was going to give the boy who lived next door to him and who was going to visit relatives in Zierikzee a "telescope [along] and a few prints...of a few important buildings in this country," since the boy was going to visit the area of his birth around Goes anyway. Alas, the bird had already flown the coop before Janse could give him his present.[31] These visitors to the old country provided so much information about the American environment of the letter writers that letters were sometimes thought to be superfluous. Krijn Goudswaard wrote in 1874, eight years after emigrating: "I will not write you about us or America. I am sure you have the opportunity now to learn all kinds of things from Johannes den Engelsman from America." And five years later he concluded, after he himself had mentioned news items about wedding anniversaries and deaths in the Netherlands, "Now you can see that not much happens there without me knowing it."[32] New arrivals kept people from the same area up to date on the latest news.

In turn, the Dutch also came to visit their relatives in America, usually for a couple of weeks. Seventy-five-year-old W. van Duren from Kampen visited his family in Holland, Michigan, in 1860. Although at the time this visit was still special enough to make the newspaper, the editors claimed that such visits occurred much more often. So many older people traveled back and forth that the paper expected younger ones to follow soon.[33]

In the Dutch-American communities there was much family contact in the workplace, for instance, in the factories and stores of Werkman, Brink, Steketee, and in church and nonchurch organizations. These mutual contacts in America bound immigrants together, both within local communities and within regions. The result was that

---

The category "all" consists of Dutchmen, Germans, Letlanders, Poles, Swedes, and diverse small groups. *Immigration Commission*, vol. 15, table 65 on page 527 and table 39 on page 584.

[30] Van Pernis, *According to Thy Heart*.

[31] Izaak Janse (Grand Rapids) to F.P. Polderdijk, Nieuw- en St. Joosland, December 14, 1886, ILC HH.

[32] Krijn Goudzwaard, March 26, 1874; December 17, 1879, ILC HH.

[33] *De Hollander*, August 22, 1860.

just a few links were sufficient to maintain contact between Dutch and American networks, and that immigrants could move easily back and forth within such communities. Contacts between various centers of Dutch immigrants were maintained by coordinating meetings in ecclesiastical assemblies, school organizations, and on the occasion of anniversaries, which were reported faithfully by the Dutch-American newspapers. Residents of a daughter colony visited their family in the mother colony with certain regularity. These grand family reunions were called excursions. In 1886 E. Bloemendaal participated in an excursion of people from Orange City to Pella. The company was welcomed at the train station with music: "Oh, what a blessed experience in a foreign country! For it may be as it is, but every person, even the one least emotionally prone, feels in America that he has left his homeland."[34]

When Sybren Bakker arrived at his family's home in South Dakota in 1927 to find work, the news was soon broadcast all over: "We read in three different papers that we had arrived here, we soon became known here. I also received a letter from a farmer in Corsica [in South Dakota]! He wanted me to work for him in the winter months, he wanted a Dutch farmhand to feed his cattle...."[35] That is how fast the Dutch grapevine worked.

**Reading Material**

In the eighteenth and nineteenth centuries, America made up a small but continuous market, especially for religious reading material, from the Netherlands. Amsterdam and Leiden booksellers provided the growing scientific world in America with ancient texts and study material. Dutch scientific books were imported into America but had a limited reach.[36]

The pioneers could only take a few books along. The books owned by the farmer from Borssel, Van de Luijster, served as a library for the reading of sermons and meditations of ministers from the pietistic tradition, such as Smijtegeld, Koelman, Hellenbroek, and à Brakel. Geertje van Oosterhout, née Frederiks, ordered a number of books by Jacob Cats to be sent from Middelburg for reading in America.[37]

---

[34] Bloemendaal, *Naar Amerika*, 157.
[35] Bakker, *Zuster*, 371.
[36] Marika Keblusek, "New York, Amsterdam, Leiden: Trading Books in the Old and New Worlds," in Harinck and Krabbendam, *Amsterdam-New York*, 117-24.
[37] "Brievenboek," Vande Luyster Collection, box 1, "Register van geleende boeken," Joint Archives of Holland, Michigan. Geertruida Van Oosterhout,

The immigrant leader Cornelius Van der Meulen from Zeeland owned at his death in 1876 a collection of 113 books, of which 16 percent were in English. Most of them were practical books such as *Webster's Dictionary, Statistics of the U.S. Census of 1850,* and the *American Lawyer and Form Book.* There were also a few theological works in the collection, such as the *Encyclopedia of Religious Knowledge* and the *Guide to Family Devotion.* Moreover, the minister owned a copy of the popular book by J.L. Motley about Dutch history, *The Rise of the Dutch Republic.* The Dutch-language part contained many collections of sermons, Bible commentaries, and devotional works. As a former carpenter, he had also taken along his *Manual of Architecture.* The value of his library amounted to $209.35.[38] The next generation of immigrants took more books along. When Christian Reformed minister Roelof T. Kuiper died in South Holland in 1894, he left behind a considerable library of five hundred books, of which only a few were English Bible commentaries.[39]

The stream of immigrants maintained a steady but small market for Dutch books. The village of Zeeland had a "Dutch Library" in 1876 containing four hundred books, of which teacher, town clerk, and book seller R.A Hijma was the librarian. A hundred people paid two dollars annually to be able to read these books.[40] Two years later the new book seller, A.J. Welmer, added new services to the sale of Bibles and hymnals. Lemonade and ice cream were sold in a "new business in Zeeland." This combination of merchandise was seen as a sign that rural Zeeland also was Americanizing.[41] Still, interest in Dutch culture continued. In May 1880, the Dutch drama society *Kennis is Macht* ("Knowledge is Power") presented the play *Het Turfschip van Breda* ("The Peat Ship of Breda"), in Grand Rapids.[42] In 1887 the well-known director of the orphanage in Neerbosch, J. van 't Lindenhout, shipped two crates of Dutch books

---

née Frederiks to Johan Samuel Frederiks in Middelburg, August 14, 1852, ILC HH.

38  File Cornelius Van der Meulen, correspondence C. van Loo to Jacob Van der Meulen, October 30, 1882. Original Cases, nr. 2593 (reel 697) Kent County Probate Court, Grand Rapids, Michigan. John Motley was an American historian who wrote three standard works about Dutch history.

39  *Catalogus van de bibliotheek van wijlen R.T. Kuiper, welke op publieke auctie zal worden verkocht door J.B. Hulst, Boekhandelaar te Grand Rapids, Mich.* [1895], 17 pages, folder 21, Heritage Hall, Calvin College.

40  *De Hollander,* April 19, 1876.

41  *De Grondwet,* July 2, 1878.

42  *De Grondwet,* May 25, 1880.

Hoekstra bookstore, Grand Rapids.
Archives, Calvin College, Grand Rapids, Michigan.

to Hope and Northwestern colleges; these books were appreciated, especially by the older generation.[43]

The original way in which B.D. Dykstra provided the Dutch network with (Dutch) literature demonstrated its closeness. Without a paying job, he made a living in the 1930s from the yield of his own garden, and from time to time he went around by train and bicycle to the Dutch colonies where he sold his collection of poems door to door, which he had written and published himself. Quite often he returned after about five days having made hundreds of dollars, while he found a warm welcome and shelter from his compatriots when he was on the road.[44]

**Merchandise**

Trade between the Netherlands and America was not very intensive. It was not until after the economy in the Netherlands was liberalized in 1870 that the rate of import and export increased. In 1850 the Netherlands exported 2 million dollars worth of merchandise to

---

[43]    *De Wereldburger*, March 22, 1888.
[44]    Dykstra, *"B.D.,"* 140-41.

the United States. In 1872 the value of export was twice that amount, 4.4 million dollars, and the Netherlands imported goods from America for 26.1 million dollars. Until the 1880s Dutch merchants sold especially gin, pewter, and coffee to the Americans; afterwards also tobacco, nutmeg, herring, and diamonds. Goods for an amount of 26 million dollars were exported in 1901. In return, on average, about twice as much came to the Netherlands in raw materials, animal fats, petroleum, cotton seed, and fertilizer. In 1900 this import had a value of 115 million dollars.[45]

Trade and immigrants had little in common with each other, unless the immigrants themselves are considered commodities. Immigrants did not come for the sake of trade but were interested in land; it was still inexpensive and increased in value rapidly. Boudewijn Nieuwenhuise kept a close eye on the movements in price and knew that the farmers who had bought land in 1851 for 15 dollars per acre sold it six years later for 62.50 per acre; less fertile land still yielded 25 to 40 dollars per acre. From his sideline in Dutch products it was evident that he intended to perpetuate his old lifestyle: he imported wool for knitting stockings, four dozen mouth pieces for small porcelain pipes (he still had the bowls), New Testaments, and psalters.[46]

Thus, immigrants played a very modest role in the promotion of trade. They imported, only for their own consumption, Dutch Bibles, pipes, and silver jewelry, objects that reminded them of the past and were of guaranteed quality. This struck an "old Dutch" resident in Albany when he saw immigrants arrive in the middle of the nineteenth century with objects that he already considered to be antiques:

> They took along furniture, clothing and jewelry, as can still be seen in old homes in Albany and Ulster and in some homes close to New York. They spoke the same language that we heard in our childhood from the mouth of old people who wanted to be nothing else but *Dutch*. The miniature cup and saucer, the foot warmer, the Bible with clasps, these were put away by us as holy remnants of the past; all of these things they had brought with them. The clothes they wore were identical to the ones we could

---

[45]  *Statistiek van den in-, uit- en doorvoer* (The Hague: Ministerie van Financiën, 1863-1915); Walter H. Salzmann, *A Market to Explore: A History of Public-Private Partnership in the Promotion of Trade and Investment between the Netherlands and the United States* (The Netherlands Chamber of Commerce in the United States, Inc., 1994), 55-63.

[46]  Brief van B. Nieuwenhuijse, April 20, 1857, and March 1854, ILC HH.

see in old family portraits whose color and gilding had faded with age.[47]

New immigrants or travelers brought packages along for friends and acquaintances. Nineteen-year-old Gerrit Roelofs, who had left Zwolle in 1872 to avoid the draft, received a sizeable package from his parents the next year via the Reverend Henry Dosker of Zwolle, who had accepted a call to Grand Rapids: socks, buttons, a coat, vases, a harmonica, cigars, a gold watch, and a set of books. These books formed the basis of a public library with American and Dutch works on history, literature and poetry, theology, and children's books, which he offered on loan, free of charge, on Saturday mornings in a room in his house. He became a citizen in 1877 and worked his way up as an independent insurance agent, realtor, and journalist.[48]

### The Dutch-American Press

Immigrants in America would publish a newspaper or magazine for one of two reasons: as a mouthpiece for the members of an association or as a commercial enterprise. Most non-English immigration magazines were directed toward workers and belonged to the first category. Their heyday occurred in the decade before the First World War when thirteen hundred titles were in circulation. This was also the high point of the Dutch-American press, but the twenty-some titles were hardly intended specifically for workers.[49]

The first Dutch newspaper, the *Sheboygan Nieuwsbode* ("*Sheboygan Messenger*"), came on the scene in 1849 in the print shop of Jacob Quintus, who had emigrated from the Zierikzee (Zeeland) area. Quintus was a newspaperman in heart and soul. He took the initiative and published four newspapers of which only the *Sheboygan Nieuwsbode* may be called a success. Quintus followed the model of the *Zierikzeesche Nieuwsbode,* a liberal paper with regional news for which he became the sales agent in

---

[47]   Conrad Bult, "Dutch Silver," *Origins* 6.1 (1988): 36-41; Jacob Quintus, " Een terugblik over vijftig jaren," *De Grondwet,* November 21, 1911 (quoting an article from 1897).

[48]   Verbrugge, *Life of a Dutch American,* 74-75. He published a weekly for the temperance movement.

[49]   D. Hoerder and C. Harwig, eds., *The Immigrant Labor Press in North America, 1840s-1970s: An Annotated Bibliography,* 3 vols. (Westport, Conn.: Greenwood Press, 1987), 21-27. The number of issues went down because of the anti-immigrant sentiment in and after the First World War and the transition to English.

America. In 1853 he tried to publish a weekly, the *Democratic Secretary*, but it failed in spite of the support of the Democratic Party.[50] In the meantime the *Sheboygan* grew into the first nationally read weekly for Dutch speakers, thanks to the favorable location of Sheboygan on the west coast of Lake Michigan between the colonies in Michigan, Iowa, and Illinois. Quintus filled his paper with news from diverse places; he repeated this concept in the Democratic weekly, *De Amerikaansche Stoompost* ("*American Steampost*") in Grand Rapids, where he moved in 1858; this weekly succumbed in the political earthquake of the Civil War.[51] After this first publication in the Dutch language in Grand Rapids, which appeared between 1859 and 1866, William Verburg and John W. van Leeuwen marketed a Republican counterpart, *De Vreijheids Banier* ("the *Freedom Banner*"), between 1868 and 1900. This paper did not become a success either. The best paper was *De Standaard* (1875-1918), published by J. Strien and Dennis Schram.

Most newspapers in the Dutch language served to make a town attractive, to support a political party, or a combination of both. The *Sheboygan Nieuwsbode* received support from the Democrats, and *De Nederlander* (from Kalamazoo) from the Whigs, the forerunner of the Republican Party. Financial support of a political party generated revenues through advertisements but could also endanger the continuity. After just one season the publisher of *De Nederlander* had to stop its publication in 1852. The *Sheboygan* joined the enthusiasm for the Republican Party, which was founded in Wisconsin in 1854. Chief Editor Quintus was even elected Republican clerk of the court that year but returned in 1857 to the Democratic camp because the Republicans saw immigrants as a danger and did not push back slavery.[52]

The cradle of the newspaper *De Hollander* did not stand in the city by that name but in Allegan, the county seat of the district. Initially the definite article in 1850 read *The*, because the paper was intended by Americans as a bilingual paper that was to reach not only those speaking

[50]  Quintus sold the *Zierikzeesche Nieuwsbode* in Buffalo (July 24, 1848) and in Albany (1849). The only issue of the *Democratic Secretary* is found in the State Historical Society of Wisconsin in Madison, dated October 7, 1853 (volume 1, number 1). It contains many advertisements, news of the Democratic Party, and various fillers.

[51]  Lucas, *Netherlanders*, 529-42. Donald Sinnema, "Dutch American Newspapers and the Network of Early Immigrant Communities," in Wagenaar and Swierenga, *Dutch Enterprise*, 43-56.

[52]  Van Hinte, *Netherlanders in America*, 311, 914-42. *De Sheboygan Nieuwsbode*, November 7, 1854 and November 3, 1857. After Quintus sold his newspaper to G.M. Groesbeck, the paper turned Republican again.

English but also the Dutch of the region.[53] Not long after its founding, Van Raalte moved it to Holland. This newspaper also promoted the interests of the Democratic Party. No wonder that after the victory of the Republicans in 1860 a competitor appeared to offer political balance: *De Grondwet*. *De Hollander* gave up the ghost in 1895, since by that time the entire colony had turned Republican. From the beginning *De Grondwet* regularly supplied news from other Dutch settlements in America and expanded this service ever farther. In 1879 the reader was presented with news about the Dutch who lived elsewhere in Michigan, and six years later this news grew into a column with the name, "Onze Correspondenten." A wide circle of correspondents contributed weekly between five and ten news items, which became so important that in 1908 they even appeared on the front page. Beginning in the 1880s, *De Grondwet* also established a network of agents who had to collect the subscription fees and bring in new subscribers. Circulation reached the four-thousand mark in 1909.[54]

In Pella also, a paper in the English language was published in 1855, called the *Pella Gazette*, but after five years Scholte, who was editor in chief, had to cease publication, probably because the population mistrusted him as a person and because of the tenacity of the Dutch language. In 1861 the Dutch newspaper *Pella's Weekblad* appeared on the scene. This Democratic-leaning paper existed until 1942.

Newspapers that gathered news from other Dutch settlements became popular, such as the Republican-leaning *De Volksvriend* of Orange City, Iowa. This weekly began publication in 1874, formed a circle of correspondents in 1892 who, from 1911 on, found their pieces on the front page. This sort of news from other immigrant circles became the trademark of the newspaper and filled half of it. Readers who often had family members or relatives in other states were able to follow the development of all those places with one subscription. The information was extremely detailed: about the arrival of new immigrants, what the crops looked like, the weather situation, church festivals, the growth of the community, birth, death and wedding announcements, and disasters. The Dutch newspapers created a close bond between Dutch in America as well as in the Netherlands; no wonder that some letter

---

[53]   Already in October 1850 Van Raalte had promised his cooperation to keep each other informed, *Classis Holland, Minutes 1848-1858* (Grand Rapids: Eerdmans, 1950), 40.

[54]   Lucas, *Netherlanders*, 536. Robert P. Swierenga, "Press Censorship: Rev. Albertus C. Van Raalte and Editor Hermanus Doesburg of *De Hollander*," in Swierenga, *Dutch-American Arts and Letters*, 171-82.

writers sighed that their private correspondence reported "old" news.[55] Although most Dutch-American newspapers fed mutual relationships, sometimes they also entered the arena of attempting to curry the favor of the voter or potential immigrants. Competition existed especially between Iowa and Michigan.[56]

It is therefore remarkable that Grand Rapids, where the greatest concentration of Dutch lived, produced only small newspapers: the *Standard-Bulletin* (begun in 1875) and the *Christian Journal* (1887). This city took the lead in publishing religious papers, with *De Wachter* being the leader as the voice of the Christian Reformed Church. The paper was founded in 1868 and had developed into a weekly by 1907, with a reach of nine thousand addresses.

From 1893 on, Chicago had the Republican weekly *Onze Toekomst* (*"Our Future"*), which the Reverend Dr. John van Lonkhuijzen, a CRC minister, turned into a flourishing publication. On the East Coast, *Het Oosten*, published in Paterson, New Jersey, also of Republican persuasion, constituted the principal reading material. Apart from these general weeklies, which numbered between two and eight thousand subscribers, scores of other Dutch periodicals appeared, varying from the *Utah-Nederlander*, which served the Dutch Mormons, and the *Stemmen uit de Vrije Hollandsche Gemeente* (*"Voices from the Free Dutch Church,"* the liberal church of F.W.N. Hugenholtz in Grand Rapids), to all kinds of short-lived local newspapers such as *De Nederlandsche Dakotiaan* (1884-1886) and *De Alto Demokraat*. Not enough readers, the departure of the editor in chief, and competition from the large papers shortened the lifespan of these papers. Typical of the Dutch as a middle-class community was the fact that a paper for workers, such as other west-European groups had, was lacking. Only in election years did papers for workers appear briefly to support their interests.[57]

The Catholic community had its own weeklies, for example, *De Pere Standaard*. In 1878 two Flemings in northern Wisconsin, Eduard Van de Casteele and John Heyrman, had taken the initiative for its publication. Heyrman sold his share in this newspaper to his partner

---

[55]  Sinnema, "Dutch American Newspapers," 48-51.

[56]  Jacob Van der Zee, *The Hollanders of Iowa* (Iowa City: Iowa Historical Society, 1912), 157-58.

[57]  P.R.D. Stokvis, "Socialist Immigrants and the American Dream," in Krabbendam and Wagenaar, *Dutch-American Experience*, 91-101. In Grand Rapids, *De Christen Werkman* (1892-1894), *Het Volksblad* (1892), *De Volksstem* (1908), in Holland, *Voorwaarts* (1914), and in Paterson, *Nieuw Nederland* (1911-1912).

Advertisement for *Onze Toekomst* (*Our Future*), the Dutch weekly in Chicago.

Archives, Calvin College, Grand Rapids, Michigan.

in 1890, who reached a circulation of approximately 2,500, until he suspended publication in 1907. Heyrman was a true newspaperman who simultaneously published an English-language newspaper, the *Brown County Democrat*, and a second Dutch-language newspaper, *De Volksstem*, in 1890. The circulation grew steadily from 1,300 copies in 1890, to its maximum of 1,750 in 1910. For thirty years *De Volksstem* was the most important medium in America for Dutch Catholics. Thanks to mutual exchange agreements this paper was able to print news from the Netherlands, while it also printed information from other Dutch/ Flemish communities, and at times even from Protestant colonies. In 1919 *De Volksstem* merged with the *Gazette of Moline*, also published by Flemish immigrants who, together with the *Gazette of Detroit*, provided Catholics with news. At that time the paper switched over to English.[58] During all this time, these newspapers were loyal supporters of the Democratic Party.

---

[58]   Kristine Smets, "The Gazette of Moline and the Belgian-American Community, 1907-1921" (M.A. thesis, Kent State Univ., 1994), 14-15. *Commemorative Biographical Record of the Fox River Valley Counties of Brown, Outagamie and Winnebago* (Chicago: J.H. Beers, 1895), 413 and 431.

Each newspaper paid attention to religious matters. The Dutch readers expected an edifying word and received a daily meditation, religious serials, theological polemics, and much church news, from America as well as from the Netherlands. Church papers had the greatest continuity, and they in turn contained also much secular news.[59]

After the Civil War, *De Hope* evolved from a news magazine connected with the college of the same name into a church paper of the Reformed Church as a counterbalance to *De Wachter*, which in 1868 became the official medium of the Christian Reformed Church. *De Hope*, the *Leader*, and the *Christian Intelligencer* were the papers that were read most. In 1903 the *Banner* became the church paper for the English-speaking segment of the Christian Reformed Church. It was the voice of Henry Beets, the progressive minister who was its editor in chief from 1903 until 1924, and it is still in print.

After the *Sheboygan Nieuwsbode* had died, *De Grondwet* and *De Volksvriend* took over its function as provider of the news for and about the scattered Dutch settlements. Other newspapers provided these same services, but on a more regional basis. *De Hollandsche Amerikaan*, published in Kalamazoo from 1892-1945 and of orthodox-Republican persuasion, offered news especially from areas where its readers had their roots, in other words, the provinces of Groningen and Zeeland. The reports kept people of the same area informed of the latest news. Thus, the issue of January 18, 1907, reported that the municipal constable of Hoedekenskerke in Zeeland, B. de Jonge, had received an envelope, with money, from the mayor as evidence of appreciation for twenty-five years of faithful service. This newspaper majored furthermore in news about thefts, appointments, accidents, choir festivals, and court cases in the Netherlands, and in much church news about the Secessionist churches in the Netherlands. The paper also drew on the church press in America.

A good example of a correspondent who brought his settlement in contact with the rest of the Dutch network was Klaas G. Feyma. For twenty-eight years Feyma wrote reports for *De Volksvriend* about the small colony of Friesland in Minnesota. Each correspondent received

---

[59] *De Wachter* and the *Hollandsche Amerikaan* were anti-English and pro-German during the First World War. When America joined the war, *De Wachter* provided little information about the war, while *De Grondwet* fully supported the war effort. Eventually all newspapers adopted a pro-allied standpoint. *Hollandsche Amerikaan*, November 1, 1918. Harry Boonstra, "Dutch-American Newspapers and Periodicals in Michigan, 1850-1925," (M.A. thesis, Univ. of Chicago, 1967), 36-90.

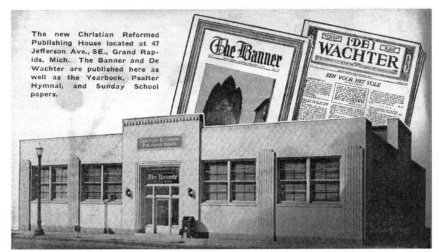

The new Christian Reformed Publishing House located at 47 Jefferson Ave., SE., Grand Rapids, Mich. The Banner and De Wachter are published here as well as the Yearbook, Psalter Hymnal, and Sunday School papers.

Printing plant of the Christian Reformed Church in Grand Rapids.

Archives, Calvin College, Grand Rapids, Michigan.

a free subscription, and the distribution was looked after by a network of agents. The number of subscriptions reached a peak in 1907.[60] This resulted in part from the free postal delivery in rural areas (Rural Free Delivery), which kept distribution costs low. However, in the long run this measure was the death knell for the local press, because newspapers from outside the region also had easy access to the local market. At the same time, the correspondents widened their horizons by writing more about the region instead of only about experiences of Dutch immigrants.

Readers were not presumed to expect a lot from these newspapers. They found the same sensational reports as in the American press, with village gossip added as attractive dessert. In the event that debates were carried on, the topics were either theological or about political intrigue. An exception was the charismatic B.D. Dykstra, the evangelist of the Reformed Church and teacher at frontier schools, who between 1928 and 1934, and also from 1949 to 1951, was editor in chief of *De Volksvriend*, the leading Dutch weekly in Orange City, Iowa.[61] He wrote

[60]   Robert Schoone-Jongen, "Klaas F. Feyma: Minnesota's Carpenter/ Correspondent," *Proceedings of the Association for the Advancement of Dutch-American Studies* (Grand Rapids: Calvin College, 2001), 44-49, and "De Volksvriend and Dutch-American Relations," in Swierenga, *Dutch-American Arts and Letters*, 183-90.
[61]   Dykstra, *"B.D.,"* 121-38.

a weekly editorial with a firm position, a Sunday school lesson, local and national news—drawn from the *Congressional Record*, not one of the most exciting newspapers. For news from abroad, the editor used the Amsterdam *Telegraaf*, which not only provided fairly old news items in view of the time interval, but also offered a European perspective. The greatest attraction, therefore, was the news from Dutch immigrant communities, full of names and facts, which everyone wanted to read.

Publications in the Dutch language were not restricted to northern Protestants and Catholics. Dutch Mormons in Ogden, Utah, published *De Huisvriend* in 1905, which appeared irregularly with some Dutch news, and was followed by *De Hollander*, which existed for only a few weeks. A third effort to publish a weekly succeeded in 1914 with *De Utah Nederlander*, "The Only Dutch Newspaper in the Inter-Mountain States," which appeared until 1935. This weekly received financial support from the leadership of the Church of Latter-day Saints and was not only intended for Dutch immigrants but was also to make new converts in the Netherlands.[62] The editor in chief, Willem De Bry—an immigrant from Rotterdam who had lived in Utah since 1890—often served as a guide for other immigrants and made regular mission trips to the Netherlands. Every Thursday he published a newspaper of four pages that was printed at a communal print shop. The contents consisted of summaries of European, Dutch, and American news, church reports, and accounts of the weekly cultural gatherings of the Dutch in Ogden and Salt Lake City. In between, De Bry provided

[62] William Mulder, "Willem Jacobus De Bry and *De Utah Nederlander*, 1914-1935," *Utah Historical Quarterly* 72.2 (2004): 100-18. Publications for other nationalities were also supported by the Latter-day Saints. More information about the Dutch Mormons may be found in William Mulder, "Hollander Immigrants to Utah," in *The Utah History Encyclopedia* (Salt Lake City: n.p., 1994), 259-60. William Mulder, "From Haarlem to Hoboken: Pages from a Dutch Mormon Immigrant Diary," *Utah Historical Quarterly* 64 (1996): 298-321. Janet Sjaarda Sheeres, "From Dikes to the Desert: The First Dutch Mormons in Utah in the Last Half of the 1800s," *Utah Historical Quarterly* 74 (Spring 2006): 114-30.
   Dutch Mormons settled in the state of Utah in 1864, three years after the first missionary activities in the Netherlands. These converts expected the literal establishment of God's Kingdom in America and wanted to be present for that. After the turn of the century, sufficient Dutchmen lived in Utah to sustain a flourishing cultural program. Scores of compatriots gathered weekly for the "Dutch Meeting," in Salt Lake City on Friday evening, and in Ogden on Tuesday, for a mixture of cultural and religious elements. The annual meeting in 1906 even mobilized a thousand people for a program of song, theater, sports, and music.

information about important events in American history and about national symbols, coupled with advice for new immigrants. The paper served as source of information about anniversaries and news items from the home country, and as an advertiser for Dutch products and services. Theatrical performances were faithfully covered, just as the accomplishments of the players of *De Voetbal Club* ("the Soccer Club"). In the midst of the economic depression of the 1930s the paper was suspended, just as the other foreign-language newspapers that the Mormons published. Immigration came to a halt, the older generation died, and Mormons were accepted more and more. The small circulation (six hundred copies at maximum) had kept the paper dependent on support and cooperation from the church. The Church of the Latter-day Saints stimulated the use of immigrant languages because in that way contacts and missionary activities in other countries were promoted. The language of the *Utah Nederlander* was a mixture from the beginning, witness the following poetry:

> Wij lijke Dutch op Zion's hill [We like Dutch on Zion's hill]
> And show it!
> Wij speaken moeders taal nog still - [We still speak our mother's tongue]
> And know it!
> We houden het hier in de West [Here in the West we continue to treasure it;]
> In waarde;
> Want Hollands language is de beste [For the Dutch language is the best]
> Op aarde! [On earth!] [63]

Love of the Dutch language and interest in matters of faith were the mainstay of the Dutch-language press.[64] It is also ironic that this same press made itself superfluous by breaking through the isolation of the Hollanders. The many efforts to start their own periodicals testified to a widespread sense of belonging in America. The high point came in the years 1910-1919 when ten new publications saw the light of day and a total of twenty-two Dutch-American newspapers were available.[65]

The loss of the ethnic press was the result of the disappearance of local autonomy in the 1950s, after this press had formed the cornerstone of the network for almost a century. With the discontinuation of Dutch-language newspapers, the supply of Dutch books also stopped. Many printers had combined the publication of newspapers with the

---

[63]  Ibid., 116. See also the plea for the Dutch language in *De Utah Nederlander*, May 21, 1914.
[64]  Lucas, *Netherlanders*, 541.
[65]  Boonstra, "Dutch-American Newspapers," 104.

publication and sale of books. The largest part of the publisher's list consisted of theological works, supplemented by a few history books and novels. They recommended their own products in their own newspapers, in which these books often had first appeared as serials. Thus, the printers filled an important social function during an entire century, especially in the newly settled areas of the country.

## Informative Ties

Dutch Americans may have visited the home country and other Dutch colonies, but they especially maintained relationships on paper. Millions of letters traveled across the Atlantic Ocean to keep family ties alive, often accompanied by Dutch newspapers and magazines. Approximately fifty periodicals, fifteen of which were publications of long standing, supplied the immigrants' need for news. Most newspapers were established for political reasons and to provide information. Afterwards they became important as a means for promoting individual colonies and as a channel for spreading local news. Newspapers stimulated, and profited from, the Dutch-American network. The breaking up of the community and the disappearance of the Dutch ethnic middle class in the 1950s weakened them. Newspapers and periodicals that were supported by an institution—first political parties, and later especially churches—had the best chance of survival. The Reformed and Christian Reformed churches did this, but also a relatively small community such as the Mormons.

The newspapers were the cement between the building blocks of the Dutch communities. Thanks to financial support and the ideas of political parties, readers were drawn into the American political system. As a result, the Dutch immigrants began to think about their identity as American citizens.

# CHAPTER 9

# Politics

The Dutch in the nineteenth century showed very little interest in American politics. Occasional travel accounts reported the basic facts of the American political system, unless the writer happened to have landed in an election campaign.[1] Immigrants, of course, did pay attention to the political culture of their new environment. They fostered positive expectations of America, even though they had second thoughts about some developments. Their leaders knew all too well that they needed Americans in order to make their plans come true, but they also realized that politicians could be competitors for their own authority position, as were businessmen and journalists.[2]

Compared to other immigrant groups, Dutch immigrants did not draw political attention. They did not organize for political change in their home country or produce sensational politicians like the Irish. They were not numerous enough to build a political machine in the

---

[1]  Steringa, *Nederlanders op reis in Amerika*, 88-90.
[2]  Victor R. Greene, *American Immigrant Leaders 1800-1910: Marginality and Identity* (Baltimore: Johns Hopkins Univ. Press, 1987), 1-16.

cities like the Italians and did not play an organizing role in the balance of power like the Jewish community. Their migration did not result from political motives like that of the Germans, who left their country in large numbers in 1849 because they were disappointed in the failure of political reforms and who would remain active participants in American politics. For the Dutch, politics was not a career path; they mainly used the American political system to strengthen their subculture.

From their first arrival as a group, Dutch immigrants sensed the advantages of the American system. In contrast to their native country, they could participate in local elections immediately after having submitted their desire to become citizens, and they obtained the right to vote in national elections after a residency of five years. Their leaders encouraged participation in the political process and obtained concrete benefits for them by having their settlement registered as soon as possible as a township. In this way they could promote the development of their settlement by constructing roads, building bridges, and establishing schools, which were being paid for by self-imposed taxes. By their involvement in the most important political debates and events (such as the Civil War), immigrants began to identify with the greater entity of "America." As a result, they began to see themselves in a new (American) light.

Participation in politics by Dutch immigrants was not the conclusion of a cultural development, but the beginning intended to secure the safeguarding of their own community, and subsequently an instrument to defend it. The urge to apply for citizenship diminished in the course of the nineteenth century, because by then most local matters had been regulated. After the Civil War, Protestant immigrants lent their support to the Republicans and became more and more conservative. When in the 1870s the communities were ever more closely linked to national networks through railroads, market expansion, contacts, and new media, they had to determine their response to national questions. The negative impact of rapid industrialization, expansion, and urbanization, which led to labor unrest, poverty, criminality, and unfair competition, could be redressed in two ways. One option was to strengthen the influence of the state. Another option was to plead for driving back this influence and for strengthening private institutions such as schools, which were not only binding agents of the group itself, but which also were able to resist the advancing influence of the state. The American historian Jon Gjerde suggests that the stronger the creedal convictions were that bound an immigrant group together, the less it was inclined to become involved in politics for fear of outside interference.[3] The Dutch immigrants in the colonies who had a religious identity fit this last profile, but that did not keep them away from politics. They wanted not only to secure their own interests; they also had a sincere admiration for the American political system, which contrasted favorably with the limitations of the European systems.

## Appreciation of the American System

The Mennonite emigrant R.J. Sijmensma concluded in 1853 that the difficult sea voyage had a leveling influence on immigrants and prepared them for the republican form of government: "I saw a heavy woman from the highlands, who just a moment earlier had looked down on us rather contemptuously, now crawl toward us in her anguish, and lay down unceremoniously next to those despised Frisians. Then the thought occurred to me, it is only very natural that the American states are republican since all delusions of grandeur are severely chastised during the voyage there, by circumstances like these."[4]

Whether this chastening would make a lasting impression is doubtful, although this line of thought was certainly illustrative of the positive attitude of the nineteenth-century immigrant toward the republican form of government in America, which offered all citizens, regardless of their stations in life, a say in the government of the country. The contrast was especially striking for immigrants who left the Netherlands before the new constitution of 1848. In the Netherlands citizens were residents with restricted rights. In America they were full-fledged citizens. Alexander Hartgerink already informed Van Raalte of this in May 1846: "Concerning civic affairs, here we have a government of the people. All government officials from the highest to the lowest are elected by the citizens. If someone in this land has owned any property for 5 years, he is a citizen and a voter, and may even be elected to the highest office...." He also extolled the freedom of religion, "the freedom all religious sects have, as long as they do not threaten the State; also the freedom of every religious denomination to establish their own schools at their own expense, and to provide an education here as they see fit, next to freedom of every denomination to preach to anyone in this country." No church received state support and for that

---

[3]    Gjerde, *Minds of the West*, 280.
[4]    D.S. Gorter, *Vijf brieven uit Amerika* in *Godsdienstige lectuur voor Doopsgezinden* (Sneek: Van Druten en Bleeker, 1854), 264. He was referring to a heavy storm.

reason there were no second-class citizens based on religious criteria.[5] This state of affairs made America attractive to religious minorities, while the members of the established church, as well as the orthodox supporters of the dissenters and political conservatives, were put off by America and did not emigrate. In that country there was no room for the privileges of the Reformed Church (*Hervormde Kerk*), no role for the aristocracy, and no central control over education. The Dutch elite saw these deficiencies as a serious threat to the good order of society.

New immigrants used the local circumstances as a standard for judging their new society. Many came to the conclusion that the roles were reversed in America. Three young men who had traveled ahead in 1845 to investigate the possibilities for emigration, sent enthusiastic reports to their coordinators in the Netherlands. Carpenter apprentice Arnoldus Hallerdijk reported from Milwaukee, Wisconsin, that the "Seceder [religion] was the most important one," and that there were "many true worshipers."[6] Jan Arend Beukenhorst, a Seceder who emigrated in the summer of 1845 with the vanguard, wrote about the sense of being liberated that he experienced when he noticed that the well-to-do did not look down on the common man: "Dear friends! It was difficult for me to leave Winterswijk, but I don't ever want to go back: the common man here is the rich man's equal, you don't have to tip your hat for anyone. The wealthy people respect us for working for them."[7] Roelof Sleijster, who prepared Van Raalte's journey as a scout, was equally excited in 1846: "Thus Brother! I am an American citizen and enjoy full voting rights in all matters, which is of great importance here for a Christian if he wants to act as a Christian and to give Christian counsel both in schools and in other matters."[8]

A decade later this enthusiasm had not cooled. Jannes van de Luijster wrote to his friend Abraham de Munck June 21, 1856, that he saw God's providence in the developments in America, which caused the conversion of many fortune hunters. He praised the possibilities offered by freedom of religion and local autonomy:

My thoughts and reflections pertain only to the founding of

---

[5]   Ligterink, *Landverhuizers*, 96; Ido de Haan, "Burgerschap, sociale stratificatie en politieke uitsluiting in de negentiende eeuw," in Joost Kloek and Karin Tilmans, eds., *Burger. Een geschiedenis van het begrip "burger" in de Nederlanden van de Middeleeuwen tot de 21ste eeuw* (Amsterdam: Amsterdam Univ. Press, 2002), 231-75.

[6]   Ligterink, *Landverhuizers*, 99.

[7]   Ibid., 101.

[8]   Ibid., 104.

Church and State in this continent. There are many signs for this trend for those who pay attention: the Lord disclosed gold in Kalvorm [California] which lures thousands, and mostly the poorest, Spaniards and Irish, an ungodly lot. But since God's Word has been translated here in over 100 languages and is brought powerfully to all people, it is spread and proclaimed also among those foreigners in California. And reports have it that many accept it....We are a separate people here, we have our own political and church government. We pay our taxes once a year. And the tax collector, who is one of our own, comes to our home to collect it.[9]

The word politics seems to have had a cultured sound for the first emigrants. Johannis Izaak Bril sent his brother Pieter in Zuidzande a list with the dates of Easter for the next thirteen years: "This shows you how political the people are. They look ahead thirteen years, which shows you that they are not the wild and savage beasts that many people say Americans are, no brother, you also find theology and scholarship here in physics, in one word politics."[10]

Emigration therefore appealed immediately to the common people: it created the chance to become one's own boss without being demoted by the higher classes. In 1847 the Frisian S.T. Krap reported enthusiastically from Indiana that he saw everybody work hard, and that "he had heard no one mention constables, bailiffs or custom officers. Everybody here bakes, distills, brews, buys, and sells without a permit, and J. Bolman says: 'everything is free, we are in *America!*'"[11] This spontaneous reaction shows how strongly the absence of monitoring authorities was experienced as liberation. The community solved its own problems. Church council meetings helped keep mutual relationships sound: quarrelsome persons were visited and had to settle their conflict on pain of exclusion. Questions and complaints about members of the community received a full hearing. A balanced church council strengthened the civic community. So, for instance, the church council of the Reformed Church in Zeeland made a member live up to a delivery contract of Indian corn (maize). The council also dispatched an elder to ask shopkeepers to remove their merchandise from the display windows so as not to tempt churchgoers by arousing their desire. It

9    RSC.
10   January 10, 1858, *In den vreemde* 5 (September 1994): 120.
11   Osinga, *Tiental brieven betrekkelijk de reis*, 28.

was not until the beginning of 1859 that the consistory of Holland, Michigan, stated that it would no longer deal with civic matters.[12]

During the same pioneer period, immigrants did have an eye for the practical objections against a weak central government that left many responsibilities to the citizens. Father Adrianus van de Braak commented that insufficient supervision of public works led to many railroad and bridge accidents that could have been prevented with proper supervision. He had counted five hundred victims in the newspapers in three weeks' time. He did, however, praise the freedom that he found and which he saw also affecting his church. The existence of a monastery with black nuns, "Moorins," filled him with pride since it showed that the Catholic Church accepted blacks as equal human beings. America compared favorably with the Netherlands; he had read in an American newspaper that the restoration of the Catholic hierarchy there had almost led to a civil war.[13]

It was precisely the contrast with the Netherlands and the appreciation of the American system it fostered which enabled it to weather the constant criticism of the spectacular election campaigns. This election circus continued to flabbergast immigrants, even after years of residence. H.W. van den Bosch, a Catholic immigrant who had witnessed his sixth presidential campaign, was still amazed in 1868 at the goings-on of the political parties that spent hundreds of thousands of dollars and left no stone unturned to deliver the next president.[14] Johan Philipsen, from the village of Auburn in New York, wrote that there were presidential elections every five [sic] years, when the citizens elected a "sort of a king," and that the Democrats were Catholic and the Protestants Republican. In spite of the not entirely correct account, the writer did know where the power lay. Teunis van den Hoek of Roseland, near Chicago, confirmed the impression of the Protestant climate in America from his Protestant perspective. He praised the president, who did a better job of maintaining the law in church and state than the king of the Netherlands. To his relief (and due to his limited perception), Catholics stood outside public life.[15]

A somewhat unimpressed but hopeful account of the presidential election came from the Dakotas in 1896: "Yesterday the people voted, but what a hullabaloo, in the cities people nearly kill each other, but the

---

[12]  Consistory minutes, Reformed Church, January 13, 1859, and May 12, 1859, Zeeland Historical Society.

[13]  Letter of May 18, 1853, from Father Adrianus van de Braak, August 1852-August 1853. Box 21, folder 136, H. van Stekelenburg Collection, RSC.

[14]  H.W. van de Bosch, November 1, 1868, Brinks, *Dutch American Voices*, 234.

[15]  Ibid., 118, December 28, 1866.

Republicans stand a good chance of winning and then life will certainly improve somewhat for everyone."[16] These observations remained superficial. Participation in the elections and immigrants' interest in political parties, and vice versa, gave the immigrants new instruments to order their lives.

## Political Parties

The leaders of the Dutch immigrants of the mid-nineteenth century realized how they could make use of American politics to achieve local autonomy. Politics was chiefly a local affair. Van Raalte knew that when people founded a village, they were allowed to elect their own justice of the peace, who had a governmental and a judicial function. The justice of the peace would be assisted by officers from the people themselves and would therefore not be imposed upon them by the authorities.[17] He also praised the involvement of the Americans in their politics: "...everybody here reads. The republican viewpoint is deeply impressed on people in every possible way, and everybody begins to realize: all the land and business belongs to us, and we govern ourselves by way of our own smartest citizens."[18]

Already before leaving the Netherlands, the first emigrants decided to become American citizens. On July 5, 1848, 186 men took an oath on the Constitution in an assembly in the Zeeland church to start the process of naturalization. This haste was prompted especially by the desire to organize local rule quickly, with as their first trophy a post office. These immigrants were allowed to vote for the first time in the presidential election of 1852, in which the Democrat Franklin Pierce won convincingly over the leading candidate of the Republicans, the Whig candidate General Winfield Scott.[19]

Hendrik Scholte knew how to find the way to the center of power quickly. At the beginning of 1848, he submitted a petition to the government of the state of Iowa to form a township committee and to grant the right to vote for local offices to everybody who had made a statement of intent to become an American citizen. He used American cooperation to further advocate emigration in the Netherlands.[20]

---

[16]   Bakker, *Zuster*, 145. The author turned out to be right: William McKinley was chosen.
[17]   Brummelkamp, *Stemmen uit Noord-Amerika*, 66.
[18]   Ibid., 76.
[19]   Jannes van de Luijster, Diary IV, Joint Archives of Holland, Holland, Michigan.
[20]   Scholte, *Eene Stem uit Pella*, 32-33.

Initially the immigrants felt most at home in the Democratic Party because of its immigrant-friendly attitude. The political opponents, the Whigs, tried to restrict immigration. Both Scholte and Van Raalte had no difficulty gaining access to the political leaders of their state. Van Raalte was a friend of Lewis Cass (1782-1866), a hero of the War of 1812, secretary of war under the Democratic presidents Andrew Jackson and James Buchanan, senator of Michigan from 1845-1856, and Democratic candidate for president in 1848. Other prominent Democrats, such as Judge Kellogg, had helped Van Raalte get land.[21] An election banner in Grand Rapids in 1856 read in Dutch, "Oppressed by aristocrats in the Old World, Protected by Democrats in the New World. We vote for Buchanan and Breckenridge."[22] However, the corrupt administration of Buchanan was disappointing. When the Republican Party removed the anti-immigration measures from its party platform, this party became attractive again to immigrants, even though the majority of them still voted Democrat and Catholic newcomers would continue to do so.

In the 1852 election year, Van der Meulen called on people to support the Democratic candidate for the House of Representatives because "he had proven to be a reliable person...by his knowledge of our most precious interests which he...desires to endorse and promote."[23] The minister found that partisanship should not exclude a fair evaluation of the candidates. The Whigs also had their defenders, but they formed a minority because the party was associated with the aristocratic interests of the Northeast.

Initially only Scholte felt at home with the Whigs, because they were better educated, pursued a sounder economic policy, and in his opinion promoted the unity of the nation. He defended the position that the states had to decide the fate of slavery, instead of the federal government. He also propagated an active policy of government investments.[24] To Scholte the democratic form of government would only succeed if the majority was of good will. In 1857 he already expressed the fear that the Union might break up as a result of "the folly and political fanaticism of the power-driven party leaders."[25] However,

---

[21]    Larry J. Wagenaar, "The Early Political History of Holland, Michigan, 1847-1868" (M.A. thesis, Kent State Univ., Ohio, 1992), 62-75.

[22]    *De Hollander*, July 9, 1856.

[23]    Ibid., October 13, 1852.

[24]    Swierenga, *Faith and Family*, 276.

[25]    Letter H.P. Scholte to J.L.L. van der Brugghen, 1857, Stellingwerff, *Iowa Letters*, 433-34. For a brief summary of his political development see C. Smits, *De Afscheiding van 1834*, vol. 3, 329-30. He joined the Whigs first,

in the same letter he expressed his longing to retire in the Netherlands: "My heart is not in it. America can never become the Netherlands for me." He maintained contact with the royal family by sending the king the *Pella Gazette*, and from time to time he would receive a reply from King Willem III.

When the Whigs proved themselves to be proponents of an immigrant stop and drastic measures against alcohol, his love flagged. When subsequently the influence of the Whigs waned quickly after the death of their leader Henry Clay in 1852, Scholte threw his weight behind the battle on behalf of the Democrats because he lost confidence in the stability of the new Republican Party. He feared that a civil war might break out, and he involved himself with much fervor in the election debates of 1856 on behalf of the Democrats, whom he considered the lesser of two evils. He even came to Michigan to speak for Buchanan. His participation in the election circus evoked quite a bit of opposition, as though he defended slavery for monetary gain. Witness the following rhyme that appeared in the *Sheboygan Nieuwsbode* of October 7:

> Did Rev. H.P. Scholte leave his pulpit?
> To talk about the Democrats?
> Instead of winning souls for Jesus?
> To waste his time on Slavery?
> From Genesis 1 vs. 28 we do not learn
> That whites have greater rights than blacks,
> Or could it be that for a few pieces of silver
> He wants to garner them some votes? [26]

Scholte thought in abstract terms and from a national perspective, but most Dutch immigrants let themselves be led by regional considerations. They had little sympathy for radical solutions, and only a few were truly interested in the fate of the slaves. This mentality slowed their defection to the Republicans. Their political preference was not determined by high ideals, but by local interests. When the Democrats did not support the creation of harbors in Michigan while the Republicans did, the latter gained the sympathy of the coastal residents. The close ties with the Dutch-American benefactors of the

found J.C. Frémont unfit as presidential candidate for the Republicans, expressed his preference in 1860 for William H. Seward as Republican candidate for the presidency in that year, but afterwards had no difficulty with the choice of Abraham Lincoln.

[26]  Lucas, *Netherlanders*, 714 note 134.

East Coast, who were Republicans, paved the way for the defection. The Republican plans to guarantee Sunday rest and to limit alcohol consumption were well received by the religious Dutch in Michigan, who had a more explicit and closed community ideal than their cousins in Iowa. Van Raalte barred taverns at first, while Scholte argued for a brewery. Both opposed the consumption of alcohol but differed in their opinions about the effects of strict legislation.

Van Raalte and Van der Meulen made the transition to the Republican Party just before the Civil War. This may have been due to their close connections with the Reformed Church, which already in 1855 had decided not to admit congregations that permitted slavery to their denomination.[27] Scholte followed in 1859 from disappointment with the Democrats, who had not kept their promises regarding a national economic policy, support for railroads, and the Homestead Act. His sudden conversion to the Republican Party astounded friend and foe. Although he was expected at the state party convention as a Democratic delegate, he turned up a few days later, to everybody's surprise, at a party gathering of the Republicans where he was elected vice chair. He felt at home with the more elitist and national Republican Party, but his fellow Pellians remained Democrats, in spite of their objections to slavery. Elsewhere, also, some Dutch continued to support the Democrats. They believed the election promise of the Democrats that only this party could end the slavery conflict, or they had personal objections to Republican representatives.

The Republican Party had a few drawbacks as well. The radical rhetoric for the abolishment of slavery scared the Dutch immigrants off, just as the proposals to ban liquor by way of legislation. Especially repellent to voters was the inclusion of the outspoken anti-immigrant party of the "Know-Nothings" from the Northeast, which had succeeded in the 1850s in gaining a large following in the West among the supporters of the Republican Party. The effect of these political debates was that this first generation cherished its citizenship, because that right was threatened for immigrants.[28] During the Civil War most of the Dutch supported the northern Union against the southern Confederacy. Scholte even attended the inauguration of "Honest Abe" in 1861 and promised land to volunteers who enlisted in the Union Army.

The lack of a strong and consistent national party ideology offered opportunities for opposition in the Dutch communities. In

[27]    *Classis Holland Minutes, 1848-1858* (Grand Rapids: Eerdmans, 1950), 180.
[28]    Lucas, *Netherlanders*, 541-51.

1860 Holland still counted a small Democratic majority but saw it shift to the Republican camp four years later.[29] In Zeeland the Democrats had a slight advantage until 1877. In February of that year there was a controversy in Zeeland because the Democrats G. van Schelven and J. van der Veen tried to show that the Republican J. den Herder was not a citizen and for that reason should not have been allowed to hold office. He was a presidential elector (the first Dutchman) in the disputed Tilden-Hayes campaign of 1876, which Hayes won.[30]

In November 1880 the Republicans were victorious, and they celebrated with a parade, music, and fireworks. The role of the Democrats was not over, however. A number of prominent Dutchmen remained loyal to the Democratic Party, which became acceptable again after slavery had ended. They won many a village election when the Republican Party was divided, or when it embraced too exclusively a controversial issue such as prohibition.[31] The attraction of the Republican tradition was that it endorsed the religious convictions of many Dutch immigrants that man's evil nature should be restrained.[32] The Dutch embraced the organizational innovations of the leading party. On July 18, 1888, young men in Zeeland started a Young Republican Club, which soon numbered a hundred members.[33]

Krijn Goudzwaard was of this mind; in 1877 he testified to the uncertainties elections brought, "... as far as that is concerned, this is a strange country, when a President is elected and all the members who are under him who govern the country, everything has to be closed, which means no work and no money." He found the political debates of little value because "providence" was not mentioned. To his orthodox-Reformed thinking, things were plain: as long as the people lived according to God's ordinances prosperity would reign; otherwise it would not. Moral questions therefore had long-lasting consequences.[34]

---

29  In Holland, 208 people voted for the Democratic candidate Douglas and 185 for Lincoln; in Zeeland the difference was even smaller: 89 to 85. Afterwards they voted Republican. Since 1864 Ottawa County has always voted for a Republican. De Hollander, November 28, 1860.

30  De Grondwet, May 8, 1877, and February 20, 1860.

31  De Grondwet, November 4, 1880; see also the battle in De Grondwet, May 12, 1885, about the election campaign, and May 10, 1887, and May 1, 1888, about the victory of the Democrats in Zeeland.

32  Van Hinte, Netherlanders, 438-43.

33  De Grondwet, July 24, 1888.

34  Letter Krijn Goudzwaard, Grand Rapids, to brothers and sisters in Poortvliet, January 27, 1877, RSC. This conclusion was widely accepted, as is shown in a sermon by Van Raalte, who did not claim to be without

Fourth of July celebration in Sioux County, Iowa.
Archives, Calvin College, Grand Rapids, Michigan.

It was the celebration of America's independence that bound the Dutch immigrants and their new country together. The Netherlands introduced August 31 as the day of the monarchy only in 1885. From the start, the Dutch joined the Americans with much fervor in their festivities. On July 4, 1849, the village of Zeeland celebrated "in a religious fashion" the Declaration of Independence:

> Rev. Van der Meulen gave the official speech in a most fitting address about the discovery of America by Columbus, Americus Vesputius [sic], and others; he further devoted the remainder of his speech to the flourishing and rise of these United States, its glorious Declaration of Independence, the difficult struggle for freedom under brave Washington, so illustriously sustained and so wonderfully brought to a close. Even though it was done in miniature here, the village of Zeeland was illuminated, the American flag with its stars was flown in front of the Zeeland Hotel; the young people demonstrated their exuberance by

sin himself. See Gordon J. Spijkman, *Pioneer Preacher Albertus Van Raalte: A Study of His Sermon Notes* (Grand Rapids: Heritage Hall, 1976), 102.

shooting off guns and pistols. Sincere prayers of thanksgiving were sent up the Great Ruler of peoples and nations....[35]

In that same year, the Classis of Holland made the decision that from now on it would join in observing the American Thanksgiving Day.[36]

Local interest showed up very clearly in the first election contest in the colony, before the villages of Holland and Zeeland were separated administratively. The election for the office of town clerk, road supervisor, school superintendent, and tax collector took place in the church of Zeeland. Together with the neighboring people from Drenthe, the Zeeland people were in the majority because the voters from Holland had to travel ten miles. They tried to get locals in all offices because they found the "Hollanders" too domineering, which brought down the wrath of their neighbors upon them. Diplomatic intervention by Van Raalte avoided a fight. This incident led to a split in county government between Holland and Zeeland in 1851, which prevented further animosity.

In the Far West, agrarian interests were usually the deciding factor for political preferences. The Dutch would organize especially when there were incompatible interests between neighboring villages, or between investors and residents. In Harrison, South Dakota, for instance, a conflict erupted about the location of the courthouse. Two Dutchmen opposed each other: the Republican banker Frank le Cocq, Jr. and the Democratic school teacher Peter Hospers. In the 1890s the support for the Populist Party grew; it defended the interests of farmers and consumers against the power of the banks and large companies. The village of Harrison was Republican, New Holland and Joubert were Populist for a while, and afterwards Democrat.[37]

**Local Politics**

In the rural areas local offices remained in the hands of the Dutch, but on the regional level and in cities the complaint was that they did not form a voters' bloc and were totally uninterested in supporting a compatriot.

The first political organization of the Dutch in Grand Rapids was born when three prominent Dutchmen formed a "Grand Rapids Hollander Association," which was to propagate the principles of the

---

[35]   Lucas, *Dutch Immigrant Memoirs*, 1:467, diary of Hendrik van Eyck.
[36]   *Classis Holland Minutes 1848-1858* (Grand Rapids: Eerdmans, 1950), 34.
[37]   Van der Pol, *Reservation*, 101-02.

**George Steketee,
businessman
and mayor of
Grand Rapids, 1881.**

Grand Rapids History & Special
Collections Center, Archives,
Grand Rapids Public Library,
Grand Rapids, Michigan

Democratic Party. The Republican Party was still too much in the hands of the anti-immigrants; in addition, the opposition of the Democrats to a central government that was too strong appealed to them because they had experienced its harmful effects in the Netherlands. In the course of the 1850s, the Dutch became more critical of slavery. After the Civil War, the most Americanized led the majority to the party that had saved the Union.[38]

The Dutch in Grand Rapids were underrepresented in local politics (they constituted one-third of the population), although at the city and county levels they did produce representatives and were strong enough to elect a compatriot, George Steketee, to be mayor. Although the Dutch were proud of him, the politicians were not their true leaders; that role remained reserved for the ministers. The lack of a well-thought-out political philosophy of their own making was a hindrance to being able to act firmly as a group and promoted a pragmatic attitude. To have their own Christian labor union and political party appeared therefore to be impractical.[39]

[38]  Vanderstel, "Dutch of Grand Rapids," 506-07.
[39]  The short-lived reflection by the study group *Fas et Jus*, which functioned for ten years in the neo-Calvinistic slipstream of the politically successful

Historian David Vanderstel explained the lack of political involvement from the strong provincial loyalty that superseded solidarity with the national (Dutch) identity. In addition, the Dutch as a group did not share a specific mutual interest.[40] This attitude was strongest in the beginning period because people from the same region sought each other out. This pattern was visible for a long time in Grand Rapids. There, immigrants from Zierikzee or Tholen concentrated in specific areas. After 1900 these concentrations slowly dissolved. The presence of an alternate, ecclesiastical support network was of greater importance. Therefore the Dutch were not dependent on politics as an alternate route to better positions, as were the Italians and Irish. They achieved social prestige by holding positions in the church, as a member of the consistory, for instance, or in associated organizations. Church responsibilities took away the necessary energy from political activities.

That the center of gravity was to be found in local politics was evident also from the vote in a big city such as Chicago. There, the Reverend Bernardus de Beij of the First Reformed Church praised the results of direct involvement of the people in politics. From 1868 he worked in "the queen of the West," where he was quite successful in gathering together the dispersed Dutch. He did not view the American city in negative terms at all:

> ...what a pleasure it is to live in the midst of such Christian people. Recently a proposal was made in the city council to tax houses of ill repute (whorehouses), and thus to grant them the right to exist. This had hardly become public when a number of women, almost 30,000, protested and the proposal was dropped. Houses of ill repute are outlawed here. The same holds true for violations...especially the abuse of liquor. Here is a Christian government that opposes the power of evil, which finds its strength for the most part in foreigners such as Germans, the Irish, and Frenchmen. Our Dutch people are partly better people, partly more modest and partly more religious, although there are also many among them who are not a credit to their nation.[41]

Abraham Kuyper, antirevolutionary prime minister in the Netherlands between 1901 and 1905, failed to make the transition to practical politics.

[40]  Ibid., 511.

[41]  B. de Beij to P. Lanting, April 1, 1874, ILC HH. De Beij had also been interested in politics in the Netherlands; see Kasboek Kerk en pastorie, 1840-1886, Archief van de Gereformeerde Kerk te Middelstum, Goninger Archieven, April 18, 1865.

The same De Beij was much more critical of national American politics. After eleven years in the New World, he sighed:

> I do not think I will ever be able to accept the republican form of government. Americans and fortune seekers may rave about such a government, not I. Misleaders and misled may claim that the People govern, but in fact demagogues and carpetbaggers rule. But when I look at the despotism of Russia, the straight jacket of Germany, the power of priests in Austria, the turbulence in France, and the weakness in Italy, then I am all confused about this world—and then I praise my old Dutch government—and especially the love between king and people, which, I believe, is somewhat sincere. However, the Netherlands is facing *humiliation*.[42]

Nevertheless, he also saw honest politicians in national politics like the presidential elections of 1880: "The Republican convention has ended and General *Garfield* is candidate for President. He rose from an orphan to his present honorable status, not through advocacy or favoritism, but through hard work, education, and competence. He has been a member of the Senate already since 1870, to which position he has been reelected every two years. Whether he will be President, time will tell."[43] Four years later, right after the elections of 1884: "Our Government has fallen into the hands of the Democrats by the withdrawal of the Independents and Prohibition Republicans. But, 'the Lord reigns!' I see that where you are things are also far from quiet. However, there must be struggle, yet it is less desirable that it is being waged between brothers, like you folks against Dr. Kuipers [Abraham Kuyper]. Such is often a struggle about minor things."[44]

In 1899, a Dutchman was elected to the Chicago city council for the first time, but without campaigning as being Dutch or by being supported by compatriots, since hardly any lived in his district. Also, the first Dutchman in the Illinois House of Representatives, John Meyer, who was active in politics from 1886 until his death in 1894, did not have the backing of a Dutch organization, although he had learned his English in the midst of the Dutch community at the home of Bernardus

---

[42]    B. de Beij to P. Lanting, May 30, 1879, ILC HH.
[43]    B. de Beij to P. Lanting, June 10, 1880, Garfield had actually been a member of the House of Representatives. He referred further to the church struggle led by Abraham Kuyper which was to lead to the Doleantie of 1886.
[44]    B. de Beij to P. Lanting, November 25, 1884, ICL HH.

de Beij in Chicago; as a businessman he had laid the foundation for the Holland Building and Loan Company in 1881, which provided loans with which the Dutch financed their homes. In spite of this solid ethnic base, the group was too small to form a political organization, and for that reason they set other priorities for themselves.[45]

Advice from the Netherlands on how to vote was not appreciated, not even from a respected leader such as Abraham Kuyper: back home, people simply did not understand American politics. Such was the conclusion of the influential minister of the Reformed Church in Chicago, Peter Moerdyke, in *Onze Toekomst* during the Bryan-McKinley campaign of 1900. He lectured Kuyper for meddling in American affairs and for his public support of William Jennings Bryan, who at least was not an imperialist like McKinley.[46]

The Dutch immigrants were hardly the victims of actions against newcomers. Only local circumstances, such as a sudden massive invasion of Dutch that took place in Orange City in the 1870s, aroused resistance from the residents, who thought they were in charge. There, in Iowa, old leaders in neighboring Calliope refused to acknowledge two elected (Dutch) officials. On a cold January day in 1872, a band of 150 angry Dutchmen proceeded to Calliope to fetch the ledgers and the cashbox from the courthouse and take them to Orange City. Both parties quickly came to an agreement and the young city succeeded in 1872 to become the county seat (this was decided through an election). Three years later the Republican Party excluded the Dutch. The latter subsequently joined forces against the party and won the elections.[47]

After the turn of the century the American authorities became concerned that recent immigrants no longer applied for citizenship. There was a slight slowdown among Dutch immigrants, but it could not be called a waning trend. Of the men employed in the furniture industry in Grand Rapids who had immigrated to the United States between five and nine years earlier as adults, only 4 percent held full citizenship, while 40 percent had submitted the initial application. Of those who had immigrated at least ten years earlier, 60 percent had been fully naturalized. In 1890 only 10 percent of the eight thousand born in the Netherlands did not have citizenship papers. Ten years later

---

45    *Onze Toekomst*, April 8, 1899. Swierenga, *Dutch Chicago*, 688. Amry VandenBosch, *The Dutch Communities of Chicago* (Chicago: Knickerbocker Society, 1927), 54-55.

46    *Onze Toekomst*, October 12, 1900.

47    Nella Kennedy, "The Sioux County Dutch," in Bruins, *Dutch in America*, 35.

this percentage had risen by one point; at that time three-quarters of the Dutch had been naturalized. In Chicago that number was even 80 percent.[48]

Support of a party produced concrete returns provided the party won the majority. Lage Prairie, for instance, received a post office with a mailman as thanks for Republican support in 1861.[49] Most Catholics in the communities in Wisconsin supported the Democratic Party, although there were also some who sympathized with the Republicans.[50] It is possible that others behaved like John VandenHoy, a wealthy Catholic farmer in Grand Chute, Wisconsin, who had the following recorded about himself: "...he is a Democrat in politics, but, though supporting that party invariably in State and national elections, he votes for the best candidate in local affairs, regardless of politics."[51]

The Dutch Catholics always remained faithful to their Democratic Party. Protestants and Catholics ignored each other completely. The only thing they agreed on was their rejection of women's suffrage.[52] The Dutch Catholics lamented the underrepresentation of their fellow countrymen in the party and in the elected offices, and just like the Irish they threatened to defect to the Republicans if their candidate was not placed on the ballot.[53]

The Protestant Dutch in Wisconsin voted first for the immigrant-friendly Democratic Party, turned to the Republican Party during the Civil War, and remained true to that party until the elections of 1912, when they appeared to be sensitive to the Dutch Reformed background of Theodore Roosevelt and voted for the Progressive Party just once.

---

[48]   *Reports of the Immigration Commission*, vol. 15, 534. For the Swedes the percentages were 33 (naturalized between five and nine years in the U.S.) and 60 (first papers), while 93 percent of those who had been in the country ten years or longer had been naturalized. Brinks, *Dutch American Voices*, 163. Swierenga, *Dutch Chicago*, 684, and Vanderstel, "Dutch of Grand Rapids," 531.

[49]   Rowlands, *Down an Indian Trail*, 57.

[50]   *Commemorative Biographical Record of the Fox River Valley counties of Brown, Outagamie and Winnebago* (Chicago: J.H. Beers, 1895): Martin van Beek (42) and Martin van de Wyngaard (261) Arnold Peerenboom (923).

[51]   *Commemorative Biographical Record of the Fox River Valley Counties of Brown, Outagamie and Winnebago* (Chicago: J.H. Beers, 1895), 593; see also the sketch of Julius Peerenboom, 900-901.

[52]   Rippley, *Immigrant Experience*, 81.

[53]   John Smith, "Een open brief aan de Hollandsch-Amerikaanse Burgers en Hunne Vlaamse Broeders in Brown County," *De Volksstem*, October 5, 1892 (with thanks to Willem Keeris).

## Officials and Politicians

That politics did not offer a career path for Dutch immigrants but was able to count on their administrative interest was evident from the posts they held. On the local level quite a number of Dutch immigrants held political office, although these were almost never full-time jobs. Only more numerous groups offered opportunities for a political career. However, the band of Dutch was too small in number to become a regional political factor of any significance. Some immigrants held office at a young age, although perhaps not in very prestigious positions. The young watchmaker from Zeeuws-Vlaanderen, Pieter van Ouwerkerk, Jr., was only twenty years old in the early 1850s when he served as mayor of Sheboygan, Wisconsin. After that, he left the office for what it was worth because he found that he had to do too much for the small remuneration of $50 per year. In other places as well, Dutch immigrants ran for office successfully.[54]

In Muskegon, Michigan, the Dutch cleared a path to the office of mayor via local part-time functions such as director of the City Poor Fund or as city councilmen for wards with many Dutch. The office was usually held by shopkeepers or merchants who had many contacts. Since a quarter of the population of Muskegon was of Dutch descent around 1900, this group was able to deliver political representatives fairly regularly and from time to time also mayors, who were reelected repeatedly.[55]

Of all the immigrant leaders, Hendrik Scholte showed himself the politician with the greatest ambition. In March 1886 he tried to cash in on his efforts on behalf of the Republican Party by applying for the post of ambassador to The Hague or Brussels. He obtained the support of the entire Iowa delegation for his candidacy and submitted as his main argument that his appointment would offer a counterbalance to the negative rumors that gave the impression that naturalized citizens were avoided in government. He claimed that the number of immigrants from the Netherlands had been reduced sharply because of the actions of the Know-Nothings who made efforts to bar new immigrants. He thought that immigration—preferably of well-educated people—should

---

[54]  Pieter van Ouwerkerk to stepson Pieter A. Bril in Zuidzande, ca. 1854/55, in A. Vergouwe, *In den Vreemde* 5 (September 1994), 118. Lucas, *Netherlanders*, 555-58.

[55]  Cornelius Steketee, "Hollanders in Muskegon 1850-1897," and Benjamin Telman, "Hollanders in Muskegon Politics, 1872-1914," in Lucas, *Dutch Immigrant Memoirs*, 2:265-70 and 276-79.

increase in the interest of America. He would be glad to cooperate in that effort. His appointment would immediately emasculate all rumors about second-class citizenship. But it was not to be. The practical argument that the state of Iowa was underrepresented in the assignment of foreign posts did not make an impression either.[56] His late conversion to the Republican Party and the loss of his influence among the Dutch did not work in his favor. Scholte's eye for national interests and his personal ambition were increasingly at odds with the local interests of his fellow immigrants and furthered the alienation between leader and followers. Van Raalte experienced this tension as well, but as a parish minister he remained closer to his people and was more democratic and consistent than Scholte.

In West Michigan the route to elected offices was relatively unobstructed. After 1871 the Dutch reached the level of state government, with delegates in the Michigan House of Representatives and Senate. Since that time the Dutch have always been represented in these political bodies. In Iowa the Dutch Americans reached the highest political layers much less often because they lacked an urban power base.[57]

Having representatives in the upper political echelons strengthened feelings of satisfaction and security among the immigrants. In 1881 Krijn Goudzwaard from Poortvliet was proud of what the Dutch in Grand Rapids had accomplished: "...this year, for the first time, a Dutch mayor has been elected who was voted in by the people. We also have Dutch council members, also Dutch tax collectors of whom there are eight in this city. Last year two of my wife's cousins were collectors, a certain Abram De Bruin from Oudvossemeer and a certain Kornelis Sonke, son of Bastiaan Sonke, also from

---

56 "Letters of application and recommendation presidents Lincoln and Johnson," roll 43, 8 and 16 March 1861 microfilm collection M650, National Archives, Washington, D.C. See also Barry J. Carman and Reinhard J. Luthin, *Lincoln and the Patronage* (New York: n.p., 1943). Even a celebrated author such as John Lothrop, writer of the bestseller, *The Rise of the Dutch Republic* (1856), could not convert his Republican support into an ambassadorship to The Hague and had to be satisfied with the post in Vienna and later in London. Six years later he tried again, this time for Berlin because he had learned that the present ambassador was ill. He spoke the major European languages, knew the secretary of state, Mr. Seward, personally, as well as the senators of Iowa. He presented himself as a powerful Republican with whom the interests of the president were safe (March 8 and May 14, 1867).

57 Van Hinte, *Netherlanders*, 896.

Oudvossemeer." This first Dutch mayor was George Steketee, who took a firm line against disturbers of Sunday rest and saloons.[58]

Toward the end of the nineteenth century, the number of Dutch politicians grew. In 1904 five of the twelve Republican candidates for the city council (aldermen) had Dutch backgrounds; two of them even had been born in the Netherlands. In 1907 three men "of Holland parentage" held elected office in the city of Grand Rapids and just as many in Kent County. In that year six of the twenty-four district representatives in Grand Rapids were Dutch.[59] Ate Dykstra (1865-1953) began his political career in 1904 as Democratic alderman in Grand Rapids and managed to become a Republican representative in the Michigan State House of Representatives, where he represented, with a few interruptions, the first district of Kent County between 1923 and 1946. His position as owner of a grocery store, political commentator for the *Standard Bulletin*, and prominent member of the Christian Reformed Church provided him a large base of support.

Only few Dutch immigrant women involved themselves in politics. In this respect Cornelia (1865-1948), the youngest daughter of De Beij, was a pioneer. She was one of the best-educated women in the immigrant community, with diplomas from the Cook County Normal School, the Chicago Art Institute, Northwestern University, and Hahnemann Medical College. After years of study and education at an advanced level, she established herself as a medical doctor in Chicago in 1895. Together with a number of other women, including the well-known social worker Jane Addams, she devoted herself to children's health, employment legislation, the rights of teacher labor unions, and

[58]   April 2, 1881. Vanderstel, "Dutch in Grand Rapids," 507.

[59]   Folder *Republican Candidates City of Grand Rapids, 1904 Spring election*, Grand Rapids Public Library "Common Council Proceedings, City of Grand Rapids, April 7, 1904, Grand Rapids City Archives. With thanks to Bill Cunningham. In 1904 the Republican candidate Sybrant Wesselius fell eight hundred votes short of being elected mayor, out of a total of thirteen thousand. However, fellow party members Dick De Bruyn and Adrian Otte were elected secretary of the police court and county supervisor respectively. In three districts (the sixth, ninth, and twelfth) Dutch-American candidates ran for the position of alderman on behalf of the Republicans and the opposing Democrats. In this mutual contest two of the three Democratic candidates won seats. In 1907 prominent Republican Dutchmen included: City Clerk John L. Boer, Justice of the Peace Nicholas Kik, Board of Assessors Gerrit H. De Graaf. See George Oggle and T.O. Williams, *Standard Atlas of Kent County, Michigan* (Chicago: G.A. Oggle, 1907).

educational reforms. During the First World War she demonstrated an unflinching pacifistic attitude.

Cornelia Van Kooij (1885-1945), an immigrant from Utrecht, followed a similar course. This Cornelia also had grown up in the Netherlands, and she came to Milwaukee, Wisconsin, in 1905, where her parents were active members of the Reformed Church. She took nurses' training and worked as a private nurse and a health information provider before taking an executive position in the fight against tuberculosis. Later she was in charge of public health organizations in the state of Wisconsin. In the eyes of most of the churchgoing Dutch immigrants, these women lived and worked in a different world.[60]

The breakthrough into national politics may be attributed to Gerrit J. Diekema (1859-1930) from Holland, Michigan. He was a scion of a well-to-do immigrant family. His father was active in local government on behalf of the Republican Party. Gerrit graduated from Hope College, studied law at the University of Michigan, and opened a law office in 1883. In 1885 he was elected to the House of Representatives in the State of Michigan, where he soon became speaker. His challengers were also Dutch, but they chose not to campaign. As far as content was concerned, Diekema was a conservative, but as to form he was a progressive: he used entertainers to add luster to his political speeches.[61] The citizens of Holland elected him mayor in 1895, after which his rise in the Republican Party began. In 1907, these involvements led to his nomination for, and election to, the national House of Representatives, where he served one more term until 1910. Although he did not succeed in acquiring another political position, his influence reached far.[62] He used his oratorical and organizational talents to introduce practical improvements and to obtain finances for construction projects (post offices and a harbor) in and around Holland, and to support business and industry. During the split in the Republican Party in 1912, when some joined the Progressive Party under the leadership of Theodore Roosevelt, he remained faithful to his party by campaigning for

---

[60]  Hans Krabbendam, "Serving the Dutch Community: A Comparison of the Patterns of Americanization in the Lives of Two Immigrant Pastors," (M.A. thesis, Kent State Univ., 1989), 84-88. Of the 533 immigrants mentioned in *Hollanders Who Helped Build America* only 22 were women, among whom 3 were immigrants, while the rest were descendants of Dutch Americans with roots in New Amsterdam.

[61]  C. Warren Vander Hill, *Gerrit J. Diekema* (Grand Rapids: Eerdmans, 1970), 11-27. The Republican Party was the majority party in the state until 1930.

[62]  Schrier, *Gerrit J. Diekema*, 206-07.

Post Office Holland, Michigan, in 1921, result of political pressure.
Archives, Calvin College, Grand Rapids, Michigan.

William H. Taft, who in the heavily Dutch counties did not stand a chance against Roosevelt. Most Dutch were not charmed by the so-called Progressives, whom they suspected of taking politics away from the sphere of influence of the common people in the name of efficiency and entrusting it to bureaucratic managers.[63]

Diekema's political defeats were in part a consequence of his conservative standpoints during the heyday of Progressivism, which made him less attractive to non-Dutch voters, while for the Dutch he ran too far ahead on the path of assimilation. This became clear from his defense of the public school system, Freemasonry, the insurance business, women's suffrage, and his fervent patriotism. Only in the struggle for the Republican nomination for governor did he achieve large majorities in the Dutch counties. His speeches brimmed with platitudes and supported the existing leadership without offering new ideas. After the Republican defeat of 1916, he was no longer available for office but devoted himself to his law practice, while periodically involving himself in the campaigns of Republican candidates.

In 1929 President Herbert Hoover rewarded "Diek" for his faithfulness to the party with a diplomatic post in the Netherlands. He was able to enjoy his honorable position only sixteen months, because he passed away suddenly in The Hague in 1930. His appointment was proof that the Dutch Americans had arrived. He felt at home in the Netherlands because it was just as conservative as he was. In his longest speech in the country that he had not visited before, he repeated his characterization of the immigrants: "The Hollander in America has

63    Bratt, *Dutch Calvinism*, 65.

**Gerrit Jan Diekema (1859-1930), influential Dutch-American politician and diplomat.**

Hope College Collection of the
Joint Archives of Holland

ever been a conservative element in the body politic. He is not swept off his feet by false propaganda or by temporary popular upheavals. He must be shown and his reason must be convinced before he acts."[64]

After a solemn commemorative service in The Hague two days before Christmas in 1930, Diekema's funeral in America attracted 8,500 visitors, the largest the city had ever seen. Thus he was honored as a leader without truly having been able to break through nationally. The tension had been too great between identification with his ethnic background on the one hand and wider public recognition on the other. Besides, as a resident of little Holland he had to compete against mighty Grand Rapids.[65] His friend and fellow tribesman, Arthur VandenBerg, was getting ready to fill the void. He began his career as a senator in 1928 with an equally conservative platform, but without the ethnic ties of his political friend. Diekema built connections with the dominant political culture without burning his bridges behind him. Thanks to his talent as a public speaker, which he had developed at Hope College, his moral-religious upbringing in the Reformed Church, and his training

---

64    "Address delivered by G.J. Diekema at The Hague on February 5, 1930, to the members of the organization 'Nederland in den Vreemde' and their guests." National Archives, RG 59 Department of State, Decimal file 123 Diekema, Gerrit J., National Archives, Washington, DC.

65    Vander Hill, *Diekema*, 67.

in modern law and business practices, he was able to operate in both worlds. Whoever lacked either of these supports remained either too provincial or lost contact with his supporters, such as the businessman and newspaper publisher Cyrenus Cole of Pella, Iowa, who at the height of Republican power from 1921 to 1933 represented his district in the House of Representatives but did not present himself as a Dutchman, witness the quick Americanization of his original surname, "Kool."[66]

Just as newspapers for the working people stood hardly a chance, Dutch Socialist candidates did not get far in election campaigns. James Hoogerheyde received only 245 votes, one-half of a percent, in the elections in West Michigan in 1909; even the Prohibition candidate received more than six times that number of votes.[67] In Chicago the Republicans also held sway over the Dutch, who supported a socially sensitive medical doctor from time to time because of his efforts on behalf of the working people or prohibitionists.[68]

**Wars**

The outbreak of the Civil War in April 1861 happened at the moment that the Dutch immigrants had found a firm footing. Engagement in this crucial event connected these Dutch with the politics of the nation and intensified relations with the federal government. Just as the "old Dutch" almost a century earlier had shared America's identity through their role in the struggle for independence, so the recent immigrants now embraced America as their country. At first the Dutch assumed something of a waiting attitude, but for those who had come to America with ideals, the war awakened new feelings of patriotism. Fewer than a thousand people, 3 percent of the total number of Dutch immigrants, lived in the Southern states, whereas the overwhelming majority of the Dutch lived in the North and identified with the Yankees. Mrs. Budde-Stomp put it into words on December 5, 1861: "Our fatherland is at war with the South." Her husband explained the cause of the Civil War from a spiritual perspective: "The American nation was too haughty with all the blessings it enjoyed above other

---

[66]   Vandenberg had an English-American mother and twice married women from that circle. C. David Tompkins, *Senator Arthur H. Vandenberg: The Evolution of a Modern Republican, 1884-1945* (Lansing: Michigan State Univ. Press, 1970). Another Dutch-American in the House of Representatives was Dow Henry Drukker (1872-1963), a Frisian by birth, who represented Passaic, New Jersey, from 1914 to 1919.

[67]   Vander Hill, *Diekema*, 93.

[68]   Swierenga, *Dutch Chicago*, 693.

nations. It forsook the Lord of heaven and earth. And then the wrath of God was spread over the earth in his judgments."[69]

The first wave of Dutch volunteers in Holland Township, Wisconsin, enlisted in September 1861 when President Lincoln asked for 300,000 volunteers. In the following year approximately 40 Dutchmen entered the service, while in 1864 some 20 men joined them. All told, 168 men became involved in the war (among them also some non-Dutch), which was a considerable part of a township where 268 people had voted in 1862. In the Holland, Michigan, colony 82 men presented themselves in August of that year, followed by some 28 more in February 1865.[70]

The motives of the volunteers who joined in fighting the war varied from idealistic ideas to wanting to rescue the union of the country to expectations of honor and reward. Many Dutch boys, especially from Pella, Holland, and the villages in Wisconsin, enlisted and filled a number of companies. More than four hundred boys and men answered the call to enlist. Some of them signed up out of enthusiasm for a good cause, others were enticed by the promise of land as a reward. A small number escaped the draft which, after 1863, was needed to obtain the necessary number of soldiers. The support for army recruits and the patriotic climate increased identification with America.[71] In 1861, the governor of Iowa forced all foreigners in the state to become citizens or else to leave. This order was used subsequently to force the men to enlist. Some objected to this method; they had lost too many family members already to the Civil War and took refuge in Oregon.

On May 3, 1861, an eager candidate-soldier, Matthijs Grootemaat, wrote from Kalamazoo to his uncle and aunt about the Civil War: "...the high government of our Republic has spared the rebels as long as it was at all possible, even to the amazement of many foreign nations, but the rebels refused to listen to reason and were the first ones to open canon fire on the fortifications of the Republic." He concluded from the fact that in ten days' time 75,000 volunteers had enlisted in the Union

---

[69]  Stellingwerff, *Iowa Letters*, 488, 495. Gerlof D. Homan, "Netherlands-American Relations during the Civil War," *Civil War History* 31 (1985): 353-64.

[70]  Pieter Daane, "Sketch of Cedar Grove and Oostburg," in Lucas, *Dutch Immigrant Memoirs*, 2:125-27. Albert H. McGeehan, ed., *My Country and Cross: The Civil War Letters of John Anthony Wilterdink, Company I, 25th Michigan Infantry* (Dallas: Taylor, 1982), 90-91.

[71]  Brian W. Beltman, "Civil War Reverberations: Exodus and Return among the Pella Dutch during the 1860s," in Krabbendam and Wagenaar, *Dutch-American Experience*, 117-41.

army, that the government was highly thought of. He would have gone himself, had not his sick mother prevented him: "...however, I hope that she will let me go if necessity requires it, for we don't draw lots here, but the soldiers are paid and clothed well, and as long as transportation is available they are fed well. Also, they are not kept in the service unnecessarily, but are sent home as soon as the country no longer needs their services." He contrasted this with the conduct of the rebels who forced anyone who was in the least capable to become a soldier and otherwise threatened them: if they refuse "... they are deported and their goods are confiscated, they are mistreated as persons, which causes many to flee to the North because they refuse to take up arms against the lawful government of their native or adopted country. For every European who receives citizenship from this Government is required to acknowledge this land as his homeland."[72]

Immigrant leaders Scholte and Van Raalte set a good example and took pride in their sons enlisting voluntarily, together with hundreds of other Dutch boys. Dirk Van Raalte expressed the feelings of the soldiers who had enlisted voluntarily and despised those who remained on the sidelines. When his father asked him for a share of his soldier's pay for the benefit of Hope College, he wrote back stridently: "We are willing to shed our blood and suffer for our country and those fellows are staying home and live off our money, and mock us to boot, there is no way in which I will give them that opportunity. We have to suffer too much, which we do gladly for the sake of our country, and the little money that we happen to earn I can use myself too well. It would look a lot better if half of those students filled the ranks here, rather than to stay home as cowards and wait until they get drafted."[73] Dirk lost an arm in the war; many endured imprisonment or did not return. The ones who did had certainly enlarged their horizon and considered themselves to be more American than those who stayed home.

Arnold Verstegen of Little Chute confirmed the optimism and initial expectations. "Concerning the revolution, the fighting is heavy, but it is far away from here and they ask only for volunteers. The North is losing forts, but they are saying that few men have been killed. Quite a few volunteers have joined from Little Chute. They are paid $8.00 per month, and will get 160 acres of land when it is finished."[74] Two and

---

[72] In ILC HH.
[73] Cited in Lagerwey, *Neen Nederland 'k vergeet u niet.*, 57 (December 20, 1862). See also H.J. Brinks, "Dutch American Reactions," *Origins* 6.1 (1988): 10-17.
[74] Arnold Verstegen to family, May 6, 1861, Brinks, *Dutch American Voices*, 56.

a half years later all enthusiasts had already joined the army and the ranks had to be filled by way of conscription. Verstegen explained:

> We have had two military conscriptions. The last group has not left yet, and they are allowed to buy substitutes for $300. Many who have the money try to be exempted. The conscription goes this way—the marshal orders someone to write the names of all the men from twenty to forty-five years of age. Those of twenty to twenty-five are first class. Unmarried men up to forty-five are also first class. Married men [between twenty-six and forty-five] are in the second class and probably will not be conscripted. Men [who claim to be] under twenty must have sworn testimony about their age.
>
> Then there are those who are not legal American citizens, although the father is a citizen and the children have not yet voted, he has to state which ones he wants to keep at home...he has to make a choice. Fathers are allowed to select one child as a breadwinner who is then free [from conscription]. Then there are quite a few others who have been excused, but if they have been drafted, they usually have to fight their case in a court of law which is expensive.[75]

Many Catholic Dutch immigrants in Brown County enlisted in the Northern army. Father Spiering even served for two years as an army chaplain. Afterwards they remained completely loyal to the Democratic Party. Until 1900 Hollandtown had not seen a single vote go to a Republican candidate, and if one was found it was discarded, because the election board was convinced that it was a mistake.[76]

The more the war dragged on, the more its high expectations evaporated, while its cruel reality was felt more deeply. After two years of war, David Lankester from Zeeland showed himself considerably more reserved about the struggle, even though he continued to identify strongly with the North. When the state of Wisconsin failed to deliver the assessed number of soldiers, a draft lottery took place to designate four thousand recruits. He was elated that he had not been chosen because he had learned that only 30 to 40 percent of the soldiers came back. Later in the war he found a substitute for himself for the amount of $600. Many died of malnutrition, illness, and exposure, and many

---

[75]    December 1863, ibid., 58. Additional paragraphs in Van Stekelenburg Collection, box 1, folder 3, RSC and in ILC HH.

[76]    Vandehey, *Wooden Shoes* West, 47. Geenen, "History of Hollandtown," 6.

Civil war veterans in downtown Holland, Michigan, 1905.
Archives, Calvin College, Grand Rapids, Michigan.

a village began to object to the lottery. By comparison, to serve in the military in the Netherlands was easy.[77]

However, faithful service in the Civil War generated nice sums of money for those who survived. Jan Vogel from Noordeloos enlisted in September 1861 and served four years. This netted him the sum of $1,500, two-thirds of which he used to visit the Netherlands after the war to fetch his parents and sister, and to invest in land and a sawmill. Also those who participated in the war later on could expect considerable "bounties." Twenty-four-year-old Gerrit Jan Hesselink received a $5.00 bounty February 18, 1865, plus $100 from Michigan, $150 from the county, and $100 from the city of Holland. He used $30 of that money to complete his evening classes. He served until February 1866 to help maintain order in the South.[78]

It is estimated that one-fifth of both armies consisted of immigrants.[79] The veterans were welcomed back with receptions, parades, and services of thanksgiving. They joined veterans' organizations and

---

[77]  March 10, 1863, Brinks, *Dutch American Voices,* 351-53, 359. Thomas H. Ryan gives examples of Dutch Catholics who enlisted, in his *History of Outagamie County Wisconsin* (Chicago: Goodspeed, 1911), 901 (Martin Coonen).

[78]  Jan Vogel, "Memoir," in Lucas, *Dutch Immigrant Memoirs*, 2:261; G.J. Hesselink, "Een verhaal van mijn soldaten leven," Gerrit J. Hesselink collection, (letters 1862-1866 and diary), Historical Documentation Center for Dutch Protestantism, Vrije Universiteit, Amsterdam.

[79]  Dean Mahin, *The Blessed Place of Freedom: Europeans in Civil War America* (Dulles, Vir.: Brassey's Inc., 2002), 10.

devoted themselves to erecting monuments. Thus, they strengthened the bond between immigrants and their new country. By making the connection between their commitment to the good cause and Dutch history, they strengthened their Dutch-American identity, as shown in a poem by Colonel Cornelius Gardenier:

> Holland's heart remained faithful, Holland's blood did flow
> In the service of freedom for hundreds of years
> Wherever or whenever, these Dutchmen sowed
> A seed that roots deeply and hates oppression.[80]

A call to sons of immigrants to participate in the struggle also caused reflection on citizenship. Those unwilling to fight had to dismiss citizenship. Young Chris Verwyst did so when he was drafted. He appealed to his Dutch nationality to avoid having to serve and even received proof of his Dutch citizenship from the Dutch consul in Milwaukee. This excuse was not accepted because his father had become an American citizen and as a minor he was included. Verwyst opted for the usual way of paying $300 for a substitute. When, a few months later, elections were held he thought he had better vote because citizenship had cost him a lot of money. His story was not believed and the poll supervisors did not allow him to vote. This damper sapped his democratic yearnings. It was not until fifteen years later that he officially became an American citizen.[81]

War forced people to make choices and stimulated reflection on citizenship. Twenty-year-old Klaas Hoekema enlisted in 1917 in the American Expeditionary Force, because in this way he obtained American citizenship and because he hoped that by being in France he might be able to visit his relatives in the Netherlands. He remained stationed in America, but in the meantime he did notice the advantages of wearing a uniform, especially with regard to social activities. Thanks to free language courses for veterans his English improved.[82] Klaas, however, was an exception. The Netherlands itself was neutral, and many an immigrant had escaped the Old World precisely because of the draft. The reverse could also happen. Lauw Allewijn, who had lived

---

[80]  Poem by Colonel C.N. Gardenier, on the occasion of the fiftieth anniversary of Holland, Michigan, June 1897. Copy RSC.

[81]  Chrysostom Adrian Verwyst, "Reminiscences of a Pioneer Missionary," *Publications of the State Historical Society of Wisconsin, Proceedings*, 1916 (Madison, 1917): 166-67.

[82]  Leonard Sweetman, "Klaas and Claude: The Evolution of a Young Frisian Boy into American Citizen," *Origins* 16.2 (1998): 27-35.

in Kalamazoo nearly two years, received a notice from the Netherlands to report for military duty at the outbreak of the First World War. He decided to answer the call and left his pregnant wife behind. She joined him in the Netherlands after their baby died, thus ending his American adventure.[83]

The strong emotions that the First World War evoked, the exaggerated grapevine rumors about traitors and conspiracies, stirred up an enormous feeling of patriotism that branded deviant behavior immediately as suspect. The Dutch communities, with the exception of a few rural areas, also contributed to the war effort and became more closely involved with America because of volunteers and the purchase of War Bonds, just as had been the case during the Civil War.

For education conducted in the Dutch language, the war meant the beginning of the end. In 1915 the Christian school in Chicago stopped teaching in Dutch due to government pressure. When six years later the superinflamed patriotic passions had calmed down again, a substantial group of parents tried to reintroduce Dutch. However, the school did not want to return to a dual-language curriculum; the same thing happened in many other communities.[84]

The Reformed Church minister and teacher B.D. Dykstra stood amazed at the patriotism among the Dutch immigrants, especially among the members of the Christian Reformed Church, who did have a strong Dutch awareness. How could they embrace two nationalities at the same time? He explained the one from the other. The feelings they had for the Netherlands were compensated by their extra-enthusiastic American patriotism and by their fear of secular liberalism, which constituted a threat to their conservative values.[85] This held true for some churches in the CRC—most firmly refused to allow American nationalism to enter their church.

## Conservatism

Because local autonomy had proven to be so important in the formation of their own subculture, Dutch immigrants looked askance at proposals that curtailed elbowroom for the family or their own tradition. This came to expression in the struggle for their own school system and in discussions about women's suffrage and the total

---

[83]  Brechtje Allewijn-Mieras from Kalamazoo to relatives in Zeeland, September 24, 1914, ILC HH.

[84]  Swierenga, *Dutch Chicago*, 379-80.

[85]  Dykstra, *"B.D.,"* 87-88.

prohibition of alcohol. Ethnic groups began to favor center field in order to protect their families and communities against the state.[86]

Prohibition was a moral theme that brought politics and religion together. The drink-demon formed a growing threat that needed to be banished forcefully from society. The Anti-Saloon League arranged meetings in the Dutch churches in Chicago, which thereby were at odds with Dutch-American churches elsewhere that wanted to acknowledge alcohol as a gift from God.[87]

Lively discussions were held in Zeeland about prohibition proposals.[88] On May 10, 1887, *De Grondwet* reported regretfully that the prohibition of alcohol had become the subject of political conflict. The Republicans had proposed to increase the license fee to $6,000, which would make for an actual prohibition, while the state of Michigan opposed it. However, the Republicans lost the election battle and this effort to drive back alcohol was lost.[89]

Zeeland went dry and remained dry till the twenty-first century. Until 1920 each of the villages of Cedar Grove and Oostburg in Wisconsin had three to four saloons, which the Eighteenth Amendment had to close.[90] Beginning in 1893 George Roelofs published a prohibition newspaper in Grand Rapids. *Een Stem des Volks* ("*A Voice from the People*") would hold out until 1910. He was an active member of the Second Reformed Church and expanded the progressive horizon with pleas for women's suffrage, civil rights for blacks, and opposition to the Spanish-American War.[91] In 1912 he would vote for the Progressive Party.

---

[86]   Gjerde, *Minds of the West*, 258, 267, and 309.

[87]   Swierenga, *Dutch Chicago*, 699.

[88]   *De Grondwet*, March 15, 1887.

[89]   *De Grondwet*, January 14, 1890.

[90]   Walvoord, *Windmill Memories*, 41. Such is the case even until today, although this prohibition is increasingly coming under pressure because of culinary services to a growing industry. The power of attraction that prohibition was supposed to have, since it advertises community responsibility and moderation, is weakening.

[91]   Verbrugge, *Life of a Dutch American*, 78-82. There was no automatic connection between orthodoxy and love of the House of Orange. Roelofs continued to be jubilant about Queen Emma and Princess Wilhelmina, in spite of his republican and socialist sympathies (84). CRC minister Herman Hoeksema had little use for emotional expressions of solidarity with the Netherlands and the House of Orange, and used to react with "Long live Orange, with nothing to eat," a phrase that would fit Socialists well. Gertrude Hoeksema, *Therefore Have I Spoken: A Biography of Herman Hoeksema* (Grand Rapids: Reformed Free Publishing Assoc., 1969), 44.

The Dutch community remained oblivious to the earliest feminist wave of the 1870s, which had women's suffrage as its objective. Very few women could operate independently, and then only in cities. In Chicago the previously mentioned Cornelia de Beij, the unmarried, youngest daughter of the minister of the First Reformed Church, developed her abilities and became a medical doctor, school reformer, and lobbyist. In Grand Rapids, Cornelia Steketee, an English high-school teacher who had no children of her own, was the most progressive woman. In 1912 a representative of the Christian Reformed Church pronounced, "We cannot afford to vote for a measure which, if carried and enacted into law, will destroy love, harmony, and intimacy, and thus strike a blow at the very foundations of the ideal home."[92] Although the official position of the Christian Reformed Church was that the church had no position because the Bible did not contain a clear rule either for or against women's suffrage, most leaders favored exclusive male suffrage based on Bible texts about the submissive position of women. Most Dutch Americans therefore voted against the Nineteenth Amendment, which forbade the exclusion of women from voting on the basis of their gender.[93]

Once women's suffrage had been secured constitutionally, a dilemma presented itself: should Dutch-American women be allowed to use the right to vote for a good cause? This cause was part of the ballot in Michigan in 1920, when a referendum took place in Wayne County over whether parochial schools could be outlawed. Since Christian day-school education enjoyed a high priority, the key question became: was it right to mobilize women to vote this proposal down? When this dilemma was submitted to the editor of the *Young Calvinist*, he rejected a compromise; he wanted to live as soundly as possible: "I would rather lose the schools in the way of the Word of God than save them in the way of the devil."[94]

At first, loyalty toward the Republican Party was not a sign of conservatism. On the contrary: toward the close of the nineteenth century it was more progressive than the Democratic Party.

---

[92]   J.G. van den Bosch, "A Burning Question: The Equal Suffrage Question," *Banner*, October 31, 1912, 684.

[93]   N. Burggraaf, "Report of the Committee on Woman's Suffrage," *Banner*, May 4, 1916, 290. Only the Rev. Johannes Groen in the CRC defended women's suffrage, because the lordship of the man was a result of the fall into sin and not part of the creation ordinance. However, he had few supporters in the CRC.

[94]   "Our Reply," *Young Calvinist* 1 (May 1920): 122-24.

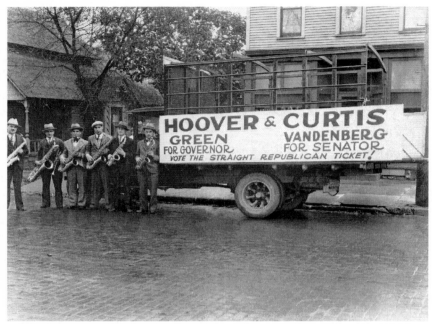

Election campaign for the Republican Party in Grand Rapids, 1928.

Grand Rapids History & Special Collections Center, Archives,
Grand Rapids Public Library, Grand Rapids, Michigan.

Economically the Republican Party (until its turnaround in the 1930s) was the party of progress, of national investments, of control by the federal government. The Republican Party was more attractive to Dutch immigrants personally and in political goals. Cornelis van Loo described the differences between the parties as follows: "One can find the frugal, educated, moral, and Christian elements of the Nation in the Republican party. In the Democratic party, on the other hand, almost exclusively the lower elements." As proof he submitted a list of Republicans who had caused Zeeland to flourish by getting the railroad to the village, by starting a flourmill, by providing equipment for the fire department, and by setting up two-thirds of the businesses.[95] The Dutch profited from political opportunities to build up and consolidate their places. From the point of view of protecting local autonomy, the 1930s ushered in a transition, with the central government becoming increasingly involved in everyday life.

In that decade the Dutch immigrants saw the expansion of the federal government's influence as a threat. Some of the Dutch,

[95]    *De Grondwet,* June 2, 1885.

being dissatisfied with Hoover, did vote for the Democratic candidate Franklin D. Roosevelt but withdrew this support when he offered the country a (lavish) menu of government-sponsored programs. A few intellectuals supported Roosevelt's approach out of solidarity, but most of the Dutch were opposed to tax increases believing that private organizations, such as churches, should offer support. They labeled Roosevelt's plans "socialism!" and feared for the future of their highly appreciated freedom. That FDR was proud of his Dutch roots did not cause them to change their minds.[96]

The antipathy toward government support was partly the result of their immigrant experience: this generation having withstood the test of poverty, the next generation had better grin and bear it and not go begging from the government. A high school student from the Passaic, New Jersey, community expected riots because government benefits would exceed minimum wages.[97] However, it was not the economic crisis that caused the end of small communities. They lost their viability precisely as a result of the recovery of prosperity. The automobile and the supermarket took their economic centers away.[98]

## From Eagerness to Protection

Contrary to later lamentations about the lack of political involvement by Dutch immigrants, the first Dutch colonies were highly motivated to participate in the political game. They recognized its importance for their own communities, felt the pressure of the anti-immigrant movements, and tasted the delight of local political successes. Within one generation their preference moved from the Democratic to the Republican Party when the first showed too little interest in wanting to invest in the well-being of the communities, and the latter demonstrated more stability. Only a rare individual understood the national political consequences, with Scholte as the best example. The rest allowed themselves to be led by local interests or personal positions.

But more than concrete election themes was involved. Initially the choice was to favor the Democratic Party, which was much farther removed from European norms than the Whigs, who adhered to

---

[96]  Ibid., 706-10; Bratt, *Dutch Calvinism*, 148-50. Swierenga, *Dutch Chicago*, 706-07.

[97]  Cornelis E. Peters to D. Boone in Ritthem, Zeeland, July 19, 1935, RSC.

[98]  Fannie Smith, "Pease, Minnesota: Saga of One Hundred years," *Origins* 7 (1989): 14-22.

hierarchical power structures, and a (negative) choice against the Old World. After they had settled in the Midwest, Dutch immigrants appeared to have more European blood in their veins than they thought, and they made a positive choice in favor of the (Republican) party that, just like them, respected moral and economic structures highly and connected them more closely to the evangelical mainstream in America. The small size and predictable voting behavior of the Dutch prevented them from becoming a significant ethnic factor in politics. However, this did not stop their political involvement. Especially on the local level, the Dutch immigrants wanted to be good citizens.

# CHAPTER 10

# Dutch-American Identity

As happened to most European immigrants in the nineteenth century, attachment to the Netherlands gradually shifted to solidarity with America. In 1852, Pieter van Ouwerkerk wrote to Pieter J. Bril in Zeeuws-Vlaanderen that newcomers lost most of their homey smell as quickly as in one year: "The American sun is already starting to dissolve the Dutch smell. In our case it is gone, but more new ones have arrived in the meantime and they are not rid of their Dutch smell yet."[1] At times those varying emotions came to expression in dreams. Krijn Goudzwaard had such a dream in 1877, twelve years after he had emigrated. He often thought of his family "...and the strange thing is that when you dream it is as if you are still in the Netherlands. Nevertheless when in my dream I am with you there, I can never return, but then, when I awake, I am sure glad that I am in America." He observed that those who actually visited

---

[1] Pieter van Ouwerkerk, Jr., to Pieter J. Bril in Zuidzande, June 11, 1852. Original in the Oggel Collection of the JAH; published in *In den Vreemde* 5 (March 1994). Remieg Aerts and Henk te Velde, "De taal van het nationaal besef, 1848-1940," in N.C.F. van Sas, ed., *Vaderland. Een geschiedenis van de vijftiende eeuw tot 1940* (Amsterdam: Amsterdam Univ. Press, 1999), 402.

317

The Rev. Henry Uiterwijk, minister in the Reformed Church in America.

Western Seminary Collection of the Joint Archives of Holland, Michigan.

their old fatherland almost always returned to America. "And why, you might ask? It is because here in America people are free, you are not the slave of the big shot, you don't have to be afraid of Your Lordship or the boss, for there is more equality here among the poor and the rich than where you live. Enough said for today."[2]

Usually, accommodation to American customs happened in stages and unconsciously, but on special occasions the process of assimilation was highlighted. Most likely inspired by the forthcoming commemoration of the twenty-fifth anniversary of the colony in 1872,

---

[2]    Letter from Krijn Goudzwaard, Grand Rapids, to brothers and sisters in Poortvliet, January 27, 1877, RSC. Sudden and intensive contact with the fatherland also caused people to dream in Dutch, even in the twentieth century; see Webber, *Pella Dutch*, 29.

the leading minister in Holland, Michigan, Henry Uiterwijk, reflected in the late summer of 1871 on the Dutch immigrants' future. In a series of articles in the weekly *De Hope*, Uiterwijk stated that he believed that God had assigned people their character through a slow growth process under the influence of geographical and governmental circumstances.[3] He characterized the Dutch as discerning, prudent, frugal, stable, and serious, in contrast to the Americans, who were quick, enterprising, generous, easy-going, and cheerful. Uiterwijk betrayed his American frame of mind when he praised the desire for independence and freedom on the part of the Dutch—notions that were equally sacred in America but were suppressed more and more in the old fatherland. "Culture may not be as fine and deeply rooted as there [in the Netherlands], but neither is it so artificial and cold, and much more common." The author was not blind to the downsides of greed, ambition, restlessness, and lack of respect for authority. Especially the conduct of women and young people filled him with concern for the future. In a paradoxical speech he mentioned as the cause of their minor influence in America the slowness with which the colonial Dutch had adjusted.

"True Americanization" consisted, according to Uiterwijk, not in the denial of one's own history, for that was impossible, but in discovering the destiny of the Dutch immigrants. He advised the Dutch community "to become an inspiring part of the American nation with our special character and our way of thinking as a people, and this under the acknowledged influence of our divine calling."[4] He pleaded for a bond as intimate as marriage, instead of one that resembled an artificial leg in a body. In his own mind the minister saw how founding settlements, preaching the gospel, providing a Christian education, learning the English language, adopting good habits, and fulfilling civic duties would bring the best characteristics of the Dutch national character into America.[5]

Ten days after Uiterwijk's final contribution, this solidarity with America was confirmed by a generous response to the terrible disaster that almost meant the end of the Dutch community. On June 9, 1871, the city of Holland was reduced to ashes (including Uiterwijk's home) by a forest fire that also destroyed Chicago. Thanks to timely warnings only one person died, but the material damage was enormous. The

---

[3]    H. Uiterwijk, "Het Hollands en Amerikaansch volkskarakter," *De Hope*, August 17, 24, and 31 and September 7, 14, 21, and 28, 1871.

[4]    *De Hope*, September 21, 1871.

[5]    *De Hope*, September 28, 1871.

work of twenty-five years was undone in two hours, and the community lost $900,000 worth of possessions, of which only $50,000 was covered by insurance, which amount could not even be collected in every case because the insurance companies went broke. Only a few houses on the south and east side were spared, as well as Hope College and Van Raalte's Pillar Church. The relief from America far surpassed that from the Netherlands, where a few church papers collected funds, and Prince Hendrik donated 500 guilders to victims in Chicago and 300 to Holland. The members of the Dutch Reformed Church on the East Coast collected $40,000. A year later, the *Holland City News* wrote, "Thank God that our misfortune befell us in a Christian land, and among Christian people, whose sympathetic hearts made willing sacrifices for our relief."[6] Holland did not doubt its future for one moment and was rebuilt, but it did not reach its former level of well-being until ten years later. The only advantage of the fire was that the last tree trunks were cleared and that more agricultural land became available. The reconstruction marked the end of the pioneer phase.

At the high point of immigration in 1906, Reformed Church pastor Peter Moerdyke articulated astutely the tension between the old and the new identities. He contended that Americanization was a reconstruction of life, not of the essential characteristics but of the accidental and external qualities. He warned against the misconception that emigrants by their departure indicated that Americans were superior. On the contrary, the immigrant imported valuable qualities into America. "The Hollander by exchanging his foreign coin for United States currency does not surrender or despise his imported treasure." Accommodation was necessary, but it was a sign of wisdom when the Americans allowed the newcomers to keep their old principles and virtues. "The gold of one land is as good as that of any other, though it may be coined differently by their respective mints."[7]

Adopting an American lifestyle could already begin on board ship. Some emigrants did so quite literally. When the twenty-five-year-old emigrant Daniel Koppenol from Hoogvliet had left half of the ocean voyage behind him in 1910, he changed clothes: "Tomorrow

---

6    *De Hope*, December 7, 1871. A collection of newspaper articles and personal memories has been assembled by Donald L. van Reken in *The Holland Fire of October 8, 1871* (privately printed, 1982). The minister of foreign affairs to envoy in Washington, December 6, 1871. National Archives, The Hague, Gezantschap vs. Legatie Washington, 1814-1946, inv. 37. *Holland City News*, October 12, 1872.

7    P. Moerdyke, "Chicago Letter," *Christian Intelligencer*, July 14, 1906.

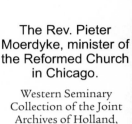

**The Rev. Pieter Moerdyke, minister of the Reformed Church in Chicago.**

Western Seminary Collection of the Joint Archives of Holland, Michigan.

is Saturday, we are making good progress, then I will take off my old duds, and change into American underwear. Got up at 7 [o'clock] on Saturday morning and went to the bathroom with my clean clothes. First I took a bath and then put on my new clothes and gave away the others. Thus I underwent another change."[8]

**At Home in America**

The public reflection by the Dutch matched a general pattern of immigrants of non-English descent who after the Civil War went looking consciously for arguments to demand their place in America. Many of them still felt caught between the Americans, who continued to see them as "aliens," and their old country, which considered them to be foreigners as well. Besides, local autonomy became subject to

---

[8]    L.W. Koppenol, ed., "Het reisverslag van een Hoogvlietse emigrant. Een door Daniel Koppenol geschreven verslag van zijn reis naar Amerika in 1910," *Historisch jaarboek Hoogvliet* 3 (1997): 81.

pressure. Toward the end of the nineteenth century, national structures in America increasingly began to dominate local communities, which at the same time became part of a much larger (ethnic) network. Participation in the political process, more often by the electors than by those elected, encouraged immigrants to consider fully their place in America.[9]

The Norwegian literary historian Orm Overland distinguished three ways in which immigrants tried to demonstrate that they belonged to America. One possibility was to prove that the group had made an important contribution to the formation of America. A second way was furnished by the memory of sacrifices that earlier generations had made in America's wars. A third strategy focused on the ideological kinship between the immigrant group and America.[10] Among Dutch immigrants, too, combinations of these three mythical tales were clearly present in commemorative speeches and historical reviews in the period of large-scale immigration between 1870 and 1930. Immigrant leaders used these myths to strengthen the self-respect of their groups and to prevent their members from assimilating into American society without leaving a trace. These efforts were not only intended to convince their own followers of their legitimate place in America, they also served to neutralize the competing claims of other national groups. When Norwegian Americans produced Leif Erikson as the discoverer of the New World, Italian Americans considered this to be an attack on their Columbus. Swedes tried to keep the Finns away from the commemoration of New Sweden with the argument that Finland was not yet an independent nation in the seventeenth century.

These strategies were only successful when public opinion favored the group. Thus, German Americans in an effort to maintain their place in the ranking during the First World War, appealed in vain to the sacrifices their compatriots had made during the struggle for independence and the Civil War, or to the values of freedom and democracy. The Irish also, at an early stage, used ideological means, such as their fight for freedom against the British. That this had minor mythological value became soon apparent: they were not welcomed

---

9    Gjerde, *Minds of the* West, 247-49. Alan Trachtenberg, *The Incorporation of America: Culture and Society in the Gilded Age* (New York: Hill and Wang, 1982).

10   Orm Overland, *Immigrant Minds, American Identities: Making the United States Home, 1870-1930* (Urbana: Univ. of Illinois Press, 2000). This part of the chapter is based on my lecture, *Dutch-American Identity Politics: The Use of History by Dutch Immigrants* (Holland: Van Raalte Institute, 2003).

when they set foot on land in impoverished droves between 1840 and 1860. Next, they called upon the fourth myth, namely, that they were considered undesirables in America. This negative myth served to guarantee mutual solidarity and to warn job seekers that the non-Catholic outside world was dangerous. This negative myth was also used to criticize the old fatherland and so to enable them to appeal to America for asylum from persecution. The Dutch Protestants did the same with their tales of the persecution of their forebears.[11]

These historical arguments were popular among the better situated citizens; workers saw little benefit in using them because it undermined solidarity with workers from other countries. Factors such as philosophy of life, location of settlement, relationships with other population groups, the presence of English descendants who dominated the scene, and historical sources (which were freely stretched if necessary) determined the preference for using this sort of argument. The most powerful argument was the presence of the group at the founding of America, followed by the sacrifice for America, and similarities in ideology. The higher classes made use of the same arguments to distinguish themselves from the recent immigrants. In the twentieth century, European governments discovered the value of these tales to strengthen their diplomatic ties and economic interests in America. During the First World War, the Dutch envoy in Washington took to the road to visit the various "Dutch" societies in the country and together with them to sing the praises of the Netherlands as the "Holy Land of Modern Europe" (as he quoted a scholar from Oxford), and thus to gain moral support for the Netherlands.[12]

## American Discovery of Dutch History

Historical references to the Netherlands were not signs of nostalgia but instruments to make the immigrants feel at home in America. Before the Midwestern Dutch immigrants began to use Dutch history as an instrument around 1900, others had already discovered its value. The American historian Firth Fabend dug up an early-nineteenth-century example of members of the Reformed Dutch Church who began to tell romanticized heroic legends about early

---

[11]   See http://tigger.uic.edu/~rjensen/no-irish.htm, visited March 21, 2009.
[12]   *Addresses Netherlands Societies of Philadelphia*, 155, 159. Sweden initiated contact with Swedish Americans in the 1930s only, when the Swedish government through the commemoration of New Sweden wanted to make a positive impact on the press to strengthen diplomatic relations.

Batavian tribes to bring to the fore the positive qualities of the Dutch as a counterbalance to English domination of the tradition. Conservative ministers in this denomination appealed to this tradition to keep out American influences of revivals and interdenominational cooperation. The arrival of the wave of pious Dutch immigrants in 1846 was a boon for both camps in the Reformed Church. The addition of a group that explicitly appealed to Dutch confessional statements and the church order of Dordt confirmed the traditional character of the church, while the progressive camp was equally thankful for growth and the opportunity to lift the poor by way of relief actions.[13]

The first scholarly attention to the Dutch in the New World was not even a product of the Dutch community. The author Washington Irving, with his historical scenes of the Dutch from the time of New Amsterdam (1809) (which he wrote under the pseudonym of Diedrich Knickerbocker) and with his tales about Rip van Winkle, had created a primarily comical picture of the Dutch founders, even though his stories contained many more reliable historical details than is often assumed.[14] During the years when the immigration from the Netherlands got under way, an American of Irish descent marketed the first serious study of New Netherland. *The History of New Netherland* by Edmund B. O'Callaghan provided a gold mine of arguments about the important role of the Dutch at the founding of America.[15] The real breakthrough of the history of the Dutch in America came ten years later with the best-seller of the English-American historian John Lothrop Motley, *The Rise of the Dutch Republic*, in 1856.[16] For three-quarters of a century this

---

[13]   Firth Haring Fabend, *Zion on the Hudson: Dutch New York and New Jersey in the Age of the Revival* (New Brunswick: Rutgers Univ. Press, 2000), 8-19, 44, 70, 214-16.

[14]   Elisabeth Paling Funk, "Knickerbocker's New Netherland: Washington Irving's Representation of Dutch Life on the Hudson," in Harinck and Krabbendam, *Amsterdam-New York*, 135-47.

[15]   *History of New Netherland, or, New York under the Dutch* (New York: D. Appleton, 1846-1849). For the anti-British and socially inclined background of the author see Jos van der Linde: "De 'Remonstrantie van Nieuw Nederland' (1649) and its special significance for Edmund Bailey O'Callaghan," in E.F. van de Bilt and H.W. van den Doel, eds., *Klassiek Amerikaans. Opstellen voor A. Lammers* (Leiden: Universiteit Leiden, 2002), 92-102.

[16]   Alice P. Kenney, *Stubborn for Liberty: The Dutch in New York* (Syracuse: Syracuse Univ. Press, 1957), 191-96. O.D. Edward, "John Lothrop Motley and the Netherlands," in J.W. Schulte Nordholt and Robert P. Swierenga, eds., *A Bilateral Centennial: A History of Dutch-American Relations 1782-1982* (Amsterdam: Meulenhoff, 1982), 171-98. Mark A. Peterson, "A Brahmin Goes Dutch: John Lothrop Motley and the Lessons of Dutch History in

book determined the favorable reputation of the Republic of the Seven United Netherlands in the English-speaking world. A Dutch traveler commented in 1870, "Because of that work the name of Holland became popular with a great many Americans."[17] This success was due mainly to the evident parallels between the Dutch and the American struggle for independence during the time of increasing tensions between North and South, with an anti-Spanish and anti-Catholic flavor. Motley also had an educational purpose in mind and hoped with this book to free the English-speaking world of its self-importance and remind it of the virtues of a confederation.

At the end of the century, in 1892, the American of Scottish descent, Douglas Campbell, went even so far in his book, *The Puritan in England, Holland, and America: An Introduction to American History,* as to deny the English the honor of being the cradle of American institutions in favor of the Dutch. They were to have influenced England directly and indirectly in every field of endeavor.

The celebration of America's centennial in 1876, the professionalization of historical research in America, and the beginning of historical tourism called attention to the old Dutch-American ties. The centennial stimulated American self-consciousness, which expressed itself in commemorations and called attention to the correct reproduction of historical events. Newspapers liked to publish stories of heroic events. In 1881 the American envoy in The Hague, James Birney, got involved in a discussion about the archival records of the first salute that was fired on St. Eustatius. Toward the close of this decade, the ceremonies in commemoration of the Puritans at Plymouth gave Envoy Samuel R. Thayer the idea also to put up a monument in the Netherlands as a reminder of the departure of the "Pilgrims" from Delfshaven.[18]

In the midst of the 1880s the Dutch-American elite of New York organized societies to safeguard the Dutch heritage. In 1885 a handful of lawyers founded the Holland Society of New York, after four "Van's"—Messrs. Van Siclen, Van Allen, Vanderpoel, and Van Vorst—had

Nineteenth-Century Boston," in Goodfriend, Joyce D., Benjamin Schmidt, and Annette Stott, eds., *Going Dutch: The Dutch Presence in America, 1609-2009* (Leiden: Brill, 2008), 109-31.

[17] A.E. Croockewit, "Amerikaansche schetsen," *De Gids* 34 (1870): 66.
[18] *Papers Relating to Foreign Relations of the United States 1881* (Washington, D.C.: Government Printing Office, 1882), 847-51 and 1889 (Washington, D.C.: Government Printing Office, 1890), 640-41.

met at a court case. For them it was a means to set themselves apart from newcomers of a lower class.[19] Membership in the club they founded was reserved for men who were able to trace their origins to the residents of New Netherland before 1675. The society set as its objective the gathering of information about the Dutch in America, to put their history in writing, and to disseminate the principles and virtues of their forebears. This seemed to meet a need, for in the first year more than two hundred "heirs" joined. The Dutch consul general J.R. Planten presented the society with replicas of the Beggars' Cup and other objects that symbolized the courage of the Dutch in their struggle for civil and religious freedoms.[20] Chapters also sprouted in other cities with Dutch-American communities. The enthusiasm was rewarded with a trip to the Netherlands undertaken by fifty members in the summer of 1888, where they were fêted by mayors and businessmen. Their position was confirmed by copious dinners with expensive Dutch dishes, adorned by "Dutch" customs and songs that applauded their ancestry: [21]

> I'm a Van of a Van of a Van of a Van
> Of a Van of a way back line;
> On every rugged feature ancestral glories shine;
> And all our band in kinship stand
> With all that's old and fine;
> I'm a Van of a Van of a Van of a Van
> Of a Van of a way back line.

Some members of this society used these stories about New Netherland as ammunition in the struggle for political reforms. Theodore Roosevelt proposed a toast to the Dutch in America during a dinner of the Holland Society in 1890 and lauded the virtues of quick assimilation, referring to the colonial Dutch as proof of prosperity: "The thoroughness with which the Dutchman Americanizes and the manner in which he is prevented from being anything else but an American, makes him an invaluable lesson for the races that followed him to America two centuries later."[22]

---

[19]  David William Voorhees, *The Holland Society: A Centennial History 1885-1985* (New York: Holland Society of New York, 1985), 6. To be sure, the St. Nicholas Society was founded fifty years earlier, in 1835, but it had a more recreational function, rather than a serious purpose.
[20]  Ibid., 31.
[21]  *New York Times*, January 11, 1890.
[22]  Ibid.

In 1903 Robert B. Roosevelt, American envoy in the Netherlands in 1888, cofounder of the Holland Society, and uncle of Theodore, seized the occasion of the commemoration of the first independent city government of New York in 1653 to encourage the city government not to pay too much attention to the corrupt party bosses in the state capital, Albany. He expressed his admiration for the courageous Peter Stuyvesant, who did not let himself be bullied by rulers from a distance. He reduced a few typical American characteristics (no taxation without representation and the right to vote) to Dutch precedents in New Netherland. Thus, he drew on the Dutch heritage to demand "the birth right of independence and autonomy" of the city.[23] He wanted to make this tradition of a fearless struggle for freedom visible by putting up a statue for William the Silent.[24] Others continued the efforts to anchor the mutual Dutch-American tradition at places in the Netherlands. In 1914, the Dutch-loving Congregational minister of English descent, William E. Griffis, boasted that he was responsible for putting up ten monuments in the Netherlands in places that were relevant to American history.[25] The Holland Society also took the initiative to

---

[23]   Robert B. Roosevelt, "The Oldest Charter of New York," Theodore M. Banta, ed., *Yearbook of the Holland Society of New York* (1903), 234. The society remained the platform for political networks, as became clear in 1924 when the president of the Holland Society spoke at the annual banquet of the Netherlands Society of Philadelphia to encourage its members to support a better rail connection between the two cities.

[24]   Voorhees, *Holland Society*, 66-68. It was to take twenty years before the statue was made and another five years before it received a place at Rutgers University in New Jersey (in 1928).

[25]   *Addresses of the Netherlands Society of Philadelphia*, 76-81; W.E. Griffis, "Thankful America," *Outlook* 106 (January 10, 1914), 88-90. See also Stott, *Holland Mania*, 78-100. Griffis set himself the task of combating the regional separation of New England. He believed that the true united powers in the U.S. were to be found in the mid-Atlantic states, where the Dutch influence was the strongest. Recognition of the European contribution to the shaping of the U.S. was often exhibited in the press: see for instance, the series of articles by Herbert N. Casson in volume 1906 of *Munsey* about twelve groups of immigrants. He wrote about the Dutch (usually from the early period) in the November issue, "The Dutch in America," 238-42. The Dutch historian H.T. Colenbrander paid scholarly attention to the Dutch element in America in the *American Historical Association Report for 1909* (1911), "The Dutch Element in American History," as did the American historian and biographer of William of Orange, Ruth Putnam, "The Dutch Element in the United States," resp. 193-201 and 205-18. Colenbrander corrected the exaggerated interpretation of the Dutch influence in Campbell's publications.

underwrite the rebuilding of Henry Hudson's famous ship the *Halve Maen* for the benefit of the commemoration of his voyage of discovery in 1609. Unfortunately, the celebration of Fulton's first steamship on the Hudson River in 1807, which took place simultaneously with the discovery by Hudson, took attention away from the role of the Netherlands.[26]

## Regional Differences

The first wave of Dutch immigrants to arrive in Michigan in 1846 and 1847 did not need an explicit confirmation of their affection for the new country that they had chosen consciously, and where they quickly felt at home. On the Fourth of July the immigrants got acquainted with a new phenomenon—a national holiday—and they wholeheartedly joined in the festivities.[27] They readily integrated civic festivals in their faith tradition, even though in the 1880s resistance arose in the Christian Reformed Church against this American novelty, which was viewed as competition with ecclesiastical feast days. In 1887 a Christian Reformed minister in Classis Holland asserted that the "Fourth of July" was a necessary evil. The editor-in-chief of *De Grondwet*, L. Mulder, took up arms against this. He considered such statements a sign of ignorance about American society, which new immigrants interpreted by Dutch standards, relating to the chasm between church and society, while American society was positively Christian. Mulder added a practical objection: rejection of the festivities disrupted the unity of the Dutch community and fostered division, such as happened in the village of Overisel where the Christian Reformed Church had withdrawn on the premise that the public holiday did not have a religious character.[28]

The celebration of the twenty-fifth anniversary of the colonies in Michigan and Iowa in 1872 was a fully religious ceremony. Seven years

---

[26]   Lincoln Diamant, *Hoopla on the Hudson: An Intimate View of New York's Great Hudson-Fulton Celebration* (Fleischmanns, N.Y.: Purple Mountain Press, 2003).

[27]   The first written account dates from 1853. *De Hollander*, July 5, 1872. This became clear in 1872 when the village of Zeeland organized a regional celebration of the 4th of July that was attended by many residents of Grand Rapids. *De Hollander* commented that the community had not celebrated the 25th anniversary of the founding of the village, but that it had observed Independence Day. Since the Dutch were not accustomed to celebrating national holidays, the festivities on the 4th of July were a sign already of Americanization.

[28]   *De Grondwet*, June 7, 1887.

**Patriotic parade in Holland, Michigan.**
Hope College Collection of the Joint Archives of Holland, Michigan.

later, the Dutch pioneers realized that they had made history. Thirty-two men founded the Old Settlers Society in the village of Zeeland, with the objective to record history. The first commemoration with a serious historical content was the celebration of the colony's fortieth anniversary in 1887.[29] Five hundred guests, mainly Zeelanders, with one woman still in the traditional costume, came from Grand Rapids for the occasion. Ministers warned against prosperity as a threat to the spiritual caliber of the colony.[30]

Impulses from outside led to reflection on how to demonstrate the nature of the Dutch character. America was the stage for the 1893 World's Fair in Chicago. The principal Dutch contribution to the "Columbian exposition" consisted of 332 paintings, which stole the show at the expense of a few modern inventions, such as the

---

[29]  *De Grondwet*, March 11, 1879, and July 19, 1887. *De Hollander* of July 8, 1874, published the programs of the Fourth of July in Holland, with musical performances, theater, good food, and a patriotic speech about the American Revolution. *De Grondwet* of July 10, 1883, called for a serious celebration of the principle of popular sovereignty, which had its antecedent in Dutch history. Pella organized a similar society on June 14, 1894. The Zeeland Settlers' Society was disbanded in 1907 after the last pioneers had died and the village had put up its own monument (Toni Van Koevering, "Zeeland's Historical Monuments," manuscript Zeeland Historical Society 1988).

[30]  *De Grondwet*, March 11, 1879, July 19, and September 6, 1887.

herring schooner and the machinery of a cocoa factory. The painting exhibition was received jubilantly and stood in sharp contrast to the old-fashioned uniforms of the Dutch soldiers in the parade that made a comical impression. Paintings of self-confident, prosperous citizens appeared to be a useful means to convey national pride. The Dutch consul general in Chicago, George Birkhoff, who was closely associated with the organization, chose August 31 as the day for Dutch festivities; but only in 1933, at the next World's Fair, did this day begin to be meaningful for Dutch immigrants.[31] The preparations for these world fairs expedited the founding of new Dutch clubs in Chicago, such as the elitist Holland Society in 1895 and the more mundane St. Nicholas Society in 1905, neither of which had the good fortune of a long life.[32] At their gatherings references were invariably made to William of Orange and the ideological similarities between the Netherlands and the United States.

After 1900, the profile of Dutch identity was enhanced, thanks to the influx of Dutch immigrants who had left with stronger nationalistic feelings and to prosperity within the Dutch community.[33] Also, within the circle of the Christian Reformed Church, the need arose to define the group. The Reverend Henry Beets, the champion of quick accommodation in this denomination, composed a "Song of the Holland-Americans,"[34] in which he extolled the virtues of the Dutch Americans on the occasion of the fiftieth anniversary of the Christian Reformed Church in 1907. In Beets's version of the Dutch national anthem, "In whose veins flows the blood of the Netherlands," the publisher saw merit, not only because it was "real poetry," but especially because the song compensated for a long-felt need in the gatherings of Dutch people in America. The words contained few religious terms but made a connection between the colonial Dutchman and the nineteenth-century immigrants by singing the praises of the United States. The second stanza shifted attention from the glorious

---

[31]  http://columbus.gl.iit.edu/bookfair/ch21.html#735, visited March 21, 2009.

[32]  Swierenga, *Dutch Chicago*, 526-50.

[33]  Henk te Velde, *Gemeenschapszin en plichtsbesef. Liberalisme en nationalisme in Nederland*, 1870-1918 (The Hague: Sdu Uitgeverij, 1992).

[34]  He perfected his arguments for proper Dutch pride in his often-held lecture, "Why we of Dutch descent claim a modest place in the sunshine of respect of our American nation with its various national origins," of which diverse versions exist, the last one of 1934 in box 24, folder 3, of the Henry Beets Collection in Heritage Hall, Calvin College, Grand Rapids, Michigan.

past of the Netherlands to the inviting future in America, and the song concluded with the wish, "Infuse the best of all our past, the noblest of our traits, into the life, into the deed of our United States!" The text created a distance with the old fatherland and made an emotional appeal to the singers and listeners to embrace America. The song brought the various generations of Dutch Americans together, because they were the only ones who could sing the song. The melody was the same as the Dutch national anthem that was used until 1933, when it was replaced by the Wilhelmus.

> Come ye, who boast of Dutch descent,
> Sons of New Netherland,
> And ye who reached our friendly shore
> With western pilgrim band
> Unite with us in festive song,
> Song which the heart elates
> And sing the praises of our land
> Our own United States,
> Our own United States.
>
> We love the land across the sea
> We glory in its past;
> We pray for its prosperity,
> May it forever last!
> But tho we love old Holland still,
> We love Columbia more,
> The land our sons and brethren fill
> From east to western shore,
> From east to western shore.[35]

In the same year that this song was distributed, Nicholas M. Steffens, a professor at Western Theological Seminary in Holland, Michigan, addressed a crowd of compatriots on the sixtieth anniversary of the founding of the colony. He proudly stated that the Dutch had

[35] This song was the first one in a collection of Dutch spiritual top songs with English translations. Henry Beets, *Herinneringen. Holland-American Songs. Holland songs with English Text. Series I* (Chicago: Paul H. Wezeman, 1907). This was the opening song of the Semi-Centennial Commission, *Gedenkboek van het Vijftigjarig Jubileum der Christelijk Gereformeerde Kerk A.D. 1857-1907* (Grand Rapids: 1907), reprinted in Lagerwey, *Neen Nederland*, 62. The song was sung at the celebration of the 400th anniversary of William of Orange April 24, 1933, in Chicago, but no longer during Princess Juliana's visit on May 12, 1942. The "Wien Neerlandsch Bloed" was still sung on the 60th anniversary of Holland and Zeeland in August 1907.

become such good citizens because they had kept the best parts of their tradition. He contrasted this praiseworthy attitude with the "new" immigrants from southern and eastern Europe, who fortunately were absorbed quickly by American society: "It may be well that Italians, Hungarians, Greeks, Poles and Russians do not establish colonies but are soon swallowed up by the powerful American spirit, but if immigrants come from countries whose citizens have something that is worthy to be preserved it will be a blessing for them as well as for the Americans if they come just like the Dutch came in 1847 A.D."[36]

On the same occasion the Reverend Matthew Kolyn explained the task of the Dutch in America: "We are persuaded that the Hollander in America has come to stay. His influence is to be powerful and lasting; it has been known and felt during the three centuries that have passed since his coming. His name is written large upon the pages of American history. His love for and devotion to the new fatherland has been unquestioned. In peace and in war, the Hollander in America has been a patriot of the noblest type." His argument was clearly historical in nature: the Dutch had not only founded New Amsterdam, but their influence had also entered the country by way of the Pilgrim Fathers who had been influenced by living in the Netherlands, as well through the person of William Penn, who had a Dutch mother. They had contributed much to order in America.[37]

Similar sounds echoed throughout the entire Midwest. Vice Consul Gerrit Klay of Orange City, Iowa, reported in 1931 that not a single Dutch person had appeared in court on a criminal charge in the last three years. In this he saw conformation of a recent statement of President Hoover, "The Dutch descendants over here are never in prison and never in the poor house."[38] Although many Dutch liked to see these facts as signs of their moral superiority, they were, in fact, the result of their settlement patterns, with strong social ties caused by family migration to agricultural areas, and by a strong religious framework. The stories of these heroes were impressed upon the minds of the young. Hope College student William C. Walvoord won a speech

---

[36]    N.M. Steffens, "Het zestigjarig feest," *Historical Souvenir of the Celebration of the Sixtieth Anniversary of the Colonization of the Hollanders in Western Michigan* (n.p., privately printed, 1908), 113.

[37]    Matthew Kolyn, "The Hollander in America," in ibid., 55-64, citation on 59.

[38]    Report to the minister in Washington, January 5, 1931, Inv. 2.05.13 Gezantschap VS, nr. 406 Orange City, 1919-1934. Nationaal Archief, The Hague.

contest in February 1908 with an argument about the significance of the siege of Leiden: "Heroism, sacrifice, and nobleness of purpose are qualities which characterize not only the defense of Leyden, but...[t]he American Revolution, qualities which are essential to every struggle for true freedom."[39] In the same year Hope College student George F. Huizinga won a prize from Edward W. Bok, the editor-in-chief of the *Ladies' Home Journal*, for his essay about the contributions of the Dutch to the development of the American West.[40]

According to historian Overland the need of the Dutch immigrants to prove that they felt at home in America was minimal. "Dutch immigrants themselves do not seem to have felt a great need to widely broadcast their own presence when America was still a colony."[41] His main proof is a 1929 editorial comment in the weekly *Onze Toekomst* that asserted that the most important contribution of the Dutch was establishing the true church (the CRC). Here we encounter a paradox: the stronger the religious identity of the group, the less it needed an explicit national identity. At the same time its religious identity was fed and governed by a Dutch mindset to which it reverted to justify its existence. The Christian Reformed Church and the western part of the Reformed Church formed tightly knit groups that completely satisfied the need to belong to something. They offered their members a self-consciousness that neutralized the fear of being absorbed by America without leaving a trace.

For the immigrants who quickly established primary American relationships and who had hardly any association with a Dutch-American church, historical roots were more important. Public references to Dutch historical personages or events provided newcomers with a connection to their own situation, as the precursor of their own involvement with America. Thus, they could resort to historical research done by those not belonging to the tribe in order to show how they were different from the dominating British. Simultaneously with the patrician New Yorkers, who solidified their positions by means of

---

[39]  Walvoord, *Windmill Memories*, 57-58. The lecture was printed in the *Anchor*, April 1908, 5-10.

[40]  George Ford Huizinga, *What the Dutch Have Done in the West of the United States* (Philadelphia: privately printed, 1909). In an editorial comment in the *Banner* of January 21, 1909, Henry Beets congratulated the winners and expressed his regret that the students of Calvin College were not allowed to participate. The later journalist and portrayer of the Dutch in America, Arnold Mulder, won third prize.

[41]  Overland, *Immigrant Minds*, 78.

ethnic societies and who unearthed their Dutch roots, the Midwestern Dutch arrived at a series of commemorative events that made them return to the same roots.

The three regions with Dutch-American settlements used different strategies. On the East Coast, the Dutch with roots in New Amsterdam appealed to their past with a view to political ends. In the Midwest and other places where immigrants settled after 1846,[42] church-connected immigrants used Dutch history to promote moral ends. The later immigrants on the West Coast used the Dutch empire, including its colonies, to promote trade interests. In view of the modest role played in America's wars by only a small number of immigrants, accounts about the origin and ideology of America offered the best points of contact.[43] The ideological myth was generally the most suitable and could be tapped also without bilateral historical ties. However, there were enough historical points of contact available to produce actual areas of commonality, and to bring to the fore the common virtues of both countries during commemorations.[44]

Fear, therefore, was not the primary motivation in this process. Historical means were used in an assertive manner rather than defensively. The old Dutch elite was fully accepted and used the three myths as answers to being belittled by the Americans. The Dutch Envoy

---

[42]  The Dutch communities in New Jersey, especially Passaic (Clifton), Paterson, Lodi, and Prospect Park, show similarities with the patterns of the Midwest. See Gerald F. De Jong, "Dutch Immigrants in New Jersey before World War I," *New Jersey History* 94 (1976): 69-88.

[43]  An example of attention received for the contribution of Dutch Americans to the wars of the American Republic is the text of the song by Isaac Rusling Pennypacker, "The Dutch on the Delaware," which was adopted as the club song of the Netherlands Society of Philadelphia in 1894. It refers to the sons of the beggars who together with General Washington crossed the Delaware and who later fought against Robert Lee. *Addresses Made at the Annual Meetings of the Netherlands Society of Philadelphia. Bellevue-Stratford Hotel 1913-1930*, II. This society was founded January 23, 1892, on the day the Unie of Utrecht of 1579 was commemorated. In 1913 the society funded a statue for Pieter C. Plockhoy in Zierikzee. This honored him as the founder of Swaanendael, Delaware, and as a "Pioneer of Christian Civilization." The city of Holland celebrated Decoration Day to remember those fallen in the Civil War (*De Grondwet*, May 29 and June 5, 1877). The Holland Soldiers' Union was founded in 1875 and erected a monument for veterans in the Pilgrim Home Cemetery, in 1894.

[44]  William E. Griffis emphasized that Holland as a republic invited a prince to accept sovereign power (*Addresses* 1914, 70). Griffis traveled through the Netherlands to put up ten memorial plaques at places that were relevant to American history.

A.C. de Graeff gave a typical example in 1924: "So often in Washington society I am greeted socially by the ladies with the question: 'How is dear little Holland?' I am sure these people feel genuine sympathy for my country. However, I take exception....It is not geographic dimensions, but strength of character of the people that fixes a country's place in the family of nations."[45] In this respect the agenda of the Dutch government coincided with that of older Dutch Americans by confirming a common tradition.

Except for the tensions of the First World War, there were no foreign attacks that stimulated these strategies, but rather societal developments of which the Dutch themselves were a part. One such trend was their participation in the founding of ethnic societies because other groups did the same.[46] Thus, the Dutch eventually strengthened the dominance of the Anglo-Saxon culture by looking for common ground in their own tradition. They received Josiah Strong's book, *Our Country*, with great enthusiasm; it "proved" the superiority of the Anglo-Saxon race because it had allowed them to obtain worldwide influence: "We, of this stock and this nation, constitute the Gibraltar of the ages that governs the future of the world."[47] Whatever the negative results may have been for the surpassed party, these ideas stimulated the Dutch immigrants to commit themselves to American society. They could draw on precedents in their own history. A clear example was the support the members of the Holland Society of Chicago offered in 1898 for the "liberation of Cuba" during the Spanish-American War, while referring to the Dutch struggle for independence from the same Spain.[48] Also, the Tulip Time festivals, which were organized toward the end of the 1920s and in the 1930s to strengthen free enterprise, confirmed the American character of the Dutch-American subculture. These festivals

---

[45]   Ibid., 357-58.

[46]   Frank Van Nuys, *Americanizing the West: Race, Immigrants, and Citizenship, 1890-1930* (Lawrence: Univ. of Kansas Press, 2002), 9-32. German-Americans succeeded in 1987 in having October 6 proclaimed "German-American Day." This day referred to the arrival of the first group of German immigrants in Philadelphia in 1683. See Don Heinrich Tolzmann, *The German-American Experience* (Amherst, N.Y.: Humanity Books, 2000), 364-66. This proclamation emphasized the German contribution to American culture, such as the Christmas tree, kindergarten, music, science, democracy, and the total integration of the German Americans, who formed the largest ethnic group in the country.

[47]   Strong, *Ons land*, 229. Pages 283-86 contain "testimonials" by six prominent RCA ministers and one CRC minister.

[48]   Overland, *American Minds*, 123.

made copious use of stereotypes such as windmills, wooden shoes, and tulips in order to stir up nostalgic longings for the simple life and to tie them to products. They bound communities more firmly together by making them more American.[49]

## International Relationships

International entanglements strengthened the Dutch immigrants' own awareness of their identity in America. The South African Boer War of the early 1880s, and especially the one between 1899 and 1902, made the Dutch swell with pride by identifying with the Boers in South Africa who so valiantly resisted British tyranny. The gruesome tales about the concentration camps, in which innocent women and children were tortured, evoked strong anti-British feelings that lasted until after the First World War. The money raised and the protest meetings in America on behalf of the cause of the Boers strengthened relations with the Netherlands, where similar sentiments offered compensation for the loss of international influence and lack of contemporary heroes. The Boers symbolized virtues, such as faith and heroic courage, with which the Dutch wished to identify. The limited role of the Netherlands in Europe and the small size of the Dutch-American group in the United States made it easy to identify with the Boers whose cause was a source of strength for their own identity.[50] Stimuli from the outside and

[49]    Suzanne Sinke, "Tulips are Blooming in Holland, Michigan: Analysis of a Dutch American Festival," in Michael Sínnocenzo, a.o., *Immigration and Ethnicity: American Society—"Melting Pot" or "Salad Bowl"* (Westport, Conn.: Greenwood, 1992), 3-14. Janet S. Sheeres, "Klompendancing through America," in Wagenaar and Swierenga, *Dutch Enterprise*, 71-82, for a survey of all tulip festivals and Dutch cultural celebrations. Just as the Italians in Europe do not celebrate Columbus Day, or the Norwegians May 17, and just as all kinds of ethnic groups in America normally participate in the Irish St. Patrick's Day, so Tulip Time is not an originally Dutch feast but a fabrication of 1929 that coupled a fair to self-promotion of the group. Overland observes that these ethnic celebrations are typical expressions of the middle class. Laborers resorted to labor unions rather than ethnic clubs, which buzzed with progress, success, and nationalism. See also Geneviève Fabre, Jurgen Heideking, and Kai Dreisbach, eds., *Celebrating Ethnicity and Nation: American Festive Culture from the Revolution to the Early Twentieth Century* (New York: Berghahn, 2001).

[50]    See Michael Douma, "Holland Michigan and the Boer War" (B.A. thesis, Hope College, 2003) and Hans Ester, "Met Louwrens Penning naar het land van de verbeelding: De Nederlandse liefde voor Zuid-Afrika," *Transparant* 2 (August 2000): 4-9; Chris van Koppen, *De geuzen van de negentiende eeuw. Abraham Kuiper en Zuid-Afrika* (Wormer: Immerc, 1992). *De Grondwet* of February 22, 1881, published a poem that called for support of the Boers.

from the non-Dutch contributed considerably to making this Dutch-American identity explicit. In the case of the Boers this was easy, and this identification had no political consequences, but in the First World War taking on a nonconformist position was more dangerous.

The position of a neutral power surrounded by warring nations made the Netherlands vulnerable in public opinion, especially after the United States publicly joined the allies. Not only did the Dutch not participate in a "heroic struggle," they were also suspected of carrying on a lucrative trade with the enemy. The growing importance of the Asian trade for the Netherlands and the U.S. made the consul general in San Francisco, Henry A. Van Coenen Torchiana, take up arms. This former cowboy who had gone into business defended the commercial interests of the Netherlands and America in 1918 with fervor and was the first diplomat who consciously practiced cultural diplomacy, because he realized that public opinion would become increasingly important in commercial relations.[51] He was not afraid of the opinion of the American press about the Netherlands, because he trusted that a country that was above reproach would be treated fairly.[52] He neutralized in advance allegations that the Netherlands had carried on trade with Germany with the argument that this was the prerogative of a neutral power and that, moreover, this was necessary in order to provide its own population with needed consumer goods. He further tried to arouse sympathy for the honorable and erudite prime minister, the tormented young queen, and the beloved former Dutch ambassador to Washington, Loudon, who was married to a respected American lady.

Van Coenen realized that a historical appeal to the services rendered by the Netherlands in the past would be impractical in this situation. On the other hand, he believed firmly that shared ideals of personal and political liberties could be used advantageously. He even saw new opportunities for commercial growth, now that Germany had a poor reputation, if Dutch exporters guaranteed that their products originated from their own country. He proffered the West Coast appealing trade perspectives with the Dutch East Indies, which had the potential of becoming lucrative if banks and transport companies

---

[51]   H.A. Van Coenen Torchiana, *The Future of Trade Between the United States of America and the Netherlands and Its Colonies: A Short Study* (San Francisco: Holland-American Chamber of Commerce, 1918), 9. See also the address of the Dutch ambassador in Washington to the Netherlands Society of Philadelphia, January 23, 1919, *Addresses*, 217-31.

[52]   Van Coenen Torchiana, *Future of Trade*, 11.

would invest.[53] Similar arguments, which confirmed the lasting mutual commitment to liberty, peace, and justice, were expressed by Willem de Beaufort, first secretary of the Dutch embassy in Washington, D.C.: "Our common past does not come at the expense of the realization of our collective present."[54]

From the Netherlands came impulses for a Dutch consciousness and the Dutch language when Abraham Kuyper during his tour of the U.S. in 1898 called on his large audiences to support the Algemeen Nederlands Verbond (ANV) and to establish chairs in the Dutch language. The ANV had been founded in 1895 to promote the interests of speakers of Dutch, and the hesitant start in Chicago in 1896 received an enthusiastic boost from Kuyper's visit and from concern for the Boers. After Kuyper left, most chapters folded; only Chicago kept the flame alive and was able to fuel it also in other localities. In the long run, the association, which at the most numbered a few hundred sympathizers in America, was not able to survive, even though the initiative was not entirely unproductive: chairs in the Dutch language and literature were established at the University of Chicago and Columbia University, which provided intellectual interest in the Netherlands with varying success. Books were given to universities and portraits of Queen Wilhelmina were distributed. In 1923 the Leiden church historian, A. Eekhof, suggested twelve ways to promote the cultural heritage in America, which for the most part were implemented by the Netherlands America Foundation that had been founded in New York in 1921. The Dutch reputation in America during the First World War had suffered from allegations that the Netherlands had profited financially from the conflict. Together with the realization that the economic interests of America were ever-increasing, this fact was the reason for renewed cultural impulses.[55]

The Second World War and America's contribution to the liberation of the Netherlands strengthened the ties between the two countries even more. The celebration of the centennial of the Dutch colonies in America in 1847 offered an abundance of opportunities to highlight the contributions of the Dutch to America. Willard Wichers, director of the Netherlands Museum in Holland, Michigan, and of the Dutch Information Service, was in charge of the planning committee and succeeded in getting the Dutch government so directly involved in the festivities that some residents of Holland complained that the Dutch had preempted the events. The interests of the Netherlands resided in strengthening cultural ties with the principal liberator of the Netherlands who, moreover, as benefactor relieved the distress of the impoverished nation. Furthermore, the intellectual ties between the countries were strengthened by philosopher Marten ten Hoor, who did his best to show that the Dutch Calvinists had established a democratic organization, even though they rejected, in principle, popular sovereignty. But the most important part of the commemoration was the exhibition of objects that were to evoke pride in the Dutch pioneers and the "spirit of Ebenezer [thus far the Lord has helped us], the spirit that enabled our fathers to build happy homes and to become productive citizens, wherever they settled."[56] That moment was the highlight for the Dutch-American subculture.

CHAPTER 11

# Conclusion: Building Blocks for Permanence

The Dutch emigrants who came to the United States in groups of a few hundred in 1846 and 1847 had a much greater effect on the creation of a Dutch-American subculture than one might expect from their number. Among the hundreds of thousands of Germans and Irishmen these Dutchmen hardly attracted attention. Still, they succeeded in building a subculture that to this day is identifiable. How did they accomplish this?[1]

It began with positive expectations of America: travel accounts, newspaper articles, letters, brochures, and occasional poems usually painted a positive picture of a free American society without a meddlesome government. Citizens had much more control over their own lives than in their home country. In the Netherlands economic crises, gloom, natural disasters, and a growing number of restrictions formed a dark contrast with the positive expectations, the openness, the promises for growth and abundance in the New World. Therefore the United States compared favorably with alternatives in the Dutch

[1]  Thomas Bender, *Community and Social Change in America* (New Brunswick: Rutgers Univ. Press, 1978), 7-8.

colonies and even with land reclamation projects elsewhere in the country. The passage of thousands of German emigrants through the country confirmed the impression that America was an attractive destination that became easier to reach all along.

The basis for the formation of a stable community in America was laid already in the Netherlands. Especially the first wave of Seceders and their sympathizers was ready and able to subordinate their self-interest temporarily to the interest of the group. Thanks to seed money, good advisors, a strong, mutual trust, and the readiness to make sacrifices the group was able to take root.[2] Ministers who decided to cast their lot with the members of their congregation were well equipped to solve problems and set priorities. Their authority kept the group together in adversities, conflicts, and dealings with authorities and businesses. The founding of a number of emigration societies produced not only a mental process about how to organize a community with concrete goals and means, but it also provided variety for richer and poorer immigrants. Hendrik Scholte functioned as the crowbar for removing philosophical hindrances to emigration. The independence of people in America appealed to him in particular. His method was more suitable for well-to-do people whom he preceded to the prairies of Iowa, rather than for the people who had fewer financial resources and who went to Michigan with Van Raalte and Cornelis Van der Meulen. Van Raalte hinted that he was not sure that the Scholte group would also act "on behalf of the impoverished brothers," while these were precisely the people that he was concerned about.[3]

The differences in prosperity among the pioneers resulted at first in differences in the colonies, which, however, began to resemble each other more and more after a decade, thanks to mutual exchanges and the central position of these ministers in the pioneer communities. The fact that these leaders themselves were pioneers sometimes led to accusations of conflicts of interest, but it eventually benefited the community as a whole, because they did the long-term planning, provided employment opportunities, new areas for agriculture, and necessary institutions.

Roman Catholic initiatives for establishing Dutch colonies originated in America itself with Father Van den Broek, who filled the vacuum that was left by the removal of Indians in Wisconsin with

---

[2]     Lewis, "Farm Settlement on the Canadian Prairies, " *Journal of Economic History* 41 (September 1981): 517-35, and "Farm Settlement with Imperfect Capital Markets," *Canadian Journal of Economics* 24 (2001): 174-95.

[3]     Brummelkamp, *Stemmen uit Noord-Amerika*, 70.

Catholic immigrants from his native country. His leadership ended when he died in 1851.

The departure from the Netherlands of hundreds of emigrants in groups called attention to emigration as a realistic possibility. Publication of the mainly positive experiences and new measures by the government kept emigration alive as a topic of conversation. Various sources of information describing the risks for immigrants had a self-selective effect. The services of the newly formed communities diminished the risk of failure and helped the poorer and more vulnerable emigrants across the threshold.[4] Immigrants were bound together especially by familial ties, church contacts, and village connections, even if they had left at different times. Whatever the connections (and they often overlapped), the most important result was that immigrants could join a community that improved their chances of success considerably.

The time for settling in America was favorable. The United States experienced a period of economic and geographic expansion that made it easy for immigrants to find work and acquire large tracts for group settlement. Protestant immigrants from the Netherlands could make use of the Dutch network in New York, something Catholic and Jewish emigrants lacked. These "quartermasters" paid a high price in hard work and personal sacrifices, but they also reaped the benefits of increased land values.

The Dutch colonies in the Midwest did not want to isolate themselves from their surroundings, but modernized from the beginning. Thus, the communities prevented a sudden paralysis when after the Second World War big corporations and the government began to regulate public life and exacted scaling-up.[5] The Dutch-American communities recognized that their viability depended on the services of neighboring cities and on efficient lines of communication among the settlements. Furthermore, the diversity that resulted from the economic development required space for growth. Especially farther west the new settlements needed the railroads and international shipping that took care of markets for their products, provided a regular supply of immigrants, and also maintained contact with the

---

[4]  Simone A. Wege, "Chain Migration and Information Networks: Evidence from Nineteenth-Century Hesse-Cassel," *Journal of Economic History* 58 (1998): 957-86. The wave of emigration included a long aftermath. See Timothy J. Hatton and Jeffrey G. Williamson, *The Age of Mass Migration: Causes and Economic Impact* (New York: Oxford Univ. Press, 1998), 14.

[5]  Bender, *Community*, 15-24.

motherland. Thanks to the stability of the first settlements and their supply cities, new daughter colonies could be founded after the Civil War, which offered new immigrants additional options for settlement. The move to the cities meant a welcome expansion of job opportunities for temporary and steady laborers, who looked each other up and formed a community. In order to create room for farmers, the colony in Iowa had to work more systematically than in Michigan, because economic alternatives outside agriculture were much more limited in the prairie states. The colonies in the northwestern part of the state formed an important link in the network. Even though the growth market attracted speculators who misled trusting immigrants, thanks to mutual contacts failed colonists could find places in another Dutch community.

In order to remain viable, the community had to be homogeneous yet guarantee variety as well. This variety could only be achieved thanks to the coordination among the settlements. Only then could the ethnic community form a channel for contacts with the outside world. The Protestant churches drew a sharper boundary with the outside world than the Catholics by forbidding members to join organizations that claimed competing loyalties, such as the Freemasons and the labor unions.

Among the institutions that the immigrants created to support their community, the churches occupied a central place. They took care of continuity, cohesion, and a network beyond the community. Even the church split of 1857 contributed to this cohesion, although that may seem contradictory: it offered these immigrants the possibility to differ on matters of faith and yet to stay within the Dutch subculture. Besides, they were given the opportunity to choose a slower pace of integration. Those for whom the experiential aspect of faith was most important felt more at home in the Reformed Church in America, which readily opened up to the emotional tradition of American Protestantism. Believers who valued doctrine more, and who put strict conditions on fellowship with nonbelievers or those of a different faith in order to keep the outside world at bay, found a spiritual home in the Christian Reformed Church. The mutual competition between the Reformed and the Christian Reformed Church to gain new members heightened their efforts in this regard. This objective to grow pulled both denominations, sometimes almost imperceptibly, into the American framework. The lessons that the Reformed Church learned in living with diversity in liturgy, organization, interchurch cooperation, missionary, and social work, caused by the different phases of the churches at the East Coast and in the Midwest, were experienced by the Christian Reformed Church thirty to forty years later.

The Dutch Catholics who wanted to remain true to themselves found a suitable place in the few homogenous rural areas where they were protected from the state and the outside world. Catholic settlements formed a subculture only after city communities had increased the number of immigrants and churches, newspapers, and businesses had strengthened the mutual connection. However, joining the Catholic Church in America did hasten the intermingling with other nationalities. More than Protestants, Catholics experienced their identity in cultural events, such as the fair and the rifle club.[6]

The high demands on the part of the church community regarding knowledge and involvement, time and money, and the expectation (especially for men) to be involved in decision making, led to a strong identification with the institution. Besides their organizational ability to attract people, Protestant churches provided an intrinsic contribution to the formation of a Dutch-American identity of its own by connecting it to the Dutch Reformed tradition. Thanks to the dominance of the strict Calvinist (*Gereformeerde*) ministers (only two Dutch Reformed [*Hervormde*] colleagues emigrated), they were able to propagate the Dutch Calvinistic body of ideas. Although its reach was limited, it was nevertheless the only Protestant system of thought from Europe that was able to compete in breadth and depth with the results of the revival of Roman Catholic thought, Neothomism.[7] Outside the Reformed and Christian Reformed churches, organized meeting places were available for the Dutch only in about ten Presbyterian churches and in cultural clubs for businessmen in the big cities.

Families formed a firm basis for the Dutch community and provided stability, prosperity, and continuity. More than any other European group the Dutch emigrated as families. This resulted from the overrepresentation of people from rural areas who, especially in the beginning, were bent on acquiring land for their offspring. Marriages could be entered into much more easily in America than in the Netherlands. Even though many more men than women emigrated, thanks to the high number of children the next generation saw a much more balanced make-up, which facilitated finding a partner in one's own circle. Families often stayed together thanks to low divorce rates, and thanks to the proximity of work for the head of the household. The

6    Gjerde, *Minds of the West*, 12-15 and 271-75.
7    Mark A. Noll, *The Old Religion in a New World: The History of North American Christianity* (Grand Rapids: Eerdmans, 2002), 248-49.

families offered stability and tended to stay put; this compensated for lost contacts and encouraged investing for the future. The presence of large numbers of children promoted the founding of social and cultural institutions, such as schools and libraries, and provided an important impetus for a conscious transfer of traditions. In this way the family became a pillar of the Dutch community in America, to which it also contributed materially.

The free American economy offered Dutch immigrants variety and room to build a future and offered surpluses for communal ends. The best opportunities were found, especially in the mid 1800s, in agriculture. There, people of limited means could build up their own businesses with determination and proper management in communities that provided their own stores and shops. After the Civil War, the cities offered a great variety of unskilled work, and the Dutch specialized in construction, transportation, the furniture industry, and truck farming. These concentrations created close communities because they provided work and contacts for newcomers. The next generation profited from the growing educational opportunities that prepared it for better paid service jobs. This development offered Dutch Americans access to better jobs in the American economy, contributed to a stronger community, and also to more interaction with other Americans.[8]

The opportunities to make quick material headway decreased over the course of the century but were nevertheless considerable compared to those in the dynamically much slower economy of the Netherlands. In the short term, possessing land and ready employable skills, such as in construction, provided rapid growth in income. In the long run, work that did not require physical strength provided more affluence. Good educational provisions in one's own circle were helpful in climbing the societal ladder without losing the group ties.

The transition from Dutch to English as a means of communication happened gradually and was always governed by the need to keep the generations together and retain access to cultural, and especially religious, sources. The use of English was never a matter of "whether" but "when." Dutch was spoken longest in the relatively isolated agricultural communities where farms were transferred from one generation to the next. The first wave of immigrants fostered ideals of cultural continuity but also understood that English could not

---

[8]    Carmel U. Chiswick, "From Ellis Island to JFK—An Economist's Perspective," *Journal of American Ethnic History* 21 (2002): 57-67.

**Eighth Street, the main street of Holland, Michigan.**
Hope College Collection of the Joint Archives of Holland, Michigan.

be avoided. It was often the second crop of immigrants, who settled in isolated areas, that found the pace of adjustment too fast and therefore made a strong case to keep the Dutch. The first generation of immigrants learned English in order to be able to function in the economy, in society, and in politics. The immigrants who followed expected more often that they would land in "little Holland," where they would be able to use Dutch longer. When modern means of communication and transportation opened these areas after 1950, they were the last ones to change to English.

Freedom of education was an important draw for emigrants in the middle of the nineteenth century. For that reason the curriculum of the early "Dutch" schools included, characteristically, Bible lessons and received a new impetus when after 1900 the religious content of the public schools diminished gradually, beginning in the cities.

The need for solid training of ministers became the stimulus for establishing educational institutions. The leaders of the community also received their education there, which in turn led to the founding of separate secondary schools. It was only in areas where thousands of immigrant families were able to generate sufficient funds, personnel, and students that a well-coordinated school system could come into being. The Dutch Catholics in Wisconsin also invested in parochial schools, but, forced by legislation, they soon changed over to English. The only "Dutch" college, St. Norbert, appealed to a broad Catholic constituency and for that reason did not become a breeding ground for a Dutch-American identity.

The conviction that worldly influences had to be kept at bay led to the creation of Christian schools, Protestant as well as Catholic. The Dutch immigrants had three motives to found their own schools: to prepare their children in a practical way for life in America, to learn the Dutch language as long as it was necessary to be able to keep in touch with the older generation, and to transfer their ideology. The result was twofold. On the one hand, the educational level increased, which improved the quality of the group, and a cadre was formed that could provide leadership to the subculture; on the other hand, this development promoted self-criticism and closer ties with American culture.

Private funds to maintain these institutions only flowed to the coffers thanks to intensive communication that kept the dispersed members of the community together. Newspapers, private correspondence, and meetings created a strong bond and fed their identity through contacts with the fatherland. The exchanges of news, reflection on trends in America, passing on of traditions, and creation of support actions for the needy contributed to intensive cooperation among immigrants.

From the publication of the *Sheboygan Nieuwsbode* in 1849 until the discontinuation of Orange City's *De Volksvriend* in 1951, Dutch-language newspapers supplied the colonies with a mixture of local Dutch and American news, supplemented with practical tips and meditations. The loss of local autonomy and the reduced number of immigrants after the Second World War meant the end of Dutch-language newspapers, magazines, and books in America. These had played a crucial role for an entire century in the exchange of information among the various Dutch-American communities and with the fatherland. Besides, they had opened the way to politics, thanks to the political news and financial support that the political parties offered the newspapers.

The first generation of immigrants was therefore eager to participate in the game of politics. They saw its importance for their own community, felt the pressure of anti-immigrant movements, and tasted the satisfaction of local political successes. During the Civil War, the preference of the Protestant Dutch immigrants shifted from the Democratic to the Republican Party when the former showed too little effort on behalf of the communities, and the latter showed more stability. After they had settled, these immigrants still proved to have more European blood than they had thought. They made a conscious choice in favor of the Republican Party, which, like themselves, attached a greater value to moral and economic structures. This connected them more closely to the Protestant mainstream in America. Their small size and predictable voting patterns prevented the Dutch from becoming an ethnic factor in politics. The political parties were not important to the Dutch for the strengthening of their ethnic group, but they were used for the protection of local interests. The churches encouraged people to assume their civic responsibilities, especially in times of transition, but did not play an active role in politics.

The Dutch immigrants who left their fatherland in groups did regret having to say goodbye to their native soil and relatives, but much less to their national identity. It was not until the Dutch had built a solid economic and regional basis that they made an appeal to history to underscore the connection with America. In doing so, they could draw from a selection of historical data on which to base their right to be accepted in America—by appealing to the role the Dutch had played when the Europeans occupied the land, by pointing to the sacrifices their ethnic group had made in America's wars, and by pointing to the basic similarities between America and their land of origin: freedom, entrepreneurship, diversity in population, relative tolerance, and democratic structures. These three strategies were aimed against the exclusive claims of the British colonists. The Dutch profited from a full arsenal of historical arguments to demand their status as true Americans, but used their historic "rights" only seldom. The New Yorkers did not consider it necessary because they already belonged to the elite, while the Christian Reformed in the Midwest not only reacted against the residents of the East Coast who had grown soft but also considered theological purity much more important than historically grown privileges.

The aim of the colonies was not to build a Dutch utopia, but to use the opportunities America offered. The purchase of English Bibles was an early indication that accommodation would be inevitable. The explicit Christian character of the early colonies testified to an ideal that could not be realized in the Netherlands, but for which America did offer room. The internal debates and conflicts made it especially clear that the immigrants wanted to retain the bond with their old fatherland without being sidelined in America. Americans were not chased out of the community or avoided; instead, they were invited to be involved in projects.

Although the Dutch-American identity was tied to a historic phase, its presence is valuable because it offered these immigrants and their off-spring access to other traditions besides the American and could mobilize opposing forces against excesses of individualism, consumerism, materialism, and patriotism.

## Long-Term Effects

A long-term perspective offers a view of the timing and transience of the nineteenth-century immigration movement. A comparison with the history of seventeenth-century New Netherland offers surprising differences: New Netherland retained an administrative relationship with the Netherlands during the first forty years, and until the close of the eighteenth century ecclesiastical ties as well. The tension experienced by the seventeenth-century colonists with the government in the mother country was unknown to those of the nineteenth century. In New Netherland the highest offices in government were beyond the reach of its citizens, who became involved only later, while "Holland" could choose its own leaders. New Netherland was more cosmopolitan, was interested in commerce more than in agriculture, and was put together more diversely, while nineteenth-century immigrant colonies were more homogenous because of regional clustering and church affinity. The arrangement of the colonies in the Midwest was more systematic and unambiguous. New Netherland gradually developed via a gradual simplification of the old Dutch structures, adjustment to the local situation, and imitation of Europe by the elite. American structures were clearly visible already in the nineteenth century, and the elite took the lead in becoming American.[9]

Those who called themselves "Dutch" in America certainly were not all of the same stripe, as the American historian Firth Fabend has shown. Some of those who in the seventeenth century had gone from Amsterdam to America had first arrived in the Dutch commercial center as immigrants. Some of the non-Dutch residents of New Netherland adopted the Dutch way of life. A third group joined the established church and not only identified with the church, but also with its ethnic origin.[10] In seventeenth-century society with its changing boundaries, nationality was less important for one's identity than religion. The religious character was stable and narrowly defined in the creeds, yet, at the same time, not narrowly national.

[9]    Jacobs, *New Netherland*, and Janny Venema, *Beverwijck: A Dutch Village on the American Frontier*, 1652-1664 (Hilversum: Verloren, 2003).
[10]   Fabend, *Zion on the Hudson*, 8-19.

But there also were parallel developments: prosperous immigrants were the first to leave the Dutch subculture. The Dutch language thrived best in rural areas in New Jersey and in the state of New York, more so than in the cities. Pietism strengthened the use of the Dutch language as a counterbalance to worldly English. However, since Dutch centered around the home and the church and lacked additional corresponding institutional support, its cultural value weakened.[11] Nineteenth-century immigrants, however, were better equipped for transmitting traditions.

This book describes the history of the prewar Dutch emigration. After the Second World War a new emigration era dawned. Almost one-third of the Dutch population indicated in a 1948 opinion poll that they would leave if given the choice. In the following years this percentage dropped, but one out of five Dutch continued to entertain thoughts of emigrating.[12] The background of this readiness lay in the recent events in international politics, in particular in the tensions caused by the decolonization of the Dutch East Indies and the outbreak of the Cold War. In addition, there were national political concerns: the threat of overpopulation, poverty, lack of housing, unemployment, repatriation of soldiers and other fellow citizens from the Dutch East Indies, the electoral success of the Communists (10 percent), the social problems that were the result of the devastation caused by the war. Not everyone who wanted to was able to leave, because right after the war there were not enough ships available and the authorities prioritized demobilization and reconstruction. When the practical impediments were cleared up around 1950, the new immigration wave could get under way thanks to new shipping connections, incentives on both sides of the ocean, and extensive information dissemination by special emigration offices and especially by Canadian information agencies.[13]

[11]  A.G. Roeber, "'The Origin of Whatever is Not English among Us:' The Dutch-speaking and the German-speaking Peoples of Colonial British America," in Bernard Bailyn and Philip D. Morgan, eds., *Strangers within the Realm: Cultural Margins of the First British Empire* (Chapel Hill: Univ. of North Carolina Press, 1991), 220-84, esp. 234.

[12]  Marijke van Faassen, "Min of meer misbaar. Naoorlogse emigratie vanuit Nederland: achtergronden en organisatie, particuliere motieven en overheidsprikkels, 1946-1967," in Saskia Poldervaart, Hanneke Willemse, and Jan Willem Schilt, *Van hot naar her. Nederlandse emigratie vroeger, nu en morgen* (Amsterdam: Stichting beheer IISG, 2001), 50-67.

[13]  Enne Koops, "Dutch Emigration to the United States," in Krabbendam, van Minnen, and Scott-Smith, *Four Centuries*, 1005-16.

The desire to leave was a continuation of the emigration tradition, which indeed was smaller in size after 1920, but which nevertheless endured because of extensive transatlantic communication and the emigration societies. Correspondence with America had been interrupted during the Second World War, but it was resumed. America's contribution to the liberation; the contrast between the devastation at home and the wealth in America, visible in the consumer goods and the generous support of private American individuals and in the Marshall Plan sponsored by the American government; employment opportunities elsewhere; and unemployment at home made emigration attractive. After the war the Holland America Line cleverly zeroed in on the need to visit relatives in North America, whom people often had not seen for a long time. This caused direct contacts to flourish.[14] Expectations for the future of a new and better postwar era did not come true, or at least too slowly. As soon as individuals left, the desire to keep families together pulled others along.

The Dutch government began to play an active role and encouraged emigration as a means to relieve the labor market. Unemployment threatened especially small farmers who were not able to keep up with the mechanization process. The government paid $260 per person, and the receiving country added another $60, so that approximately half of the needed $600 for the voyage across was covered.

Not everybody received the same treatment. The Dutch government was afraid to lose too many well-educated citizens, and the receiving countries were afraid to get the failures. All kinds of rules and regulations were invented to counteract undesirable trends and improper practices. But in view of the fact that most measures were put into operation and adjusted after the peak year of 1952 when 48,000 emigrants left the Netherlands—20 percent to America and almost 40 percent to Canada—this intervention was not the most important factor. The government considered its task finished as soon as the emigrant put foot on foreign soil. The emigration offices went much further: their concern was the interest of the emigrant, and they wanted to exclude interference on the part of the government as much as possible. In spite of the limited influence of the government, its involvement did constitute a marked difference with emigration in the long nineteenth century.

Not only did the attitude toward emigration change in the Netherlands, the same thing happened in America. Presidents Truman

[14]   Folder Holland Amerika Lijn, Municipal Archives Rotterdam.

and Eisenhower recognized the importance of giving impoverished Europeans a new chance in America and, thus, to alleviate tension on the continent. A new ordinance created extra room for refugees and other people in distress to be admitted to America. Thanks to this liberalization, twenty thousand more Dutch than the annual quota of three thousand were able to enter America. The concept of "refugee" was interpreted quite broadly for the Netherlands, so that also those who suffered indirectly, for instance, from the disastrous flood of 1953, as well as those who returned from Indonesia, were categorized as such. When many Dutch citizens wanted or had to leave Indonesia, the quotas were expanded twice by nine thousad persons. Thus, thirty-five thousand more people were allowed to emigrate to the U.S. than were permitted under the old law. In 1965, Congress adopted a broader immigration policy for people who could deliver an essential contribution to the American economy, and to reunite families. But precisely in that period the successful Dutch industrial policy and the building up of the welfare state lessened the need to emigrate. The main difference with the prewar emigration was that the Dutch government began to carry out an active emigration policy. After the war, America lost its position of preferred country to Canada, and inside America the destination of the immigrants shifted more and more to the West Coast at the expense of the Midwest. Thus, no new Dutch colonies were founded because no new areas were being developed, and because emigration became more and more an individual enterprise.

**Freedom**

To what extent did the Dutch immigrants acquire their desired freedom? In America they received all sorts of incentives to build up their lives. Most immigrants came in the prime of life, at a phase in which they wanted and could build up their own families, their businesses, schools, churches, and communities. Doing all of this, they did not experience any opposition from the authorities, as was the case in the Netherlands. Whoever emigrated in the nineteenth century could own a larger slice of life without high taxes, military draft, divisions between the classes, and limits on future opportunities. The rise of prosperity (not for everyone, but nevertheless for many) afforded the opportunity to make plans and to realize them.

As a result of emigration the Seceders began to pay less attention to, and lamented less about, the past but became focused on the future. They reformulated "God, the Netherlands and Orange" to "God, America and the Constitution." Of course, a national church, in the sense of a conscience of the entire nation, was out of the question. Seceders in their informal discussion groups were certainly much more democratic than in their churches. Besides, there was sympathy in America for dissenters, while state institutions were looked upon with suspicion.[15]

The Dutch immigrants who were visible as a group met the expectations of the American government, which liked to see that immigrants came as families and settled in the countryside. Thus, they had an easier start than people of other nationalities who were more numerous and different, and who were seen as more threatening.

In fact, the small size of the stream of Dutch immigrants was not an obstacle for their own subculture, but rather a stimulus, as long as it arose from explicit plans to found a community. The relatively small number made it necessary to use all available resources well, and it kept mutual contacts personal.

Today's descendants of these immigrants feel right at home in American society, where they continue to leave their mark. The most visible remnants of Dutch immigration to the United States are found in concentrations of communities in Iowa and Michigan, in the spiritual heritage (present in religious denominations and in a modest immigrant literature), and in a threatened material legacy.

## Spiritual Legacy

The postwar immigrants in America found existing communities that they could join, but since the emigration wave quickly subsided after 1960, the total number remained limited and since the newcomers wanted to integrate quickly, not much changed in the subculture as a result.

Changes came from within. The shocking events of the 1960s directed the attention of Dutch Americans to issues outside their subculture: the political assassinations, Watergate, Vietnam, civil rights, and the environment.[16] On the one hand, the polarization strengthened feelings of patriotism and identification with America; on the other hand it also fed feelings of criticism vis-à-vis America and the isolated position of their own churches.

The Reformed Church initiated new discussions about a merger with Presbyterians, which was prevented at the last minute by the western half of the denomination. It appeared to be a victory for the ethnic side of the church with which two-thirds of the members in the

---

[15]    Brummelkamp, *Stemmen uit Noord-Amerika*, 85.
[16]    Bratt, *Dutch Calvinism*, 204-21.

western part identified. But below the surface, opposition to liberal political agendas and perceived centralistic tendencies, which were contested with an appeal to local autonomy, also played a role. In the Christian Reformed Church, the guardians of the Calvinist tradition lost their dominant position and the roles were reversed: the most conservative theologians looked to America for inspiration, whereas the progressives drew their inspiration from the Netherlands, where traditional sociopolitical barriers were breaking down. As the various factions joined American evangelical brothers and sisters they sought an umbrella to preserve their unity.

The existence of a Dutch Protestant subculture became evident especially as a result of the opposing forces that it evoked from those who extricated themselves from it and who wrote about it. That the Protestant circle was much more tightly knit than that of the Catholics may be deduced from the relatively extensive literature about the Protestants from the pens of insiders and outsiders. The Dutch are not portrayed positively in this literature: they are narrow-minded, adverse to art, hypocritical, intolerant, and coarse. This image was promoted by authors who were outsiders, such as Edna Ferber and Lucy F. Perkins, and who used the stereotypical Dutchman to make a plea for openness and authenticity. Those who had grown up in a Dutch colony wrote from a need to expose conservatism. An author such as Arnold Mulder published autobiographical novels in which he distanced himself from his past. David C. De Jong was an immigrant himself and wrote books about the inner tensions of immigrant life. The prolific Frederic Manfred (pseudonym for Feike Feikema) used immigrant families for his novels, situated in "Siouxland," the border region of Iowa, Dakota, and Minnesota, but he was more interested in the mutual relationships of his main characters than in their immigrant status. When fellow countrymen appear, such as in the book *Of Lizards and Angels: A Saga of Siouxland*, they do play a negative role. Manfred saw himself as a midwestern author who wrote about the Midwest rather than as an ethnic writer. In this respect he could be compared to Peter De Vries, who chose as the setting for *The Blood of the Lamb* (1961) his Dutch Calvinistic community in Chicago, but whose theme was the battle against cancer. Historian Henry Lucas found this image so negative that he sighed: "After reading these books, one wonders how so many people could come to have so many objectionable qualities."[17]

---

[17]  Edna Ferber, *So Big* (Garden City: Doubleday, Page, 1923); Lucy F. Perkins, *The Dutch Twins* (Boston: Houghton Mifflin, 1911); Novels by Arnold Mulder: *The Dominie of Harlem, Bram of the Five Corners*, and *The Outbound*

In spite of these prominent authors who all originated from the Protestant part of the Dutch-American subculture, literary critics thought that they ignored the immigration experience. The American literary historian, C.J. Ter Maat, complained in the 1960s with regard to the work of Arnold Mulder and David C. De Jong (about Michigan) and Frederic Manfred (about Iowa and Dakota) that "so little has been overtly done with the usable past in the Dutch community."[18] Ter Maat explained this weakness as the strong dislike these authors felt toward their own religious and ethnic background. They not only feared that their style might be impaired if they gave free rein to such feelings, but also that they would be seen as too provincial if they made their regional frustration their main theme. The result was that their subculture remained virtually invisible in America at large. The immigrants who published stories and poetry in Dutch to give expression to their own feelings remained unnoticed because of the language barrier. The treatment of both the brighter and the darker aspects of the former immigrant life is due to be reevaluated.[19]

Since the 1970s a change has occurred. Younger authors have written, and continue to write, much more positively about life in a Dutch-American community but have received much less national recognition. A poet such as Stanley Wiersma/Sietze Buning, and authors such as James Schaap, Ronald Jager, and Arthur Versluis have lovingly described (while observing a certain distance) the simple life on

---

Road. Books by David C. DeJong: *With a Dutch Accent: How a Hollander Became an American* and *Belly Fulla Straw*. Lucas, *Netherlanders*, 631. David C. DeJong's book *Old Haven* (published in a Dutch translation in 1939 as *De veilige haven*) hardly qualifies as immigrant literature since emigration is mentioned only in the form of an unsympathetic "American" who returned home, or as an escape for fellow villagers who had lost the connection with their hometown and therefore left for the Dutch East Indies or America. Emigration was the alternative for social isolation for the person who did not adjust to the cultural codes of the village or who crossed the boundaries of the separation between men and women.

18    C.J. Ter Maat, "Three Novelists and a Community: A Study of American Novelists with Dutch Calvinistic Origins" (Ph.D. diss., Univ. of Michigan, 1962), 181.

19    Lagerwey, *Neen, Nederland 'k vergeet u nie*, and "The Netherlandic Muse in the Forests, on the Plains, and in the Cities of America from 1850-1975," in Wolodymyr T. Zayla and Wendell M. Aycock, eds., *Ethnic Literatures since 1776: The Many Voices of America*, 2 vols. (Lubbock: Texas Tech Press, 1978), 2:353-74. A beginning is made in the volume edited by Swierenga, Nyenhuis, and Kennedy, *Dutch American Arts*.

Dutch-American farms in small communities in Iowa and Michigan.[20] Nature and the landscape play a much more positive role in their books than in the earlier mentioned works. The difference in approach has undoubtedly to do with the phase of the immigrant community. The older group of authors wrote from the perspective of the hardships of the first generations and the tight connection from which they wanted to extricate themselves, the more recent ones write from a more comfortable position about a disappearing phenomenon that they wanted to preserve. The older generation experienced their own tradition as a hindrance to participation in the cultural life of Americans, the younger generation appreciates the value of past traditions as an alternate lifestyle in a commercialized society. From the perspective of the history of the strong family-oriented Dutch-American community, these books take a stand against the disintegration by modern capitalism, which allows the value of the land to be determined by the real estate market rather than by its fertility, by investments made in the past, and by the consequences for community life.

## Material Legacy

There is more that is bound to disappear. The most noticeable legacy of the Dutch in the American Midwest is shown in the homes that were built with bricks from the brick factory of Jan Hendrik Veneklasen and his son Berend Jan. This family had come from Holten to west Michigan in 1847. Father Veneklasen was a mason and sent his son to Allegan to find work in an American brick kiln. There he discovered that the demand for brick was growing, at first for the construction of smokestacks, but later also for homes. In 1848 father and son started their own business in the rich clay soil between Holland and Zeeland. Fifteen years later prosperity permitted the building of brick homes, and the market for this product grew, but the business got a boost especially after the Holland fire of 1871. The great demand for building materials, the deforestation of the region, and the great vulnerability of wooden structures provided the Veneklasen Brickyard with a large

[20]  Sietze Buning, *Purpaleanie and Other Permutations* (Orange City, Iowa: Middleburg Press, 1978), and *Style and Class: Poems* (Orange City, Iowa: Middleburg Press, 1982), James Schaap, *Romey's Place* (Grand Rapids: Baker, 1999). Ronald Jager, *Eighty Acres: Elegy for a Family Farm* (Boston: Beacon Press, 1990), and Arthur Versluis, *Island Farm* (East Lansing: Michigan State Univ. Press, 2000), and Jim Heynen, *The One-Room Schoolhouse: Stories About the Boys* (New York: Vintage, 1994).

**The Schaap family in front of their Veneklasen house, ca. 1890.**
Archives, Calvin College, Grand Rapids, Michigan.

clientele when after ten years the city had recuperated economically and the railroad opened new markets.[21] Schools, churches, and stores were built of the more durable brick and raised the prestige of the architecture. Style also began to play a role: besides the standard red-brown brick, white bricks were being produced, which enabled the creation of patterns, arches, ornamental borders, and playful variations. The designs were reminiscent of the building styles in the northeast of the Netherlands, and were adjusted by masons in Michigan to fit the American taste. The floor plans, often in an L-shape, the standard sizes, basements, and the small windows were typically American in style.

This "Dutch" business flourished until the 1930s and provided hundreds of jobs until the competition from other states (which had access to larger clay areas that they could exploit more efficiently) became too strong, and cement tiles crowded out bricks. It is estimated that more than three hundred houses were built from bricks from the Veneklasen kilns, and certainly a hundred public buildings stand out because of their fine masonry. These unique buildings were not only a fitting metaphor for the motives, the fluctuation, the creative style in

[21]  Michael Douma, *Veneklasen Brick: A Family, a Company, and a Unique Nineteenth Century Dutch Architectural Movement in Michigan* (Grand Rapids: Eerdmans, 2005).

an American environment and the socioeconomic consequences of the Dutch-American subculture, but also of the legacy of Dutch emigration to America. Just like the church buildings mentioned in the beginning of this book, these structures also are threatened with demolition. Their stories are too valuable to be lost.

APPENDIX 1

# Statistical Overview: Dutch Emigrants to the United States per Year, 1840-1940

Statistical surveys of emigration are never entirely transparent: every country used different norms, not everybody agreed to be registered, data have been lost, definitions of an emigrant changed, etc. The higher the number of single persons from urban areas and the less control by the police, the bigger the chance some will fall outside of the official statistics.

Structurally, little changes in the global composition of an emigrant group, but the total number can only be estimated. This number lies between 75,000 and 100,000 persons for the period 1835-1880. The American immigration expert, Dr. Robert P. Swierenga, found the Dutch records to be the most complete compared to American sources.[1]

---

[1]  Robert P. Swierenga, *Faith and Family: Dutch Immigration and Settlement in the United States: 1820-1920* (New York: Holmes & Meier, 2000), 40-42 and 293-309.

| | | | | | | | |
|------|------|------|------|------|------|------|------|
| 1840 | 2    | 1874 | 991  | 1908 | 2889 | | |
| 1841 | 5    | 1875 | 537  | 1909 | 4266 | | |
| 1842 | 23   | 1876 | 222  | 1910 | 5350 | | |
| 1843 | 72   | 1877 | 180  | 1911 | 5255 | | |
| 1844 | 176  | 1878 | 223  | 1912 | 4184 | | |
| 1845 | 445  | 1879 | 738  | 1913 | 4338 | | |
| 1846 | 1059 | 1880 | 2425 | 1914 | 3134 | | |
| 1847 | 3319 | 1881 | 7380 | 1915 | 1552 | | |
| 1848 | 1997 | 1882 | 7230 | 1916 | 1585 | | |
| 1849 | 1855 | 1883 | 4798 | 1917 | 597  | | |
| 1850 | 680  | 1884 | 3654 | 1918 | 541  | | |
| 1851 | 1113 | 1885 | 2121 | 1919 | 1429 | | |
| 1852 | 1112 | 1886 | 2004 | 1920 | 4790 | | |
| 1853 | 1565 | 1887 | 5018 | 1921 | 3099* | | |
| 1854 | 3365 | 1888 | 4298 | 1922 | 1912* | | |
| 1855 | 1827 | 1889 | 5050 | 1923 | 5373* | | |
| 1856 | 1778 | 1890 | 3282 | 1924 | 2604* | | |
| 1857 | 1475 | 1891 | 3923 | 1925 | 2688* | | |
| 1858 | 406  | 1892 | 6211 | 1926 | 2817* | | |
| 1859 | 193  | 1893 | 5476 | 1927 | 2991* | | |
| 1860 | 341  | 1894 | 1102 | 1928 | 2553* | | |
| 1861 | 287  | 1895 | 1036 | 1929 | 2709* | | |
| 1862 | 549  | 1896 | 1445 | 1930 | 2554* | | |
| 1863 | 833  | 1897 | 675  | 1931 | 207* | | |
| 1864 | 603  | 1898 | 749  | 1932 | 79*  | | |
| 1865 | 1464 | 1899 | 1136 | 1933 | 113* | | |
| 1866 | 3006 | 1900 | 1451 | 1934 | 133* | | |
| 1867 | 3967 | 1901 | 1893 | 1935 | 175* | | |
| 1868 | 2883 | 1902 | 2272 | 1936 | 140* | | |
| 1869 | 3330 | 1903 | 3133 | 1937 | | | |
| 1870 | 1795 | 1904 | 2627 | n.a. | | | |
| 1871 | 1828 | 1905 | 2733 | 1938 | 213 | | |
| 1872 | 3412 | 1906 | 3437 | 1939 | 696 | | |
| 1873 | 3793 | 1907 | 5778 | | | | |

\*     including Canada (about one-third to one-half). Source for 1921-1939 Centraal Bureau voor de Statistiek, *Jaarcijfers voor Nederland*, 1929-1940 ('s-Gravenhage: Drukkerij Albani, 1930-1942). The suppliers of these numbers were the committees of oversight on the emigrants and the municipalities of Amsterdam and Rotterdam. It concerned the number of Dutch emigrants who left from Dutch ports. American statistics indicate greater numbers but differ in the counting unit (with the fiscal year ending on June 30) and definitions (sometimes including travelers).

# Historiography of the Dutch in America

In various phases, amateurs and professionals have kept busy with the history of Dutch emigration to America. In every phase, the authors accentuated that which suited the interest of emigration in their own situations.

## Personal Experience (1845-1900)

From the very beginning of organized mass emigration to the United States in 1846 and 1847, the movement has been well documented. The leaders of this movement were ministers who had seceded ten years earlier from the Dutch Reformed Church (*Hervormde Kerk*) because they did not find this church orthodox enough, and they believed they lacked the space to work according to their conviction. They justified their undertaking in brochures that found an eager market. Opponents stood ready to respond and warned unsuspecting readers against expecting too much. This opposition, in turn, elicited defensive brochures that confirmed the chances of success through detailed accounts of pioneer life. When the stream of emigrations got underway, it was only natural that a market in advisory literature would be created. The clergy leaders of the movement had their letters printed because it was impossible to correspond with everybody individually. At the same time these publications served to advertise the undertaking.

Following the pioneer phase, there was relatively little public interest in the experiences of those who had left. The Netherlands had its hands full with its own developments. News about ups and downs in the colony reached especially the homes of relatives and friends. A split in the Dutch immigrant churches in 1857 was noticed only by one or two people in the mother country. This split in the time-honored Reformed Dutch Church caused an initial wave of publications to appear among Dutch Americans and was also commented on by the church press in the Netherlands. At first, the mutual justification for the turn of events was courteous and polite, but it became more angry as time went on. In spite of the theological character of the debate, the conflict dealt especially with the relationship to American culture and the choices of the first generation of colonists.[1]

In 1872 the twenty-fifth anniversary of the Dutch settlements was celebrated, and the pioneers who were still alive realized that the number of eyewitnesses of the often dramatic settlement period was diminishing fast. Dingeman Versteeg therefore published *De Pelgrim-Vaders van het westen* in 1886. In it he placed the Dutch colony on the same level as the Puritans who had come to the New World as pilgrims. "Just as Joshua, after wandering in the desert for forty years, gathered the children of a new generation around him and proclaimed to them the great deeds of God, so also the gray-haired old man, who was part of the struggle, gathered the youth around him and told them of the anxious days when distress often ran high, but the deliverance was from God." Kommer van Stigt also, who chronicled and concluded the pioneer phase of Pella, had an explicitly religious purpose in mind. "In all sincerity we can testify that it is our desire through this work to be profitably engaged for the benefit of the present generation and for those who will arise after us. And that all of us by studying history may be led more to see God in History, and History in God."[2]

Information about "America" kept people in the Netherlands curious. The Dutch colonies regularly received visits from compatriots

---

[1]    John Kromminga, *The Christian Reformed Church: A Study in Orthodoxy* (Grand Rapids: Baker, 1949), 45-48.

[2]    Dingman Versteeg, *De Pelgrim-Vaders van het westen* (Grand Rapids: C.M. Loomis, 1886), 10 and Kommer van Stigt, *Geschiedenis van Pella, Iowa en omgeving* (Pella: Weekblad Print Shop, 1897), v.

who later published accounts of the peculiarities they had encountered. Depending on their own positions with respect to the orthodox Protestants, they were either positive or critical. The orthodox Remonstrant minister M. Cohen Stuart had been deeply impressed by the fact that "a respectable, sound shoot of our national trunk is able to grow, prosper, and bear fruit upon this fertile soil, in the pure, fresh air of American liberty," while engineer R.P.J. Tutein Nolthenius expressed himself critically about these "little men in wooden shoes."[3]

## Inventory (1900-1965)

In the twentieth century, scholars became interested in the history of the Dutch colonies in the Midwest. Church historians such as Albert Eekhof of Leiden, who had spent his own youth in America, expanded their interest in the stay of the Pilgrim Fathers in Leiden and the genesis of the Dutch Reformed Church to a study of the still existing Dutch settlements in America.

In the meantime, the Dutch-Americans had founded their own colleges, which had nurtured their own cadre of scholars. These used their abilities to put into writing their own history and to save their Dutch background. Especially the Reverend Henry Beets (1869-1947) made the historiography of the Reformed immigrants his life's work. This ecumenically inclined Christian Reformed minister was the editor of various newspapers and magazines and published numerous articles about the origin of the Dutch settlements and the official history of the Christian Reformed Church. His goal was to strengthen the self-identity of the Reformed Americans, which meant that his outreach remained limited, for the most part, to that circle.[4]

The first milestone on the way to an encompassing survey of the Dutch in America was put in place by geographer Jacob van Hinte (1889-1948) in 1928; he was a student of the Amsterdam sociogeographer S.R. Steinmetz and the social historian I.J. Brugmans.

---

[3]    M. Cohen Stuart, *Zes maanden in Amerika* (Haarlem: Tjeenk Willink, 1879), 215. R.P.J. Tutein Nolthenius, *Nieuwe Wereld. Indrukken en aanteekeningen tijdens eene reis door de Vereenigde Ststen van Noord-Amerika* (Haarlem: Tjeenk Willink, 1902), 212-32. For a colorful survey of Dutch impressions in America, see A. Lammers, *Uncle Sam en Jan Salie. Hoe Nederland Amerika ontdekte* (Amsterdam: Balans, 1989).

[4]    Herbert J. Brinks, "Henry Beets (1869-1947): Historian of the Christian Reformed Church," in George Harinck and Hans Krabbendam, eds., *Breaches and Bridges: Reformed Subcultures in the Netherlands, Germany, and the United States* (Amsterdam: VU Uitgeverij, 2000), 125-40.

His monumental dissertation, *Nederlanders in Amerika*, was the result of a thorough study and a rigorous investigative journey that enabled him to leave behind a goldmine of information for all later historians. Van Hinte had fallen under the spell of this subject at a young age, as he revealed in his diary of his American trip in 1921: "Emigrants: the word captivated me already as a boy, and continues to convey to me a feeling of deep tragedy. Nothing fascinated me more than to trace the lives of those people who, far from their native soil, tried to carve out a new existence....Small groups of emigrants make me think of everything I had read about these economic exiles, and filled me with compassion." He saw tragedy all around him when he arrived at Ellis Island, the immigration gateway near the city of New York: "How sadly some of them stare, how expressionless others look around. And then the resignation of others. After handing in their hand baggage there is the medical examination: like horses and cows people are inspected one at a time, the head turned from left to right, lifting the eyelids. Human meat!"[5]

Van Hinte's detailed survey of Dutch settlements had the Americanization process as its leitmotiv. However much Van Hinte deplored that the Dutch element was absorbed by the American melting pot, he acknowledged its inevitability. Van Hinte wrote with undisguised pride about the assets of "our Dutchmen" in America. His careful, scholarly approach did not disguise a personal identification with his "fellow tribesmen." Although religion did not play a big role in his own life, he nevertheless kept a sharp eye out for the religious motivations and developments that formed the basis of the Dutch colonies. His sympathy lay with the Reformed Church in America. The Reverend Albertus Van Raalte (1811-1876) was Van Hinte's hero, in contrast to the much more individualistic minister Hendrik Scholte (1805-1868), whom he labeled as haughty, revolutionary, and elusive. On the other hand, he felt more at home in the somewhat worldlier Pella than in the city of Holland. He saw through the theological and ecclesiastical differences that were interspersed with contrary aspirations regarding assimilation to America, a theme that since then has marked Dutch immigration studies. The book derives its charm partly from Van Hinte's emotional involvement with the subject, which he expressed regularly.[6] His own experience led him to conclude that going from east

---

5    Dagboek "Naar Amerika" (1921), 1 and 3, Van Hinte Collection, Historisch Documentatiecentrum voor het Nederlands Protestantisme, Vrije Universiteit, Amsterdam.

6    Robert P. Swierenga, "Editor's introduction," in Jacob Van Hinte,

to west the Dutch immigrants became more open-minded, and that the urban immigrants in Grand Rapids, Paterson, and Chicago were more conservative than agrarian settlements in Michigan, which were again more conservative than their companions in Iowa. Van Hinte measured the success of the Dutch by their prosperity and stability, but above all by the literary and essayistic qualities of their publications. The results of his research made him plead for suspension of the American immigration restrictions for the Dutch, because America by doing so would be greatly enriched with useful citizens, while the Netherlands would be served well by having an outlet for job-seekers.

The outbreak of the Second World War and the occupation of the Netherlands once again directed the attention of Dutch immigrants to their native land. The Dutch diplomats had to bring the cause of the fatherland to the attention of the American public. At the request of the Netherlands Information Bureau, Bertus Harry Wabeke wrote a small book about immigration to the United States in the period of 1624-1860. He dealt with the settlement of New Amsterdam, business relationships, and the beginning of the great emigration until 1860, the beginning of the Civil War, because at that time the settlement patterns were established, and afterwards the nature of emigration changed. The book was intended to give the Dutch in America information about their background and thus to unite them, since their country of origin had been overrun.[7] Wabeke himself was an example of a mutual immigrant stream between South Africa, where he was born, and the United States, where he had lived since 1917. In the 1930s he studied history in Leiden, which he left just in time to escape the German invasion in May 1940.

The scholarly interest from America for a similar reference work as that of Van Hinte came from Henry S. Lucas (1889-1961), descendant of an immigrant generation that moved from the German Graafschap Bentheim to Michigan. Nurtured in the Christian Reformed tradition, which was heavily oriented Dutch, he had already become interested in his heritage at a young age. He turned this interest into the study

---

*Netherlanders in America: A Study of Emigration and Settlement in the 19th and 20th Centuries in the United States of America*, Robert P. Swierenga, gen. ed., Adriaan de Wit, chief trans. (Grand Rapids: Baker, 1985), xxxv-xliv. His characterization may be found on p. 450 of the Dutch edition.

7    B.H. Wabeke, *Dutch Emigration to North America 1624-1860* (New York: Netherlands Information Bureau, 1944). This effort to strengthen national pride was preceded by a biographical dictionary with names of influential Americans of Dutch origin. H.M. Vlekke and Henry Beets, *Hollanders Who Helped Build America* (New York, 1942).

of history, which later led to his appointment as chair of European Medieval Studies. His efforts toward commemorating the centennial of the colony resulted in 1955 in two important works, *Netherlanders in America* and *Dutch Immigrant Memoirs and Related Writings*, the first one completely in English and the second one (for the greater part) in both English and Dutch. Lucas did a geographic survey similar to Van Hinte's, but wrote as a descendant who was tried and tested in the Dutch-American church tradition from which he had just disassociated himself in 1947, the year of the commemoration, by joining the Roman Catholic Church. He did this because he was dissatisfied with the discord among Protestants and admired Roman Catholic art and liturgy. His specialty and his schooling outside the established Dutch-American institutions also contributed to this break. Because of his religious choice he was more aware of the Roman Catholic emigrants, who were not forgotten in his list of source materials, although the city of Holland and its immediate surroundings remained his main interest. The commemoration of the centennial also produced a number of monographs. Albert Hyman, professor of history at the University of Michigan, published a study about Van Raalte and the Dutch colony in the United States in 1947. It was not until 1964 that a similar book appeared about Scholte in the form of a dissertation which the American theologian Lubbertus Oostendorp defended at the Free University. However, this work paid little attention to Scholte's American experiences.[8]

In the commemorative year of 1947, the Dutch American journalist Arnold Mulder published a popularized book, *Americans from Holland*, which highlighted especially the "leaders and more dramatic personalities" and which confirmed once again the solid reputation of the Dutch. Also in the Netherlands the anniversary of a century of emigration drew renewed interest. H.J. Prakke, sociologist of religion, described the settlement of Drenthe, Michigan, from the perspective of the regional, personal nature of the Drents, and Risseeuw published the trilogy that was mentioned earlier.[9]

---

[8]    Henry S. Lucas, *Netherlanders in America: Dutch Immigration to the United States and Canada, 1789-1950* (Ann Arbor: Univ. of Michigan Press, 1955; repr. Grand Rapids: Eerdmans, 1989); Henry S. Lucas, *Dutch Immigrant Memoirs and Related Works* (Assen: Van Gorcum, 1955; repr. Grand Rapids: Eerdmans 1997); Albert Hyma, *Albertus C. Van Raalte and His Dutch Settlements in the United States* (Grand Rapids: Eerdmans, 1947); Lubbertus Oostendorp, *H.P. Scholte: Leader of Secession of 1834 and Founder of Pella* (Franeker: Wever, 1964).

[9]    Arnold Mulder, *Americans from Holland* (Philadelphia: Lippincott, 1947);

Gerald F. DeJong, a historian connected with the University of South Dakota, himself a third-generation Dutch American from Orange City, Iowa, presented in 1975 a total overview of the Dutch in America from the early seventeenth century to the seventies of the twentieth century. He emphasized that the Dutch with their own peculiarities had the same motivations as other groups of European immigrants.[10]

None of these scholars made immigration their specialty. Their discipline was theology, geography, journalism, or medieval studies. They produced especially detailed descriptions and wanted to keep alive the consciousness of Dutch descent and the formation of a Dutch-American identity. This generation lauded what the Dutch in the Midwest had accomplished and praised the rich cultural heritage which the Dutch had taken with them to America. Especially their mental and moral influence, which had led to flourishing settlements and institutions, deserved to be appreciated.

**Quantitative Analysis (1975-1986)**

After the war the focus of research shifted increasingly from the Netherlands to America. In the 1960s and '70s this trend became stronger. The quantitative method in particular, which had quickly gained popularity in America, gave the research a new impulse. In this period various historians of immigration to the United States began to look at emigration from a broader perspective, both by comparing it with other destinations and by looking at earlier moves of the emigrants in their home country.

Robert P. Swierenga, whose grandparents had emigrated from Groningen and who himself had grown up in the tight-knit Dutch-American community of Chicago's west side, was the first one to apply the quantitative method to Dutch immigrants to determine the yield of land speculation. He began by studying the political preference which the Pella Dutch had for the Democrats in the 1860 elections, which was won by Abraham Lincoln.[11] As professor of history at Kent State University in Ohio, he created a data bank with a hundred thousand names of Dutch emigrants between 1835 and 1880 by linking the

---

H.J. Prakke, *Drenthe in Michigan* (Assen: Van Gorcum, 1948); P.J. Risseeuw, *Landverhuizers* (Baarn: Bosch en Keuning, 1946).

[10] Gerald F. DeJong, *The Dutch in America, 1609-1974* (Boston: Twayne, 1975).

[11] "The Ethnic Voter and the First Lincoln Election," *Civil War History* 11 (March 1965), 27-43, reprinted in Swierenga, *Faith and Family*, 274-89.

lists of Dutch immigrants to the passenger lists of the ships that transported the emigrants and the data gathered by the censuses. The results of his research and methods gave the research a new impulse, not only because it enabled him to determine much more precisely trends and developments and to map elusive groups, such as women, children, and religious minorities, but also because his model was followed in many monographs. In America, Gordon Kirk and David Vanderstel conducted joint studies in the 1970s and '80s which charted the mobility and economic development in the centers of the Dutch immigrants, Holland and Grand Rapids, while Richard Doyle did the same for Pella.[12] A distinguishing trait of the American researchers is that they almost always focus on the area where they grew up themselves. The urban settlements of the East produced fewer authors and therefore received less attention.

## Reflection on Church and Faith (1975-1990)

A renewed interest in the religious factor in emigration arose simultaneously in the Netherlands and America. Attention was paid not only to the change in religious views, but also to the significance of religious convictions in the cultural developments in America.

In the Netherlands the research done by J. Stellingwerff, P. Stokvis, C. Smits, and J. Wesseling drew attention again to the role of the Secessionists, to regional differences, and demographic factors. Although it was quite clear that the Secessionists had not made up the majority of the immigrants and had shown great differences among themselves, yet their influence on the development of a lasting and tight Dutch network appeared to be of sufficient importance that could not be overestimated.[13]

---

[12]   Gordon W. Kirk, Jr., *The Promise of American Life: Social Mobility in a Nineteenth-Century Immigrant Community, Holland, Michigan 1847-1894* (Philadelphia: American Philosophical Society, 1978); David W. Vanderstel, "The Dutch of Grand Rapids, Michigan, 1848-1900: Immigrant Neighborhood and Community Development in a Nineteenth Century City" (Ph. Diss., Kent State Univ., 1986); Richard L. Doyle, "The Socio-Economic Mobility of the Dutch Immigrants to Pella, Iowa 1847-1925" (Ph.D. diss., Kent State Univ., 1982).

[13]   J. Stellingwerff, *Amsterdamse emigranten. Onbekende brieven uit de prairie van Iowa 1846-1873* (Amsterdam: Buijten en Schipperheijn, 1975) translated and expanded in Johan Stellingwerff, Robert P. Swierenga, ed., and Walter Lagerwey, trans., *Iowa Letters: Dutch Immigrants on the American Frontier* (Grand Rapids: Eerdmans, 2004); P.R.D. Stokvis, *De Nederlandse trek naar Amerika*, 1846-1847 (Leiden: Universitaire Pers, 1977); C. Smits,

Johan Stellingwerff and Pieter Stokvis worked independently from each other on a description of the initial phase of the Dutch migration to America. Stellingwerff edited a publication of source materials together with correspondence between emigrants from Amsterdam living in Iowa and those who stayed behind. With this, he supplemented an image of rural migration with a description of emigrants from the cities. In Sweden, Stokvis had become acquainted with the subject of emigration to America and became fascinated by the Dutch form of this phenomenon. He began to research the motives of the first wave of emigrants. He put "the great migration" in a broader economic and emigration perspective and corrected the misconception that the Secessionists had always dominated the migration numerically.

The publications of sources pertaining to the Secession of 1834 by C. Smits and J. Wesseling especially produced detailed material about the circumstances and personalities of the Secessionist emigrants. The availability of sources in the United States itself has also advanced the portrayal of the churchgoing emigrant and his relationship with the small Reformed churches. The churches were the first institutions and their archives have been well preserved. They were the engines behind the founding of schools and many other institutions for healthcare, missions, and learning. Through the church connection the dispersed Dutch settlements were forged together into a tight network. At the same time, they offered a counterbalance to quick assimilation because they stayed in touch with the Netherlands.

In America, church historian Henry Zwaanstra and historians Herbert Brinks and James D. Bratt discovered patterns and variants in the development of a Dutch-American subculture. Zwaanstra described the continuity of the Dutch Reformed tradition in America, which received a sequel in James D. Bratt's *Dutch Calvinism in Modern America: A History of a Conservative Subculture*, published in 1984. This study about the intellectual relationship between the Dutch Protestant subculture and its American surroundings named four different streams in the Reformed American world and their corresponding cultural strategies. The first waves of immigration (1846-1857 and 1865-1873) consisted of two streams, both of which were based on a pietistic pattern. The one group felt immediately at home in the United States and appreciated the nation as a Christian country where its people could live comfortably. It

---

*De Afscheiding van 1834*, 9 vols. (Dordrecht: Van den Tol, 1971-1991); J. Wesseling, *De Afscheiding van 1834 in ...*7 vols. (Groningen: De Vuurbaak, 1973-1984).

had a practical orientation and participated in moral campaigns, such as the temperance movement. The other group was more introspective and wanted to protect its faith and lifestyle from the world by holding on to the Dutch confessional statements. Two streams were added after 1880, both of which walked in the footsteps of the enterprising neo-Calvinists of Abraham Kuyper and which wanted to Christianize society. One part of them considered the difference with the world too big to be able to work together with non-Christians and encouraged the formation of their own Christian organizations, while another part sought to work together as much as possible with others who pursued similar goals.[14]

### Specialization (1990 – the present)

Robert Swierenga and other historians on both sides of the ocean continued to build on the statistical basis that he himself had built at the beginning of the 1980s. The results of this research corrected the sometimes one-sided memories of those involved and provided geographical balance. The American Yda Schreuder and the Dutchman Henk van Stekelenburg centered their attention on Catholic emigrants. The American historian Suzanne Sinke examined the position of women between 1880 and 1920, while the Dutch Annemieke Galema analyzed the movements and cultural baggage of ten thousand Frisians in the period of 1880-1914. Swierenga himself added a detailed study about the contribution of the Dutch Jews to the American mosaic. Also the Amsterdam Americanist Rob Kroes contributed to the image of the Dutch with a portrait of the Dutch in a remote corner of America: Amsterdam, Montana.[15]

---

[14]    Henry Zwaanstra, *Reformed Thought and Experience in a New World: A Study of the Christian Reformed Church and Its American Environment, 1890-1918* (Kampen: Kok, 1973).

[15]    Suzanne Sinke, "Home is Where You Build It: Dutch Immigrant Women in the United States, 1880-1920" (Ph.D. diss., Univ. of Minnesota, 1993), published as *Dutch Immigrant Women in the United States, 1880-1920* (Urbana: Univ. of Illinois Press, 2002); Yda Schreuder, *Dutch Catholic Immigrant Settlement in Wisconsin, 1850-1905* (New York: Garland, 1989); H.A.V.M. van Stekelenburg, *Landverhuizing als regionaal verschijnsel. Van Noord-Brabant naar Noord-Amerika, 1820-1880* (Tilburg: Stichting Zuidelijk Historisch Contact, 1991), and his *"Hier is alles vooruitgang." Landverhuizing van Noord-Brabant naar Noord-Amerika, 1880-1940* (Tilburg: Stichting Zuidelijk Historisch Contact, 1996); Annemieke Galema, *With the Baggage of the Fatherland: Frisians to America, 1880-1914* (Detroit/Groningen: Wayne State Univ. Press and Regio Projekt Groningen, 1996); Rob Kroes, *Nederlanse pioneers in*

The interest on the part of historians; the establishment of centers that gathered systematic archives, sources, and photos about immigration; and the founding of the Association for the Advancement of Dutch-American studies in 1977 have given the research a new impulse. Biennial conferences and the semiannual publication of *Origins*, with its richly illustrated articles about Dutch people of every kind in North America, which has been published by the archives of Calvin College in Grand Rapids since 1983, saw to it that the acquired knowledge was disseminated among Dutch Americans. As a result of the translation into English of Van Hinte's main work in 1985, the reprinting of the books of Henry Lucas and of representative immigrant letters, the basic texts became available for research.[16] The founding of the A.C. Van Raalte Institute at Hope College in Holland, Michigan, in 1994, gave a new impulse to the historical research of the Dutch in America in the nineteenth and twentieth centuries.

In view of the character of the supporters and of the majority of the professional participants, ecclesiastical and religious topics are often found on the programs. A need for knowledge and pure nostalgia remain the foundations of continued interest.

Also from the Dutch side the flame was kept alive. In 1977 the Netherlands American Studies Association was founded, which focused more on Americanism in the broad sense of the word, but which also paid regular attention to immigration research. The growth of Americanism in the Netherlands contributed to the expansion of research into the emigration experience and offered the possibility of putting emigration into a broader perspective of cultural-political relationships.[17]

Occasional conferences to mark the celebration of two hundred years of diplomatic relations, the Columbus year, and the beginning of mass emigration to America provided new material. Swierenga's lists appeared to be popular especially with genealogists and kept the interest and exchange alive. Publicity and publications that covered

---

*het Amerikaanse westen. Geschiedenis van Amsterdam, Montana* (Amsterdam: Bataafsche Leeuw, 1989), Robert P. Swierenga, *The Forerunners: Dutch Jewry in the North American Diaspora* (Detroit: Wayne State Univ. Press, 1994).

16  Lucas, Henry S., *Dutch Immigrant Memoirs and Related Works* (Assen: Van Gorcum, 1955; repr. Grand Rapids: Eerdmans 1997); H.J. Brinks, *Dutch-American Voices: Letters from the United States, 1847-1920* (Ithaca: Cornell Univ. Press, 1995).

17  Rob Kroes and Henk-Otto Neuschäfer, eds., *The Dutch in North America: Their Immigration and Cultural Continuity* (Amsterdam: VU Uitgeverij, 1991).

the entire range of Dutch American relationships attracted new researchers. Also the attention paid to the earlier emigration to New Amsterdam experienced a revival. Historians showed the continued influence of New Netherland into the nineteenth century, which makes a long-range perspective possible.[18]

The expansion to a more comprehensive perspective did not mean that the attention for the religiously tinted immigration disappeared. On the contrary, the majority of nineteenth-century immigrants had church backgrounds, and the Dutch identity remained strongest among church members, which is the reason that cultural changes could also be traced best in this group. Without suggesting that the Reformed immigrant would be entitled to preferential treatment, TV documentaries do show that the Reformed settlements in the American Midwest spoke most to the imagination. In these documentaries the sparkling successes of the economy and the church are steady ingredients which present the viewers with a mixture of amazement at, and criticism of, "the world in a glass bowl." Expositions about the immigration movement in maritime and regional museums supplement the written sources with images that have lost nothing of their attraction. Even though the Secessionists constituted a majority among the immigrants only in the years 1846 and 1847, while their average share in the period of 1835 and 1880 was not even twenty percent, their presence nevertheless draws most of the attention.[19]

Research into the "Dutch-American experience" done by Dutch scholars or by Americans with Dutch roots often produces strong

---

[18]    Joyce D. Goodfriend, "Amerikaans onderzoek naar Nederlandse kolonisatie: de kinderschoenen ontgroeid," in *Jaarboek van het Centraal Bureau voor Genealogie* 50 (1996),17-29; Jacobs, Jaap, *New Netherland: A Dutch Colony in Seventeenth-Century America* (Leiden: Brill Academic, 2005; orig. Dutch 1999); Lucas Ligtenberg, *De wereld van Peter Stuyvesant. Nederlandse voetsporen in de Verenigde Staten* (Amsterdam: Balans, 1999).

[19]    Robert P. Swierenga, "Religion and Immigration Behavior: The Dutch Experience" in Philip R. Vandermeer and Robert P. Swierenga, eds., *Belief and Behavior: Essays in the New Religious History* (New Brunswick: Rutgers Univ. Press, 1991), 176-78. Examples of documentaries about Dutch emigrants include "Van Afgescheidene tot miljonair" (NCRV 1982) and "Amsterdam Montana" (VPRO 1991), "De Overtocht" (VPRO 2000). An exhibition catalog is Annemieke Galema, Wolfgang Grams, and Antonius Holtmann, *Van de ene naar de andere kant. Noordnederlandse en Noordwestduitse migratie naar de Verenigde Staten in de negentiende eeuw* (Groningen: Bibliotheek der Rijksuniversiteit Groningen, 1993). Agnes Amelink, *Gereformeerden overzee. Protestants-christelijke landverhuizers in Noord-Amerika* (Amsterdam: Bert Bakker, 2006).

admiration, sometimes even reverence for their own group. Studies into remigration or into negative aspects of emigration are rare.[20] The more an immigrant group had become integrated, the more the need for affirmation of its own group decreased, while the concern that the small Dutch stone in the American mosaic will disappear completely, along with the awareness of belonging to a multicultural society, led to renewed interest. Thanks to the higher educational level, scholarly production increased.

---

[20]  The collection of interviews by H. Speerstra, *Cruel Paradise: Life Stories of Dutch Emigrants* (Grand Rapids: Eerdmans, 2005) is an exception.

# Bibliography

**Unpublished Sources**

Calvin College, Grand Rapids Michigan, USA. Immigrant Letter Collection, Archives of the Christian Reformed Church, Genealogy Collection.

Grand Rapids City Archives. "Common Council Proceedings, City of Grand Rapids, April 7, 1904."

Grand Rapids Public Library. Folder *Republican Candidates City of Grand Rapids, 1904 Spring Election.*

Historisch Documentatiecentrum voor het Nederlands Protestantisme (1800-heden) Vrije Universiteit, Amsterdam. Jacob van Hinte Collection, Gerrit J. Hesselink Collection

Hope College, Joint Archives of Holland, Holland Michigan, USA. Van Schelven Collection, Van de Luijster diaries.

Municipal Archives of Goes. Archives of the Particular Synod of the Gereformeerde Kerken in Nederland, inv. 3. Minutes of the Particular Synod of Zeeland.

Municipal Archives of Rotterdam. Archives Holland Amerika Lijn.

National Archives, The Hague. Inv. 2.05.13 Gezantschap VS, Legatie Washington, 1814-1946

National Archives, Washington D.C., USA. Microfilm collectie M650, "Letters of application and recommendation presidents Lincoln and Johnson," reel 43.

Roosevelt Study Center, Middelburg, the Netherlands. Van Stekelenburg collectie, Immigrant Letter Collection.

Zeeland Historical Society. Keppel-Moerdyke Collection, consistory minutes Reformed Church.

**Published Private Sources**

*Aan welke personen is de landverhuizing aan te bevelen? Een woord aan allen, die het voornemen hebben, om hunnen geboortegrond te verlaten en naar* Noord-Amerika *te verhuizen.* Zwijndrecht: J. Boden, 1846.

Bakker, Ulbe B., ed. *Zuster, kom toch over. Belevenissen van een emigrantenfamilie uit Friesland. Brieven uit Amerika in de periode 1894-1933/ Sister, please come over. Experiences of an immigrant-family from Friesland/The Netherlands. Letters from America in the period 1894-1933.* Kollum: Trion G.A.C., 1999.

Beltman, Brian W. *Dutch Farmer in the Missouri Valley: The Life and Letters of Ulbe Eringa, 1866-1950.* Urbana: University of Illinois Press, 1996.

*Beschrijving en inlichtingen over de nieuwe Hollandsche Kolonie Prinsburg in Renville, Kaniyohi, en Chippewa Counties, Minnesota.*

Bloemendaal, E.J.G. *Naar Amerika.* Arnhem: Arnhemsche Drukkerij en Uitgeverij, 1911.

Borgman, C. *Bezoek in de Verenigde Staten van Noord-Amerika in het jaar 1850.* Groningen: n.p., 1854.

Brinks, Herbert J., ed. *Dutch American Voices: Letters from the United States, 1850-1930.* Ithaca: Cornell University Press, 1995.

Brummelkamp, A. *Stemmen uit Noord-Amerika.* Amsterdam: Hoogkamer, 1847.

*De landverhuizers in het kanaal door Voorn, in mei 1847.* Amsterdam: Hoogkamer, 1847.

De Smit, C. *Naar Amerika? Schetsen uit de Portefeuille, op reis naar en door de nieuwe wereld.* Winterswijk: H. Bulens, 1881.

Eekma, O.J. *Amerika-Loevestein. Twee zangen des tijds.* Maastricht: W.J. van Haren Nomen, 1846.

Elsen, G. van den *Twintig brieven uit Amerika*. Nederlandsche Christelijke Boerenbond, (1907).

Hospers, Henry. *Jowa: de vraag: Zal ik naar Noord-Amerika gaan? Kort en praktisch beantwoord door een geboren Nederlander* (Gorinchem 1875). *In den vreemde* (1989-1994).

Jeremias. *Naar Amerika. Toeroep aan allen die't geluk zoeken*. Rotterdam: Mensing & Van Westereenen, (1840).

Koppenol, L.W., ed. "Het reisverslag van een Hoogvlietse emigrant. Een door Daniël Koppenol geschreven verslag van zijn reis naar Amerika in 1910," *Historisch jaarboek Hoogvliet* 3 (1997).

Kuiper, R.T. *A Voice from America about America*. Grand Rapids: Heritage Hall, 1970; orig. Dutch ed., 1882.

Lagerwey, Walter, ed. *Letters Written in Good Faith: The Early Years of the Dutch Norbertines in Wisconsin*. Green Bay: Alt, 1996.

Lennep, J. van. "De droom van Californië (1849)," *Poetische werken*. Vol 10.3. Rotterdam: M. Wijt en Zonen, 1862.

Lucas, Henry S. *Dutch Immigrant Memoirs and Related Works*. Assen: Van Gorcum, 1955; repr. Grand Rapids: Eerdmans 1997.

Osinga, S. *Tiental brieven betrekkelijk de reis, aankomst en vestiging naar en in Noord-Amerika, van eenige landverhuizers vertrokken uit De grietenijen Het Bildt en Barradeel in Vriesland*. Franeker: T. Telenga, 1848.

Picard, H. *The Little American. Handleiding om in korten tijd zoo veel van de Engelsche taal te leeren als noodig is, om zich verstaanbaar uit te drukken*. Amsterdam: Hoogkamer, 1847.

*Reglement der Zeeuwsche Vereeniging ter verhuizing naar de Vereenigde Staaten van Noord-Amerika*. Goes: Wed. P. Crombouw, 1847.

Rodenhuis, Sieger. *Nog zoo gaarne wil ik vanalles van holland weten. Brieven van Klaas Schuiling en verwanten aan de fam. Hoogland 1898-1940*. Hogebeintum: eigen beheer, 1994.

Rutte, J.M. *Levensbeschrijving en verantwoording van en door Ds. J.M. Rutte*. Paterson: De Telegraaf, (1888).

Scholte, H.P. *Eene stem uit Pella*. Amsterdam: Hoogkamer, 1848.

Stellingwerff, Johan, Robert P. Swierenga, ed., and Walter Lagerwey, trans. *Iowa Letters: Dutch Immigrants on the American Frontier*. Grand Rapids: Eerdmans, 2004.

Sweetman, Leonard, ed. *From Heart to Heart. Letters from the Rev. Albertus Christiaan Van Raalte to His Wife, Christina Johanna Van Raalte-De Moen, 1836-1847*. Grand Rapids: Heritage Hall, 1997.

Swierenga, Robert P., and William Van Appledorn, eds. *Old Wing Mission: Cultural Interchange as Chronicled by George and Arvilla Smith in their Work with Chief Wakazoo's Ottawa Band on the West Michigan Frontier.* Grand Rapids: Eerdmans, 2008.

*Ter nagedachtenis aan Rev. Cornelius van der Meulen.* Grand Rapids: De Standaard Drukkerij, 1876.

Tris, A.C. *Sixty Years' Reminiscences and Spiritual Experiences in Holland and in the United States of America.* Lebanon, Penn.: Report Publishing, 1908.

Ubbens, H. *Amerika! Kan de landverhuizing niet op betere voet worden geregeld en op voordeeliger wijze worden ondernomen? Eene vraag met het oog op het landgebruik toegelicht en beantwoord.* Veendam: E.J. Bakker, 1881.

*Vaarwel aan eenige inwoners van Oud-Vossemeer bij hun vertrek naar Noord-Amerika* [1852]. Zeeuws Documentatiecentrum, Middelburg, knipsels Oud-Vossemeer.

Van Malsen, A., *Achttal brieven mijner kinderen uit de kolonie Holland in Amerika.* Zwijndrecht: J. Boden, 1848. For an English translation see John Yzenbaard, "'America,' Letters from Holland," *Michigan History* 32 (March 1948): 37-65.

Van Steenwijk, G., "Milwaukee," *De Recensent. Algemeen Letterkundig Maandschrift* (1851).

Van Steenwijk, G., *Report of the State Commission of Emigration* (1852).

Verbrugge, Frank, ed., *Brieven uit het verleden/Letters from the Past.* Minneapolis: Department of Printing and Graphic Arts of the University of Minnesota, 1981.

Vos van Steenwijk, Carel de. *Een grand tour naar de nieuwe republiek: Journaal van een reis door Amerika, 1783-1784.* Verzorgd door Wayne te Brake. Hilversum: Verloren, 1999.

Vries, N.A. de. *De Nieuwe Wereld. Amerika 1923. Reisbrieven.* Groningen: Wolters, 1924.

## Published Public Sources

*Acts and Proceedings of the General Synod of the Reformed Protestant Dutch Church in North America at New-Brunswick, June 1845-1849.* New York: Post/J.A. Gray, 1845-1849.

*Annual Reports of the Board of Domestic Missions to the General Synod of the Reformed Church in America* (New York 1900).

*Classis Holland Minutes 1848-1858.* Grand Rapids: Eerdmans, 1950.

*Hearings Before a Subcommittee of the Committee on Foreign Relations United States Senate, Eighty-Second Congress, First Session on United States Economic and Military Assistance to Free Europe.* Washington D.C.: Government Printing Office, 1951.

*Jaarboekjes* (yearbooks) Christian Reformed Church 1881-1890.

*Papers Relating to Foreign Relations of the United States* 1881. Washington, D.C.: Government Printing Office, 1882. Also 1889. Washington, D.C.: Government Printing Office, 1890.

*Reports of the Immigration Commission. Vols. 1, 4, 15, 37.* Washington, D.C.: Government Printing Office, 1911-1912.

*Statistiek van den in-, uit- en doorvoer.* 's-Gravenhage: Ministerie van Financiën, 1863-1915.

*Survey of 2,300 Female Domestics in Michigan Agriculture, 1895, Michigan Bureau of Labor and Industrial Statistics, Twelfth Annual Report, Year Ending February 1, 1895.* Lansing: Robert Smith., 1895.

Survey of 5,419 Michigan Furniture Workers, 1889, Reported in the Seventh Annual Report of the Michigan Bureau of Labor and Industrial Statistics.

http://eh.net/databases/labor/codebooks/mi07.asc, visited April 3, 2009.

*Tabular Statements of the Census Enumeration...of the State of Wisconsin....* Madison: Democrat Printing Company, State Printer, 1895. "State Census of 1895."

U.S. Immigration Service, Bureau of Immigration Records, Microfilm reel 1. "Powderly Report, European Investigation, 1906-1907," July 1906.

*Verslagen aan de Koning betrekkelijk den Dienst der Posterijen, der Rijks-Postspaarbank en der Telegrafen in Nederland* (1878-1892), *...aan de Koningin-Weduwe/Koningin betrekkelijk de Dienst der Posterijen en der Telegraphie in Nederland* (1893-1904) en *Verslag aan de Koningin betrekkelijk den Dienst der Posterijen, der Telegrafie en der Telefonie in Nederland* (1905-1919).

*Verzameling van consulaire en andere verslagen en berichten over nijverheid, handel en scheepvaart.* Den Haag: Ministerie van Landbouw, Handel en Nijverheid, 1865.

**Newspapers and Periodicals**

*Banner,* 1912, 1916
*Christian Intelligencer,* 1846-1850, 1891-1907

*Drentsche Volks-Almanak,* 1847

*Goessche Courant,* 1847

*De Grondwet,* 1877, 1880-1890

*Holland City News,* 1872

*De Hollander,* 1852, 1856, 1860, 1872, 1874, 1876

*Hollandsche Amerikaan,* 1918

*De Hope,* 1870-1876

*De Landverhuizer,* 1872-1874

*Leader,* 1906

*Mission Field,* 1888-1908

*Nieuwe Rotterdamsche Courant,* 1847

*Onze Toekomst,* 1907

*De Volksstem (De Pere),* 1890, 1892

De Wachter, *1920*

*De Wereldburger,* 1888-1891

*Young Calvinist,* 1920

## Secondary Literature

Aay, Henry. "The Making of an Ethnic Island: Initial Settlement Patterns of Netherlanders in West Michigan," *Great Lakes Geographer* 2.2 (1995): 61-76.

Aerts, Remieg, e.a., red., *Land van de kleine gebaren. Een politieke geschiedenis van Nederland, 1780-1990.* Nijmegen: Sun, 2001.

Barnouw, A.J. *Monthly Letters on the Culture and History of the Netherlands.* Assen: Van Gorcum, 1969.

Bender, Thomas. *Community and Social Change in America.* New Brunswick: Rutgers Univ. Press, 1978.

Berrol, Selma Cantor. *Growing up American: Immigrant Children in America Then and Now.* New York: Twayne, 1995.

Billington, Ray Allen. *Westward Expansion: A History of the American Frontier.* New York: MacMillan, 1960.

Blaas-Rademaker, Joke M. "Van Walcheren naar de Verenigde Staten: Emigratie in de periode 1900-1920." *Nehalennia* 137 (2002): 37-46.

Boody, Bertha M. *A Psychological Study of Immigrant Children at Ellis Island.* New York: Arno Press, 1970 (c1926).

Bras, Hilde. "Tussen twee werelden. De migratiemotieven van Klaas jans Beukma (1789-1860) een Groningse pionier in Amerika." M.A. thesis Rijksuniversiteit Groningen, 1993.

Bratt, James D. *Dutch Calvinism in Modern America: A History of a Conservative Subculture.* Grand Rapids: Eerdmans, 1984.

Bruijn, J. de, and G. Harinck, eds. *Groen van Prinsterer in Europese context.* Hilversum: Verloren, 2004.

Bruins, Elton J. and Robert P. Swierenga. *Family Quarrels in the Dutch Reformed Churches of the Nineteenth Century.* Grand Rapids: Eerdmans, 1999.

Bruins, Elton J. *The Americanization of a Congregation*, 2nd ed. Grand Rapids: Eerdmans, 1995.

Bruins, Elton, J., comp. *The Dutch in America. Papers presented at the Fourth Biennial Conference of the Association for the Advancement of Dutch-American Studies.* Holland: Hope College, 1984.

Buchen, Gustave William. *Historic Sheboygan County.* Privately printed: 1944.

Burmanje, Piet Hein. "The Dutch Calvinist Press and the Social-Religious Development of Dutch Immigrants in the United States, 1850-1885." M.A. thesis, University of Amsterdam, 1988.

Canny, Nicholas, ed. *Europeans on the Move: Studies on European Migration, 1500-1800.* Oxford: Clarendon Press, 1994.

Cole, Cyrenus. *I Remember I Remember: A Book of Recollections.* Iowa City: State Historical Society of Iowa, 1936.

*Commemorative Biographical Record of the Fox River Valley Counties of Brown, Outagamie and Winnebago.* Chicago: J.H. Beers, 1895.

Cowan, Ruth Schwartz. *More Work for Mother: The Ironies of Household Technology from the Open Hearth to the Microwave.* New York: Basic Books, 1983.

Dassen, Annelie, Christine Van Eerd, and Karin Oppelland, eds. *Vrouwen in den vreemde. Lotgevallen van emigrantes en immigrantes.* Zutphen: De Walburg Pers, 1993.

De Jong, Gerald F. *The Dutch in America, 1609-1974.* Boston: Twayne Publishers, 1975.

De Jong, Gerald F. *The Dutch Reformed Church in the American Colonies.* Grand Rapids: Eerdmans, 1978.

De Klerk, Peter and Richard De Ridder, eds. *Perspectives on the Christian Reformed Church: Studies in Its History, Theology, and Ecumenicity.* Grand Rapids: Baker, 1983.

DeBoutte, Guy. "Pater Franciscus Eduardus Daems, O.S.C. (1826-1879) en de eerste kruisheren in de Verenigde Staten. Verwezenlijkingen en problemen." M.A. thesis, Catholic University Leuven, 1982.

Deddens, D. and J. Kamphuis, eds. *Afscheiding - wederkeer. Opstellen over de Afscheiding van 1834.* Barneveld: De Vuurbaak, 1984.

Degler, Carl N. *At Odds: Women and the Family in America from the Revolution to the Present.* New York: Oxford University Press, 1980.

DeHaan, Kathleen Anne. "'He looks like a Yankee in His new suit': Immigrant Rhetoric: Dutch Immigrant Letters as Forums for Shifting Immigrant Identities." Ph.D. dissertation, Northwestern University, 1998.

Dekker, Gerard, Donald A. Luidens, and Rodger R. Rice, eds. *Rethinking Secularization: Reformed Reactions to Modernity.* Lanham: University Press of America, 1997.

Delos Van Den Berg, Delbert. "'Building Castles in the Air:' Andreas Wormser, Immigrant Locator and Land Developer." M.A. thesis, Montana State University, 1996.

Dijk, G.B. van. "Geloofsvervolging of broodnood: Hollanders naar Michigan," *Spiegel Historiael* 5.1 (1970): 31-36.

Douma, Michael. *Veneklasen Brick: A Family, a Company, and a Unique Nineteenth Century Dutch Architectural Movement in Michigan.* Grand Rapids: Eerdmans, 2005.

Doyle, Richard L. "The Socio-Economic Mobility of the Dutch Immigrants to Pella, Iowa 1847-1925." Ph.D. dissertation, Kent State University, 1982.

Dunbar, Willis F. and George S. May. *Michigan: A History of the Wolverine State.* 3rd rev. ed. Grand Rapids: Eerdmans, 1995.

Dykstra, D. Ivan. *"B.D." A Biography of my Father, the Late Reverend B.D. Dykstra.* Grand Rapids: Eerdmans, 1982.

Dykstra, Richard, and Patricia Premo, eds. *Cedar Grove, Wisconsin. 150 Years of Dutch-American Tradition.* Cedar Grove, Wis.: Standard Printing, 1997.

Edelman, Hendrik. *The Dutch Language Press in America: Two Centuries of Printing, Publishing and Bookselling.* Nieuwkoop: De Graaf, 1986.

Eerenbeemt, A.J.J.M. van den, *De Missie-Actie in Nederland (1600-1940).* Nijmegen: Berkhout, 1945.

Ester, Peter. *De stillen op het land. Portret van de Amish-gemeenschap in de Amerika.* 3rd ed. Kampen: Agora, 2001.

Fabend, Firth A. *A Dutch Family in the Middle Colonies, 1660-1800.* New Brunswick: Rutgers University Press, 1991.

Fabend, Firth A. *Zion on the Hudson: Dutch New York and New Jersey in the Age of Revivals.* New Brunswick: Rutgers University Press, 2000.

Ferrie, Joseph P., "The Wealth Accumulation of Antebellum European Immigrants to the U.S., 1840-1860." *Journal of Economic History* 54 (1994): 1-33.

Fessler, Paul, Hubert R. Krygsman, and Robert P. Swierenga, eds. *Dutch Immigrants on the Plains.* Holland, Mich.: Joint Archives of Holland, 2006.

Galema, Annemieke, Barbara Henkes, and Henk te Velde, eds. *Images of the Nation: Different Meanings of Dutchness, 1870-1940.* Amsterdam: Rodopi, 1993.

Galema, Annemieke, *With the Baggage of the Fatherland: Frisians to America, 1880-1914.* Detroit/Groningen: Wayne State University Press/Regio Projekt Groningen, 1996.

Ganzevoort, Herman, and Mark Boekelman, eds. *Dutch Immigration to North America.* Toronto: Multicultural Society of Ontario, 1983.

Gates, Paul Wallace, "The Homestead Law in an Incongruous Land System," in Vernon Carstensen, ed. *The Public Lands: Studies in the History of the Public Domain.* Madison: University of Wisconsin Press, 1962.

*Gedenkboek van het Vijftigjarig Jubileum der Christelijke Gereformeerde Kerk A.D. 1857-1907* (1907).

Gjerde, Jon. *The Minds of the West: Ethnocultural Evolution in the Rural Middle West, 1830-1917.* Chapel Hill: University of North Carolina Press, 1997.

Goodfriend, Joyce D. *Before the Melting Pot: Society and Culture in New York City, 1664-1730.* Princeton: Princeton University Press, 1991.

Goodfriend, Joyce D., Benjamin Schmidt, and Annette Stott, eds. *Going Dutch: The Dutch Presence in America, 1609-2009.* Leiden: Brill, 2008.

Gould, Charles J. *History of the Flower Bulb Industry in Washington State.* Mount Vernon, Wash.: Northwest Bulb Growers Association, 1993.

Greene, Victor R. *American Immigrant Leaders 1800-1910: Marginality and Identity.* Baltimore: Johns Hopkins University Press, 1987.

Handlin, Oscar. *Boston's Immigrants: A Study in Acculturation.* Rev. ed. New York: Atheneum, 1975.

Harinck, George, and Hans Krabbendam, eds. *Amsterdam-New York: Transatlantic Relations and Urban Identities Since 1653.* Amsterdam: VU University Press, 2005.

Harinck, George, and Hans Krabbendam, eds. *Breaches and Bridges: Reformed Subcultures in the Netherlands, Germany, and the United States.* Amsterdam: VU University Press, 2000.

Harinck, George, and Hans Krabbendam, eds. *Morsels in the Melting Pot: The Persistence of Dutch Immigrant Communities in North America, 1800-2000.* Amsterdam: VU University Press, 2006.

Harinck, George, and Hans Krabbendam, eds. *Sharing the Reformed Tradition: The Dutch-North American Exchange, 1846-1996.* Amsterdam: VU University Press, 1996.

Hartland, J.A.A. *Geschiedenis van de Nederlandse emigratie tot de Tweede Wereldoorlog.* Den Haag: Nederlandse Emigratiedienst 1959.

Hatton, Timothy J., and Jeffrey G. Williamson. *The Age of Mass Migration: Causes and Economic Impact.* New York: Oxford University Press, 1998.

Hecht, Irene W.D. "Kinship and Migration: The Making of an Oregon Isolate Community," *Journal of Interdisciplinary History* 8 (1977).

Heitink, Gerben. *Biografie van de dominee.* Baarn: Ten Have, 2001.

Hentoff, Nat, ed. *The Essays of A.J. Muste.* Indianapolis: Bobbs-Merrill, 1967.

Hildebrand, Janice, ed. *The Heart of Sheboygan County: Sheboygan Falls, Plymouth, Lima and Lyndon Townships.* Curtis Media Corp., 1992.

*History of Sheboygan County Wisconsin. Past and Present,* 2 vols. Chicago: S.J. Clark, 1912. Vol. 2:568.

*History of the Board of Domestic Missions of the Reformed Church in America, 1786-1921.* New York: Abbott, (1922).

Hoezee, Scott, and Christopher H. Meehan. *Flourishing in the Land. A Hundred-Year History of Christian Reformed Missions in North America.* Grand Rapids: Eerdmans, 1996.

Holt, Marylin Irvin. *Children of the Western Plains: The Nineteenth-Century Experience.* Ivan R Dee, 2003.

Holthoon, F.L. van, ed. *De Nederlandse samenleving sinds 1815. Wording en samenhang.* Assen: Van Gorcum, 1985.

Hudson, John C. *Plains Country Towns.* Minneapolis: University of Minnesota Press, 1985.

Hutchinson, E.P. *Immigrants and Their Children, 1850-1950.* New York: Wiley, 1956.

Hutchinson, E.P. *Legislative History of American Immigration Policy 1798-1965.* Philadelphia: University of Pennsylvania Press, 1981.

Jacobs, Jaap. *New Netherland: A Dutch Colony in Seventeenth-Century America.* Leiden: Brill Academic, 2005; orig. Dutch 1999.

Jacobson, Jeanne, Elton J. Bruins, and Larry J. Wagenaar. *Albertus C. van Raalte: Dutch Leader and American Patriot.* Holland, Mich.: Hope College, 1996.

Jakle, John A., and James O. Wheeler. "The Changing Residential Structure of the Dutch Population in Kalamazoo, Michigan," *Annals of the Association of American Geographers* 59 (September 1969), 441-460.

Janssen, Allen J. *Gathered at Albany: A History of a Classis.* Grand Rapids: Eerdmans, 1995.

Japinga, Lynn Winkels. "Responsible for Righteousness: Social Thought and Action in the Reformed Church in America, 1901-1941." Ph. D. dissertation. Union Theological Seminary, New York 1992.

Keeling, Drew. "The Transportation Revolution and Transatlantic Migration, 1850-1914," *Research in Economic History* 19 (1999): 39-74.

Kenney, Alice P. *Stubborn for Liberty: The Dutch in New York.* Syracuse: Syracuse University Press, 1975.

Kirk, Gordon W. Jr. *The Promise of American Life: Social Mobility in a Nineteenth-Century Immigrant Community, Holland, Michigan 1847-1894.* Philadelphia: American Philosophical Society, 1978.

Krabbendam, Hans. "Avant La Lettre: The Use of Dutch Immigrant Letters in Historical Research," in Richard H. Harms, ed. and comp. *The Dutch Adapting in North America: Papers Presented at the Thirteenth Biennial Conference for the Association for the Advancement of Dutch-American Studies.* Grand Rapids: Calvin College, 2001.

Krabbendam, Hans. "'But tho we love old Holland still, We love Columbia more,' The Formation of a Dutch-American Subculture in the United States, 1840-1920," in Joyce D. Goodfriend, Benjamin Schmidt, and Annette Stott, eds. *Going Dutch: The Dutch Presence in America, 1609-2009.* Leiden: Brill, 2008, 135-155.

Krabbendam, Hans, and Larry Wagenaar, eds. *The Dutch-American Experience: Essays in Honor of Robert P. Swierenga.* Amsterdam: VU University Press, 2000.

Krabbendam, Hans. "Forgotten Founding Father: Cornelius VanderMeulen as Immigrant Leader." *Documentatieblad voor de Geschiedenis van de Nederlandse zending en overzeese kerken* 5.2 (Fall 1998): 1-23.

Krabbendam, Hans, Cornelis A. van Minnen, and Giles Scott-Smith, eds. *Four Centuries of Dutch-American Relations, 1609-2009.* Amsterdam/New York: Boom/State University of New York Press, 2009.

Krabbendam, Hans. "Rituals of Travel in the Transition from Sail to Steam: The Dutch Immigrant Experience, 1840-1940," in Margriet Bruyn Lacy, ed. *From De Halve Maen to KLM: 400 Years of Dutch-American Exchange.* Münster: Nodus Publikationen, 2008, 269-287.

Krabbendam, Hans. "Serving the Dutch Community: A Comparison of the Patterns of Americanization in the Lives of Two Immigrant Pastors." M.A. thesis, Kent State University, Kent, Ohio, USA, 1989.

Krabbendam, J.L. "Van Zeeland naar Zeeland. De ontwikkeling van het dorp Zeeland in Michigan, 1847-1860." *Nehalennia* 114 (September 1997).

Kranenborg, Reender, and Wessel Stoker, eds. *Religies en (on)gelijkheid in een plurale samenleving.* Leuven/Apeldoorn: Garant, 1995.

Kroes, Rob, and Henk-Otto Neuschäfer, eds. *The Dutch in North America: Their Immigration and Cultural Continuity.* Amsterdam: VU Uitgeverij, 1991.

Kroes, Rob. *The Persistence of Ethnicity: Dutch Calvinist Pioneers in Amsterdam, Montana.* Urbana: University of Illinois Press, 1992.

Lacy, Margriet Bruyn, ed. *From* De Halve Maen *to KLM: 400 Years of Dutch-American Exchange.* Münster: Nodus Publikationen, 2008.

Lagerwey, Walter. "The Netherlandic Muse in the Forests, on the Plains, and in the Cities of America from 1850-1975," in Wolodymyr T. Zyla and Wendell M. Aycock, eds. *Ethnic Literatures since 1776: The Many Voices of America,* 2 vols. Lubbock: Texas Tech Press, 1978. Vol. 2: 353-374.

Lagerwey, Walter. *Neen, Nederland 'k vergeet u niet. Een beeld van het immigrantenleven in Amerika tussen 1846 en 1945 in verhalen, schetsen en gedichten.* Baarn: Bosch en Keuning, 1982.

Lammers, A. *De jachtvelden van het geluk. Reizen door historisch Amerika.* Amsterdam: Balans, 1998.

Lammers, A. *Uncle Sam en Jan Salie. Hoe Nederland Amerika ontdekte.* Amsterdam: Balans, 1989.

Lewis, Frank D. "Farm Settlement on the Canadian Prairies, 1898 to 1911." *Journal of Economic History* 41 (September 1981) 517-535.

Lewis, Frank D. "Farm Settlement with Imperfect Capital Markets: A Life-Cycle Application to Upper Canada, 1826-1851." *Canadian Journal of Economics* 24 (2001).

Licht, Walter. *Industrializing America: The Nineteenth Century.* Baltimore: Johns Hopkins University Press, 1995.

Ligterink, G.H. *De landverhuizers. Emigratie naar Noord-Amerika uit het Gelders-Westfaalse grensgebied tussen de jaren 1830-1850.* Zutphen: De Walburg Pers, 1981.

Linssen, G.C.P. "Limburgers naar Noord-Amerika." *Economisch- en sociaal-historisch jaarboek* 35 (1972): 209-225.

Lucas, Henry S. *Netherlanders in America: Dutch Immigration to the United States and Canada, 1789-1950*. Ann Arbor: University of Michigan Press, 1955; repr. Grand Rapids: Eerdmans, 1989.

Lucassen, Jan. *Migrant Labour in Europe 1600-1900: The Drift to the North Sea*. London, etc.: Croom Helm, 1987; orig. Dutch ed. 1984.

Marle Jaap van, and Caroline Smits. "Deviant Patterns of Lexical Transfer: English-Origin Words in American Dutch," in Jetske Klatter-Folmer and Sjaak Kroon, eds. *Dutch Overseas: Studies in Maintenance and Loss of Dutch as an Immigrant Language*. Tilburg: Tilburg University Press, 1997, 255-272.

Marle, Jaap van, and Caroline Smits. "De ontwikkeling van het Amerikaans-Nederlands: een schets," in J.B. Berns and J. van Marle, eds. *Overzees Nederlands*. Amsterdam: Meertens Instituut, 2000, 63-83.

Mees, Jan Rudolf. *Dagboek van eene reis door Amerika 1843-1844*. Ingeleid en van aantekeningen voorzien door drs. B. Schoenmaker. Rotterdam: Stichting Historische Publicaties Roterodamum, 1988.

Meijer, Hendrik G. *Thrifty Years: The Life of Hendrik Meijer*. Grand Rapids: Eerdmans, 1984.

Merwick, Donna. *Possessing Albany, 1630-1710: The Dutch and English Experience*. Cambridge: Harvard University Press, 1990.

Nieuwenhuis, G. Nelson. *Siouxland: A History of Sioux County, Iowa*. Orange City: Sioux County Historical Society, 1983.

Noll, Mark A. *America's God: From Jonathan Edwards to Abraham Lincoln*. New York: Oxford University Press, 2002.

Noll, Mark A. *The Old Religion in a New World: The History of North American Christianity*. Grand Rapids: Eerdmans, 2002.

Nyenhuis, Jacob E. *Centennial History of the Fourteenth Street Christian Reformed Church, Holland, Michigan 1902-2002*. Holland: privately printed, 2002.

Oostendorp, Lubbertus. *H.P. Scholte: Leader of Secession of 1834 and Founder of Pella*. Franeker: Wever, 1964.

Overland, Orm. *Immigrant Minds, American Identities: Making the United States Home, 1870-1930*. Urbana: University of Illinois Press, 2000.

Peereboom, Freerk, e.o., ed. *Van scheurmakers, onruststokers en geheime opruijers: De Afscheiding in Overijssel*. Kampen: N.P., 1984.

Ranson, Frank Edward. *The City Built on Wood. A History of the Furniture Industry in Grand Rapids, Michigan, 1850-1950*. Ann Arbor: n.p., 1955.

Rippley, LaVern J. *The Immigrant Experience in Wisconsin.* Boston: Twayne, 1985.

Robinson, Jo Ann Ooiman. *Abraham Went Out: A Biography of A.J. Muste.* Philadelphia: Temple University Press, 1981.

Rowlands, Marie K. *Down an Indian Trail in 1849: The Story of Roseland.* Repr. 1949. Palos Heights, Ill.: Dutch Heritage Center 1987.

Ryan, Thomas H., ed. *History of Outagamie County Wisconsin.* Chicago: Goodspeed, 1911.

Salamon, Sonya. *Prairie Patrimon: Family, Farming and Community in the Midwest.* Chapel Hill: University of North Carolina Press, 1992.

Salzmann, Walter H. *Bedrijfsleven, overheid en handelsbevordering. The Netherlands Chamber of Commerce in the United States, Inc. 1903-1987.* Ph.D. dissertation, Universiteit Leiden, 1994.

Schoone-jongen, Robert. "A Time to Gather, a Time to Scatter: Dutch American Settlement in Minnesota, 1885-1920." Ph.D. dissertation, University of Delaware, 2007.

Schreuder, Yda. *Dutch Catholic Immigrant Settlement in Wisconsin, 1850-1905.* New York: Garland, 1989.

Schulte Nordholt, J.W., and Robert P. Swierenga, eds. *A Bilateral Bicentenial: A History of Dutch-American Relations 1782-1982.* Amsterdam: Meulenhoff, 1982.

Schulte Nordholt, J.W. *The Dutch Republic and American Independence.* Chapel Hill: University of North Carolina Press, 1982; orig. Dutch ed. 1979.

Schulte Nordholt, J.W., *The Myth of the West: America as the Last Empire.* Grand Rapids: Eerdmans, 1995; orig. Dutch ed. 1992.

Schwieder, Dorothy. *Iowa: The Middle Land.* Ames: Iowa State University Press, 1996.

Selleck, Trudy Vermeer. "'Land of Dreams and Profits': Social Networks and Economic Success among Dutch Immigrants in Southern California's Dairy Industry, 1920-1960." Ph.D. dissertation, University of California, Riverside, 1995.

*Sesquicentennial of St. John Nepomucene, Little Chute, Wisconsin 1836-1986.* St. Johns Parish, 1986, 64-69. *Little Chute. A Century of Progress 1899-1999.* Little Chute, Wis.: Village of Little Chute Centennial Committee, 1999.

Setten, Henk van. *In de schoot van het gezin. Opvoeding in Nederlandse gezinnen in de twintigste eeuw.* Nijmegen: SUN, 1987.

Sinke, Suzanne M. *Dutch Immigrant Women in the United States, 1880-1920.* Urbana: University of Illinois Press, 2002.

Smets, Kristine. "The Gazette van Moline and the Belgian-American Community, 1907-1921." M.A.thesis, Kent State University, 1994.

Smith, A.A. *A Pioneer Woman.* Lansing: privately printed, 1981.

Sollors, Werner. *The Invention of Ethnicity.* New York: Oxford University Press, 1989.

Stekelenburg, H.A.V.M. van. *"Hier is alles vooruitgang". Landverhuizing van Noord-Brabant naar Noord-Amerika, 1880-1940.* Tilburg: Stichting Zuidelijk Historisch Contact, 1996.

Stekelenburg, H.A.V.M. van. *Landverhuizing als regionaal verschijnsel. Van Noord-Brabant naar Noord-Amerika, 1820-1880.* Tilburg: Stichting Zuidelijk Historisch Contact, 1991.

Stokvis, P.R.D. *De Nederlandse trek naar Amerika, 1846-1847.* Leiden: Universitaire Pers Leiden, 1977.

Stokvis, Pieter. "Nederland en de internationale migratie, 1815-1960," in F. van Holthoon, *De Nederlandse samenleving sinds 1815. Wording en samenhang.* Assen: Van Gorcum, 1985, 71-92.

Swierenga, Robert P. "'Better Prospects for Work": Van Raalte's Holland Colony and Its Connections to Grand Rapids. *Grand Valley History* 15 (1998): 14-22.

Swierenga, Robert P., Jack Nyenhuis, and Nella Kennedy, eds. *Dutch American Arts and Letters in Historical Perspective.* Holland, Mich.: Van Raalte Press, 2008.

Swierenga, Robert P. *Dutch Chicago: A History of the Hollanders in the Windy City.* Grand Rapids: Eerdmans, 2002.

Swierenga, Robert P., ed. *The Dutch in America: Immigrant, Settlement, and Cultural Change.* New Brunswick: Rutgers University Press, 1985.

Swierenga, Robert P., Don Sinnema, and Hans Krabbendam, eds. *The Dutch in Urban America.* Holland, Mich.: Joint Archives, 2004.

Swierenga, Robert P. *Faith and Family: Dutch Immigration and Settlement in the United States, 1820-1920.* New York: Holmes & Meier, 2000.

Swierenga, Robert P., and Joel Lefever, eds. *For Food and Faith: Dutch Immigration to Western Michigan, 1846-1960.* Holland, Mich.: Holland Museum and A.C. Van Raalte Institute, 2000.

Swierenga, Robert P. *The Forerunners: Dutch Jewry in the North American Diaspora.* Detroit: Wayne State University Press, 1994.

Swierenga, Robert P. "The Settlement of the Old Northwest: Ethnic Pluralism in a Featureless Plain." *Journal of the Early Republic* 9 (1989): 73-105.

ter Maat, C.J. "Three Novelists and a Community: A study of American Novelists with Dutch Calvinistic Origins." Ph.D. dissertation, University of Michigan, 1962.

Trachtenberg, Alan. *The Incorporation of America: Culture and Society in the Gilded Age.* New York: Hill and Wang, 1982.

Van Brummelen, Harro. *Telling the Next Generation. Educational Development in North American Christian Schools.* Lanham, Md.: University Press of America, 1986.

Van Coenen Torchiana, H.A. *The Future of Trade between the United States of America and the Netherlands and Its Colonies: A Short Study.* San Francisco: Holland-American Chamber of Commerce, 1918.

Van der Pol, Henry, Sr. *On the Reservation Border: Hollanders in Douglas and Charles Mix Counties.* Stickney, S.D.: Argus, 1969.

Van Hinte, Jacob. *Netherlanders in America: A Study of Emigration and Settlement in the 19th and 20th Centuries in the United States of America,* Robert P. Swierenga, gen. ed., Adriaan de Wit, chief trans. Grand Rapids: Baker, 1985.

Van Hoeven, James W. *Piety and Patriotism: Bicentennial Studies of the Reformed Church in America, 1776-1976.* Grand Rapids: Eerdmans, 1976.

Van Nuys, Frank. *Americanizing the West: Race, Immigrants, and Citizenship, 1890-1930.* Lawrence: University of Kansas Press, 2002.

Van Pernis, Gerard M. *According to Thy Heart: A True Story of An Immigrant's Life.* Privately published, 1967.

Van Reken, Donald L. *The Holland Fire of October 8, 1871.* Privately printed, 1982.

Vancius, Conevery Bolton. *The Health of the Country: How American Settlers Understood Themselves and Their Land.* New York: Basic Books, 2002.

Vandehey, Scott. *Wooden Shoes West: A Saga of John Henry Vandehey.* Times Litho 1979.

Vanden Bosch, Mike. *A Pocket of Civility: A History of Sioux Center.* Sioux Falls, S.D.: Modern Press, 1976.

Vandergon, Gertrude Braat. *Our Pioneer Days in Minnesota.* Holland: Holland Letter Service, 1949.

Vanderstel, David W. "The Dutch of Grand Rapids, Michigan, 1848-1900: Immigrant Neighborhood and Community Development in a Nineteenth Century City." Ph.D. dissertation, Kent State University, 1986.

Vecoli, Rudolph J. "An Inter-Ethnic Perspective on American Immigration History." *Mid-America* 75 (1993): 223-235.

Veenendaal, August J. *Slow Train to Paradise: How the Dutch Helped Build American Railroads.* Stanford: Stanford University Press, 1996.

Velde, M. te. *Anthony Brummelkamp (1811-1881).* Barneveld: De Vuurbaak, 1988.

Venema, Janny. *Beverwijck: A Dutch Village on the American Frontier, 1652-1664.* Hilversum: Verloren, 2003.

Verbrugge, Cora Helen Roelofs. *The Life of a Dutch American George Roelofs (1853-1919) of Zwolle, the Netherlands and Grand Rapids, Michigan.* Privately printed, 1994 .

Versteeg, Dingman. *De Pelgrim-Vaders van het westen.* Grand Rapids: C.M. Loomis, 1886.

Verwyst, Chrysostom Adrian. "Reminiscences of a Pioneer Missionary," *Publications of the State Historical Society of Wisconsin, Proceedings, 1916.* Madison, 1917.

Vlekke, H.M., and Henry Beets. *Hollanders Who Helped Build America.* New York 1942.

Voorhees, David William. *The Holland Society: A Centennial History 1885-1985.* New York: Holland Society of New York, 1985.

Wagenaar, Larry J. "The Early Political History of Holland, Michigan, 1847-1868." M.A. thesis, Kent State University, Ohio, 1992, 62-75.

Wagenaar, Larry J., and Robert P. Swierenga, eds. *Dutch Enterprise: Alive and Well in North America.* (n.p., 1999).

Walker, M. *Germany and the Emigration, 1816-1885.* Cambridge: Harvard University Press, 1964.

Walvoord, William C. *Windmill Memories: A Remembrance of Life in a Holland-American Community before the Turn of the Century.* Cedar Grove, Wis.: Villager Publications, 1979).

Webber, Philip E. *Pella Dutch: The Portrait of a Language and Its Use in One of Iowa's Ethnic Communities.* Ames: Iowa State University Press, 1988.

Wege, Simone A. "Chain Migration and Information Networks: Evidence from Nineteenth-Century Hesse-Cassel." *Journal of Economic History* 58 (1998): 957-986.

Wilterdink, Willem. *Winterswijkse pioniers in Amerika.* Winterswijk: Het Museum, 1990.

Zeidel, Robert F. *Immigrants, Progressives, and Exclusion Politics: The Dillingham Commission, 1900-1917.* DeKalb: Northern Illinois University Press, 2004.

Zevenbergen, C. *Toen zij uit Rotterdam vertrokken. Emigratie via Rotterdam door de eeuwen heen.* Zwolle: Waanders, 1990.

Zwaanstra, Henry. *Reformed Thought and Experience in a New World: A Study of the Christian Reformed Church and Its American Environment, 1890-1918.* Kampen: Kok, 1973.

Zwart, David E. "Formed by Faith: The Dutch Immigrant Community in Kings County, California: 1890-1940." M.A. thesis, California State University, 2004.

Zwemer, Adrian, and Samuel M. *Genealogy and History of the Zwemer-Boon Family.* Harrisburg: Nungesser, 1932.

# Index of Persons

# Index of Places

(The locations of the Dutch places can be found on Map 3 p. xxvi)